Inside the Castle

Senior civil servants of the final

Dublin administration

1920-1922

JOHANNA LOWRY O'REILLY

D1388857

Copyright © Johanna Lowry O'Reilly

First published in Ireland, 2022, in co-operation with Choice Publishing, Drogheda, Co Louth, Republic of Ireland.
www.choicepublishing.ie

ISBN: 978-1-913275-68-6

The moral right of the author has been asserted.

A CIP catalogue record for this book is available from the National Library.

Printed and bound in Ireland by Choice Publishing Ltd.

Cover: Keilah Cass

Index: Eileen O'Neill

Dublin Castle Photographs: Kelan Lowry O'Reilly

For Brendan and our family, especially Elle

Table of Contents

FRONT MATTER

Title Pages
Acknowledgements   v
Illustrations and Tables   vi
Abbreviations   vii
Prologue   ix

PART ONE
1   Gathering the threads of administrative and educational change   2

PART TWO
2   Legislation for intermediate education, 1878-1920   18
3   Towards meritocracy and equality   44

PART THREE
4   MacMahon and Anderson: A dual biography   80

PART FOUR
5   Warren Fisher and a new look administration   132

PART FIVE
6   The 'Old Castle Gang': core Irish group   160
7   A seconded British cohort 1920-1922   198

END MATTER

Epilogue   242
Bibliography   244
Index   268

Acknowledgements

Grateful thanks to Prof Marie Coleman and Prof Peter Gray of Queen's University Belfast and Dr Marnie Hay, Dublin City University.

Many thanks also to the archivists, librarians and curators I met with, or spoke to, during my research in the National Library of Ireland; Berkley Library, TCD; James Joyce Library, UCD;   British Library; Bodlean Library, Oxford; National Archives of Ireland; TCD Manuscripts and Archives; Jesuit Archives, Dublin; GPO Archives Dublin; Cardinal Tomás Ó'Fiaich Memorial Library and Archive, Armagh; Freemason's Hall, Dublin; Knights of Columbanus, Dublin; National Archives, Kew; Parliamentary Archives, Westminster; British Postal Museum and Archives; London Metropolitan Archives, City of London; Lambeth Archives, London; Hugh Lane Gallery, Dublin, National Portrait Gallery, London, National Galleries of Scotland and the OPW.

I would particularly like to thank the archivists of the following schools for their assistance:

Ireland: Alexandra College, Milltown, Dublin; Blackrock College (French School), Dublin; Clongowes Wood College, Naas, Co Kildare; Crescent College, Limerick (Sacred Heart College); Mount Anville School, Dublin; The High School, Rathgar, Dublin.

Northern Ireland: Coleraine Grammar School (Coleraine Academical Institute); Foyle College, Londonderry (Londonderry Academical Institute); St Malachy's College, Belfast; St Mary's CBGS, Belfast; St Patricks Dioscean College, Armagh; St Patrick's Grammar School, Armagh; Victoria College, Belfast.

Scotland: George Watson's College; Kingussie High School.

England: Downside School, Bath; The Dragon School Oxford; Emanuel School, London; Eton College, Windsor; Manchester Grammar School, Manchester; Rugby School, Rugby; St Paul's School, London; Westminster School, London; Winchester College, Winchester.

Special thanks to:

The MacMahon, McKee and Doolin families and Sr Nora Smith.
Keilah Cass whose design vividly depicts my concept for the book cover.
As always my family and friends for the distraction of coffees, brunches and dinners, and the 'Friday Lunch Club'.

Illustrations

Brennan, Joseph (courtesy Clongowes Wood College Archives).

Clarke to Street (courtesy the National Archives, Kew).

Doolin, Walter (courtesy Clongowes Wood College Archives).

Livingston Place (No1) and the Meadows (photographs by author, July 2019).

Letter re appointment of James MacMahon (courtesy the Military History Archives).

Letter of appointment of John Anderson (courtesy The National Archives, Kew).

Lord FitzAlan and the Rt Hon James MacMahon (*The Graphic, 21 Jan. 1922*).

Map of Sailortown (courtesy Sailortown Regenertion).

MacMahon family (courtesy Eilish Tennent and Pauline Arthurs).

Rt Hon James MacMahon (courtesy Blackrock College Archives).

Rt Hon James MacMahon and his brother (private collection).

Rt Hon James MacMahon and son John MacMahon (private collection).

Rt Hon James MacMahon in Parknasilla (private collection).

Sir Alfred Cope (courtesy collection & image © Hugh Lane Gallery, Dublin).

Sir John Anderson (courtesy National Portrait Gallery, London).

The British 'Junta' (unknown).

Wedding of Mark Sturgis, *Tatler,* 15 July 1914.

Tables and charts

Ngram re usage of 'elite' and 'superior'.

Students who gave notice to attend examinations, 1879,80,81

Students who presented for examinations, 1879,80,81

Commisioners on Intermediate Board, 1879

Expenditure of the board, 1879

Six top placed boys' schools, 1879,80,81

Intermediate results for boys and girls, 1879

Boys' middle grade resultes 1879

Irish born students at Downside 1883

Abbreviations

ACA	Alexandra College Archives
AUS	Assistant Under Secretary
BCA	Blackrock College Archives
BMH	Bureau of Military History
BPM	British Postal Museum
BPP	British Parliamentary Papers
CAB	Cabinet Office Files
CB	Companion of the Order of the Bath
CBE	Commander of the British Empire
CCA	Castleknock College Archives
CM	Congregation of the Mission
CRS	Central Registry Service
CS	Chief Secretary
CSC	Civil Service Commission
CSO	Chief Secretary's Office
CSORP	Chief Secretary's Office Registered Papers
DAA	Downside Abbey Archives
Deb	Debate
DHR	Dominion Home Rule
DIA	*Dictionary of Irish Architects*
DIB	*Dictionary of Irish Biography*
DNB	*Dictionary of National Biography*
DSA	Downside School Archives
DV or de V	Eamon de Valera
EPPI	Enhanced British Parliamentary Papers on Ireland
FCA	Foyle College Archives
GAI	Governess Association of Ireland
GDPR	General Data Protection Regulation
GOC	General Officer Commanding
GRO	General Registry Office
GSR	Great Southern Railway
GWCA	George Watson's College Archives
GWS	George Watson's School
HC	House of Commons
HCS	Home Civil Service
HL	House of Lords
HSDA	High School Dublin Archives
Ibid.	In the same place
IRA	Irish Republican Army
IRB	Irish Republican Brotherhood
ISB	Irish Statute Book

KBE	Knight of the British Empire
KCB	Knight Commander British Empire
KSA	Kingussie School Archives
LAI	Londonderry Academical Institution (Foyle College)
LMA	London Metropolitan Archives
MC	Michael Collins
MP	Member of Parliament
MS	Manuscript
NAI	National Archives of Ireland
NLCS	North London Collegiate School
NLI	National Library of Ireland
NRS	National Records of Scotland
NUI	National University of Ireland
NUIG	National University of Ireland, Galway
OBL	Oxford Bodleian Library
ODNB	*Oxford Dictionary of National Biography*
PA	Parliamentary Archives
PM	Prime Minister
PQ	Parliamentary Question
PRO	Public Record Office
PS	Private Secretary
QUB	Queen's University Belfast
RBAI	Royal Belfast Academical Institution
RC	Roman Catholic
RIC	Royal Irish Constabulary
SHA	Sacred Heart Archives
SHC	Sacred Heart Circular
Strath Papers	Strathcarron Papers
TCD	Trinity College, Dublin
TNA	National Archives UK
(The) Board	Intermediate Education Board for Ireland
UCD	University College Dublin
UCDA	University College Dublin Archives
US	Under Secretary
VCA	Victoria College Archives
Vict.	Queen Victoria
Vol.	Volume
WCA	Winchester College Archives
WS	Witness Statement
WSA	Westminster School Archives

Prologue

During April 1920, the administration in Dublin Castle had the appearance of stability. This followed a period of unrest with sectarian divisions, unionist domination and inter personnel intrigues dominating between 1918 and 1920. The ex-Chief Secretary, Ian MacPherson was in London and his replacement Hamar Greenwood had been appointed on 12 April 1920 but was most likely still based in Whitehall. Unionist Assistant Under Secretary John Taylor, was in London on 'French leave', that is the Lord Lieutenant had recommended he take a break for rest and recuperation.

Under Secretary James MacMahon was effectively acting as Chief Secretary, with the endorsement of the Lord Lieutenant. This short-lived respite was to end a month later with the arrival in Dublin of Sir Warren Fisher, Head of the Civil Service, Alfred Cope, of Pensions and R.E. Harwood, Treasury, to examine the workings of the Irish administration, with the resultant secondment of a British cohort. That group of civil servants, with their diverse life experiences and educational backgrounds, provide a basis for comparative biographical studies with core Irish personnel, highlighting a connection between education and the administration across both cohorts and broader administrative departments.

PART ONE

1

Gathering the threads of administrative and educational change

These are the materials for reflection which history affords to those who choose to make use of them.

Plutarch *Parallel Lives**

*Quotes from Plutarch's Parallel lives and his other writings appear at the start of each chapter. While these epigraphs could be regarded as individual introductions to specific sections, they are intended to be much more than that. In primarily choosing *Parallel lives* the objective is to draw together not only themes of administration in relation to the Irish and British cohorts of Dublin Castle 1920-1922, but biographical studies of the people whose lives were impacted by many factors including education legislation. In the Irish context the key implementation was the Intermediate Education (Ireland) Act, 1878. Plutarch's insightful reasoning that 'by the study of their biographies, we receive each man as a guest into our minds and we seem to understand their character as the result of a personal acquaintance', is a driving force behind this book. It has generated research into the lives behind the names of the personnel of the final Dublin Castle administration and the contribution of those civil servants to the establishment of the Irish Free State.

There is a blindness, ostensibly a deliberate one, when it comes to the recognition of the final Dublin Castle administration within the historiography of the 'New Ireland', post 1922. Over the past century, the narrative of the Free State has been focused on revolution and the heroes of violent and murderous outrage. However, there is another side to the 1922 coin. The Irish and British senior civil servants in the Chief Secretary's office, Dublin Castle, provided a counter balance to the physical force brigade. Both cohorts within the administration were ideally placed to effect a solution to the 'Irish question'. In doing so they contributed in a non-revolutionary but highly effective way to the realisation of Ireland's independence. As much as revolutionaries define Irish historiography, recognition is due to the Dublin Castle civil servants.

The 1920 to 1922 administration in Ireland combined two cohorts, the

'Old Castle Gang' and seconded British civil servants. The British group which was mainly from Whitehall presents an interesting basis for comparison with the civil servants already in Dublin Castle in terms of early lives, education and career trajectories. The majority of these personnel had reached senior positions through access to education and enhanced career opportunities. From an Ireland perspective, most histories of the administration have failed to connect educational change and increased provision to advancement in the civil service. With regard to popular recognition, they remain grey men or faceless bureaucrats. In order to bridge that gap and create a greater awareness of who they were, the human face of these civil servants is portrayed through their families, schools, academic profiles, sporting achievements (even successes in fun events at school sports days), university attendance, and careers prior Dublin Castle. Such a 'through the lens' biographical style is utilised to reveal the persons behind the administrative masks. In the interest of seeking a balanced historiography, the personnel of the last administration are profiled individually, while they are likewise portrayed within the framework of Dublin Castle, as a form of prosopography or collective biography.

Educational opportunities saw these civil servants rise to the upper levels of the administration, bringing together two groups that combined and exceeded cultural and normative experiences among the greater part of the population in Ireland and Britain. Nonetheless, in the Irish context the educational levels in the general population following the 1878 intermediate legislation, often paralleled that of civil service personnel. Their educational achievements and subsequent careers point to an upward mobility that was sometimes beyond that of the existing Catholic merchant middle class. Such academic successes highlighted the impact of the intermediate examinations and created a broad spectrum of change, into which the advancement of meritocracy over privilege ostensibly fits. Inclusive of a broad grouping across England and Scotland, educational advantage and career opportunities provide the main emphasis of the comparative biographies of the personnel of the Dublin Castle administration of 1920 to 1922. However, a focus on these Irish and seconded British senior civil servants places them within the history of a deeply fractured and unsettled country, both politically and administratively.

In the years prior to 1920, the Irish Convention of 1917, established by Lloyd George, under the chairmanship of Horace Plunkett, primarily addressed the 'Irish Question', but ended inconclusively after twelve months. This setback and the attempt to link conscription with Home Rule, which by default boosted Sinn Féin, giving it sweeping success in the 1918 General Election, resulted in widespread outrages, with the militant nationalists proving difficult to control. Britain's initial response 'was to allow the civil authorities in Ireland, based at Dublin Castle and heavily reliant on the enforced powers of the Royal Irish Constabulary, to deal with the situation'.[1] This coupled with the imposition of coercion in Ireland was, 'a policy that led increasingly to the militarisation of the administration'.[2] According to Richard Murphy, 'the murder of two policemen, the first Royal Irish Constabulary fatalities since the Easter rising, and the capture of a wagonload of explosive at Soloheadbeg, County Tipperary, on 21 January 1919', were proof that physical force measures were very much active'.[3] For Lloyd George there could be no concessions. Despite this, when policies of coercion failed to deliver social order, the failure was laid at the door of the civil service administration, not the policy.[4] While according to Eunan O'Halpin, criticising the performance of the Irish administration was easy, he claims that 'the blame for many of the disasters of the final years of British rule should not lie solely with the Irish authorities' and that 'administrative ineffectiveness under British rule was the product, not the cause, of the failures of British policy in Ireland'.[5]

The unsettled position in Ireland and the perceived weakness of the Castle administration were exacerbated by the War of Independence, which started in January 1919 and ended with an official truce that began on 11 July 1921. Beyond revolutionary activity or administrative action, legislative provision exerted an influence on the pre-Free State years. Set within the historical framework of Anglo-Irish affairs in the period 1918-22 and having a long-term effect, comparatively little attention has been paid

---

[1] John Ainsworth, 'British security in Ireland, 1920-1921: a desperate attempt by the Crown to maintain Anglo-Irish unity by force', *11th Irish-Australian Conference*, Perth Western Australia, p.11.
[2] Martin Maguire, *The civil service and the revolution in Ireland: Shaking the blood-stained hand of Mr Collins* (Manchester, 2008) p.69.
[3] Richard Murphy, 'Walter Long and the making of the Government of Ireland Act, pp. 82-96.
[4] Maguire, *The civil service and the revolution in Ireland*, p.69.
[5] Eunan O'Halpin, *The decline of the union, British government in Ireland 1892-1920* (Dublin, 1987) pp. 216-7.

to the making of the Government of Ireland Act, December 1920, although it was this piece of legislation, which laid the basis for partition of north and south.[6] Murphy asserts that, 'the act is something of an historical aberration in that its application within nationalist Ireland was superseded within less than a year of reaching the statute book, for the Treaty of 6 December 1921 effectively repealed it by granting full dominion status'.[7] James MacMahon, Under Secretary for Ireland, 1918 to 1922, had his finger on the pulse. Disagreeing with the Government of Ireland Bill, 'from early 1919 (if not earlier), he had favoured a county option under a dominion home rule system with fiscal authority'.[8] Furthermore, 'he opposed the escalating repression from the second half of 1920, which the Lloyd George government ... saw as necessary to assert the authority of the law and force Sinn Féin to the table'.[9]

With a focus on the Irish administration and the changes that occurred in Dublin Castle, Ainsworth contended that 'in 1920 however, with a demoralised administration in Ireland perceived to be lacking in resolution in the increasingly violent struggle against nationalists, London finally intervened'.[10] John McColgan argued that British 'on-the-spot action was threefold: to install new personnel at the top ... to reinforce the military strength of the army and of the police ... and to revitalise the bureaucracy of the Irish executive'.[11] In this regard, British governmental attention was turned to the efficacy of Dublin Castle. Administrative reform was to follow the completion of a report by Sir Warren Fisher into the workings of the Dublin administration. This led to the secondment from Whitehall of a British cohort of civil servants, who joined with the existing 'Old Castle Gang' of the pre-1920 Irish administration.

In profiling this administration, education and the provision of schools are essential, indeed over-riding considerations. Greater access to intermediate level schooling and competitive examinations were, in terms

---

[6] The Government of Ireland Act 1920 (10 & 11 Geo. 5 c. 67).
[7] Murphy, 'Walter Long and the making of the Government of Ireland Act 1919-20', pp. 82-96.
[8] Patrick Maume, 'MacMahon, James (1865-1954)', *DIB*.
[9] Ibid.
[10] Ainsworth, 'British security in Ireland, 1920-1921'.
[11] John McColgan, *British policy and the Irish administration, 1920-22* (London, 1983).
p.3.

of the administration, tied in with the emphasis of the Northcote-Trevelyan report on meritocracy. The trigger for what was to be increased provision in the late 1800s in Ireland and Britain was legislative enactment. Debates on education legislation in Ireland highlighted similar areas of concern to those raised England and Scotland in 1870 and 1872, although these enactments in the main concerned primary level. They included religious teaching and the setting up of education boards. A common linkage is shown between political appointments, administrative structure, access to higher-level positions, increased educational provision, competitive examinations for entry to the civil service, patronage versus meritocracy as outlined in the Northcote-Trevelyan report and the impact of the Warren Fisher report on the 1920-22 administration.

With regard to education and administrative history in Ireland, there is a demarcation that has been imposed by most available publications, which are segmented into these two areas. A number of works on both topics have been produced but they rarely interconnect. Investigative studies on Irish schools and educational provision are relatively limited. The Dublin Castle administration pre-1922 has been more extensively documented with publications providing a linkage of common themes, for example Irish Catholic advancement within the civil service.[12] There is however, a failure to emphasise the connection between enhanced educational provision and entrance to the upper levels of the administration. For example it has been contended that author Lawrence McBride 'focuses too much on the upper echelons of the administration and too little on the changes in the Irish educational system'.[13] Kieran Flanagan is of the opinion that 'the relationship between educational supply and competitive examinations did have a meritocratic influence which McBride acknowledged, but is not adequately explored'.[14] Mary Daly also links education and the

---

[12] John McColgan, *British policy and the Irish administration, 1920-22* (London, 1983); Eunan O'Halpin, *The decline of the union: British government in Ireland 1892-1920* (Dublin, 1987); Lawrence McBride, *The greening of Dublin Castle: the transformation of bureaucratic and judicial personnel in Ireland 1892-1922* (Washington, 1991); Fergus Campbell, *The Irish establishment 1879-1914* (Oxford, 2009).

[13] Kieran Flanagan, review of Lawrence McBride, *The greening of Dublin Castle: the transformation of bureaucratic and judicial personnel in Ireland 1892-1922* (Washington, 1991) in
Irish Historical Studies, vol. 29, issue 113, May 1994, pp.131-133.

[14] Ibid.

administration, asserting that 'although competitive examinations undoubtedly increased Catholic and nationalist access to government positions, the transition was limited by inequalities of access in the Irish educational system'.[15]

Among historians of the administration, there is inadequate recognition of the impact of the Intermediate Education Act (Ireland) 1878, and a lack of investigation into the educational backgrounds of top civil servants. There is a regrettable loss of valuable records in many Irish schools, with a marked differentiation between the available records and archival approach of Irish secondary schools and their Scottish and English counterparts. For example, English public schools meticulously preserve their records and school magazines. However, any failure in the availability of data in Irish schools, is to an extent mitigated through primary sources such as intermediate examination results, Royal University applications, school magazines, individual memoirs and obituaries.

An anachronistic focus on the term 'elite' in respect of nineteenth and early twentieth century educational establishments, not only in England but also in Ireland, creates an image that is modern rather than being contemporaneous. The term was not widely used at the time to describe schools and in fact, the word itself was not in common usage. By utilising the word 'elite', which has a resonance today of privilege and wealth, some current writers sensationalise and heighten the desirability of what are perceived to be exclusive schools. Such institutions in the nineteenth century were known as 'superior schools' in Ireland and public schools in England. The definition of 'superior schools' related to the subjects taught, that is one or more foreign languages, rather than social status. While it could be argued that 'elite' is a sociological term used to denote relative wealth and position in society, the point being made relates to its usage to describe certain schools at a time when it appears the term was not in vogue. As the Ngram below illustrates, the term 'superior' was prevalent in the early nineteenth century and declined steadily by 2000 with subsequently a slight increase.[16] Conversely, 'elite' showed little usage in the 1800s, but

---

[15] Mary E. Daly, 'The formation of an Irish nationalist elite? Recruitment to the Irish civil service in the decades prior to Independence 1870-1920', *Paedegogia, Historica,* vol. 30:1, (1994), pp 281-301.

[16] Google Ngram is a search engine that charts word frequencies from a large number of books printed between 1500 and 2008.

increased marginally from approximately 1920 to its peak in 2000, although then remaining below the rate for the designation 'superior'.

Ngram showing usage of the words 'elite' and 'superior' from 1800-2000 – 'superior' in red and 'elite' in blue.[17]

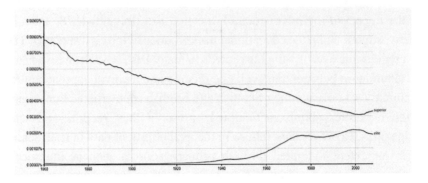

Within that timescale, the years 1878 to 1900 show increased provision and availability of schools in Ireland, negating the need to travel abroad, as had been the case for both Catholic and Protestant pupils, whose parents could afford high fees and travel costs. Despite the valuable contribution of Ciaran O'Neill's book of the same name, it could be contended that *Catholics of consequence* rather than being from a landed monied grouping, became those whose success in the intermediate examinations combined with access to the Royal University and later UCD, obtained a level of upward mobility through educational provision.

Although not directly connected to the upper levels of the 1920-22 administration, inclusion of girls in the 1878 act was to impact on a number of issues, particularly in relation to financial resources for implementation of the legislation. This was due in the main to the success of female candidates. The involvement of girls was to give rise to dissent, with headmasters from both Catholic and Protestant schools highlighting the threat to available funding for boys. Anne O'Connor writes that nineteenth century Ireland showed 'the emergence of two dominant influences on girls' secondary education, one French and primarily religious, the other English

---

[17]https://books.google.com/ngraMS/graph?content=anxiety&year_start=1800&year_end=2016&corpus=15&smoothing=3&share=&direct_url=t1%3B%2Canxiety%3B%2Cc0. [Accessed 19 Nov. 2019].

and mainly utilitarian'.[18] As such, the utilitarian emphasis was focussed on work and the 'view that girls should take the same examinations as boys if they hoped to compete for jobs'.[19] The movement gave rise to two educational enterprises, the Queen's Institute and Alexandra College, both associated with Anne Jellicoe, a Quaker. The influence of these organisations initially extended to Protestant schools in Dublin, Belfast, Cork, and Mountmellick.[20] French educational methods related to Catholic convents, such as those founded by the Ursuline, Sacred Heart, the Faithful Companions of Jesus, St Joseph of Cluny, Loreto and Dominican orders.[21]

Setting the issue of female education firmly within a broad perspective, Mary Hatfield and Ciaran O'Neill contend that 'since the inauguration of feminist history, there has been a persistent tension between the progressive narrative of widening access and enfranchisement against a cultural critique of the narrowed content, quality, and purpose of female education'.[22] These tensions were not unique to Ireland, but 'echo many of the concerns present in British, American, and French literature'.[23] A little known area of the Irish educational system, is the contribution of governesses, who from the 1840s until the 1860s 'formed almost ten per cent of the total teaching force. The majority of governesses were Protestant'.[24] There are however, few records of this form of teaching in Ireland'.[25] Nonetheless, links existed 'between the Governess Association of Ireland (GAI), Alexandra College, Dublin and the movement for higher education for women'.[26]

Highlighting the 'Irish University Question' shows Irish Catholics had limited access to third level. This was ostensibly not due to any lack of provision but to an insistence by the Catholic hierarchy on a denominational university with recognised degrees and under the Church's control. While

---

[18] Anne V. O'Connor, 'Influences affecting girls' secondary education in Ireland', *Archivium Hibernicum,* vol. 41 (1986), pp. 83-98.

[19] Ibid.

[20] Ibid.

[21] Ibid.

[22] Mary Hatfield and Ciaran O'Neill, 'Education and empowerment: cosmopolitan education and Irish women in the early nineteenth century', *Gender & History,* vol.30, no.1, (2018), pp. 93–109.

[23] Ibid.

[24] Deirdre Raftery and Karin Fisher (eds.), *Educating Ireland: schooling and social change 1700-2000* (Kildare, 2014), p.117.

[25] Ibid, p.116.

[26] Ibid.

the Intermediate Education (Ireland) Act, 1878 demonstrated the need for increased provision of schools at secondary level, the university sector was well provided for prior to and beyond that date. However, despite a more than adequate provision in Ireland, the Protestant ethos in the case of Trinity College and the non-denominational status of the Queen's colleges made them unacceptable to the Catholic hierarchy. 'The Catholic Church required 'access, control of appointments and curricula'.[27]

The founding of the Queen's colleges was an attempt by the British government to provide non-denominational third level education as 'the majority of the population claimed to be denied access to university facilities on religious grounds'.[28] These were considered to be godless by the hierarchy. Catholics made up seventy-seven percent of the population but less than twenty-five percent of student numbers. In 1866, a memorial from the Catholic hierarchy stated that Protestants at twenty-three percent of population accounted for seventy-five percent of student places.[29] Mr Edward Horsman MP, speaking on Questions regarding the University Education (Ireland) Bill, 1873, stated, 'in 1866 and 1868 the then Cabinets were in communication with the Roman Catholic hierarchy, and finding a settlement hopeless, the attempt failed'. He further stated, that a memorial and resolutions by the Roman Catholic Archbishops and Bishops had been submitted prior to the current debate on the University Bill, by Lord Granard.

Third level provision was not ostensibly the problem for Irish Catholics, but the issue was one of religion and the dictates of the hierarchy, which deterred them from attending Trinity, or the Queen's colleges. This left access to the Catholic University, which was a private college (Papal degrees only) and not a state recognised awarding body. The attendance figure alone testified to the lack of success of the Catholic University. Full-time students for the years 1854-1879 numbered 521, an average yearly intake of approximately twenty.[30] This did not include medical students from the Catholic University Medical School, founded in 1855 and situated in Cecilia Street, Dublin. 'The medical school was the Catholic University's

---

[27] Ibid, p.131.
[28] Ibid.
[29] Ibid, p.146.
[30] Catholic university register of students, UCDA, IE CU5, records of the Catholic University, 1850-1911.

great success story: by the end of the century it had become the largest medical school in the country. After 1908 it became the medical faculty of UCD'.[31]

Although discussion of higher-level educational provision in Ireland acceptable to all religions, preceded the Intermediate Education (Ireland) Act, 1878, little progress was made in terms of religious exclusivity, 'although the problem had been debated in earnest since since the establishment of the Queen's colleges in 1845'.[32] Nonetheless, despite the insistence of the Catholic and Presbyterian Churches on religious autonomy in third level provision, all denominations ostensibly accepted the secular nature of intermediate education. In 1793, the University of Dublin, or Trinity College, then the only university in Ireland, was enabled by an act of the Irish Parliament (section of the Catholic Relief Act, 1793) to admit and confer degrees upon students without religious tests'.[33] The removal of the religious bar was further cemented by the disestablishment of the Church of Ireland in 1869. In 1908 two new universities, the National University of Ireland and the Queen's University, Belfast replaced the Royal University, leaving Trinity College untouched.

University provision in Ireland had a number of distinct phases; the removal of the religious bar in Trinity in 1793; the setting up of the Queen's colleges under the Queen's College (Ireland) Act, 1845 and the foundation of the Catholic University in 1854, following the Synod of Thurles in 1850. The failed Irish University Bill, 1873 brought forward by the first Gladstone government, preceded the Intermediate Education (Ireland) Act, 1878 by five years. Legislation followed to enable the setting up of the Royal University under the University Education (Ireland) Act, 1879. Two new universities were subsequently created by the provision of the Irish Universities Act, 1908. These were the National University of Ireland, with three constituent colleges established by charter: University College, Dublin; University College, Cork; and University College, Galway, while the second university established under the 1908 act was Queen's University, Belfast, with the Royal University dissolved in 1909.

---

[31] Donal McCartney, *UCD: A National Idea: the history of University College Dublin* (Dublin, 1999), p.7.
[32] Pašeta, *Before the revolution,* p.5.
[33] Ibid, p.90.

Despite ongoing demands by the hierarchy for a university with total Catholic control and registration, the new National University of Ireland did not realise a fully Catholic college. The only denominational colleges were Maynooth founded in 1795 and the Presbyterian College Londonderry, 1865. These provided for clerical education for Catholics and a more complete education for Presbyterians, with, according to Moody, the Londonderry college replacing a theological one established in Belfast in 1853.[34] In fact, Magee College, Londonderry, did not replace Assembly College in Belfast, but co-existed with it. According to McCartney, UCD was a response to 'a sixty-year-old demand for a university that would be acceptable to the religious majority and that would place Catholics on a footing with the hitherto privileged minority'.[35] The existing colleges of University College, under Jesuit sponsorship and a constituent of the Royal University since 1882, and the medical school were subsumed into University College Dublin, as were the female colleges at Eccles Street and Loreto College St. Stephen's Green.[36] Clongowes Wood, Blackrock, Belvedere, and Castleknock College provided the bulk of the first year students.[37]

John Healy, Catholic Bishop of Clonfert, 1896-1903 and Archbishop of Tuam from 1903-1918, stated in 1890, that 'we have examinations enough to spare in the Royal University but we have no adequate means of preparing for them, no centre of light and culture for the teaching and residence of our students'.[38] A graduate of the Royal University of Ireland writing in the same year highlights a college, which as portrayed appears to be the antithesis of other institutions and an example of what could be achieved in college provision. He stated that 'the Queen's College, Belfast stands on a different footing. The practical genius of the north of Ireland has already discovered that a college to be of use must be popularised and suited to the needs of people for whom it was established'.[39]

---

[34] Ibid, p. 98.
[35] McCartney, *UCD: A national idea*, p. 41.
[36] The Catholic University of Ireland changed its name to University College in 1882 and was placed under the management of the Jesuits in 1883.
[37] Ibid, p.33.
[38] John Healy, 'University education in Ireland', *Dublin Review*, vol. xxxii, (1890), p.26.
[39] Graduates of the Royal University: *The present provision for higher education in Ireland plainly stated*, (London, 1890).

It has been claimed that from the time of the Northcote-Trevelyan report into the civil service published in 1854, 'higher positions required a university education'.[40] This is negated by to an extent by the career of the Rt. Hon. James MacMahon, who did not have the benefit of a university education but made his way from a second-class clerkship to the top of the Post Office hierarchy. Subsequently, in 1918 he was appointed Under Secretary to the Lord Lieutenant of Ireland, making him the most senior civil servant in the Irish administration. Highlighting the viewpoint that experience was more valuable than third level education, Edwin Chadwick, Commissioner of the Board of Health in his comments on the Northcote-Trevelyan report questioned what particular advantages a civil servant would gain from 'several years passed in the university learning the classics … instead of being in the field … learning by actual practice'.[41] University provision and access in Britain, with a comparison between English and Scottish universities and those in Ireland highlights disparities. The influence of the Northcote-Trevelyan report in terms of the entrance examination for first division posting to the civil service and the maintaining of a form of privilege, regrettably did little to encourage meritocracy. A bias towards students studying for Oxford 'Greats' in the examinations is an important consideration, as it left students not only in Irish universities, but those outside Oxford in England and Scotland at a disadvantage.

Potential upward mobility and expansion of middle classes of Catholic members of the Irish cohort in the Dublin Castle administration, 1920 to 1922 and the population at large based on increased educational access, focusses attention on class formation in Ireland. The concept of middle class has been described as being 'notoriously fuzzy… it is the class that occupies the space between the upper (landowning or industrialist) and the lower (working or landless), in Ireland's case as indeed in other European countries'.[42] Among those countries, the British highly defined stratification extended from working class to middle class and beyond the upper middle

---

[40] Mary Clarke, 'The origins and impact of the Northcote-Trevelyan report on civil service reform in Britain', (PhD, Queen's University, Belfast, 2010).

[41] Heather Ellis, 'Efficiency and counter-revolution: connecting university and civil service reform in the 1850s', *History of Education*, vol. 42, no. 1, (2013), pp. 23–44.

[42] Joseph Ruane and Jennifer Todd, 'The role of the middle classes in twentieth-century Ireland' in E. Biagini and M. Daly (eds.) *The Cambridge social history of modern Ireland* (Cambridge, 2017) p.177.

classes to the aristocracy. Of particular relevance to the importance of education is Bourdieu's concept of the habitus as a 'structuring structure'.[43] This is an example of how 'the Irish boarding school habitus privileged particular forms of social and cultural accomplishments that fit within the institution's pedagogical vision. Rather than economic or monetary assets, a child's capital could consist of cultural accomplishments, social connections and relationships or educational credentials'.[44] Furthermore, 'during the mid-nineteenth century schools and universities became more important gate-keeping institutions regulating entry to the professional classes'.[45]

Ruane and Todd ascribe the expansion of the middle classes in Ireland to 'the development of university education … with professions such as law, medicine and the civil service providing new opportunities and outlets'.[46] For Tony Farmar, the passing of the Land Act, 1881, saw a shift from land ownership by the ascendancy transferred to small farmers in Ireland. However, this is debatable, as the 1881 act did not make provision for land purchase. He argues that 'space was left for the Catholic urban middle class to expand socially and economically'.[47] However, according to Ruane and Todd the middle class escaped 'the absolute want and dependence of the working class but without the manoeuvrability or security of those above them'.[48] Nonetheless, they claim on the plus side that the middle class had 'the reciprocally supportive relationship that often exists between it and the state'.[49] Ruane and Todd further highlight the argument that 'Protestants were over represented in the civil service and the judiciary, particularly in the higher ranks … although by the early twentieth century Catholics were making inroads even to the senior ranks'.

---

[43] Pierre Bourdieu, *The Logic of practice* (Cambridge, 1990), p.63.

[44] Mary Hatfield, *Growing up in nineteenth century Ireland: a cultural history of middle-class childhood and gender* (Oxford, 2019), p.12.

[45] Ibid p.13.

[46] Ruane and Todd, 'The role of the middle classes in twentieth-century Ireland' p.177.

[47] Tony Farmar, *Privileged lives: a social history of the Irish middle class 1882-1989* (Dublin, 2012), p.3.

[48] Ruane and Todd, 'The role of the middle classes in twentieth-century Ireland', p.178.

[49] Ibid.

There is an acceptance that 'the administration of Ireland through the Chief Secretary's office at Dublin Castle ground to a halt in 1920'.[50] Is this perhaps a tacit agreement by a number of historians with the findings of Warren Fisher report of 12 May 1920? Fisher stated that, 'the Castle administration does not administer. On the mechanical side it can never have been good and is now quite obsolete'.[51] For historians of Dublin Castle administration this is almost a mantra and lends weight to the decision to augment the Irish administration with a British cohort. Coming to Ireland ostensibly to rectify the inadequacies in the Chief Secretary's office, the seconded British civil servants in arriving 1920 had 'London', for which one could read Whitehall, connections. Were those links, which would not have been common to the Irish core group, beneficial in terms of administrative cohesion and governmental policy?

It is an exaggeration to claim that Anderson, Cope and Sturgis 'seemed to have changed the face of civilian administration at the Castle overnight'.[52] The perception that the British cohort totally dominated the administration from 1920 to 1922, is likewise suspect. The purported lack of success of Dublin Castle and its relationship with other departments, within both the Irish and British administrations and government offices, however, highlights a difficult relationship between Ireland and the Treasury, which 'disliked Irish departments as much as they disliked it'.[53] Given Warren Fisher's Treasury background, did that subsequently influence his report into the Dublin Castle administration of 1920?

The Lord Lieutenant or Viceroy, with all the trappings of a monarch was the head of British government in Ireland answerable to the Prime Minister and UK parliament. As a political appointment, the position was decided by the ruling party and normally ended with a change of government. According to Martin Maguire, 'unlike the non-political Crown, the Lord Lieutenant occupied several politically powerful posts. As head of the government boards, he exercised independent political judgement and he gave an account of his ministry to parliament'.[54] It was obligatory for those

---

[50] McColgan, *British policy and the Irish administration,* p.14.
[51] Warren Fisher report into Dublin Castle administration carried out by A.W. Cope and R.E. Harwood, 12-15 May 1920 (TNA, HO 317/50).
[52] McColgan, *British policy and the Irish administration,* p.14.
[53] O'Halpin, *The decline of the union,* p.3.
[54] Maguire, *The civil service and the revolution in Ireland,* p.3.

holding the office to be peers of the realm, with their appointment ratified by the Crown. The role of Lord Lieutenant was an influential one in terms of policy and the incumbent was entitled to a seat in cabinet, as Lord French chose to have in 1918. The holder of the position was at the head of the Irish executive, with the Chief Secretary and Under Secretary answering to him. With the resignation of Lord French on 30 April 1921, Lord FitzAlan, an English Catholic, became the last Lord Lieutenant of Ireland. On being asked his view of the appointment, Cardinal Logue acidly retorted that 'Ireland would as soon have a Catholic hangman'. Within days of the handing over of Dublin Castle to Michael Collins, Edward J. Byrne, Archbishop of Dublin lost no time in disassociating the Church from FitzAlan and cementing its hold on political matters, which was to be a mark of the Free State. A letter from the Archbishop suggesting that FitzAlan did not attend the memorial mass for Pope Benedict XV for fear of jeopardising the acceptance of the Treaty was addressed to James MacMahon and not the Lord Lieutenant himself.[55] FitzAlan's response was coolly polite but he insisted on attending, which he did, albeit not in uniform with an escort.[56]

Also outside the civil service administration was the Lord Lieutenant's immediate subordinate, the Chief Secretary. In 1920, Ian MacPherson, was succeeded by Sir Hamar Greenwood. Appointed by the government on 12 April 1920, his role was political, with much of his time spent in Whitehall on parliamentary business. Under the control of the Chief Secretary, the Dublin Castle administration was made up of civil and military divisions. By the end of the eighteenth century, a judicial division was added. According to McBride, the Chief Secretary 'had to give department heads freedom to make decisions on how to conduct departmental policy and manage office procedure.[57] The Chief Secretary's office was abolished in October 1924. Looking beyond political appointments, the Under Secretary or from 1920-1922, the joint Under Secretaries headed the civil service. They represented the most senior civil servants in the Irish administration. Until 1821, there had been separate civil and military Under Secretaries, so the dual role of 1920-22 was not without precedent.

---

[55] TNA, LG/F/20/1/17 Archbishop Byrne to James MacMahon, 29 Jan. 1922.
[56] TNA, LG/F/20/1/17 (b) FitzAlan to Archbishop Byrne, 29 Jan. 1922.
[57] McBride, *The greening of Dublin Castle* p. 11.

PART TWO

2

Legislation for intermediate education, 1878-1920

It is a thing of no great difficulty to raise objections against another man's oration, it is a very easy matter; but to produce a better in its place is a work extremely troublesome.[1]

Plutarch, *Parallel Lives.*

Following the passing of the Catholic Emancipation Act, 1829, an important question for Irish Catholics was that of education. Thomas Bonaparte Wyse MP presented a memorial on primary, intermediate and university education to the British Prime Minister, Earl Grey at the end of 1830.[2] While this was to be influential in the setting up of the national school system the following year, there was no provision for secondary or third levels. Forty years later in early 1870, a declaration was published on the orders of the House of Commons based on a motion by the O'Conor Don, in relation to university education in Ireland. It was signed by 960 Catholic gentlemen, including members of parliament, deputy lieutenants, magistrates, and professional men.[3] They sought changes in relation to higher education for Catholics in Ireland. In 1878, Mr Timothy McCarthy Downing MP, Liberal Party, speaking in response to Queen Victoria's speech, delivered to both Houses of Parliament on 17 January 1878, stated:

> Let the House observe the different way in which matters affecting Ireland and England were dealt with in the speech from the throne ... in the case of Ireland all that was said was that attention would be invited to the subject

---

[1] This epigraph, while perhaps enigmatic, suggests a theme of parliamentary debate and opposing viewpoints, for example finance, the conscience clause, and cramming, as raised during the stages of the Intermediate Education (Ireland) Bill 1878 and the ongoing demand for university provision.

[2] D.G. Paz, 'Wyse, Thomas (1791–1862)', *ODNB*.

[3] *Hansard Parliamentary Debates*, HC, 1 Apr. 1870, vol. 200 cc 1090-146, W.E. Gladstone, Prime Minister, 'The declaration signed by, I think, thirty-six Members of this House, and by a great number of other persons connected with the Roman Catholic Communion in Ireland'.

of Intermediate Education and the Grand Jury Laws. The people of Ireland wanted a Catholic University, but all that the Government offered to them was a scheme of intermediate education.[4]

While the O'Conor Don's motion had essentially failed in the short-term, the introduction of intermediate education in 1878 was followed by university provision a year later. Although less than was sought, being non-denominational and without a built environment or lecture facilities, the Royal University of Ireland was founded in the University Education (Ireland) Act, 1879, as an examining and degree-awarding university. From 1878, post-primary education in Ireland underwent a change, from limited access to secondary level schooling to a gradually expanded provision for schools and countrywide competitive intermediate examinations with monetary awards.

Questions as to what drove nineteenth-century educational reform and what steps were taken to enforce it, initially focus on legislation. The Intermediate Education (Ireland) Act, 1878 was the first legislative provision for post-primary education for the whole of Ireland, regardless of religion or class. Examinations were to be open to all students. The act made provision for financial assistance to both individuals and schools through its payment by results fees and awards, while imposing strict guidelines for teaching within a competitive framework. This structure tied in with the perception of a move towards meritocracy rather than patronage, as a means of career advancement in the public sector. The initiative was essentially driven by the recommendations of the Northcote-Trevelyan report on the permanent civil service, which was commissioned by William Gladstone, Chancellor of the Exchequer in 1853 and signed by Sir Stafford Northcote MP for Dudley and Sir Charles Trevelyan.[5]

The report recognised the importance of increasing numbers in the civil service recruited by way of competitive entry. It recommended a system of examinations ahead of entry and promotion on merit through open competition. Professor Hennessy described it as 'the greatest single governing gift of the nineteenth to the twentieth century: a politically disinterested and permanent civil service with core values of integrity,

---

[4] *Hansard Parliamentary Debates*, HL, 17 Jan. 1878, vol. 237 cc3-7.
[5] *Report on the organisation of the civil service, together with a letter from the Rev. B. Jowett*, 1854, H.C. [paper 1713].

propriety, objectivity and appointment on merit, able to transfer its loyalty and expertise from one elected government to the next'.[6] In Ireland, the lack of access to university education or patronage had ostensibly denied Catholic applicants access to first class clerkships within the civil service. This however, was not entirely the case, with other factors in terms of the recommendations of the Northcote-Trevelyan report and the underlying meaning behind its focus on meritocracy, creating a broader picture.

Candidates for Class 1 service positions 1877-1886 [7]

College or non-university	Per cent
Oxford	46.5
Cambridge	22
Universities in Scotland	2.5
Universities in Ireland	4
Non-university	23

The table above highlights the lack of first class entry not only by students in Ireland but also in Scotland, with the established Oxbridge colleges showing a near monopoly. This demonstrates the advantages of patronage did not disappear instantly with the move towards meritocracy advocated by the Northcote-Trevelyan report and raises questions on what exactly was intended by the authors of the report and how broad social access would be? According to Heather Ellis 'the old patronage system with its ties of favour and kinship was simply too unreliable, often resulting in the appointment of individuals who were either incompetent or were considered to be of dubious moral character'.[8] With regard to broader access, Northcote and

---

[6]Professor Peter Hennessy, Founder's Day address, Hawarden Castle 8 July 1999, cited in 'Whither the civil service', research paper 03/49, House of Commons library, May 2003.

[7] *Thirty-fourth report of the civil service Commissioners 1890* [c.6142] XXVI, appendix, p.24. Despite being sourced from the official report, this table is inaccurate in that figures add up to 98 rather than 100 percent. It highlights the dominance of Oxford candidates. That Durham University and University of London are not included in the table may be indicative of the fact that these universities had a different focus, for example medicine and law in the University of London and theology in Durham and did not present candidates for the civil service in in those years.

[8] Ellis, 'Efficiency and counter-revolution: connecting university and civil service reform in the 1850s, p.23.

Trevelyan 'saw the reform of the civil service as a means of stabilizing the polity and removing the pressures for undesirable radical or populist politics'.[9] Far from envisaging increased access across social divides, Gladstone wrote in a letter to Lord John Russell in January 1854 that reforms in civil service entry 'would strengthen and multiply the ties between the higher classes and the possession of administrative power'.[10]

Likewise, Northcote and Trevelyan argued 'that recruiting civil servants by means of a competitive academic examination would work more effectively to select the right kind of people'.[11] The examination to decide who would obtain the higher access posts in the civil service favoured those educated at Oxford taking 'Greats'.[12] According to Ellis, inspection of the examinations proposed in the Northcote-Trevelyan report, showed 'a specific privileging of those who had completed the recently reformed classical studies course at Oxford known as 'Greats' (study of Ancient Rome, Ancient Greece, Latin, ancient Greek, and philosophy).[13] The socialising aspect of the course was designed 'to produce men of character with a strong sense of duty to Queen and country, and a loyalty to the established political and social order'.[14] In 1915, Sir Mathew Nathan, Under Secretary, persuaded John Redmond to agree that Ireland would continue to use the British civil service commissioners for recruiting and examining candidates for the Irish civil service.[15] This effectively left all Irish applicants at a disadvantage and perpetuated the stranglehold of Oxbridge on entrance to the higher divisions of the civil service.

With a legislative focus mainly on secondary or intermediate provision, separating it from third level would be to ignore a piece of the jigsaw. This is particularly important in terms of access to higher-level positions in the civil service, both for Irish and British personnel. Following the Intermediate Education (Ireland) Act, 1878, and subsequent university

---

[9] John Greenaway, 'Celebrating Northcote–Trevelyan: dispelling the myths', *Public Policy and Administration'*, vol. 19, no.1, (2004), pp. 1-14.

[10] Gladstone to Lord John Russell, Jan. 1854, MS. 44291 ff. 93–103, W.E. Gladstone Papers, British Library.

[11] Edward Hughes, 'Sir Charles Trevelyan and Civil Service Reform, 1853–5', *The English Historical Review,* vol. 64, no. 250 (1949) p.72.

[12] Ellis, 'Efficiency and counter-revolution', p.31.

[13] Ibid, pp. 131-32.

[14] Ibid, p. 32.

[15] TCD, Dillon papers', MS 6801/167, 'meeting, 5 Mar. 1915'.

legislation of 1879, progress was slow to impact on Irish Catholics in relation to senior administrative positions. A level of parity was only gradually realised with the foundation of University College Dublin in 1908, a constituent college of the National University of Ireland. However, in terms of entry to the upper division of the civil service, restrictions did not only apply to Irish Catholics but to applicants from Irish universities regardless of religion and likewise as mentioned to those in Scotland and England who had not attended an Oxbridge college.

In this regard, university provision for the middle classes in Britain in comparison to that in Ireland and Scotland highlights similar issues, particularly in relation to religion. Action to remove religious barriers in English universities was by no means as early as in Trinity College, Dublin, which had occurred in 1793. The Universities Tests Act, 1871, removed religious restrictions in Oxford, Cambridge, and Durham Universities, except for the study of divinity. The Oxford University Bill, 1854, had abolished such limitations for BA degrees only. Degrees without religious tests in arts, law, music and medicine were extended by the Cambridge University Act, 1856. Despite the removal of these barriers, the emphasis on an Oxbridge education, especially a degree in 'Greats', points to a class and privilege driven system that limited entrance to the upper levels of the civil service for most English and Scottish applicants, as much as for Irish ones.

Distinguishing between England and Scotland, Arthur Conan Doyle wrote in 1881. of the privilege associated with nineteenth century English universities in comparison with Edinburgh University. He found that in Scotland 'there is none of the atmosphere of an enlarged public school, as is the case in English universities but the student lives a free man in his own rooms with no restrictions of any sort. It ruins some and makes strong men of many'.[16] The contrast between Scottish and English universities was likewise, highlighted by the Secretary for Scotland in 1888. Schomberg Henry Kerr stated in 1888 that students at English universities were what

---

[16] Robert Anderson and Stuart Wallace, 'The universities and national identity in the long nineteenth century, c. 1830-1914 in Robert Anderson, Mark Freeman, and Lindsay Paterson, (eds.), *The Edinburgh history of education in Scotland*, (Edinburgh, 2015), p. 273.

'might be called the higher classes, whereas the universities of Scotland were attended by all classes of the community'.[17]

He claimed that 'nothing could be a greater test of the difference ... than the single fact that while the proportion of the population of England that attended the Universities of Oxford and Cambridge was about one in 5,000, in Scotland the proportion that attended the universities was about one in 600'.[18] Kerr went on to say that, there were other differences between the universities. For example, he maintained Scotland had no residential students in the colleges, which was also the case as has been shown in the Royal University in Ireland. Confirming what Conan Doyle had said, Kerr claimed the authorities had no control over students unless they were in the universities, although the awarding of degrees depended on compulsory attendance and the payment of fees. He also stated that Scottish university fees were lower than in England, allowing for broader access.[19]

The English public schools in the nineteenth and early twentieth centuries prepared students for Oxford and Cambridge and for public service. This association saw many graduates apply for and obtain first class positions in the administration. However, at that time these universities were not without their detractors. The chief criticism was that their neglect of the sciences meant they could contribute little to the needs of industrialisation. Oxford and Cambridge produced clergy, gentlemen and after 1850, civil servants. In contrast, the University of London, founded in 1828, was the antithesis of the ancient universities. It was free of religious tests, cheaper than traditional universities, catered for 'middling rich people' and had a strong emphasis on the medical, legal, engineering and economic studies neglected by Oxbridge. In 1878 the University of London, on which the Royal University of Ireland was modelled, was the first in the UK to award degrees to women. The Royal University of Ireland followed in 1884, with Charlotte M. Taylor achieving a Bachelor of Music degree. In 1888, the Royal University awarded the first Bachelor of Laws in Britain or Ireland, to a woman, Letitia Alice Walkington.

---

[17] *Hansard Parliamentary Debates,* HL, 3 May 1888, vol. 325 cc1180-206vol., Schomberg Henry Kerr (The Marquis of Lothian), Secretary for Scotland speaking on the Universities (Scotland) Bill.
[18] Ibid.
[19] Ibid.

In 1850, Ireland had two universities, the University of Dublin and the Queen's University of Ireland, while England had four, Oxford, Cambridge, London, and Durham. However, at that time, a new layer of provision in Britain saw the rise of the civic or redbrick universities, broadening not only the number of institutions but also the scope of education provided. The term redbrick often denotes non-ancient universities, but was coined by Bruce Truscot to describe the Victorian brick used in their construction; for example, Birmingham University was built from Accrington red brick.[20] The six original civic colleges in Birmingham, Bristol, Leeds, Liverpool, Manchester, and Sheffield achieved university status before the First World War. They were based in cities that had seen a growth following the industrial revolution and specialised in science or engineering.

D.P. Moran and Arthur Griffith claimed that 'higher education in nineteenth-century Ireland was not geared towards producing industrialists, scientists or engineers. The emphasis on a classical curriculum encouraged the growth of a professional and bureaucratic sector'.[21] Griffith blamed the Irish education system for Ireland's lack of industrial development, which he claimed saw the increase of 'the struggling clerkdom in Ireland'.[22] An overview of university attendance by members of the British cohort, 1920-1922, in relation to civil service entry and advancement, in comparison with that of the Irish group in Dublin Castle, provides an essential element of and linkage between education and administration.

Prior to consideration of university provision, intermediate education was a necessary step for Ireland, which was to an extent influenced by Scottish and English legislation. There was an inter-relationship between education enactments in Ireland, England, and Scotland, although in the case of England and Scotland the pre 1878 provision mostly applied to primary education. In this regard, the intermediate legislation effectively followed the setting up of the Irish non-denominational national school system in 1831, rather than English provision. However, as these enactments were relevant to members of the Irish and British cohorts in the 1920-22 Dublin Castle administration, a brief summation of the English and Scottish acts and the separate report into English public schools is included.

---

[20] Bruce Truscot, *Red Brick University* (London, 1951), pp. 24-25.
[21] Pašeta, *Before the revolution*, p.122.
[22] Ibid, p.123.

The Education Act for England and Wales, 1870, was to an extent the basis for the Education (Scotland) Act, 1872. The English act stands as the first piece of legislation to deal specifically with the provision of education in Britain on a national scale. The act permitted voluntary schools to remain unchanged, but established a system of boards to provide and manage non-denominational schools. The boards were locally elected bodies, with funding derived from local rates. This was mirrored in Scottish provision but differed from the central Intermediate Education Board for Ireland, the members of which were appointed by the Lord Lieutenant. W.E. Forster who introduced the bill in the House of Commons, stated 'there are too few schools and too many bad schools. I believe that the country demands from us that we should at least try to do two things, and that it shall be no fault of ours if we do not succeed in doing them, namely cover the country with good schools, and get the parents to send their children to those schools'.[23] Lord Cairns, Lord Chancellor, when introducing the Intermediate (Ireland) Bill, 1878, echoed this sentiment in slightly different words but with the same meaning.[24] However, rather than intermediate education, Forster was referring to elementary schooling similar to the establishment of the Board of National Education in Ireland in 1831.

The later Education (England and Wales) Act, 1902, also known as the Balfour Act, was radical and controversial. In the House of Commons debate, it was stated that some elementary schools claimed to have secondary level provision.[25] This anomaly was likewise raised in parliamentary debate on the 1878 Irish intermediate act. In relation to the English legislation, it was argued by Mr A. J. Balfour that 'authorities for primary education have exaggerated their capacity for dealing with the problem of secondary education'.[26] He further asserted that many of them seem to suppose that by merely putting a certain number of classes dealing with subjects higher than elementary at the top of an elementary school, a system of secondary education was thereby immediately established.[27] Balfour contended that this would not suffice and that a proper system of

---

[23] *Hansard Parliamentary Debates,* HC deb., 17 Feb. 1870, vol. 199 cc438-98438, William Edward Forster MP for Bradford, Liberal.
[24] Richard Hawkins, 'Cairns, Hugh McCalmont (1819–85), 1st Earl Cairns', *DIB*.
[25] *Hansard Parliamentary Debates*, HC deb., 24 Mar. 1902, vol. 105 cc846-965 846.
[26] Ibid, Mr A. J. Balfour, First Lord of the Treasury.
[27] Ibid,

secondary schools where pupils could go at thirteen or fourteen needed to be established. In order for these to be successful, a focus on teacher training was essential.[28] The legislation as enacted, led to the rapid growth of secondary schools in England and Wales with over one thousand new buildings opening by 1914. However, according to G.R. Searle, the act was a religious minefield, outraging nonconformists, such as Methodists and Baptists among others and creating a political fall-out for the Conservatives; while a short-term political disaster for the party, which lost badly to the Liberals in the 1906 elections, in education terms, it was a long-term success.[29]

The 1872 Education (Scotland) Act, was ostensibly based on the English Education Act 1870, which as stated was focussed on elementary education but it made some provision for secondary education, although not in terms of a universal system. The act provided for denominational schools, the largest of which were those run by the Church of Scotland, Free Church of Scotland, Catholics and Episcopalians, to become incorporated into the new state-funded system. Such a focus was not acceptable, particularly to the Scottish Catholic Church. Unlike the Irish act, the Scottish legislation did not include provision for a national examination system. In fact, it was 1888 before the Scottish Leaving Certificate was introduced. This was a final school examination, the results of which influenced not only career advancement but also university access and scholarships. However, the 1872 act had far-reaching consequences for Scottish education, which are still current today.

An archivist at a well-known Edinburgh school stated in relation to current regulation that statutory provision is still very much rooted in the 1872 Act.[30] However, the Education Scotland Act, 1918, brought an end to the administrative system introduced in the 1872 act. Thirty-nine county and city authorities replaced the nine hundred and eighty-seven school boards introduced in the previous legislation. While the focus of the 1872 act had been primarily on elementary schools, that of 1918 was on secondary provision. In particular, Catholic schools benefitted from the increased

---

[28] Ibid.
[29] G. R. Searle, *A new England? Peace and war, 1886-1918* (Oxford, 2005), pp. 333–34.
[30] Author's conversation with Fiona Hooper, archivist, George Watson's College, Edinburgh, 19 June 2018.

opportunity given to denominational schools to enter the state-funded system, while retaining their religious ethos and modus operandi. Such schools were to be sold or leased to the state and not handed over without compensation

The Clarendon Commission, 1861-64, which had led to the enactment of the Public Schools Act 1868, was concerned with the reform and regulation of leading boys' schools of the time. This it is interesting on two counts. Firstly, it could be claimed that such an education had some influence on the exclusive schools in Ireland that colloquially came under the category of the 'Eton of Ireland'. For example, according to Ciaran O'Neill, 'Clongowes was often referred to as the Irish Eton ... it shared this distinction with the main Protestant boarding school, St Columba's College'.[31] Secondly, a number of the nine schools under review by the commission and particularly the seven boarding schools included in the legislation, were the alma maters of some of the British cohort seconded to Dublin Castle in 1920. These were Eton, Winchester, Rugby, Westminster, and St. Paul's. That the Clarendon Commission had limited its scope to nine schools, could lead to an erroneous assumption that these were the only public schools in England. Conversely, the Taunton Commission, 1864-67, which followed directly on from the Clarendon Commission, considered almost 800 endowed schools.[32]

The ensuing Public Schools Act, 1868, covered only 'the schools of the highest political and social importance, i.e. the schools catering for the sons of the aristocracy and influential upper classes'.[33] While education centred, the act embedded class and privilege firmly into British social delineations. The 1868 enactment was followed by the Endowed Schools Act, 1869, which legislated for the recommendations of the Taunton Commission.[34] Under this legislation, grammar schools were described as day schools to age sixteen but with a fee paying option for middle classes, an educational provision likely to have impacted on the higher levels of the civil service.

---

[31] Ciaran O'Neill, 'Rule Etonia: educating the Irish Catholic elite 1850-1900' (unpublished PhD, University of Liverpool, 2010), p.53.

[32] Colin Shrosbree, *Public schools and private education: the Clarendon commission 1861-64 and the Public Schools Acts* (Manchester, 1988), p.90.

[33] Nigel Middleton, 'The Education Act of 1870 as the start of the modern concept of the child' *British Journal of Educational Studies*, vol. 18, no. 2 (1970), pp. 166-179.

[34] According to the act such schools were defined as 'wholly or partly maintained by means of any endowment'

A year later, the Education Act, 1870, formulated a national system of schools for the children of manual workers.[35]

Lord Cairns, the Irish born Conservative Lord Chancellor in Disraeli's second government, introduced the Intermediate Education (Ireland) Bill, 1878 in the House of Lords on 21 June 1878.[36] Prior to the introduction of the bill, the Prime Minister, Benjamin Disraeli, had written to the Chief Secretary for Ireland, Sir Michael Hicks Beach in 1874 reminding him 'that any attempt to deal with national education in Ireland, even in quieter times, had broken up two governments'.[37] In opposition, the Conservatives under Disraeli had voted against the Irish University Bill, 1873, leading to the defeat of Gladstone's Liberal government in 1874. John Pope Hennessy wrote that 'Mr Disraeli's Irish policy was of course controlled by party exigencies'.[38]

While Disraeli's stance on the University Bill may have been motivated by political expediency, he subsequently opposed the boycott of Irish history by Castle authorities, the National Board, and the Queen's colleges. Pope Hennessy ascribed this prohibition of the teaching of history to 'the hard headed logical schools of statesmen ... on the grounds that it leads inevitably to Irish nationality'.[39] Conversely he quotes Disraeli as saying, 'I have no faith in any statesman who attempts to remedy the evils of Ireland, who is either ignorant of the past or who will not deign to learn from it'.[40] Hennessy claims that 'in this, the guiding principle of his Irish policy, he is apart from every English statesman of his time'.[41]

In 1878, Lord Cairns referenced the intermediate bill as 'a step much needed and much too long delayed towards improving the material and intellectual welfare of large classes of our fellow subjects in Ireland'.[42] Such

---

[35] Commonly known as Foster's Education Act (33 & 34 Vict. c. 75) [Eng.] (9 August 1870).
[36] 41&42 Vict. Intermediate Education (Ireland), 1878 {HL}.
[37] Disraeli to Hicks-Beach, 17 Dec. 1874, Gloucestershire archive, St Aldwyn MSS, PPC/75.
[38] John Pope Hennessy, *Lord Beaconsfield's Irish policy: two essays on Ireland* (London, 1885), p.29.
[39] Ibid, p.35.
[40] *Hansard Parliamentary Debates*, HC deb., 16 Mar. 1868, vol. 190 cc1688-792.
[41] Pope Hennessy, *Lord Beaconsfield's Irish policy,* p.35.
[42] *Hansard Parliamentary Debates*, HL, first reading of Intermediate Education (Ireland) Bill, HL deb., 21 June 1878, vol 241 cc7-19.

inclusivity was also stressed twenty-two years later when John Redmond MP stated during the debate on the Intermediate Education (Ireland) Bill 1900, that the 1878 provision enabled children of poor parents to obtain a first class education, which was denied them prior to the act.[43]

Lord O'Hagan, an Irish Catholic from Belfast[44], speaking on the 1878 bill, said the first question that must be asked was whether there was a need for intermediate education in Ireland.[45] In answer to his own query, he referenced the introduction of primary education and the conflicting views on the existence and operation of the National Board, which he said had been responsible for spreading education throughout Ireland, although to youth not at the high class now proposed. Was 'high class' intended to mean an education superior to that of the national schools, or was it a reference to the social status of the pupils? If the latter was the case surely such a statement was at odds with the inclusive nature of the proposed legislation, which was open to all students with the assistance of monetary awards intended to break economic and class barriers?

O'Hagan went on to say that the figures showed that an Irish boy could succeed at the lower level of the public service but then, 'he must bound his ambition and abandon hope'.[46] He continued by blaming this situation on the lack of educational provision in Ireland beyond fifteen years of age and the failure of governments which barred advancement. However, referring to 'high class youth', he pointed out that in 1866 there were 1,504 private schools in Ireland; this had fallen to 612 by 1871.[47] The decrease in pupil numbers in that period was 24,782. Lord O'Hagan said that there must be some provision for middle class intermediate education. The question is whether he meant the financially secure upper middle class or the less well-off putative Catholic middle class, with his own words perhaps indicating

---

[43] *Hansard Parliamentary Debates*, HC deb., 19 July 1900, vol. 86 cc487-526 487, John Redmond, MP for Waterford and then Leader of the (reunited) Irish Parliamentary Party.

[44] Patrick M. Geoghegan, 'O'Hagan, Thomas (1812-85), Lord Chancellor of Ireland, and 1st Baron O'Hagan', *DIB*. He was Lord Chancellor from 1868-74 and again from 1889-81. O'Hagan.

was educated at a Protestant school (RBAI), being the only Catholic registered..

[45] *Hansard Parliamentary Debates*, HL deb., 28 June 1878, vol. 241 cc415-46, Lord O'Hagan speaking on the second reading of the Intermediate Education (Ireland) Bill, 28 June 1878.

[46] Ibid.

[47] Ibid.

the former.[48] Dr William Drennan, a founder of the RBAI, Lord O'Hagan's alma mater, might well have answered the question. Although Drennan was speaking thirty-six years later at the opening of the school in 1814, his words had resonance. Drennan stressed the aim 'to diffuse useful knowledge, particularly among the middling orders of society, as one of the necessities rather than of the luxuries of life; not to have a good education only the portion of the rich and the noble, but as a patrimony of the whole people'.[49]

The Rt. Hon. Hugh Cairns, Lord Chancellor, in introducing the bill described intermediate education in Ireland as 'defective in quality, and ... inadequate in quantity'.[50] He attributed this to the actions of the state. He said that the government had gone far to dry up the intermediate schools of Ireland by provision of a primary education system which was, he said, one of the most efficient in the world. However, he highlighted the financial cost of this, which had mostly been borne by the state unlike in England and Scotland, where the people contributed to their primary education. While the success of primary education was undisputed, the lack of state intermediate education impacted mostly on poorer students for whom education beyond the age of fourteen or fifteen years was almost financially impossible and meant lower level access to the civil service and other competitive careers.[51]

The French College, Blackrock, later Blackrock College, under the auspices of the Holy Ghost Fathers, claimed to have been instrumental in suggesting a payment by results system of intermediate examinations for Ireland.[52] Such an incentive had been introduced in Trinidad in 1869, where St Mary's College a sister school, benefitted from its provision.[53] Fr Leman, President of the French College encouraged Edward Howley, a barrister who had worked in the school in Blackrock, to write a pamphlet on the

---

[48] Ibid.

[49] Belfast Royal Academical Institute, 'History aims and ethos', http://rbai.org.ukl/ [accessed 20 Mar. 2021].

[50] *Hansard Parliamentary Debates*, HL deb., 21 June 1878, vol. 241 cc7-19, Lord Cairns, the Lord Chancellor, first reading of Intermediate Education (Ireland) Bill, 1878.

[51] Ibid.

[52] French School Blackrock, founded in 1860 with a separate civil service college added in 1875.

[53] Sean Farragher, *Blackrock College, 1860-1995* (Dublin, 1995), p.53.

benefits of the payments and recommending its introduction in Ireland.[54] This was further advanced when Sir Michael Edward Hicks Beach, then Chief Secretary for Ireland, requested Sir Patrick Keenan, Commissioner of National Education, who had set up the scheme in Trinidad to write a proposal for a similar system for intermediate examinations in Ireland.[55] Hicks Beach presented Keenan's proposal to cabinet late in 1876. It formed the basis of the bill drawn up the following year.[56] Although the government was disinclined to assist denominational intermediate education through public funding, the competitive results-based concept was acceptable and already established in national schools since 1872.[57]

The schedule of rules in the intermediate education bill was drafted in three sections. These were examinations, prizes, exhibitions, and results fees. The initial schedule did not specify that examinations would be divided into junior, middle, and senior grades, as they were in fact from the first examinations in 1879. The schedule of rules covered the provision of lists of authors for literary sections of examinations, names of examiners in the various subjects and the relevant ages of students for each year's course. Students were required to be under sixteen years on the first day of June. After 1879 and 1880, no student could sit a higher grade examination unless he had been examined in and passed at least two subjects in the previous year. In 1879, a student younger than seventeen years could present for the second year's course and likewise one of under eighteen for the third year's course. This grading commenced in 1879 and was the delineation in use up to and including the examinations in 1921, with the addition of a preparatory grade in 1892.

According to the schedule, applications sent to the board were to be submitted in the previous October and accompanied by a certificate of age. The schedule of prizes and exhibitions specified that first year students obtaining the highest places and passing in three subjects were to be awarded exhibitions tenable for three years, not exceeding £20. Exhibitions, not to exceed £30, were to be awarded for two years to the highest placed students passing three subjects in the second year. The examiners could recommend

---

[54] Ibid.
[55] Ibid.
[56] W.E. Vaughan (ed.), *A new history of Ireland: Ireland under the union 1870-1921* (Oxford, 2010) p.524.
[57] John Coolahan, *Irish education, history, and structure* (Dublin, 1981), p.61.

the awarding of silver medals and prizes to students who passed three subjects in any year and obtained certificates of merit in two, but failed to get an exhibition. Prizes were proposed in the bill in the proportion of one in every ten students who shall pass three subjects at a minimum. These 'shall be awarded to the students obtaining the highest places at the examination'.[58]All the prizes and exhibitions were to be awarded on a countrywide, rather than local basis.

The rules specified that the examinations would be held between the first day of June and the first day of August. They were to be located at centres such as town halls, or other public buildings to be decided by the board, with the approval of the Lord Lieutenant. The subjects to be examined included 'the ancient languages, literature and history of Greece and Rome; the English language, literature and history; French, German and Italian languages; mathematics, including arithmetic and book-keeping; natural sciences and other subjects of secular education as the board may for time to time prescribe'.[59] Although it was not specified in the memorandum of the bill, the Irish language, titled 'Celtic', was examined from the outset in 1879. Its initial omission in the 1878 bill was contentious during debates on the legislation.

Proscriptions in relation to payments to school managers directed that no pupils attending schools receiving such payments should be permitted to remain in any religious instruction, which had not been sanctioned by parents or guardians.[60] Such pupils were not be excluded from the secular education of the school. The 'conscience clause' ensured the right of parents to withdraw a child from religious instruction without such action influencing secular teaching, but was considered unnecessary by some speakers in debates on the bill. This so-called 'conscience clause' was one of the most contentious sections of the Intermediate (Ireland) Bill, 1878, and was raised frequently during the debates in both Houses of Parliament. Given the non-denominational nature of the provision for Intermediate

---

[58] (41&42 Vict.) Schedule of rules, prizes, and exhibitions.
[59] Ibid.
[60] *Hansard Parliamentary Debates*, HL deb. HL Deb 21 June 1878, vol. 241 cc7-1, as stated by the Lord Chancellor; Deb 28 June 1878 vol 241 cc415-46, among those speaking against the conscience clause were Viscount Midleton, Lord Carlingford, the Earl of Belmore and Lord Inchiquin.

education, which defied the existing religious status quo of Irish education, the negative reaction to the clause in the bill was to be expected.

Lord Inchiquin among others also highlighted the issue. He approved of the bill, but thought the clause an unnecessary part of the proposed legislation and that Catholics and Protestants would welcome its omission in Ireland.[61] Lord Carlingford in opposition to the clause, doubted 'the wisdom or the prudence of extending the conscience clause system from primary schools, where it is necessary, to intermediate schools ... I hope the noble and learned Lord will consider the advisability of giving up that clause'.[62] The conscience clause had also been a feature of the Scottish Act, 1872.[63] The act provided for denominational schools, the largest of which were the Church of Scotland, Free Church of Scotland, Catholics, and Episcopalian, to become incorporated into the new state-funded system. However, the Catholic and Episcopalian Churches declined to be involved due to the clear delineation between secular and religious teaching in schools. The Catholic Church in particular was concerned that what it perceived, as a 'non-denominational' emphasis would in fact mean a Church of Scotland agenda. It was also concerned that Catholic schools would be assimilated by the state without compensation.[64] Thomas Collins, Conservative MP for Boston and Skegness, during the Irish debate in 1878 considered that it failed to address the issue of religion fairly.[65]

In highlighting the Scottish act as a precursor to the Intermediate Education (Ireland) Act, 1878 the aim is to show areas of discussion and dissention common to both. However, if any real comparison were to be made it would be with the provisions of the Irish national board in 1831. This saw the introduction of a non-denominational, results based primary school provision in Ireland. While contested by both Catholic and Protestant churches, the schools proved highly popular with the people. At the close of the year 1850, there were 4,547 schools connected to the national system

[61] Lucius William O'Brien, Baron Inchiquin, Co. Clare, *HL Deb 28 June 1878 vol 241 cc415-46.*

[62] *Hansard Parliamentary Debates*, HL deb., 28 June 1878, vol. 241 cc415-46.

[63] An act to amend and extend the provisions of the law of Scotland on the subject of Education [6th Aug. 1872].

[64] Stephen J. McKinney and Raymond McCluskey (eds.), *A history of Catholic education and schooling in Scotland: new perspectives* (London, 2019), p.24.

[65] Thomas Collins MP for Boston and Skegness, Conservative.

with more than half a million children on the rolls.[66] The figures quoted showed a slight increase in provision from the previous year when around 500,000 children were attending the 4,321 national schools.[67] However, by the turn of the century, the education system in Ireland was despite its name, denominational in practice.

The Irish Act in 1878 directed the Commissioners of the Church Temporalities in Ireland to make payments for the use of the Intermediate Board under the Irish Church Act, 1869. This act enabled the disestablishment of the Church of Ireland, leaving it independent of the Church of England. However, with regard to the property of the Church of Ireland the act decreed:

> Whereas, it is expedient that the union created by act of parliament between the Churches of England and Ireland as by law established, should be dissolved and that the Church of Ireland as so separated should cease to be established by law and that after satisfying so far as possible upon principles of equality, as between the several religious denominations in Ireland, all just and equitable claims; the property of the said Church of Ireland, or the proceeds thereof, should be applied in such manner as Parliament shall hereafter direct.[68]

Among the provisions of the Intermediate Education (Ireland) Act 1878, section eight concerned finance for the board. It stated that 'the Commissioners of the Church Temporalities shall ... provide for the use of the board, either in cash or in securities, rent charges of an equivalent value, such amount, not exceeding in the whole one million of pounds sterling, as the board shall estimate to be required'.[69] It was further stated that 'the annual income arising from the amount so provided shall be applied by the board for the purposes of this act and if and so far as the same shall not in each or any year be required to be so applied, the same shall be invested by the board by way of accumulation in the purchase of government

---

[66] Patrick F. O'Donovan, 'Ireland's national school system in the time of the Great Famine: an overview', *History of Education*, 2021, https://doi.org/10.1080/0046760X.2021.1906455 [accessed 29 Jan. 2021].
[67] R.F. Foster, *Modern Ireland 1600 -1972* (London, 1988), p.341.
[68] David Charles Douglas, and W.D. Handcock (eds.), *English historical documents* 1833-1914, 'Ireland and Irish affairs, 1833-1914' (London, 1977) p.294.
[69] 41 and 42 Vict c.60 [Ire.].

securities'.[70] The board was directed to provide annual accounts and reports to the Lord Lieutenant, which were to be laid before the Houses of Parliament. The onus was put on the board under the direction of the Treasury, to prepare annually or within a shorter timeframe 'accounts of the receipts and expenditure of the capital and revenues derived from all funds under the control of the board'.[71]

Following auditing, reports of the Comptroller and Auditor General were required to be laid before both Houses of Parliament, with the cost of the audit to be included in the expenses of carrying out the provisions of the act.[72] From the enactment of the 1878 Act and the introduction of the first intermediate examination in 1879, and the provisions of the act in conjunction with the rules as laid down by the board, certain financial changes and challenges not anticipated in the 1878 legislation, necessitated the introduction of the Intermediate Education (Ireland) Acts of 1882 and 1890. The amending act, 1882 was concerned with financial distribution and the 'application of future surplus' and the 'prohibition on anticipation of income'.[73] The former clause made it lawful for the board to apply a surplus of income in one year, in whole or part to another year or years. The latter stated that it would be unlawful for the board to anticipate in one year the income of other years in the future, but not unlawful to hire or assign a salary to any officer involving payment in that year but also in future years. This act created an impression of financial stability that for reasons outlined by headmasters in Ireland was not accurate.[74] The amendments of 1882 were to cause outrage among school principals and parents, eroding the initial trust in the examinations.

During the debate on the bill, some of the main arguments raised were in relation to the failure of the Chancellor to name the intended members of the Intermediate Board, which was to be called 'the Intermediate Education Board for Ireland, in this act referred to as 'the Board'.[75] At the Committee stage Charles Lewis, the Conservative MP for Londonderry, brought up the

---

[70] Ibid.
[71] Ibid.
[72] Ibid.
[73] Intermediate Education (Ireland) Act, 1882 (61 & 62 Vict. c. 22) (18 Aug. 1882).
[74] *Remonstrance of the headmasters of Ireland against the financial changes made by the board of Intermediate education in their rules for 1882* (Dublin 1882).
[75] 41 and 42 Vict. c.66 [Ire.] clause 2.

issue of the names of the proposed commissioners. This matter had been raised in both Houses during the debates. He was concerned that when the bill passed, the House would have no control whatever over the board. He claimed that 'the bill was so shaped, that although certain rules were laid down in the schedule to the bill, the commissioners would have the power with the sanction of the Lord Lieutenant to abrogate every one of the rules and substitute an entirely new system'.[76] With perhaps a certain foresight he feared that there was nothing to prevent the board as contemplated by the bill from being wholly an ecclesiastical board, or it might even be constituted of worn-out judges.[77]

The board was to be a 'body corporate and have a common seal'.[78] It was however, specified in the bill that the board would be made up of seven members appointed by the Lord Lieutenant. The board's composition in terms of denominational representation was hotly debated in both the House of Lords and the Commons. It was also to be a contentious feature of the 1890 legislation twelve years later. Other matters related to the composition of the board including the filling of vacant places and the annual appointment of a chairman. These were matters at the discretion of the Lord Lieutenant. Additional points covered included the delineation of three members to form a quorum; the periodic appointment of assistant commissioners to assist the board also acting as secretaries and inspectors; salaries for assistant commissioners were not to exceed £1000 per annum and other expenses were all included. The Earl of Belmore speaking on the second reading of the bill questioned the role of the assistant commissioners.[79] He wished to know if they were to be 'in all respects equals of the other commissioners and to vote as members of the board'.[80] The Lord Chancellor in response stated 'the assistant commissioners will not be co-ordinate; they will be inferior to the commissioners, as their name obviously implies'.[81]

---

[76] Ibid.
[77] *Hansard Parliamentary Debates*, HC deb., 25 July 1878, vol 242 cc261-327.
[78] 41 and 42 Vict. C.66 [Ire.].
[79] Somerset Richard Lowry-Corry, 4th Earl Belmore, Fermanagh, Conservative.
[80] *Hansard Parliamentary Debates*, HL deb, 28 June 1878, vol. 241 cc415-46.
[81] Ibid.

Lord Waveney[82] speaking on the debate stated that 'the advantages offered to the country were not to be over-rated and the country would only have itself to blame if it did not take advantage of the opportunity now offered. If ever there was a scheme which had a fair prospect, a more than fair prospect, a certainty of success, it was this one'.[83] He then made an important reference to an issue that was also to be raised by other speakers, namely the extension of the provision of the bill to females.[84] Lord Waveney went on to say that he had received a letter from the secretary of a leading school in Dublin in which the secretary 'begged that at the proper time he would move that the benefits of the bill be extended to the ladies of Ireland'.[85] Subsequently, on 5 July 1878, Earl Granville [86] presented a petition from the 'Ladies' General Educational Institute' to the House of Lords, 'praying that female students might be permitted to share the benefits of the Intermediate Education (Ireland) Bill'.[87]

Earl Granville highlighted the fact that strong feelings existed in England on the question of girls' education and that he was sure the same applied to Ireland. Rather than hold up the passage of the bill, Earl Granville said he believed that the matter was covered by the assurance of the Lord Chancellor that there was nothing in the bill to prevent the board from admitting females to the advantages of intermediate educational provision. However, Catholic clergy and educators in Ireland were not of the same opinion. However, William Ewart Gladstone, MP for Greenwich, endorsed the call for the benefits of the bill to be extended to women, this being especially important he said at a time when those who stop short of supporting their political enfranchisement, support their inclusion. On 25 July, the bill was considered in committee with a divergence of opinion on the inclusion of female candidates. Attorney General, J. Lowther, moving an amendment on the issue, suggested that the following words should be introduced into the bill: 'For applying, as far as conveniently may be, the benefits of this act to the

---

[82] Robert Alexander Shafto Adair, 1st Baron Waveney, Liberal Party speaking on HL deb., 28 June 1878.

[83] Ibid.

[84] *Hansard Parliamentary Debates,* HL deb, 28 June 1878.

[85] Ibid.

[86] George Leveson-Gower, Second Earl Granville, Liberal.

[87] Hansard Parliamentary Debates, HL deb., Intermediate Education (Ireland) Bill Petition, 5 July 1878, vol. 241 c.848.

education of girls'.[88] Isaac Butt, MP for Limerick City,[89] opposed the amendment on the grounds that, 'when this bill passed the House of Lords there was not the slightest intention of providing for the education of girls'.[90] Another objector noted that 'the fund to be disposed of under the bill was not very large, and indeed was not sufficient to provide for the requirements of the male youth of Ireland'.[91]

The discussion appears to have reflected more than one view on the subject in relation to education being for boys. Whether through an omission or assumption the bill referred to 'students' and in one instance to 'pupils' but these were not specified as being male. However, despite protestations, the amendment passed. The matter was further raised by way of a parliamentary question in the House of Commons in 1879.[92] While it could be argued that the passing of the Attorney General's amendment and proposed wording for its inclusion in the bill, could have hinged on defeat of a patriarchal assumption that students or pupils were boys, this was not the entirely the case. The defeat of those who spoke against the inclusion of females was primarily due to the impact of petitions as referenced by Lowther and the support of English MPs, who were perhaps more conscious of the implications of the rising suffragette movement, as highlighted by Gladstone among others, than perhaps their Irish counterparts.

Girls went on to do very well in the intermediate examinations. They did so despite the objections from the Catholic Church. However, the petition of Irish headmasters highlighted the reaction to the female position vis-à-vis monetary rewards: 'The weaker sex is sure to go to the wall in a fierce struggle for the endowments, and it is surely worthwhile considering what effects an improved education for girls would produce on the next generation'.[93] When the bill was passed, the ensuing Intermediate Education (Ireland) Act 1878 contained the amendment in relation to the inclusion of girls as proposed by the Attorney General.[94] It was to be twenty-four years

---

[88] Hansard Parliamentary Debates, HC deb., 25 July 1878, vol. 242 cc261-327.

[89] Isaac Butt, MP, leader of the Home Rule party, 1874-79.

[90] Hansard Parliamentary Debates, HC deb., 25 July 1878.

[91] Ibid, Sir Joseph M'Kenna MP, Youghal, Irish Parliamentary Party.

[92] *Hansard Parliamentary Debates*, HC deb., 07 Apr. 1879, vol. 245 cc445-644.

[93] *Remonstrance of headmasters of Ireland against the financial changes made by the Board of Intermediate Education in their rules for 1882* (Dublin, 1882).

[94] 41 and 42 Vict. c.66 [Ire.]

after the enactment of the intermediate act, before the first women were employed in the Irish civil service in 1902.

The issue of cramming, which still resonates today, was raised during the debate on the Intermediate Education (Ireland) Bill, 1900, by James Rentoul MP, Down East.[95] He argued that if anyone wanted to encourage cramming there was no better means by which it could be achieved than by the intermediate system, as it had existed hitherto.[96] Furthermore he stated that many Irishmen considered that it would have been better if not a single farthing had been spent on intermediate education since 1879. He contended that 'a vast number of shattered constitutions and early graves were the result of the system.[97] With a tie-in to a contention that many Irishmen regretted the spending of money on intermediate education and that it caused health problems, Rentoul was not only confusing separate issues but making a broad statement with regard to the popularity or otherwise of intermediate provision. John Redmond said that the system of secondary education in Ireland 'led merely to a training of the memory, that it did not train the intellect, that it simply crammed the mind'.[98]

The matter of inspection of schools was to be vehemently opposed by Catholic schools, supported by the hierarchy. Bishop Conroy writing to the Chief Secretary stated: 'I trust that your plan for the improvement of intermediate education will not include a demand of the right to inspect Catholic schools, otherwise than by testing their results in the examination.[99] We should be jealous of such an inspection and to claim the right of making it would interfere with the success of the proposed scheme'.[100] Lord Carlingford further insisted, 'we do not want a general inspection of the schools. We do not undertake a responsibility of that kind; but there are certain things mentioned in the bill, conditions as to the number of pupils and the attendances, as to which it may be necessary to have some limited inspection, and so far as it is necessary that duty will be performed by the

---

[95] *Hansard Parliamentary Debates*, HC deb, 19 July 1900, vol. 86 cc487-526, James Rentoul MP, Down East, Conservative.
[96] Ibid.
[97] Ibid.
[98] Ibid, Mr John Redmond MP for Waterford.
[99] Bishop Conroy to the Chief Secretary, 20 Feb. 1886. Quoted by T.J. McElligott, *Secondary Education in Ireland, 1870-1921* (Dublin, 1981).
[100] Ibid.

assistant commissioners'.[101] Unlike the debates on the 1878 Irish enactment, the issue of inspection does not seem to have been contentious in the Education (Scotland) Bill, 1872.

Just prior to the foundation of the Irish Free State, the MacPherson Bill of 1919 (Education Ireland Bill, 1919) was initiated and was intended to be the first far-reaching legislation since 1878.[102] The bill was based mainly on the English Education Bill, 1918, or as it was known, the Fisher Bill, and would have had a major influence on post 1878 Irish educational provision if Chief Secretary Ian MacPherson had succeeded in his proposals. H.A.L. Fisher recognised not only the benefit of education to the individual but to society.[103] While his bill was the first attempt to raise the leaving age to eighteen in England, after the First World War, spending cuts meant that such a proposal was not immediately implemented. Its provisions however, allowed for increased salaries and pensions, which Fisher hoped would attract more teachers. It was enacted on 8 August 1918.[104]

MacPherson introduced the Irish bill in light not only of the Fisher legislation, but following a report on the Viceregal commission on Intermediate Education, Ireland (Maloney) in March 1919, which in tandem with the Killanin report demonstrated the need for extensive change.[105] The bill, which drew on both reports, provided for compulsory attendance, a department of education and local maintenance.[106] Provision such as evening and continuing education, abolition of payment by results and the introduction of superannuation schemes for teachers based on the recommendations of Killanin report were also included.[107]

---

[101] *Hansard Parliamentary Debates,* HL deb., Lord Carlingford, 28 June 1878.

[102] Ian (John James) MacPherson, Chief Secretary for Ireland 10 Jan. 1919-2 Apr. 1920.

[103] Herbert Albert Laurens Fisher, historian, vice chancellor Sheffield University and president of the board of education.

[104] Education Act 1918, known as the Fisher Act (8 & 9 Geo. V c. 39) [Eng.]

[105] Report of Vice-Regal Committee of Inquiry (Killanin), HC 1919 (Cmd. 60), XXI 741).

[106] Tony Fahy, 'State, family and compulsory schooling in Ireland', *The Economic and Social Review,* vol. 23, (1992), pp. 369-395.

[107] At the direction of the Lord Lieutenant of Ireland, Lord French a Vice Regal Committee was to be set up to enquire into matters connected with primary education in Ireland, particularly in relation to teachers' salaries and conditions of service. The Right Honourable Lord Killanin was appointed Chairman and other nominees included Maurice Headlam, Treasury Remembrancer, and

However, failing to reach a second reading, the bill was formally withdrawn in December 1920. Its collapse left intermediate education in a poor state. Sean Farren argued that 'the failure to enact the bill marked the last British attempt to reform education in the whole of Ireland'.[108] The proposed legislation caused outrage in the Catholic Church, local councils and in the press. MacPherson's 1919 bill was described as 'merely an attempt by Dublin Castle to mould the minds of Irish youth in the British fashion'.[109] However, it was not just Catholics, who strongly objected to the bill. Farren pointed out that 'ironically while the Protestant churches appeared to endorse the principles of the 1919 bill and had allied themselves with the stand taken by unionist politicians, their endorsement was soon revealed to be less than wholehearted.[110] He further contended that 'they were to prove just as capable as the Catholic Church of protecting their interests whenever they perceived them to be endangered by a political power'.[111]

The report of the board for 1919 stated 'matters have been getting steadily worse in the schools and a complete collapse seems to be not far distant'.[112] The aborted bill was not only a failure in educational amendment and advancement but also a career defeat for MacPherson. He was described as being in an hysterical state during a debate in the House of Commons on the Condition in Ireland, on 14 May 1919. Suffering from purported ill health he took increasingly long periods of absence in London and on resigning the post of Chief Secretary, left Ireland permanently on 2 April 1920. On 4 April, two days after the Chief Secretary's departure, French wrote to Macpherson, 'I am glad you will now have a measure of peace and rest. I have noted sadly how you terribly stood in need of it'.[113]

Most likely influenced by his experience of Scottish and English legislation, the setting up of a department of education had been one of the

---

Andrew Nicholas Bonaparte Wyse. Official notification was given at His Majesty's Castle of Dublin on the 12th Aug. 1918, signed by Under Secretary, James MacMahon.

[108] Sean Farren, *The politics of Irish education 1920-65* (Belfast, 1995), p. 34.
[109] *Weekly Irish Times*, 17 Jan. 1920.
[110] Sean Farren, *The politics of Irish Education*, p.34.
[111] Ibid.
[112] *Report of the Intermediate Board for Ireland for the year 1919*, [cd. 904], H.C. 1920.
[113] French to Macpherson, 4 Apr. 1920 (Strath. papers, MS 490 (186)).

central focusses of MacPherson's bill. The civil service in Ireland in the early 1850s had in fact provided an efficient National Education Office, which in conjunction with the Northcote-Trevelyan Commission was satisfactory with systematic procedures.[114] Reports on the Education Office in London found it to be far less satisfactory than the Dublin office.[115] The push in the Bill for a department of education was very much in line with a similar attempt in Scotland. However, the Duke of Richmond had referred to the Scottish Education Department, as 'simply a room in Whitehall with the word "Scotland" painted on the door'.[116] The department did not move to Edinburgh until 1939 although pressure led to the creation of a Secretary for Scotland in 1885.[117]

Despite the inevitable discord centred on areas such as secular provision, finance and the inclusions of female candidates, legislation in relation to intermediate education in Ireland was a watershed moment. Its competitive emphasis, whether driven by the provisions of the 1831 Irish primary system, or a new era of examinations for civil service advancement following the Northcote-Trevelyan report, changed the profile of education in Ireland. When taken on face value, the intention by Northcote-Trevelyan to replace privilege with meritocracy in selection for upper level civil service entry seemed laudable and progressive.

However, beneath the aspiration lies another level, that of the meritocracy of the privileged. Effectively the new entrance examinations favoured those educated at Oxbridge, especially Oxford University, perpetrating the old concept of privilege, with few middle or working class students attending Oxbridge. The second point relates to university provision and Catholic access in Ireland, with the hierarchy barring entry to all colleges with the exception of the Catholic University of Ireland. It is apparent that Irish Catholics were not deprived of third level education by a lack of university provision. It could however be argued that it was the dogmatic action of their own church in demanding nothing less than a state

---

[114] Aine Hyland, 'An analysis of the administration and financing of national and secondary education in Ireland, 1850-1922' (PhD thesis, University of Dublin, Trinity College, 1982), p.564.
[115] Ibid.
[116] James Scotland, *The history of Scottish education* (London, 1969), p.5.
[117] Ibid.

university under its total control that deprived Catholic students of adequate third level education.

3

Towards meritocracy and equality

To receive a proper education is the source and root of all goodness.

Plutarch, *De Liberis Educandis**

*Edmund G. Berry, 'The De Liberis Educandis of Pseudo-Plutarch' Harvard Studies in Classical Philology, vol. 63, (1958), pp. 387–399. De Liberis Educandis is considered to be the work of Plutarch, despite some contention.

The impact of intermediate legislation on the Irish population and profiles of high achieving examination candidates, especially in the early years of the intermediate examinations, show interesting if not always expected outcomes. Balancing the progression of a core established Catholic merchant and professional class, socially secure and with access to secondary education prior to 1878, against any increase in upward mobility dependent on expanded educational provision, shows an uneven distribution. A comparison of examination results from the first few years following the introduction of the examinations to approximately a decade later, demonstrates what educational and social changes there were and how rapidly they progressed.

With the passing of the potentially ground breaking Intermediate Education (Ireland) Act, 1878, implementation posed the next hurdle. There were indubitably successes and pitfalls in the introduction of a competitive intermediate examination structure in Ireland. The impact of the legislation on the population, particularly the heretofore under-funded and under-recognised Catholic education sector brought about change. How successful was the provision and how effective were the rules and schedules outlined in the act? In order to create an overall picture of the impact of the intermediate legislation, an overview of the practical running of the examinations and the participation of schools and individual candidates is necessary. The workings of the Intermediate Education Board, its reports and results-lists published annually from 1879 in tandem with other primary and secondary sources, provide a comprehensive picture of the implementation of the legislation and its contribution to educational practice and standards. The reports are particularly relevant as they provide an annual account of the necessary adjustments to the rules and regulations, financial outlay, male and female pass rates, the number of results fees awarded, and the schools receiving exhibitions and prizes. Subject reports by individual examiners were also provided annually, starting in 1879, the first year of the examinations.

What exactly did the results of the first year's examinations indicate? How, for example, did Catholic schools compare with their Protestant counterparts and what educational facilities did they have? An overview of secondary schools prior to 1878 shows uneven provision. Other than efforts made by some national schools to extend their curricula to include a couple of years of intermediate teaching, Catholic superior schools in Ireland were the alternative for some. As these did not have state endowments they were costly and beyond the reach of the average family. However, they provided a less expensive alternative to education abroad for the Catholic merchant or professional classes seeking denominational education at a relatively affordable cost. Conversely, according to O'Neill, for those who could afford a foreign education, 'it is also possible to argue that religion had little to do with this tradition, and that it was wealth and status that motivated the decision'.[1]

Nonetheless, O'Neill states that in 1872 a 'committee of Irish Catholics' under Cardinal Cullen and members of the Catholic laity produced a pamphlet listing 47 schools in Ireland providing an intermediate education.[2] In *Secondary Education in Ireland,* T.J. McElligott argues that educational provision was not lacking in Ireland before intermediate legislation, asserting that prior to 1878, 'every county had a small but varied collection of schools for those who wanted a 'superior' education'.[3] Far from being under-represented, there was a preponderance of Catholic students from 1861, which could be ascribed to a greater Catholic population. What these figures do not highlight is the financial outlay necessary to access such schooling or the recognition by parents of its benefits. In comparison to the figures for 1861, the post 1878 figures show a marked increase in Catholic attendance with the total for 1911, three times that of 1861. Protestant numbers declined marginally, while Presbyterian totals had fallen off slightly in 1881 but rose to just above previous levels by 1911. The total

---

[1] O'Neill, 'Rule Etonia', p.24.
[2] Ibid, p.23.
[3] McElligott, *Secondary education in Ireland 1870-1921,* p.1.

number of superior schools had declined from 729 to 572 in the ten years from 1861-71.

According to McElligott, 'the question of secondary education for Catholics had not become a matter for serious discussion until the second half of the nineteenth century'.[4] He goes on to make the point that even then there were not many Catholics, whose social and financial standing was such as to make them feel the want of such an education. He claims that 'the inherited notion that secondary education was the exclusive privilege of children of higher social position prevailed in this country as well as in England for many years, in the case of Ireland even after the introduction of the Intermediate Education (Ireland) Act, 1878'.[5] Prior to that time in what was seen as an imitation of English public schools, a number of Catholic fee-paying schools for boys under the direction of religious orders were founded in the years before 1878. Among the most notable of these was the French School Blackrock, as previously mentioned. Founded in 1860 by the Holy Ghost or Spiritan order, it provided education at junior and secondary levels and incorporated a university preparation college and also one aimed at preparation for the civil service examinations. Rockwell College in Co. Tipperary was founded four years after the Blackrock school, also by the Holy Ghost order.

The Jesuits were responsible for the establishment of Clongowes Wood College, which was arguably the most exclusive of the Catholic colleges. According to O'Neill, 'the first deliberately elitist boarding school to open in Ireland was the Jesuit Clongowes Wood College in north Co. Kildare, founded in 1814'.[6] James McLorinan of Dublin was first to enrol in the school. His parents were drapers and belonged to the evolving prosperous class of Catholics who were willing to take advantage of a classical education for their son.[7] St Stanislaus College, Tullabeg, just over six miles from Tullamore, and the Sacred Heart College (now Crescent College), Limerick were also prominent Jesuit schools. The order has been associated with Limerick since 1565. A stated aim of the 1878 intermediate education legislation was to provide secondary schooling across all social levels.

---

[4] McElligott, *Secondary Education in Ireland*, p.3.
[5] Ibid p.30.
[6] O'Neill, 'Rule Etonia', p.34.
[7] Brendan Cullen, *A Short History of Clongowes Wood College* (published privately by the author, 2011).

While empirical evidence does point to an increased provision of schools and educational opportunities under intermediate legislation, it was perceived that 'the chief defect of the Bill ... was its failure to make any provision for new reasonably cheap schools for the sons of struggling professional or business men'.[8] This 'was all the more necessary in view of the fact that the bill was bound to have important consequences as regards the future status of our population and the position which they are destined to hold hereafter in the social scale'.[9]

McElligott, while giving consideration to the option of continental schools, focused primarily on the increasing numbers of secondary schools in Ireland, which provided an alternative to sending pupils abroad and increased provision for those unable to pay for such exclusive foreign schooling. When Ciaran O'Neill discussed Catholic pupils attending French and German schools in *Catholics of consequence*, he was, as previously mentioned, referring to education for boys. However, in an article in the *Irish Times* in 2014, he referred to the richest families sending their sons to England and daughters to the continent stating that 'transnational education offered even more exclusivity and for girls would guarantee fluency in French or German, highly prized in the marriage market'.[10]

In terms of those girls who were educated in Ireland and who wished to avail of the provisions of the Intermediate Act of 1878, 'the Dublin Catholic convents were discouraged by the Catholic Church from taking part in public competition. This was justified as being due to potential dangers to modesty involved in entering examination centres remote from their schools'.[11] Perhaps a more credible reason for this discouragement of female participation was the Church's fear that they would take prize money away from male students. This theme was taken up in a letter from Cardinal Paul Cullen of Dublin to the Chief Secretary in response to preceding correspondence from the Chief Secretary.[12] In the letter to Cardinal Cullen,

[8] Ibid.

[9] *The Irish Times,* 27 June 1878.

[10] Ciaran O'Neill, 'Paying for privilege, whether we benefit or not' *Irish Times,* 21 Oct. 2014.

[11] Robert Dudley Edwards cited in McElligott, *Secondary education in Ireland,* p.53.

[12] Cardinal Paul Cullen to Chief Secretary for Ireland to Sir Michael Hicks-Beach, 7 Feb. 1878 (Cardinal Cullen's correspondence, Holy Cross College, Clonliffe, Dublin).

the Chief Secretary stated that 'the term "student" is intended to include girls as well as boys, but it might be advisable to reduce the value of payments to the former and of their prizes and exhibitions below that named for boys'.[13] However, the cardinal was reluctant to see any of the available funding go to female students, stating in relation to the proposals for the intermediate act that: 'In intermediate schools, boys begin to train themselves for the army or navy, for the bar or magisterial bench, for the medical or surgical professions, or for other occupations to which men alone can aspire. Females go in a different direction and require other sorts of training and teaching and it seems strange that regulations for the two classes should be united in one bill'.[14]

There is ample scope in the results of the intermediate examinations to examine the effect of the expanded educational provision on education for females, following the Intermediate Education (Ireland) Act of 1878. Despite the exhortations of Cardinal Cullen, 'by 1914 women had arrived in Irish government offices'.[15] According to R.B. McDowell, following a couple of appointments of females from 1902, there were seventeen women officials and twenty card tellers in the health insurance commission and 60 female typists were employed in Irish offices by 1914. However, Sir James Brown Dougherty, Under Secretary, claimed that 'it was impossible to employ them in the Chief Secretary's office because it was relatively small and 'public opinion would insist on segregation of the sexes'.[16] McDowell went on to reference 'Robinson' of the Local Government Board stating that he 'hoped that public opinion would not penetrate into his old age pensions branch where men and woman were working side by side'.[17]

Data presented in the reports of the intermediate board from 1879-1919 highlights the total number of students who gave notice of their intention to present and those who actually sat for the examinations. A question arises whether changes in the regulations of the board, a lack of educational provision in terms of secondary schools, or personal circumstances caused

---

[13] Sir Michael Hicks-Beach, Chief Secretary for Ireland to Cardinal Cullen, Jan.1878, Gloucestershire archives, St Aldwyn MSS, PCC/64.
[14] Cardinal Paul Cullen to Chief Secretary, 7 Feb. 1878 (Cardinal Cullen's correspondence, Holy Cross College, Clonliffe, Dublin).
[15] R.B McDowell, *The Irish administration 1801-1914* (London, 1964), p. 35.
[16] Ibid.
[17] *Royal commission on the civil service,* fourth report, evidence pp. 189, 206, 1914 [Cd.7340] xvi.

students to withdraw. The candidates who presented in 1881 exhibited an increase of 25 percent on those in 1880 and nearly 76 percent of the total for 1879.[18] An average of approximately 90 percent of those who gave notice of the intention to present in 1881, actually sat the examinations at 174 centres in 64 localities. According to the annual report, the figures in all regards for that year show 'the progressive development of the intermediate system and the appreciation on the part of the public of the benefits which it offers'.[19]

Students who gave notice to attend examination in 1879, 1880 and 1881 [20]

Years	Boys	Girls	Total
1879	3,473	798	4,271
1880	4,493	1,633	6,126
1881	5,694	2,034	7,728

Students who presented for examination in 1879, 1880 and 1881 [21]

Years	Boys	Girls	Total
1879	3,218	736	3,942
1880	4,114	1,447	5,561
1881	5,147	1,806	6,953

Exhibitions and money prizes in 1881 were gained by 224 boys and 68 girls, a total of 292 students. Prizes of books were awarded to 512 boys and 166 girls, making a total of 678 recipients. Given that the board had an outlay of £15,431 for results fees in the same year, as compared to a total of £9,681 in results fees in 1880 and results fees of £7,462 in 1879, it was not remarkable that the first financial changes were proposed for 1882. With an overall shortfall of £10,000 for 1881, the board submitted a proposal to the Lord Lieutenant to diminish the scale of results fees by a half for 1882, which he approved. It was also proposed to reduce the exhibitions in junior and middle grades and prizes in the senior grade from £20, £30 and £50 to

---

[18] *Report of the Intermediate Board for Ireland for 1881* [c.2919], H.C. 1882.
[19] Ibid.
[20] Ibid.
[21] Ibid.

£15, £25 and £40 respectively while also reducing the number of exhibitions and prizes by one third.[22]

Under new regulations, students were required to pass at least two of the following subjects: Greek, Latin, English and arithmetic, as opposed to passing one as in the first two years of the examinations. While it was stated that this change was to encourage students to give their attention to these subjects, the move also had the effect of making conditions under which exhibitions were awarded more stringent. The proposal was met with outrage by the headmasters of Ireland and with confusion and dismay by parents and students.[23] The changes ostensibly caused a steady decline in numbers sitting the examinations. The board recognised problems for schools that had incurred considerable expense to meet the requirements of the intermediate act. The programme had introduced a broad range of subjects not formerly available in some schools in Ireland such as languages, commercial subjects and extended mathematical provision, with attendant costs. It was accepted that the reductions would possibly embarrass and discourage school managers. However, the board noted that parliament should not be permitted to cripple the intermediate system due to an inadequacy of funding.

In 1883, the board reported that the numbers, which had fallen in 1882, were down again. This showed the impact of the decision to reduce the value of exhibitions and prizes from 1882. It was in fact pre-emptive and in hindsight proved to be an unnecessary step. The board again showed a surplus, in this instance of £7,077,16s,7d. It then decided to increase the scale of results fees by approximately 33 percent and exhibitions, and prizes to one in ten students, instead of the revised figure of one in fifteen in 1882/3. However, the damage had been done, as already mentioned. It seems that the public faith in the system was slow to recover. Although figures for those examined rose somewhat in 1888 and 1889, this was not maintained, as the numbers decreased again in 1890. This was the year of the second amendment bill to the 1878 Act. Like the 1882 act it was primarily focused on administration but impacted on educational provision.

The fall in the numbers of students sitting the examinations from 1881 was indicative of school and parental reaction to what seemed to be a

---

[22] *Report of the Intermediate Board for Ireland*, 1882.
[23] *Remonstrance of the headmasters of Ireland* (Dublin, 1882).

diminution of the core principles of the original legislation. While this is possible, it must be considered that 1881 was a year of acute rural crisis with an associated decline in farming incomes and likewise farm dependent urban incomes, potentially making the payment of school fees difficult. However, by 1892 an indication of the perceived success of the intermediate system was as previously mentioned the introduction of a preparatory grade, which remained a feature of the examinations until 1913. This innovation came about despite the unfounded fear of a financial deficit. The introduction of commercial certificates and prizes also added a new dimension to the examination system. According to the report of the board, 'those who did not aim at obtaining commercial certificates availed themselves of the opportunity of presenting themselves for examination in certain commercial subjects'.[24]

While the improvement in educational standards and methods intended by the framers of the 1878 Act were being realised, the ability of the board to meet the increasing financial demands of awards was being threatened by its success. This was again attributed in the 1881 report to the extension of the scheme to girls. The number of students passing the examinations in 1881 was boys 3,439 and girls 1,235, a total of 4,674 out of the 6,953 who presented. Of those who presented 2,279 candidates failed the examinations. It was contended that making provision for girls out of the money provided played a major part in the shortfall of funding. However, what is not cited at any stage is the fact that girls achieved a higher percentage of passes than boys in the first five years of the examinations.[25]

The much requested list of names of all the Commissioners by MPs during the parliamentary debates on the Intermediate Education (Ireland) Act, 1878 was officially published in 1879, in what was the first report of the Intermediate Education Board. It is interesting to note from this report on the first intermediate examinations held following the 1878 legislation, the name of the Rt. Hon. Christopher Palles, Lord Chief Baron of the Exchequer in Ireland, and one of the most prominent Catholics in Irish

---

[24] *Report of the Intermediate Board for Ireland for 1895* [c.6324], H.C. 1896.
[25] *The report of the board for 1879* shows that 57.5 percent of boys passed compared to 65.4 percent of girls; in 1880, 70.4 per cent of boys passed and 76.7 percent of girls; 1881 shows that 66.8 percent of boys passed with 68.3 of girls. In 1882 and 1883 the percentage of girls was again higher. It was to be 1892 before the boys achieved a higher percentage of passes than the girls.

judicial and administrative circles, was cited as being among the Commissioners of the Intermediate Board for Ireland. He was in fact chairman for a number of years up to 1910, with the exception of 1895. During the debate on the Intermediate Education (Ireland) Bill, 1900, [HC] 19 July 1900, his inclusion brought a colourful and irate reaction from T.M. Healy MP, with acerbic remarks on judges needing to fill their time with extraneous matters. Palles who was indeed most likely included for his legal rather than his educational expertise, was nonetheless to chair the Viceregal Commission on Education in 1889. However, the perceived lack of direct educational experience of some members was not the only cause of dissention. Church leaders such as the Catholic Archbishop Walsh of Dublin and others raised the inequity of the religious divide, which was maintained on a ratio of four Protestant members to three Catholics from its inception until the change to twelve members in 1902.[26] Such concern about the possibility of an inequitable religious divide was initially raised during the debate on the Intermediate Education (Ireland) Bill, 1878 when calls for the names of commissioners were made, but were not revealed at that time.

Commissioners on the Intermediate Education Board for Ireland, 1879 [27]

Chairman: The Right Hon. John Thomas Ball LL.D., P.C., Lord High Chancellor of Ireland.

Vice- Chairman: Hon. Lord O'Hagan, P.C

The Right Hon. the Earl Belmore, P.C., K.C.M.G.

The Right Hon. Christopher Palles, LLD., Lord Chief Baron of the Exchequer in Ireland.

The Rev. George Salmon, D.D., D.C.L., F.R.S., Regius Professor of Divinity, University of Dublin.

The O'Conor Don, M.P., D.L.

James Porter Corry, Esq., M.P., J.P.

Of the Catholics appointed to the board, Christopher Palles (1831-1920) came from a relatively privileged background. Born in Co. Cavan to Andrew Palles, a solicitor and his wife Eleanor, both Catholics, he was educated at Clongowes Wood College and despite the ban by the Catholic hierarchy, at Trinity College, Dublin. He graduated from King's Inns in 1849 and two years later from Gray's Inns, London. In 1874, at the relatively young age of forty-three he was appointed Chief Baron of the Irish Exchequer by

---

[26] William J. Walsh, Archbishop of Dublin, *Statement of the chief grievances of Irish Catholics on the matter of education, primary, Intermediate and university* (Dublin 1890).

[27]*Report of the Intermediate Board for Ireland for 1879* [c.2600], H.C. 1880.

outgoing Prime Minister, William Ewart Gladstone.[28] Another prominent Catholic, Lord O'Hagan was briefly profiled during the discussion on the debate on the Intermediate Education (Ireland) Act, 1878.

Board member, The O'Conor Don, Charles O'Conor (1838-1906), was educated at Downside School. He was elected Liberal MP for Roscommon in March 1860 and held the seat until his defeat in the 1880 general election. He was appointed High Sheriff of Sligo for 1863 and of Roscommon for 1884.[29] O'Conor had a background in seeking educational change having, as previously mentioned, presented a motion to the House of Commons in 1870 relating to university education in Ireland. George Salmon (1819-1904) studied mathematics and theology at degree level in Trinity College, Dublin and was ordained in the Church of Ireland in 1845. A native of Cork, he attended Hamblin Porter's school, prior to Trinity. He was a mathematics tutor in Trinity for twenty-five years but on being elected Regius Professor of Divinity in 1866 his mathematical reputation was overshadowed by his theological scholarship. He was provost of the Trinity College from 1888 until his death.[30]

John Thomas Ball (1815-1898) was born was in Dundrum, Dublin. He studied law at Trinity College, Dublin and was a barrister, judge, politician, and Lord Chancellor of Ireland. He was appointed vicar-general of the province of Armagh following calls for the disestablishment of the Church of Ireland, which he opposed. Subsequently Disraeli appointed him to the royal commission into the property and organisation of the Church of Ireland, which was of course relevant to the 1878 intermediate legislation.[31] From the north of Ireland, Sir James Porter Corry (1826-1891) did not on the face of it, appear to have qualifications that would make him an obvious choice for the board. However, he was a Presbyterian and his appointment would have ensured representation for that denomination. He was born in Co. Down and educated at the Royal Belfast Academic Institution, afterwards joining the family timber business. He was elected as a Conservative MP in 1874 to 1885 and appointed 1st Baronet of Dunraven,

[28] W.N. Osborough, 'Palles, Christopher (1831-1920)', *DIB*.
[29] John P. McCarthy, *Ireland: A Reference Guide from the Renaissance to the Present* (New York, 2006) p. 379.
[30] Roderick Gow, 'Salmon, George (1819-1904)', *DIB*.
[31] Helen Andrews, 'Ball, Thomas John (1815-1898)', *DIB*.

Antrim at the end of that period.[32] Also appearing to have experience outside educational matters in Ireland, Somerset Richard Lowry-Corry (1835-1913), the 4th Earl of Belmore, was born in London and educated at Eton and Trinity College Cambridge. He was a Conservative politician, who having governed New South Wales was subsequently appointed Lord Lieutenant of Tyrone.[33]

Following the 1900 act to amend the law relating to intermediate education in Ireland, the number of commissioners on the Intermediate Board for Ireland increased from seven to twelve. The act, which brought the first major changes since 1879, also saw the examinations run under revised rules and regulations. Names of candidates were replaced with anonymous examination numbers. Apart from the names of the gold and silver medallists, it was then impossible to identify any of the examination candidates. Another change saw the subject previously titled 'Celtic' denoted as 'Irish' under the new regulations. Reports show Douglas Hyde, who was to become the first President of Ireland in 1938, was an examiner in intermediate Celtic in 1897 and again in 1898.[34]

As early as 1880, the second year of the intermediate examinations, the board came under financial pressure, as previously mentioned. While acknowledging this possibility during the parliamentary debates on the 1878 Bill, it was not envisaged that either the success of the scheme or the fact that the original provision was intended for boys alone, would see the commissioners facing funding difficulties so soon. Likewise, in the 1879 report the commissioners did not see the problem as likely to arise in the near future, although it was accepted that claims would inevitably increase.

---

[32] *The London Gazette,* 15 Sept. 1885, p. 4334.
[33] Kate Newman, 'Somerset Richard Lowry-Corry (1835-1913)' *Dictionary of Biography* (Belfast 1993)..
[34] *Reports of the Intermediate Board for Ireland for 1897 and 1898* [c.8798], H.C. 1898 and [c.9294], H.C. 1899.

Expenditure of the board in 1879. The total outlay amounted to £23,230 8s. 8d.[35]

	£	s.	d.
Administration	5,753	8	2
Cost of examinations	5,474	0	6
Rewards	4,541	0	0
Results fees	7,462	0	0

However, a year later the situation was 'occasioning the Board considerable worry regarding financial sustainability'.[36] Given a projected figure of 7,000 bona fide candidates for 1881, the cost was assessed as being approximately £36,000. The number actually presenting totalled 6,953, not far short of the prediction.[37] Unless additional funding was placed at the disposal of the board, it foresaw a necessary reduction of rewards and results fees. The intermediate was in fact a victim of its own success, educationally and socially, with an uptake that challenged available resources in respect of changed attitudes to schooling.

References to the grievances of the headmasters of schools throughout Ireland, particularly in relation to the participation of girls in the intermediate examinations, were made previously. However, focus is on the steps taken by the headmasters in reaction to a perceived withdrawal of funding for schools. In response to the cutbacks of 1882, the Standing Committee of Catholic and Protestant Headmasters united to send a memorial to the Lord Lieutenant. They hoped that such a statement would draw the attention of members of parliament and the public to the crisis. Not only did they send a memorial but also a deputation was formed representing every part of the country and all religions, Catholics, Episcopalians, Presbyterians and Methodists.[38] The unanimity of purpose of masters of schools was unprecedented, in terms of both religious affinity and the diversity of schools represented. In coming together to fight what was seen as an injustice, the Protestant and Catholic headmasters were giving tacit endorsement to the success of the Intermediate Board for Ireland, which ensured that 'persons of any religion or of no religion may share alike in the

---

[35] *Report of the Intermediate Board for Ireland for 1879* [c.2600], H.C. 1880.
[36] Ibid, *1881* [c.3176], H.C. 1882.
[37] Ibid.
[38] The deputation met with the Lord Lieutenant on 24 Jan. 1882.

benefits conferred, whilst no person or class of person feels aggrieved by exclusion'.[39]

However, loss of essential funding, which seemed secured under the 1878 act, threatened new schools and those which had increased spending to make teaching more efficient in line with the demands of the intermediate examinations. Such innovations included both more teaching staff and equipment, which could not have been undertaken in most cases, without the promise of recompense. The Catholic headmasters felt so strongly about the matter that they sent a letter to each member school. This asked if the authorities of the schools and colleges would continue the work of the intermediate system if parliament failed to provide the necessary funding. The matter became irrelevant the following year, 1883, when the surplus of funding allowed an increase in results fees and prizes thus averting a crisis. While the schools and parents felt justifiably angry, the onus was on the board to produce funding, given the increasing numbers participating in the intermediate examinations. Although the board had no means of anticipating the numbers for the years following 1882, the annual increase to that date gave reason to suppose that this would continue, which it did not. Did the actions of the board in reducing fees and awards cause the fall-off in numbers or the lack of foresight on behalf of the 1878 legislation? Furthermore, did the board actually believe that by reducing rewards and results fees it would incite public outrage to such an extent that Parliament would be forced to agree to further funding? This was surely not the case, as the board had no assurance that the Government would ask parliament for the further sums required and they were 'therefore reluctantly compelled to make wholesale reductions'.[40]

Inevitably, comparisons in terms of funding were made with English schools in what was seen as a contrast to the financial provision for Irish intermediate pupils. According to the Royal Commission of 1864, Eton College had an income of £20,569 during the previous seven years from endowments alone. During the same period, Winchester College received an income of £15,494. These two schools collectively had a larger income than that at the disposal of the Intermediate Commissioners for the entirety of Ireland. It is acknowledged that such a comparison is at best superficial as the English schools were endowed colleges, as opposed to those in Ireland

---

[39] *Remonstrance of the headmasters of Ireland,* p.2.
[40] Ibid p.4.

coming under the provisions of the intermediate act. However, no matter what arguments were put forward by the deputation, the Lord Lieutenant consistently stated that they should have made their submission to the Chancellor of the Exchequer and not to himself. It was reported by the *Dublin Evening Mail* that 'Mr Forster's relegation of the schoolmaster's deputation … is a shabby evasion of responsibility'.[41] This however was a Conservative newspaper criticising a Liberal Chief Secretary.

Among the much-quoted grievances raised by the headmasters and also cited in the reports of the board was the fact that the interest on the initial provision of £1,000,000 was intended to cover rewards for boys only. The inclusion of female candidates, they reiterated, had placed an undue burden on available finance which was not adjusted accordingly. The deputation also highlighted the already referenced facts that the examinations were at risk due to the extraordinary success of the 1878 Act. They asserted that schools had taken on extra financial burdens to increase teachers and equipment. For example, in Castleknock College, an extra teacher was employed to coach candidates for the exam at the exorbitant annual salary of £130.[42] While in general it was noted that teachers were so badly paid there was little inducement for men of ability to take up the profession, this was not the case in Castleknock where teachers were promised bonuses if their pupils did well in the examinations.[43]

Significant points raised by the headmasters were the prospect of the development of 'an educated middle class in Ireland and for exceptionally gifted children in the humbler classes to improve their condition in life'.[44] The deputation highlighted the benefits of the intermediate examination to the country as a whole and by extension to the Empire. Not only was the potential rise of a Catholic middle class seen as desirable but the progress of boys attending intermediate schools was perceived to extend to all classes and occupations. These were cited by the Rev. Dr Gerald Molloy, Vice-Rector of the Catholic University, in an introductory statement on behalf of the headmasters, as being future lawyers, solicitors, doctors, and likewise

---

[41] *Dublin Evening Mail*, 24 Jan. 1882.
[42] James H. Murphy, *Nos Autem: Castleknock College and its contribution* (1996), p.71.
[43] Ibid.
[44] *Remonstrance of the headmasters*, p.6.

manufacturers, traders, landowners and farmers.[45] This is very much in keeping with the question with respect to the role played in education in the rise or extension of a Catholic middle class, in the late nineteenth and early twentieth centuries. Ascribing the educational advancements as being not only for the individual in Ireland but within the Empire, had implications for the civil service, military and other areas requiring specific competencies. Nonetheless, with regard to the civil service in nineteenth century England, which employed Irish applicants, it was claimed it did not want to widen the social base.[46] However, according to Clarke, 'the civil service commissioners were careful to criticise the educational deficiencies of their rejected candidates rather than their status as gentlemen'.[47]

The intermediate acts, particularly that of 1878, were potentially watersheds in Irish education and social advancement in the nineteenth century. The acknowledgement of this by the headmasters is concrete affirmation that those years were in fact, not only educationally, but socially significant. Coolahan however, disputes this when he says 'schooling was not viewed as a means of achieving greater social equality'.[48] What's more, he states that 'leaders of the church and state viewed the poor and working classes as requiring only a limited education in basic literacy and numeracy'.[49]The secular nature of the Intermediate Act, 1878, was seen as an integral part of the system and in no way interfered with the unity of the headmasters. The efficiency of the teaching was highlighted by the success of their pupils in the examinations of the Intermediate Education Board, of the Royal University and of the Civil Service Commissioners. However, eight years later Archbishop Walsh stirred up the question of rivalry between Catholic and Protestant schools.[50] He stated that the Intermediate Act of 1878 did not attempt to remedy the injustice of the existing regulation with regard to educational endowment. He said it 'merely permitted the

---

[45] Ibid.

[46] J.M. Bourne, *Patronage and society in nineteenth century England* (London, 1986), p.31.

[47] Clarke, 'The origins and impact of the Northcote-Trevelyan report'.

[48] Coolahan, *Irish education, history, and structure* p.55.

[49] Ibid.

[50] William J. Walsh, Archbishop of Dublin, *Statement of the chief grievances of Irish Catholics* (Dublin, 1890).

Catholic schools absolutely un-endowed as they were, to enter into competition with the richly endowed Protestant schools of the country'.[51]

What changes in rules and regulations took place as the examinations moved on from the initial provision of the 1878 act? Certain practical amendments evolved as the examinations attracted increasing academic and public feedback. For example, the practice of recording the names of failing candidates was discontinued after 1884. Likewise, anonymous examination numbers replaced the publication of the names of candidates in the annual intermediate results in 1902. The highlighting of individuals by name had been a feature since 1878. This change was one of a number of radical breaks with the structures put in place by the legislation. By 1905 the examinations were divided into classical, modern literary, mathematical, and experimental science courses, inclusive of the previous introduction of a commercial section.

While there was a marked difference in the schools submitting candidates for examination particularly in the first years, a cross section of the results of the junior, middle, and senior grades in the first three years shows the distribution of success between Catholic and Protestant schools with a perfect divide in each of those years. The success of Catholic schools in the first intermediate examinations was said to have surprised the commissioners of the board, 'they having shown ability to compete successfully with the scholars of the most richly endowed Royal Schools'.[52] With the French College, Blackrock topping the list for the three years, other schools retained their places with the exception of the Academical Institution, Coleraine which was replaced by Wesley College Dublin in 1880. Subsequently Wesley lost out to the High School Dublin for a place in the top six schools in 1881. The schools listed were all well-established prior to 1878, with the results indicating a high level of academic performance.

---

[51] Ibid p.218.
[52] *Belfast Morning News*, 18 Sept. 1879.

Six top placed boys' schools for years, 1879, 1880, 1881[53] **(C) Catholic (P) Protestant**

1879	1880	1881
French College, Blackrock (C)	French College	French College
St Stanislaus College, Tullamore [54] (C)	Royal Academical Inst	Royal Academical Inst
Royal School, Armagh (P)	St Stanislaus College	St Stanislaus College
Royal Academical Institution, Belfast (P)	St Vincent's College	Royal School Armagh
St Vincent's College, Castleknock(C)	Royal School, Armagh	St Vincent's College
Academical Institution, Coleraine(P)	Wesley College, Dublin (P)	High School, Dublin (P)

Among those sitting the examinations in 1880, the second year of the examinations, was James MacMahon, the future Catholic Under Secretary in Dublin Castle, who took the junior and middle grades in two different schools in 1880 and 1881. MacMahon's participation ties in with the question of whether increased academic opportunities following 1878, were a driving force in the opening of higher administrative positions to Catholics. His education and broader career is looked at in a comparative biographical study with that of Sir John Anderson, Joint Under Secretary from 1920 to 1922.

Studies in relation to some of the most successful examination candidates among the general population, especially those involved in the early years, highlight those who presented for the examinations and whose performances could be seen to have justified the intermediate initiative and driven career advancement and social mobility. While the main emphasis is on the civil servants in Dublin Castle, such an investigation of the examinations and the biographical details of some of the candidates gives a broad overview of the general educational and social position in Ireland in the latter years of the nineteenth and early stages of the twentieth centuries. These biographies will ostensibly show that the Castle administration did not operate in a vacuum and was in fact only one area that potentially benefitted from increased educational provision. Conscious of their importance, T.J. McElligott highlighted the names of the top three boys and girls who gained exhibitions in the 1879 intermediate examinations, as he was concerned 'lest

---

[53] Compiled from the *Intermediate Education Board for Ireland, results of the examinations for the years*, 1879,1880, and 1881.

[54] The college address was given in official results as Tullamore rather than the more usual location of Tullabeg.

history fail to record their claim to distinction'.[55] However, while their names may not be commonly known they are recorded in the intermediate examination results for 1879. Biographical studies of these students and others who excelled in the early years of the examinations, will provide an historical record of an aspect of Irish society and in particular potential Catholic advancement.

Intermediate examination, individual results, 1879 (first year of examinations)[56]

BOYS

Junior Grade: Charles Francis Doyle, 56 George Street, Limerick/Sacred Heart College Limerick.

Middle Grade: Peter Paul Greer, Dunmore, Co. Galway/St Stanislaus College, Tullamore.[57]

Senior Grade: William Andrew Russell, Academical Institution Londonderry.

GIRLS

Junior Grade: Alice Mary Baxter (Exhib), Ladies Collegiate School, Belfast.

Middle Grade: Kathleen Morrow (Exhib), St Helier's Dalkey, Co. Dublin/Alexandra College, Dublin.

Senior Grade: Lucy Moore (Exhib), Ladies Collegiate School, Belfast.

While lists of names and grades and schools attended are informative, the human faces and lives behind the statistics have never been investigated in a countrywide perspective. What were the backgrounds of these students and what were their family circumstances? Attempting to bring them and their stories to life through brief biographical studies, is intended to create a picture of the educational and social advancement across Catholic and Protestant schools, and the engagement of students and families following the introduction of competitive intermediate examinations. Also under consideration is the broader impact of countrywide examinations and competitiveness. Where possible the candidates' later lives and careers will be referenced.

The top students across the girls' and boys' junior, middle and senior grades in 1879, the first year of the intermediate examinations, showed an

---

[55] McElligott, *Secondary education in Ireland,* p.47.

[56] List compiled from *Report of the Intermediate Board for Ireland for the year 1879.* Although some home addresses were given, details of schools attended were more widely provided the following year.

[57] Tullabeg.

even distribution between south and north of the country among those coming first in each section.[58] In some cases the prize-winning students gave home addresses. Most probably there was confusion in the first year of the examinations as to what was required on the application form. Giving a home address could indicate home tutoring, but if that were not the case it could have posed problems for result fees to be paid to the schools in question. The first placed students in the 1879 examinations across the three grades deserve their place in what was an historical achievement that paved the way for pupils of all denominations to compete for sought after places, for example in the civil service and the military. That these high achievers were representative of not only boys' schools but also those that educated girls, was ground breaking.

In the 1879 examinations Charles Francis Doyle (Exhib), with an address at 56 George Street, Limerick, was placed first in the boys' junior grade.[59] Doyle who was born in 1866, was the second son of Daniel Doyle, a solicitor of Limerick, who died in 1873, six years before his son's first intermediate success. Charles had two brothers, the younger of whom became Assistant Registrar General, Dublin and three sisters, all of whom attended third-level colleges. In 1880, Doyle gave a school address of the Jesuit run Sacred Heart College, Limerick and won a middle grade exhibition, coming in first place again. He went on to achieve first place in 1881, this time in the senior grade, also winning the gold medal for modern languages.

After his success in the intermediate examinations, Doyle graduated with a BA from Trinity College, Dublin.[60] One of his sisters told a story of how during his early days in university 'a report went through Ireland that this very clever boy had overworked himself and was now dead'.[61] Acting on the rumour, Archbishop Walsh of Dublin had a requiem mass celebrated for 'an outstanding ornament to Catholic education'.[62] While the story was most likely exaggerated and Doyle was in fact very much alive, a worry with regard to cramming was raised by Dr James Rentoul, MP Down East, during the debate of the 19 July 1900 in the Commons on the Intermediate Education (Ireland) Bill, 1900. As previously mentioned he drew attention

---

[58] *Report of the Intermediate Board for Ireland,* 1879.
[59] Ibid.
[60] *The Limerick Chronicle*, 1928.
[61] Francis Finegan S.J., *Limerick Jesuit centenary record 1859-1959,* p.23.
[62] Ibid.

to the fact that a 'vast number of shattered constitutions and early graves were the result of the system'.[63] This raises the possibility that such concerns may have been readily accepted at that time.

Doyle became an examiner in Greek and Latin in the intermediate examinations for a number of years from 1895.[64] In 1900, he was elected to the position of Clerk of Convocation of the Royal University, at a salary of £100 per annum. He was one of five candidates for the position. The method of voting was contentious and despite general surprise Michael Morris, Vice-Chancellor, Royal University, accepted a proposal of a show of hands to decide the winner.[65] The procedure caused a great deal of dissatisfaction among the graduates present.[66] Doyle who got 46 votes beat his nearest rival J.C. Meredith, MA by only one vote.[67]

In 1901, Doyle was living at 56, Lourigan's Lane, Dock, Limerick with his widowed mother, three sisters, and two brothers. The census of that year painted a picture of a high achieving Catholic family. Eliza Lily Doyle, head of family, was not described as a widow but as having an occupation of 'house property, furids etc'.[68] Charles gave his occupation as barrister, Clerk of Convocation, 'RUJ' a transcription error that should have read 'RUI' and MA. His brother James is entered as 'solicitor, rotary'.[69] Two sisters were art students and the third an undergraduate at the 'RUI', again copied as 'RUJ'. One female servant, Bridget Weeks, a Roman Catholic, was also listed.[70] Doyle, who was called to the Bar in 1888, took silk eighteen years later and ended his career as Circuit Judge of the counties of Wicklow and Kildare. He died on 29 September 1928.[71]

In marked contrast to the opportunities afforded to the Doyle brothers and others in the Sacred Heart College, the position for girls in a nearby

---

[63] *Hansard Parliamentary Debates*, HC deb., 19 July 1900, vol. 86 cc487-526.

[64] *Reports of the Intermediate Education Board for Ireland 1895-1907.*

[65] Patrick M. Geoghegan, 'Morris Sir Michael (1826-1901) 1st Baron Morris and Killanin', *DIB.*

[66] *The Lancet,* 3 Nov. 1900 pp. 1313-1314.

[67] Ibid.

[68] The term 'furids' is not in common or legal usage today but a reference to 'public furids', which denote 'funds' was sourced in a HC debate on Tithes (Ireland), 20 Mar. 1835.

[69] Rotary is an official transcription error with notary clearly written on Form A.

[70] Census of Ireland, 1901.

[71] Obituaries and funeral reports, 1880-1922, www.limerickcity.ie/media/Media,9269,en.pdf (accessed on 23 Nov. 2018).

Limerick school up to the late 1890s was far from progressive. In 1895, the Bishop of Limerick boasted in a prize-day speech at Laurel Hill Convent that 'we have no girl graduates here nor even intermediate students but we are working away on old Catholic rules and principles and I am not aware that we lose anything thereby'.[72]

Boys' middle grade results 1879[73]

	Name	School	Home Address
1.	**Peter Paul Greer**		**Dunmore, Co. Galway**
2.	John Harding Tibbs	Grammar School Galway	
3.	Edmond Bohan	St Stanislaus' College Tullamore	
4.	David R. Parke Smith		14 Montenotte, Cork
5.	Wm. Andrew Vinycomb		28 Melrose Tce., Belfast
6.	Mathew John Clarke	St Malachy's College Belfast	

The highest placed student in the boys' middle grade of 1879, was Peter Paul Greer, (Exhib), Dunmore Co. Galway.[74] The following year he came second in the senior grade with a £50 prize and silver medal. He gave a school address of St Stanislaus College, Tullamore, Co. Offaly.[75] Greer was a pupil in the school from 1878-1881.[76] Born in Abbeyleix in 1864,[77] Peter Paul lived in Dunmore West, Co. Galway from at least 1878-81, as his father James W. Greer, was an inspector of national schools there for those three years.[78] Following the death of Greer Snr in 1880, Peter Paul died of consumption in 1882 aged eighteen years.

In the senior grade of 1879, the first placed student was William Andrew Russell (Exhib), Londonderry Academical Institution (now Foyle College).[79] With first place in the junior and middle grades going to pupils from Catholic schools, Russell's achievement at senior level highlighted the strength of established Protestant colleges. William, was the son of a

---

[72] Eileen Breathnach, 'Women in higher education in Ireland' in Alan Hayes and Diane Urquhart (eds.), *Women's history reader* (London, 2001), p.45.
[73] Results of the Intermediate examinations, held in 1879.
[74] Ibid.
[75] Fee-paying Jesuit school, which amalgamated with Clongowes Wood College in 1886.
[76] Peter Paul Greer registration details, Jesuit archives, Leeson Street, Dublin.
[77] Ibid.
[78] *Thom's Directory*, 1878, 1879, 1880, Galway County.
[79] Results of Intermediate examinations held in 1879.

Presbyterian minister from Strabane.[80] The eldest son of the second family of the Rev W. A. Russell and his wife Hessy Nesbit Dill, he was born 1863. He had two older half-brothers, Samuel, a professor of astronomy and mathematics in Peking, China and James a banker in Canada.[81] His older sister, Hester and his younger brother both studied medicine.[82] His second sister Annie was one of a small number of nineteenth century female astronomers in Britain. Annie, like her sister attended the Ladies Collegiate School, Belfast. She came second in the senior grade in the intermediate in 1885. Gaining a three-year scholarship to Girton College Cambridge, she studied mathematics. She married Walter Maunder, a widower and a fellow astronomer. They are principally known for their work on sunspots and the associated influence on climate, with their findings still of relevance to weather forecasters today. A crater on the moon commemorates both the Maunders.[83]

Despite his father being a clergyman, William attended a merchant's school, the first non-clerical college in the area. William Andrew Russell, entered Londonderry Academical Institution, on 12 February 1873, at ten years of age.[84] The reason for this was most likely that he was awarded a scholarship. According to school records, a Mr Bigger nominated him on 15 January 1873.[85] In the intermediate examination results for the year 1879, Russell took Greek, 839/1000, Latin, English 865/1000, Euclid, algebra, plane trigonometry, elementary mechanics, natural philosophy and his weakest subject, descriptive astronomy.[86] Although he studied German, drawing and music at school, he did not take them for the intermediate.[87] His results were remarkable given that he was only sixteen years of age and could have taken the middle or even junior grade. Russell played on the school's Rugby XV, 1878-79 and was mentioned as being on the committee

---

[80] *Strabane and Lifford Trades Directory,* 1880, Rev. William Andrew Russell, Second Presbyterian Church, Derry Road, Strabane.

[81] Enda Leaney and Patricia M. Byrne, 'Maunder, Annie Scott Dill Russell (1868–1947)', *DIB.*

[82] Ibid.

[83] Michael Kennedy, 'Annie Scott Dill Maunder 1868-1947', *Strabane History Society,* http://strabanehistorysociety.org/annie-scott-dill-maunder-1868-1947/ [accessed 20 July 2020].

[84] School register, 1873, [FCA].

[85] Ibid.

[86] Results of the Intermediate examinations held in 1879.

[87] Ibid.

for the Londonderry Academical Institute team in the Schools League.[88] A classicist, he studied at Magee College, Derry and subsequently as an exhibitioner at Cambridge from where he graduated in 1887. He became headmaster of a school in Capetown, South Africa.[89]

Research among decomposed MA application forms in the NUI led to the discovery of a candidate with an interesting family history. In 1886, Arthur Conan, applied to the Royal University to take examinations in ancient classics. His application form showed that he paid the fee in 'Gold'. This fact alone set him apart from many of his generation. Looking through the forms, the usual method of payment was primarily by cheque or bank order.

The Conan family was the perfect microcosm of the social and educational standing of established and developing Catholic and Protestant middle classes in Ireland from the middle of the nineteenth century. Four of the family were sent abroad in line with the 'Rule Etonia' model.[90] The two older sons were educated in France, while Arthur and his brother, Walter attended Blackrock College. Two of their sisters went to school in London and two in Dublin, benefitting from the early years of intermediate education in Ireland. While in many respects the Conans could be considered to be an example of the evolving middle-class, the family were already successful and being well educated prior to 1878.

Arthur Conan, the second youngest of eight children, four boys and four girls was born on 14 December 1866 to Joseph, a Catholic, and Agnes Conan, Church of Ireland, in 'Roseneath', Sandymount Avenue, Dublin. His father was a wealthy military and merchant tailor with a business at 4 Dawson Street, Dublin.[91] Given that it was a mixed marriage the family followed the custom of the time whereby girls were brought up in the religion of their mothers and boys that of their fathers.[92] Arthur was a pupil

---

[88] *The Origins and development of football in Ireland*, being a reprint of R.M. Peter's 'Irish football annual of 1880', p.87.

[89] M. T. Bruck & S. Grew, 'The Family Background of Annie S. D. Maunder (nee Russell)', *Irish Astronomical Journal*, vol.23, no. 1 (1996), pp. 55-56.

[90] O'Neill, 'Rule Etonia'.

[91] *Thom's Official Directory of the United Kingdom of Great Britain and* Ireland (Dublin 1880).

[92] Irish tradition regarding mixed marriages, where boys followed the religion of their fathers and girls that of their mothers, pre the *Ne Temere* papal decree of 1908.

at the French School and University College Blackrock. He took tenth place in the boys' junior grade in the intermediate examinations in 1879, gaining an exhibition. He repeated the same grade in 1880, which seemed to be a common occurrence, whether on grounds of age, to improve results, or a change of school. He then achieved second place and a gold medal for modern languages. He again came second in 1881, this time in the middle grade (exhibition and silver medal) and in 1882, he was placed third in the senior grade. Arthur subsequently entered the University College in Blackrock and prepared for the Royal University examinations at Trinity College Dublin.

Having matriculated in 1882, Arthur, gained first class exhibitions in first and second arts and a first honours classics degree. He was awarded a fellowship premium by Trinity College in 1890. He also graduated with a degree of Master of Arts (ancient classics). According to Conan Kennedy, an application for the post of Lecturer Examiner in the Royal University highlighted these achievements.[93] In 1891, he was appointed examiner for intermediate examinations for two years at University College, Blackrock. Following a successful career in academia Arthur left Ireland, becoming a travelling tea salesman and photographer in South Africa. He is believed to have died during the Boer War.[94]

Arthur Conan, was named after author Arthur Conan Doyle, a second cousin of his father, Joseph Conan. In another linkage of the author to Ireland, the *Blackrock College Yearbook, 1914* claims that the character of 'Moriarty' in Arthur Conan Doyle's *Sherlock Holmes,* is based on the Rt. Hon John Francis Moriarty KC, Attorney General for Ireland. The Conan name seems to have been interchangeable as a surname and a first name within the family, being the maiden name of Conan Doyle's maternal grandmother. Whether the author, famous for the Sherlock Holmes books, had a double-barrelled surname or if 'Conan' was in fact a forename is contested.[95] While the Dublin family definitively used Conan, as a surname,

---

[93] Conan Kennedy, *Grandfather's house,* letter of application, headed 34, Trinity College Dublin, 18 Apr. 1891, p.32.
[94] Ibid.
[95] Owen Dudley Edwards, 'Doyle, Sir Arthur Ignatius Conan (1859-1930)', *ODNB.*

it was subsequently utilised as a forename for a grandson of Alexander Conan, Joseph Conan's eldest son.[96]

Walter (1867-1936), Arthur's younger brother, who was also educated at the French School, Blackrock, joined his father in the family business. In the 1890s, he set up his own firm on Kildare Street, which became the official 'Robe Makers to the University', hiring out gowns and other requirements to students and graduands.[97] The university, referred to the Royal University of Ireland and later the NUI. Graduates over the years to the present day have hired their robes and caps from Conan's, with the firm today trading as Phelan Conan Ltd., 'Robemakers since 1845'. In tandem with his tailoring business, Walter was an inventor and innovator of great talent. He was also a director of a number of companies including the De Selby Mining Company of Tallaght. Walter invented and patented the keyless lock (combination lock), incandescent gas lamps, and devices for preserving meat. In 1913, he patented the 'Conan fuse', which was an integral part of the depth charge used by the British navy in anti-submarine warfare. During the First World War, he worked on the manufacture of ferro-tungsten in England. Returning to Ireland in the 1920s, he lived in Dalkey. He tested his explosive devices at what was then known as the 'men's bathing place, which was in an area developed by his family who owned property nearby. Stories of his exploits led to his being the inspiration for Flann O'Brien's fictional character 'De Selby' an eccentric Dalkey inventor and sage.[98]

Alexander, the second eldest of the Conan siblings and his brother Robert, were educated at the Collège Chaptal in Paris, founded in 1844 by Prosper Goubaux, writer and educationalist. Following financial difficulties, it was taken over by the city of Paris in 1848. The college was recognised as being one of the two great municipal schools of Paris, the other being the École Turgot. Collège Chaptal did not initially teach Latin or Greek but focused on modern languages and technology. It was aimed at the sons of the prosperous merchant classes who would make careers in manufacturing.[99] Alexander, who followed his father into the business at 4

---

[96] Conan Kennedy, author of *Grandfather's house* (Mayo, 2008).
[97] Ibid.
[98] *Irish Times* 3 July 2010.
[99] Matthew Arnold, R.H. Super (ed.), *Schools and universities on the continent* (Michigan, 1990), pp. 121-126.

Dawson Street, was listed in the 1901 census as living in Monte Alverno in Dalkey. In fact, there was a recording error and the house was referenced as 'Monte Aherno'. Undoubtedly influenced by his education in Paris, Alex Conan, the eldest of the Conan sons, who took over the family business in 1891, was known not only for his business acumen but also flair and creativity. From two 'plain regency villas 'built in the early 1800s in Dalkey, Co. Dublin and bought by Joseph Conan, as holiday accommodation, Alexander who inherited them in 1889 designed a neo-gothic castellated mansion with a tower modelled on that of Kylemore Abbey in Connemara.[100] Today it is one of the most sought after properties in the Killiney/Dalkey district.. Alexander was married twice and had a large family, including among his grandchildren, Mary White, the former Green Party politician and Deputy Leader of the Green Party.[101]

The Conan family represented an eclectic mix of nineteenth century educational provision. Not only did they send their eldest sons to a school abroad but also two of their daughters, Agnes (b.1863) and Josephine (b.1864), attended the North London Collegiate School. They both proved academically successful and won school scholarships/exhibitions and prizes.[102] Sophie Bryant (Willock), the mathematician and suffragette who like the Conan sisters was born in Sandymount, Co. Dublin and lived there until she was ten years old, was teaching mathematics at the school. However, neither Agnes nor Josephine took prizes in the subject, excelling in languages, scripture, and political and social economy.[103] In 1882, prior to leaving the school, they were both in sixth form and both prefects.[104]

After passing the matriculation examinations of the Royal University of Ireland, Agnes and Josephine joined a group of female students in a memorial to the standing committee of the college, complaining that the senate provided classes given by fellows of the university for examination

---

[100] Kennedy, *Grandfather's house*, p.97.
[101] Ibid.
[102] Agnes and Josephine Conan, North London Collegiate School [NCLS] Magazines, 1879-1882.
[103] *Irish Times*, 23 Aug. 1916, 'Sophie Bryant, mathematician, suffragette, pioneer of education for women.'
[104] Agnes and Josephine Conan, North London Collegiate School archives, [NLCSA], by email from Sue Stanbury, librarian, 03 Dec. 2018.

preparation but that women were not allowed to avail of them.[105] However, they were subsequently among the first female graduates of the Royal University of Ireland, being named in the report of the university with their brother Arthur, as having gained Bachelor of Arts degrees.[106] Agnes, who later became Lady Hamer, taught for a period at her alma mater. The archives record an 'Irish cycling trip' in 1896 but it is unclear which of the Conan sisters went on this holiday with Sophie Bryant and a friend, Sophie Nicholls.[107]

The other two Conan daughters, Jeanette and Florence, attended Alexandra College, a Protestant school in Dublin and then the Dublin Metropolitan School of Art, with Jeanette becoming a successful artist and Florence engaging in social work. Looking ahead, although the 1901 census does not contain the names of all of the family, Florence, who was unmarried, lived with her mother in Sandymount. Under 'religion', both mother and daughter are listed as Church of Ireland and sons Alexander and Walter, as Roman Catholic.[108] Their father, Joseph Conan, was deceased.[109] All the Conan siblings would most likely have been assured of an education abroad, just as had been the case for the eldest four. However, leaving aside possible financial difficulties, changes brought about by the 1878 legislation, with its emphasis on countrywide competitive examinations, may have been a strong factor in the decision of their parents to educate them in Ireland. They were as outlined, sent to established Catholic and Protestant schools in keeping with their status in the merchant middle class. University provision was perhaps the greatest gain for the family with Arthur and his sisters, Agnes and Josephine benefitting from Royal University access.

Looking at the results of the intermediate examinations, one thing in particular stands out. It comes across as erroneous, certainly with regard to the performances of Catholic schools in the early years of the examinations, to talk about the creation of a Catholic middle class. What research shows is the potential expansion of an established societal grouping, which was

---

[105] Janet Horowitz Murray, Myra Stark (eds.), *The Englishwoman's Review of Social and Industrial Questions: 1883* (Oxford, 2017) p.67.
[106] *Fourth report of the Royal University of Ireland,* (Dublin, 1886).
[107] Agnes and Josephine Conan, [NLCSA].
[108] 1901 Census of Ireland, National Archives.
[109] In what were the years prior to the Ne Temere, Papal decree of 1907, the family had followed the custom in Ireland relating to mixed marriages.

already in existence, albeit in a minority. Catholic families of the nineteenth and early twentieth centuries with an established educational background demonstrated that their lifestyles and social positions certainly equated to any concept of middle class Protestants.

This viewpoint has come across strongly in the investigation into the record of the top students in the early years of the intermediate examinations. The competitive element, which was a focal point of the legislative provision, undoubtedly led to a comparison between the achievements of Catholic and Protestant schools, with Church leaders such as Archbishop Walsh, highlighting the success of Catholic schools in opposition to the highly endowed Protestant colleges. However, this must be tempered with the inescapable fact that in the early years of the examinations it was the superior fee-paying schools, both Catholic and Protestant that excelled. Much of this can possibly be attributed to the fact that families that might have sent their children abroad were now availing of the new educational provision in Ireland.

Archbishop Walsh drew attention to the success of the Christian Brothers schools (originally Christian Schools). In doing so, perhaps by default, he got to the real heart of the competition among schools, that of the superior Catholic schools, which followed in the English traditions of education and those providing for less well-off pupils from lower socio- economic groups. It was in the rise of these schools, whose success is shown in the breakdown of results from the mid-1880s, that the ideological basis of the 1878 Intermediate Act was demonstrated. This success resulted in a blurring of the academic divide among Catholic school students. The range now encompassed superior boarding schools under the authority of Catholic priests and more accessible day schools, the majority of which were run by the Christian Brothers and followed previous provision, which combined primary and secondary education.

In his review of Barry Coldrey's book on the Irish Christian Brothers, Patrick J. Corish, cites Coldrey as saying that the best decision taken by the order was to stay outside the national system of education of 1831.[110] According to Corish, 'because the Christian Brothers had never committed their schools to the national system they were free to enter their pupils for

---

[110] Patrick J. Corish, review of Barry Coldrey, *Faith and fatherland: the Christian Brothers and the development of Irish nationalism*, in *The Historical Journal*, 1989, vol. 32, no. 2, pp. 504-506.

the secondary examinations, where they were soon strikingly successful'.[111] However, it was to be 1890, before a pupil from a Christian School came to the fore in the intermediate results. This was as opposed to just passing the examinations. It is debatable if by that time the Brothers' emphasis on educating the poor had shifted. Coldrey argues that they had 'moved into middle class education and to an extent away from teaching the very poor within a generation of their founder's death'.[112] The Christian Brothers founded middle class schools in Waterford and Cork in the 1890s. These were at the 'express request of the appropriate bishops'.[113] With the schools well established, Coldrey contends that their success in the intermediate examinations was 'embarrassing, even frightening to many of the upper-middle class Catholic colleges'.[114]

However, Coldrey quotes Brother J.B. Duggan, as giving evidence to the Endowed Schools Commission in 1879, supporting the work of the Christian Bothers with the less well off. Duggan stated, 'it is a remarkable thing that among the twenty-eight who succeeded in the recent intermediate examinations, the first on the list is the son of a carman and the second who has lost both his father and mother and is totally dependent on an uncle, who has a large family'.[115] Coldrey concluded that given their work in schools, orphanages and industrial schools, the accusation that the Brothers deserted the children of the poor for the middle classes was not proven.[116]

According to Archbishop Walsh, the report of the board for 1888 shows that results fees were paid to 1,584 Catholic schools. 'Of the entire number no fewer than 913 were from schools of the Christian Brothers'.[117] These were initially designated as 'Christian Schools' in the results, with the first major success being that of James Tighe, Christian Schools, Belfast, who

---

[111] Ibid, p.506.

[112] Barry Coldrey, *Faith and fatherland: the Christian Brothers and the development of Irish nationalism* (Dublin, 1988), p. 71.

[113] Ibid, p.70.

[114] Ibid, p.71.

[115] *Report of the commissioners appointed by the Lord Lieutenant of Ireland to enquire into the endowment, funds and conditions of all schools endowed for the purpose of education in Ireland,* HC 1881, vol. xxxv, 1(c.2831) p.1503.

[116] Coldrey, *Faith and fatherland,* p.79.

[117] W.J. Walsh, 'Statement of the chief grievances of Irish Catholics, in the matter of education, primary, Intermediate and university', *The Irish ecclesiastical record: a monthly journal under episcopal sanction ,* Ser. 3, Vol. XI, Sept. 1890, pp. 859-863.

gained first place and gold medal in the middle grade in 1883 (Jnr Ex. 1881). He also gained gold medals for Greek and English in the same year. Research however, failed to find any trace of his family or his future career. Given the preponderance of exclusive high fee-paying schools excelling in the early years of the examinations, his success is a validation of the intention of the 1878 act to provide intermediate education to all students in Ireland.

The Christian Brothers educated boys in a similar manner to the national schools up to the age of fifteen, when they were in a position to take the civil service examinations for lower level positions, such as boy clerk. Nonetheless, the schools were attracted by payments based on examination results, under the Intermediate Education Board. They added classical and modern foreign languages, thus shifting their emphasis from elementary to superior schools.[118] Many pupils enrolled in intermediate classes until the age of fifteen or sixteen, perhaps sitting the junior grade examinations. They then competed for boy clerkship examinations and attended night school while working in these positions before competing for a second division clerkship.[119]

The requirements for boy clerkships and other examinations such as Customs and Excise officers included neither classics nor modern languages, though one of these could be taken as an optional subject after 1900. Examinations concentrated on précis writing, handwriting, composition, indexing, bookkeeping, and English history.[120] While the Christian Brothers educated a considerable number of civil servants, Daly argued that 'Ireland provided an excess of boy clerks and second division clerks, considerably in excess of the country's needs'.[121] She further contended that 'the lower grade clerks employed in Dublin were almost exclusively Irish: Many of them had worked in London on appointment to the civil service and then had transferred to Dublin; there was a waiting list of Irish clerks in London awaiting such transfers'.[122] Changes brought about by participation in the intermediate examinations did not put them in a position to achieve first division clerkships. This not only applied to boys in

---

[118] Daly, 'The formation of an Irish nationalist elite?' p.295.
[119] Ibid, p.296.
[120] Ibid, p.294.
[121] Ibid, p.297.
[122] Ibid.

Christian Brother schools but to established superior colleges. No matter what their achievements in competitive examinations in Ireland they all suffered the same disadvantage. They were not educated at English public schools and Oxbridge, which as previously outlined, had the correct educational emphasis for the new system based on 'meritocracy'.

While the participation ratio of south to north in the boys' section of the intermediate examinations was 2:1 favouring the south, the position in the girls' was 2:1 to the north of the country. Noting as he did, that comparatively few of the leading Catholic girls' schools prepared girls for the examinations, Archbishop Walsh had failed to acknowledge that a number of bishops and priests had discouraged their participation on such tenuous grounds as the unsuitability of exam centres for girls, as previously mentioned. The Archbishop quoted figures showing that out of 881 girls passing the examination in 1888, only 207 were from Catholic schools.[123] When the first intermediate examinations were held there were only two girls' schools that had college entry provision, Victoria College, Belfast and Alexandra College, Dublin. By 1895, there were five colleges, the aforementioned plus the Dominican College, Eccles Street, St Angela's College (Ursuline Order), Cork, and Loreto College, Stephen's Green, Dublin. These schools consistently appeared in the top results of the intermediate examinations, balancing the religious divide. In marked contrast, the Sacred Heart Convent, Mount Anville, was known for its ability to turn out 'Catholic ladies' rather than for its scholastic achievements. According to Pašeta, 'a search through the list of female students successful at Royal University' matriculation examination in 1885, 1890, 1895, and 1900 reveals no student listed as attending Mount Anville'.[124]

While ground needed to be made up in respect of the success of Protestant girls' schools in the early years of the examinations, students from Catholic convents were to take their place in the high achiever bracket of the results within five years of the first examinations. The Census of 1881 noted a 'very decided advance in the superior education of females in the last decade'.[125] Females studying Latin had increased from 292 to 770 and Greek from 35 to 122, mathematics from 510-1,082.[126] These were requisite

---

[123] Walsh, 'Statement of the chief grievances of Irish Catholics', pp. 859-863.

[124] Pašeta, *Before the revolution*, p.37.

[125] Census Ireland, 1881

[126] Ibid.

subjects for university entrance and just as the barrier to their secondary education fell, so too did the Royal University provide a gateway to the third level education of female students.

Although Greek had a relative low participation by girls in the early years, the number was greater than that for Celtic. This was also relatively low among entrants in the boys' sections, with only six in total from junior and middle grades taking the subject in 1879. In the same year, four girls took Greek, with each giving a private address, indicating home study or small private schools. Three were from the north of Ireland, with one girl from Kerry. No female student sat the Celtic paper. In 1880, seven girls are listed as taking Greek, with six coming from the south and one from the north. Brigid J. Duffy, Loretto Convent, Nth. Great George's Street, Dublin, the sole entrant in that year passed Celtic with a mark of 450/600. Results in 1885 again showed a zero entry for Celtic by girls (187 boys took the exam). In 1886, the number of girls taking Greek was down to three, while again one pupil took Celtic, Barbara Bell, Dominican Convent, Eccles Street, Dublin.[127]

The results of the 1879 examination show that the following were the highest achieving female students: Girls' junior grade: Alice Mary Baxter (exhib.), Ladies Collegiate School, Belfast; middle grade, Kathleen Morrow (exhib.), St Helier's Dalkey, Co. Dublin and Lucy Moore (exhib.), Ladies Collegiate School, Belfast was first in the senior grade as shown in Table 12. The Ladies Collegiate School, Belfast (renamed as Victoria College in 1887 the year of Queen Victoria's Jubilee), achieved a double in the 1879 examinations. Unfortunately, there is no record of Alice Mary Baxter or Lucy Moore in the school's archives. During a move from the Crescent, Belfast to Cranmore Park, in the 1970s, historic registers were mislaid.[128]

The Collegiate School, which was modelled on Cheltenham Ladies College and North London Collegiate School, was founded in 1859, twenty years prior to the first intermediate examination. Its mission was to provide girls with an education 'adapted to their wants, as thorough as that which [was] afforded to boys in schools of the highest order'.[129] According to Judith Harford, 'the curriculum offered was equally rigorous and exacting

---

[127] All results from the Intermediate Board for Ireland results' lists 1879.
[128] Victoria College archives [VCA].
[129] Prospectus, Ladies' Collegiate School, 1882, Victoria College Archives, Belfast.

and mirrored that offered at Alexandra College Dublin'.[130] She further contended that 'the notion of providing girls with such an academic education was not universally welcomed and both Alexandra and Victoria College encountered some public scepticism in the early years. Despite this, students of both colleges excelled in the public examination arena'.[131]

Although Kathleen Morrow, first place middle grade, was listed for the 1879 examination under her home address in Dalkey, she was in fact a pupil at Alexandra School, based at 6 Earlsfort Terrace, Dublin at that time. The school roll showed that she was registered in October 1878, giving an address of Frederick Street, Dublin.[132] Kathleen's father Robert was a coal importer and contractor based 16 Frederick Street South.[133] Mr Morrow does not show up in the 1901 census although there is a good chance that a Robert Morrow (Church of Ireland), aged 31 years living in Waltham Terrace Blackrock, with a four-year-old daughter named Kathleen and two other young children, was a brother of the Alexandra College pupil.[134]

Kathleen entered the intermediate examinations under the school address in 1880 when she took first place in the senior grade. Anne Jellicoe founded Alexandra College, which was the first academic institution providing university education for females, in 1866. A secondary department, Alexandra School opened in 1873, just six years prior to the first intermediate examinations. Attending a well-established Church of Ireland school for girls, Kathleen did not directly benefit from the increased educational provision provided by the intermediate act. She did however make history, as what could be considered a pioneering female with her success in both middle and senior grades. She was to the forefront of female candidates who justified the inclusion of girls in the examinations and the money provided for their participation.

One of the most remarkable success stories of intermediate education for girls was that of Hannah Moylan, who was the first woman in Ireland to be conferred with a Bachelor of Science degree, which was awarded by

---

[130] Judith Harford, 'An Experiment in the Development of Social Networks for Women: Women's Colleges in Ireland in the Nineteenth Century', *Paedagogica Historica*, 43:3, pp. 365-381.
[131] Ibid.
[132] School register, Alexandra College archives, [ACA].
[133] Thom's Dublin Directory, 1878, 'nobility, gentry, merchants, and traders', p. 1702.
[134] Census of Ireland, 1901.

Queen's College Galway in 1897.[135] Previously Moylan gained a BA from the Royal University in 1891, with first class honours in mathematical science and won the Wilkins Memorial Exhibition in mathematics from Trinity College, Dublin. Highlighting her unique achievement John Lucey argued that 'had Miss Moylan achieved such success at an English university, her name would be sounded far and wide'.[136]

Hannah, the second youngest of ten children of a Catholic family, was born in Newcastle Road Galway, in 1867, to Jerimiah and Mary Moylan, both Commissioners of National Education in Ireland, 1872. Her father was the headmaster of the model school in Newcastle Road, Galway and subsequently in Limerick. Such schools in Ireland were established in 1834 with the chief objectives being to 'promote united education ... the most improved methods of literary and scientific instructions and to educate young persons for the office of teacher'.[137] Hannah received her early education in the model schools.[138] At secondary level, she was placed third in the intermediate junior grade (exhibition) in 1882 with an address of Madame de Prins' College, 5 Upr Mallow Street, Limerick. In 1883, Hannah was ninth in the middle grade, while attending Ladies' School, 43 George's Street, Limerick and in 1884, third in the senior grade at the Ladies Intermediate School, 49 Catherine Street, Limerick.

Following an unusual secondary education, having ostensibly attended three different Limerick secondary schools in three consecutive years, Hannah was enrolled at Alexandra College in Dublin to prepare for the Royal University matriculation. The first women's university classes for Catholic students were held in 1885, at the Dominican College, Eccles Street, Dublin. These were merely an extension of the provision in the secondary school. However, in 1893, the Dominicans expanded university provision, founding St Mary's University College at 28 Merrion Square, Dublin. At this stage, Hannah had completed her pre-university education at Alexandra University College and matriculated in the Royal University in

---

[135] John Lucey, 'Hannah Moylan (1867-1902): Educationist who was first woman bachelor of science in Ireland', *Irish Journal of Education,* vol. 41, (2016), pp 61-77.

[136] '*New Zealand Tablet*, Dublin Notes', 25 Sept. 1891, vol. XIX, issue 51.

[137] W.E. Ellis, *Irish education dictionary and scholastic guide* (Dublin, 1887), p.194.

[138] Lucey, 'Hannah Moylan (1867-1902), *Irish Journal of Education,* 2016, vol. 41 pp 61-77.

1887. Following her BA degree, Hannah became a teacher at a number of schools including her alma mater, Alexandra College. She took a break from teaching in 1895 to study for and complete her BSc degree in Queen's College, Galway.[139] She then took up a teaching post in Egypt, where she died of typhoid fever in Cairo in 1902, aged thirty-four.[140]

While religion, allied with the lack of proper provision for a Catholic university, came across strongly during the debates on the intermediate legislation, it is interesting to note that high achieving Catholic students, Arthur Conan and Charles Francis Doyle attended Trinity College and Hannah Moylan, Alexandra College. Although their attendance may have been the exception rather than the rule given church opposition, Catholic students and their parents may have been prepared to step outside such restrictions, in the interest of educational advancement.

It was to be well into the early years of the twentieth century following ongoing developments of the intermediate system, before the opening of University College Dublin in 1908. The college evolved from the foundation of the Catholic University of Ireland in 1854 and the Royal University founded under the University Education Act 1879, leading to the dissolution of the Queen's colleges in 1882. Fr Peter Byrne C.M., writing in 1915 said that the progress made in intermediate education in the last thirty years had been comparable with that in other countries. He hoped that 'with the National University in full working order as a teaching body, and silently but effectively exercising its educational influence mainly upon our Catholic schools, as Trinity does upon Protestant schools, the whole system of Intermediate education will improve more in the future than it has improved in the recent past'.[141]

---

[139] Lucey, 'Hannah Moylan (1867-1902), '*Irish Journal of Education,* 2016, vol. 41 pp 61-77.
[140] *Irish Times,* 17 June 1902.
[141] Byrne C.M., 'The Irish Intermediate Act, 1878: before and after', p.144.

PART THREE

4

James MacMahon and John Anderson: A dual biography

By the study of their biographies, we receive each man as a guest into our minds, and we seem to understand their character as the result of a personal acquaintance.

Plutarch, *Parallel Lives.*

The original concept of dual biography as demonstrated in Plutarch's *Parallel lives,* is of a comparison of two groups, for example the ancient Greeks and Romans. This approach has been superseded by more recent works, which have considered political allies, rivals or enemies and even friends. In employing a broader methodology utilising more readily available primary as well as secondary sources, the scope of such works is greater than the original classical biographies. Alvin Jackson highlights dual biography in Irish history in his recent study of Redmond and Carson.[1] According to Jackson, comparative or dual biography is 'remarkably underdeveloped within Irish literature and history'.[2] He attributes this to the sensitivities of the Irish situation, particularly with regard to political biography.[3] Preceded by R.F. Foster's *Vivid faces*, a thematic generational biography of revolutionaries, Jackson's book while also along thematic lines, is comparative and to a point non-chronological. In an Irish political context, Jackson confronts the sensitivities, which he claimed had been instrumental in the under development of dual biography within Irish history.

However, Jackson was not alone in comparing Redmond and Carson, albeit the earlier work was in another genre and the comparison was by the figures themselves. John Lavery painted both men on condition that they allow their portraits to be hung side by side. They continually compared the

---

[1] Alvin Jackson, *Judging Redmond and Carson: comparative Irish lives* (Dublin, 2018).
[2] Ibid, p. xvii.
[3] Ibid.

paintings: 'Each thought the other's portrait was better'.[4] Redmond remarked that 'I have always had an idea that Carson and I might someday be hanged side by side in Dublin and now it has come to pass'.[5]

Taking a cue from Jackson and comparing the backgrounds and careers of the two men sharing the role at the head of the Irish administration from 1920 to 1922, highlights lives that were parallel in many respects. The Rt. Hon. James MacMahon and Sir John Anderson are viewed with an emphasis on their educational and career experiences as a means of social and career advancement. Despite a lack of available primary source material, school records provide a valuable insight into an individual, his family, and often his future career trajectory. To paraphrase the often quoted Jesuit maxim in relation to giving them the boy at eight and they will give you the man. The key to an assessment of a particular individual and his character can often be found in his earliest achievements and personality traits.

James MacMahon and John Anderson, joint Under Secretaries for Ireland, benefitted from educational provision in Ireland and Scotland in the latter part of the nineteenth with both of them lacking traditional patronage. In relation to MacMahon, he was at the coalface of intermediate education in Ireland, taking the junior grade in 1880, which was only the second year of the examinations. It is debatable what extra benefit in terms of career advancement this gave him, if any. Anderson, was to an extent a beneficiary of the 1872 Education (Scotland) Act, which unlike the English Act of 1870 on which it was based, was not entirely limited to elementary education but extended to some secondary provision, such as the leaving certificate examinations, which followed in 1888.

Following the impact of competitive examinations for second level students, what upward mobility and career advancement can be found within the administration? With an emphasis on the Irish civil service, any assumption of a marked increase in Catholic representation at the top of the administration, as suggested by Lawrence McBride, is debatable.[6] With MacMahon faced by unionist hostility and virtually out on a limb in his role as Under Secretary from 1918 to 1920, McBride's contention seems overstated. Fergus Campbell strongly disputed McBride's argument that a new Catholic and nationalist administration replaced the old Protestant and

---

[4] John Lavery, *The life of a painter* (London, 1940), p.217.

[5] Ibid.

[6] McBride, *The greening of Dublin Castle*.

unionist establishment in Dublin Castle, throughout the entire second chapter of his book on the Irish Establishment.[7]

However, McBride made some valid points on which to base his hypothesis. He outlined the reasons advanced by the Conservative and Liberal administrations for the appointment of Irish-born Catholics and nationalists.[8] On the one hand, he tied in what seemed like the inevitability of Home Rule with Liberal party thinking.[9] Conversely, the legitimisation of the Act of Union, 1800 and making of the government of Ireland more acceptable to the Irish people provided what McBride considered the incentive for such action by the Conservatives.[10] According to Fergus Campbell, 'the result was in McBride's view, the replacement of the old Protestant and Unionist establishment in Dublin Castle with a new Catholic and nationalist administrative elite'.[11]

Campbell argued that although accepted by historians, McBride's hypothesis did not tie in with what he described as contemporary perceptions of the nature of Dublin Castle.[12] He referred to the bigotry encountered by Catholic Under Secretary, Sir Antony MacDonnell, appointed in 1902. MacDonnell told his wife, 'there is an atmosphere of suspicion and espionage. I could not stand it for any length of time and if I cannot improve it, I must go'.[13] He felt that 'he was being watched'.[14] Campbell failed to reference a similar experience sixteen years later for James MacMahon, whose career in Dublin Castle was likewise fraught by suspicion and accusations of spying.

While referring to another Catholic Under Secretary, T.H. Burke, whose appointment in 1869 pre-dated MacDonnell's tenure, Campbell mentioned the unusual circumstance of his having come up through the ranks.[15] However, this was not from a lowly position and would appear to have resulted from privileged access. Burke was born into the Catholic landed

---

[7] Campbell, *The Irish establishment 1879-1914*.
[8] McBride, *The greening of Dublin Castle* p.71.
[9] Ibid.
[10] Fergus Campbell, *The Irish establishment,* p.53.
[11] Ibid.
[12] Ibid, p.54.
[13] Antony MacDonnell to his wife, 18 Nov. 1902, Bodleian Library Ms Eng. Hist. e. 216, MacDonnell Paper, fo.16[r-v].
[14] Ibid, 16 Nov. 1902, fos.13[v]-14[r].
[15] Campbell, *The Irish establishment* p. 59.

gentry. He started as a supernumerary clerk, in the Chief Secretary's Office, Dublin Castle in 1847. Subsequently in 1851, he became private secretary to Under Secretary, Thomas Nicholas Redington who was also from the Catholic landed gentry.[16] Although, while making the point in relation to coming through the ranks, Campbell again had the example of MacMahon, who rose to the most senior position in the civil service starting as a second division clerk in the post office in London, he did not refer to this. It is argued that MacMahon's promotion, which followed that of another Irish born Catholic Under Secretary, Sir Antony MacDonnell, ten years later, should have been referenced, as MacMahon's ostensibly non-privileged background, set him apart from the background of Burke.

Given their positions as joint Under Secretaries for Ireland, a comparative or dual biographical study of the Rt. Hon. James MacMahon PC and Sir John Anderson [later 1st Viscount Waverley] reveals much of similarities but likewise divergences in career pathways. The emphasis vis à vis the administration, will be on MacMahon as Under Secretary from 1918-20, and on his rise to that position. However, the dual biographical study will set the stage for their work in the Castle administration between 1920 and 1922. While their names are known, relatively little has been written about them particularly in the case of MacMahon. His two years in Dublin Castle, in the period 1918-1920, prior to Anderson's appointment will be covered more extensively in this chapter than Anderson's postings in Whitehall during that time.

James MacMahon and John Anderson, were not only the joint Under Secretaries of the Dublin Castle administration and therefore the most powerful figures in the civil service; they were respectively the heads of the Irish and British cohorts within the Chief Secretary's office. It was ostensibly their role to unite both groups. This was applicable only to the years 1920-1922, as MacMahon, as previously stated, had been Under Secretary at the head of the administration from 1918 to 1920. At that time, MacMahon had inherited a divided unionist/nationalist and Protestant/ Catholic administration with attendant bias and resentments. However, from 1920, MacMahon and Anderson were contemporaneous within a particular situation, most likely as colleagues rather than friends or enemies.

---

[16] James Quinn, 'Burke, Thomas Henry (1829–82)', *DIB*.

Nonetheless, MacMahon was to say that 'he held very high tribute to Sir John Anderson who was appointed joint Under Secretary with him during the trouble period, and he kept the situation under control to a very large extent'.[17] Anderson wrote that MacMahon, 'is a colleague who has always treated me exactly as I should have wished'.[18]

That MacMahon had found himself no longer the sole Under Secretary but sharing the role with John Anderson, came about due to the recommendations of the Warren Fisher report.[19] It is contended that it was essentially a means to an end, setting the stage to bring a British cohort into the Irish administration. There is no extant record of MacMahon's reaction to the change in his circumstances although he did send a telegram of welcome to Anderson. Perhaps the initial 'baptism of fire' of 1918, helped ease a situation that could otherwise have proved difficult for both men. His establishment within the system, his networks in Ireland extending across a spectrum from the Catholic Church to the most influential in Irish society, combined with his urbane manner and easy personality, most likely cushioned the arrival of the new joint Under Secretary and his team.

The focus of the biography is on the early lives and careers of these two top civil servants before the final administration from 1920 to 1922. In firstly narrowing the research down to dual biographies, who were the individuals behind the names MacMahon and Anderson? What were the influences of education on their future advancement; and how did their backgrounds and careers set them up for their positions in Dublin Castle? Comparing the lives of MacMahon and Anderson is difficult given that no biography of MacMahon has been written and he did not leave a collection of personal papers. Likewise, John Wheeler-Bennett wrote in the introduction to his official biography of Anderson, that 'in writing Lord Waverley's life I have not been over blessed with a richness of written material'.[20] G.C. Peden further expanded on this by stating that Anderson 'preferred to give advice orally rather than in detailed memoranda and consequently the full impact of his influence cannot be followed in official

---

[17] Col. Joyce, in conversation with the Rt. Hon. James MacMahon, 18 Oct, 1949, BMH, S. 1374, J.V.

[18] Anderson to Bonar Law, 2 Sept. 1920, PA, BL102/7/2.

[19] Warren Fisher, memoranda (TNA, HO 317/50).

[20] John Wheeler-Bennett, *John Anderson, Viscount Waverley* (London, 1962), p.viii.

papers'.[21] However, Wheeler-Bennett did add that he had been fortunate in having access to letters that Anderson had written to his father and first wife. This wealth of primary material is not available in the case of MacMahon, with the exception of a few letters, although research for a MA thesis by this author shed some light on his life. The only obvious links between the Rt. Hon. James MacMahon and Sir John Anderson were the civil service and in the context of the last two years of the pre-Irish Free State administration, holding the positions of joint Under Secretary for Ireland.

Entries in the *Dictionary of Irish Biography,* with reference to MacMahon and Anderson and the *Oxford Dictionary of National Biography,* relating to Anderson, provided a valuable overview of both men and an initial starting point in secondary source research. In the Irish dictionary, Patrick Maume contributes biographical details on both MacMahon and Anderson. G.C. Peden provides an extensive entry in the *Oxford Dictionary of National Biography* on Anderson, which covers the totality of his career in the civil service. Peden's entry on Anderson provides a comprehensive overview of each stage of his career, with however, details of his early life and education being covered in a short paragraph. His posting to Dublin Castle comes under the sub heading of 'Ireland, the Home Office, and India' and does not receive much prominence.

However, Maume's entries on both MacMahon and Anderson are interesting. These provide a strong contrast, with for example Maume giving a far greater insight into Anderson's early life and education than that of MacMahon. This is perhaps understandable as he had Wheeler-Bennett's book as a secondary source. Nonetheless, reading both entries, one cannot help feeling that Maume is to an extent swayed by the broad accomplishments of Anderson on the British, Irish, and world stages. With regard to the position of joint Under Secretary, he essentially belittles the contribution of MacMahon, writing that although Anderson was nominally equal in rank to James MacMahon, 'the latter's functions were mainly diplomatic and the bulk of the administrative work was left to Anderson'.[22] This point is further stressed in Maume's writing on MacMahon, when he stated that Anderson, 'took over many of MacMahon's nominal functions. He also states that MacMahon's principal task became the cultivation of moderate (mainly clerical) opinion in the hope of preparing the ground for

---

[21] G.C. Peden, 'Anderson, John, first Viscount Waverley (1882-1958), *ODNB*.

[22] Patrick Maume, 'Anderson, John (1882-1958), 1st Viscount Waverley', *DIB*.

a peace settlement[23]. It is true that the men were very different but the the breakdown of roles was far less definitive than this, as were their backgrounds and early careers.

By providing an overview of their early lives, education, and civil service careers prior to 1920 it is hoped that linkages and similarities, perhaps even coincidences will be discovered. It is not intended to compare or suggest that their academic records for example were necessarily on an equal footing but to demonstrate that the availability of educational provision in Ireland and Scotland, as outlined in the Introduction, may be considered as a contributing factor to their rise to the top of the Irish administration. MacMahon was a Roman Catholic from Armagh, northern Ireland and Anderson a Presbyterian from Edinburgh, Scotland. Apart from a religious divide, there was seventeen years between them, with MacMahon being the elder. They were also very different personalities. Patrick Maume described MacMahon, as 'a courteous and gracious man, he was liked by all'.[24] Mark Sturgis, a member of the British cohort spoke of MacMahon as being 'the best fellow in the world'.[25] Anderson came across as less approachable, being perceived as dour and humourless, or at the least having 'a gravity of mien'.[26]

James Stanislaus MacMahon, was born on 20 April 1865, at 24 Fleet Street in Belfast's Sailortown.[27] For the year 1865, number twenty-four is listed in the provincial directory as being occupied by a James MacMahon, flax buyer.[28] Strangely, for a city known for its linen industry MacMahon was the only one associated with it, living in the street. He and his wife had neighbours who were sea captains, ship carpenters, sail-makers, labourers, clerks, a violin maker and a resident named Adam Carrigan, listed in the street directory as 'hall door'.[29] It is not stated in the directory if MacMahon

---

[23] Patrick Maume, 'MacMahon, James (1865-1954)', *DIB*.

[24] Ibid.

[25] Hopkinson, *The last days of Dublin Castle*, p.45.

[26] Ibid, p. vii.

[27] James Stanislaus MacMahon, GRO, F4838 1ED, birth registered in Belfast Urban District 1.

[28] *The Belfast and province of Ulster directory for the year 1865*, p.132.

[29] Ibid, list of Fleet Street houses, residents and their occupations. The origin of the term 'hall door' is unknown although occupations are given, for residents. It may have meant he was in charge of the building or had the room next to the hall door.

owned or leased his house, or indeed if the family were the sole occupants.

In the heart of Sailortown, which ran from York Street to the Belfast docks, Fleet Street was situated between Ship Street and Dock Street, among cobblestoned roadways and mostly small red-bricked houses. These were in a relatively poor location just on the edge of Sailortown, built in 1860, five years before MacMahon's birth. Although deprived, Sailortown, which at one stage had a population of 5,000 people living in tiny terraced houses, was a cosmopolitan community due to the influx of foreign seafarers. It also had a number of fine large houses mostly occupied by well-off sea captains.[30]

Recognised as Belfast's first waterfront village, Sailortown was established in the mid nineteenth century. It boasted facilities such as a hotel and boarding houses, a fire station, factories and taverns. For many families life was hard with men and boys away at sea. Women worked in the linen mills and cigarette factories. Houses which were small and damp were often occupied by more than one family, when in reality they were barely big enough for one. In the main, the area provided housing for transient sailors and dockworkers, as well as those who worked in the factories and linen mills. It was in this socially mixed location that James Mac Mahon started life with his parents.

On his birth certificate, MacMahon's mother was named as Mary MacMahon, née McConnell.[31] Mrs MacMahon who was born in 1845, which meant she was only twenty when James was born, was from a relatively well-off family.[32] Her husband who was born five years before her in 1840, was described by a family member as a self-made man.[33] Mrs MacMahon was a mere four feet in height, while in contrast her husband stood over six feet tall.[34] Mary was considered by her family to be 'outstandingly gifted'.[35] The MacMahons were originally connected to Ballybay, Co. Monaghan. Facing strong family opposition to their marriage

---

[30] Sailortown regeneration project 'St Joseph's open doors project'.

[31] GRO, F4838 1ED.

[32] Eilish Tennent, née McKee, family recollections.

[33] Ibid.

[34] Sacred Heart Archives [SHA] *Circular*, Sr. Teresa MacMahon 1880-1965, S C/118 (8).

[35] Ibid.

they were, according to relations, forced to elope.[36] Seventeen children were born to the couple.[37]

Seven of the MacMahon's sons including James the eldest, Joseph, 1866; Frank, 1868; John, 1869; Charlie, 1875; Vincent, 1876, Harry 1883 and five daughters, Maggie, 1868; Mary, 1871; Lizzie, 1872; Katie, 1878 and Teresa, 1880, were photographed in 1887.[38] With five of the children born to the MacMahons not featured, it could be that they died shortly after childbirth or at a young age. There are gaps between 1876 and 1883 with the other dates of birth being closer together. Following MacMahon's appointment as Under Secretary to the Lord Lieutenant of Ireland, his family were described in a newspaper article as talented, with two working as barristers, one practicing in New York.[39] His other brother in the legal profession was John MacMahon, Barrister-at-Law, who worked in the purchase department of the Irish Land Commission.[40] According to the same article, another of MacMahon's siblings left the civil service for the army and was killed in the Boer War; while one was a prominent journalist in America. Joseph MacMahon, who was next to James in age with only a year between them, was a national schools' inspector.[41] The report did not give details of MacMahon's sisters.

Moving from Belfast to Armagh was to bring about a change of circumstances for MacMahon's father and the family as a whole. According to an appreciation written shortly after his death on 1 May 1954, the fact that the Rt. Hon. James MacMahon started life in Belfast, was 'an accident of birth.' The author notes that 'he belonged, as did his family to the city of Armagh and throughout his long and fruitful life, he never forgot it'.[42] From working in what was a relatively low-level job as a flax buyer, MacMahon Snr. became a hotel proprietor and gained a position of some stature in the Armagh community. The 1880 register of the French College, Blackrock

---

[36] Eilish Tennent.

[37] *Sacred Heart Circular*, S C/118 (8).

[38] MacMahon family photograph dated 1887, with names and birth dates recorded on the back, courtesy of family members.

[39] *Irish Independent,* 5 July 1918.

[40] *Irish Times,* 31 Aug. 1942, obituary of John MacMahon.

[41] *Irish Independent,* 5 July 1918.

[42] Ibid., 3 May 1954, an appreciation, on the death of the Rt. Hon James MacMahon.

shows the family's home address was in Irish Street, Armagh.[43] In 1910 the Northern Hotel in Railway Street was recorded as being under the management of 'J. M'Mahon, proprietor'.[44] Added to this, Mr MacMahon also ran the Charlemont Arms Hotel in Upper English Street.[45] Such a business profile was a long way from the overcrowded position of flax-buyer and life in Fleet Street, Belfast. In fact, the family was regarded as 'being in comfortable circumstances'.[46]

Mr MacMahon's funeral in 1912 was an indication of his success, social position and popularity in Armagh. It was reported that the procession was long and that it represented all sections of the community.[47] The article recorded that businesses along the route were shut, with lowered blinds as an 'expression of the respect universally entertained for the deceased'.[48] Showing the regard with which Mr MacMahon was held among the Catholics of the diocese and with an indication of the support that was to be accorded to the future Under Secretary, Cardinal Logue, Archbishop of Armagh and Primate of All Ireland from 1887, presided at the requiem mass. This was a link in the chain of the strong connection, which James MacMahon subsequently fostered over the years with the Catholic Church, as likewise it did with him. He had an entrée to the world of the Catholic hierarchy before and during his time in Dublin Castle, which his fellow Under Secretary, John Anderson could not have matched. Newspaper coverage of the funeral shows that the four of the sons of Mr MacMahon, James, Joseph, John, and Vincent were among the mourners but none of his daughters was acknowledged. Sons-in-law, H.J. McKee, husband of Elizabeth (Lizzie) MacMahon and John Cromie, married to Mary MacMahon, were also cited as being among the congregation along with grandsons H.J. McKee, James McKee, F.W. McKee, and James Cromie.[49]

John Anderson, later first Viscount Waverley, had similarly humble origins to MacMahon. At 3am on 8 July 1882, Anderson was born in a two-roomed flat in a stone tenement building, 1 Livingstone Place, in the district

---

[43] BCA, school register 1880.

[44] 'Ulster Directory' www.libraryireland.com/UlsterDirectory1910/Armagh [accessed 14 Feb. 2017]

[45] Eilish Tennent, family member.

[46] *Irish Independent,* 3 May 1954.

[47] *Freeman's Journal,* 1 Nov.1912, funeral of Mr James MacMahon.

[48] Ibid.

[49] *Freeman's Journal,* 1 Nov. 1912.

of Newington, Edinburgh.[50] As Anderson was entering the world, James MacMahon was just two months away from taking up his first civil service position as a second division clerk. Like MacMahon, Anderson was the eldest of his family albeit a much smaller one, with four children born to the Andersons. According to his birth certificate Anderson's parents were David Alexander Parsons Anderson, a 'fancy stationer' and Janet Kilgour Anderson née Bregelmann.[51] Janet was the descendant of a German sailor who landed in Leith, Edinburgh in the early nineteenth century.[52]

John's younger brother, Charles born in 1884, died of cerebro-meningitis at the age of seventeen months.[53] Two sisters, Catherine B. (Katie) and Janet J.P. (Nettie) were born on 10 October 1886 and 8 January 1889 respectively.[54] At the time of John's birth the family's flat was in a house that was part owned by Janet Anderson's father, Charles Bregelmann, for which they paid an average annual rate for the area of £19, 9s. p.a.[55] The stone building was at the 'Meadows' end of Livingstone Place. This poor environment marks a parity between the very early lives of Anderson and MacMahon. However, the area around Livingstone Place, deprived though it might have been, was very different from Fleet Street, Belfast in the heart of docklands. A current photograph of the house in Livingstone Place, taken by the author shows that the young Anderson and his siblings would have enjoyed the open spaces and grassy expanse of the Meadows, which was just across a roadway from number 1 Livingstone Place. There is no currently available comparison between the Edinburgh and Belfast properties, as houses in Sailortown, Belfast were demolished in the 1960s.[56]

David Anderson expanded his business interests from a small start, as had James MacMahon Snr. The family's position and social standing in Edinburgh was likewise improved. Mr Anderson made his way from relative poverty to comfortable circumstances.[57] Having initially started with one shop in the Princes Street Arcade for his stationary business, Anderson leased two further premises there for photographic and leather goods. Such

---

[50] John Anderson, NRS, ref. 685/5966. Registration required exact time of birth.
[51] John Anderson, national records of Scotland.
[52] Wheeler-Bennett, *John Anderson*, p.1.
[53] Ibid.
[54] Ibid.
[55] Wheeler-Bennett, *John Anderson*, p.2.
[56] Information provided by the 'Sailortown regeneration project, Belfast'.
[57] Wheeler-Bennett, *John Anderson*, p.16.

was the strength of his personality that the shopping area became known as 'Anderson's Arcade'.[58] Extending his interests into publishing, 'he later became a director of a well-known firm of printers and publishers, 'Valentine & Sons of Dundee', which had in fact bought out his own publishing business.[59] With a further eye to expansion, Anderson had also developed an interest in property.[60]

According to Wheeler-Bennett, the family moved from Livingstone Place to 17 Braid Crescent in Braid Hills, which Anderson bought for £700 in his wife's name, when John Anderson was eight years old. Braid Crescent is situated on the south side of Edinburgh in the Morningside district. The house was a vast improvement on the small flat of his early childhood, although it meant a walk of two miles to school for the young Anderson. Ten years later in 1900 when he was eighteen, his father purchased Westland House, Eskbank at a cost of £1,700. The house was seven miles from Edinburgh University, which John was then attending. It was conveniently near the railway station, which had opened in 1849.

The original Eskbank and Dalkeith railway station was closed (along with the Waverley Route) in 1969.[61] In a local publication, it was later erroneously claimed that 'Viscount Waverley, Chancellor of the Exchequer until 1945, whose name was given to the famous First World War Anderson shelters, was born at Westland House'.[62] This mistake was also made by his alma mater in an obituary in the George Watson's College yearbook, following Anderson's death in 1958. However, the family enjoyed life in a 'pleasant rambling property of which the centre portion was of some age. Two wings, of which one was an octagonal tower, were of later addition'.[63] To all intents and purposes the Andersons had prospered and integrated within the local community and they were particularly friendly with the Mackenzie family nearby.[64] Andrew Mackenzie, a commercial traveller and his wife Mary had a family of five daughters; one of them, Chrissie, five

---

[58] Ibid, p. 3.

[59] Peden, 'John Anderson'.

[60] Wheeler-Bennett, p. 3.

[61] 'Borders to Edinburgh railway opened as longest line in UK in a century', *BBC News*, 6 Sept. 2015.

[62] F. House, 'Eskbank and Ironmills Conservation Area Appraisal', Midlothian Council.

[63] Wheeler-Bennett, *John Anderson,* p.7.

[64] Ibid, p.10.

years his junior was to become John's future wife.[65] Sadly, on a holiday with the Mackenzies in the summer of 1903 John's sister Nettie died tragically.[66] Anderson was badly affected by the tragic drowning of his younger sister. He wrote to Chrissie almost a year later of his concern for his parents and how for himself 'little things continually occur to freshen the pain'.[67]

In setting out the dual lives of James MacMahon and John Anderson, a number of similarities and connections are evident. Perhaps the strongest parallel was the commitment of both their families to their education. This aspiration was supported by the fact that there was a structure of academic provision in place in both Ireland and Scotland that provided secondary education and ultimately prepared them for the civil service. While the old saying that schooldays are the best in your life may not be strictly true, they are certainly formative. Both MacMahon and Anderson were conscious of the influence of their secondary schooling and paid fulsome tributes to their respective colleges. MacMahon is recorded as stating that 'my obligations to the college have grown and multiplied in such number and such fullness that I cannot hope to repay them in my lifetime'.[68] According to Wheeler-Bennett, Anderson likewise never forgot the gratitude he owed to his school. For example in an appreciation of his mathematics teacher John Alison, Anderson wrote 'my debt is greatest to Alison for he first guided my faltering footsteps along the path that it has been my lot to tread'.[69] In relation to MacMahon the impression that Blackrock College made on him was remarkable given that he was only there for two years. Conversely, Anderson attended George Watson's 'Wee School', the lower division of Watson's College from 1888 and the upper school or college, from 1896 until he left at seventeen years of age in 1899.[70]

In comparing the educational provision afforded to both MacMahon and Anderson there is a lack of personal or anecdotal material from which to gain an insight into their schooldays, particularly in relation to MacMahon. Nonetheless it was the influences that both were exposed to in relation to

---

[65] Ibid.

[66] Ibid, p.11.

[67] Wheeler-Bennett, *John Anderson* p.12.

[68] *Blackrock College Yearbook*, 1954, obituary p. 105.

[69] *The Watsonian,* vol. xxiv, no 2, 2 Apr. 1926.

[70] Wheeler-Bennett, *John Anderson,* p.4.

religion, ethos and type of schools that likely had a profound effect on their future development. The Intermediate Education (Ireland) Act, 1878 while legislating for secular education, conversely improved access for Catholic students. The Education (Scotland) Act 1872 'may be viewed as an attempt to revive Presbterian educational traditions by seeking to ensure common provision across the country'.[71] This was in relation to parity among the 987 school boards established under the Act.[72]

MacMahon, the boy from a northern Irish town left his familiar home environment to be a boarder in Dublin at Blackrock College, or the French College as it was then. Conversely, Anderson remained in the familiar landscape of Edinburgh as a day-boy associating with the sons of the less well off of the town and extended area, in an environment driven by a strict Scottish protestant religion and work ethic, that saw him engaged in a personal pursuit of academic excellence. He was described by the school as 'one of our most brilliant pupils'.[73] James MacMahon attended three different schools from primary to secondary levels. He received his elementary education at the Christian Brothers Schools Armagh.[74] St Patrick's College, Armagh (now St Patrick's Grammar School), provided his secondary education for at least one year. A description of the school in 1879, when he was registered as a pupil states that 'this establishment was opened in 1838; it is affiliated to the Catholic University and under the direction of the Vincentian Fathers'.[75] The president of the college was listed as Patrick Boyle C.M. The course of studies comprised, Latin, Greek, mathematics, English, French, and history.[76] While it is not highlighted in Thom's Directory, the college was 'devoted chiefly to the preliminary instruction of young men intended for the priesthood'.[77] This raises the question as to whether MacMahon was considering becoming a priest at that time. However, attendance at such schools did not necessarily imply

---

[71] Jane McDermid, 'Education and society in the era of the school boards, 1872-1918' in Robert Anderson, Mark Freeman and Lindsay Paterson (eds.). *The Edinburgh History of Education in Scotland*, (Edinburgh, 2015), p.190.

[72] Ibid.

[73] *The Watsonian*, Dec. 1905.

[74] *Irish Independent*, 3 May 1954.

[75] *Thom's Dublin Directory*, 1879, p.817.

[76] Ibid.

[77] George Henry Bassett, *The book of County Armagh* (Dublin, 1888), p.101.

commitment to the religious life. Some seminaries were also open to general secondary school pupils.

MacMahon's sisters attended the local girls' school run by the Sacred Heart order. His mother and aunt had been among the first pupils to attend the Armagh school, which was founded in 1851.[78] Mount St. Catherine's Convent National School was within the Armagh parish and both the school and the nuns played a large part in the lives of the MacMahon siblings, with Teresa going on to join the order.[79] Katie, another sister of James MacMahon is thought to have entered the Sisters of Mercy.[80] Three of the daughters of H.J. McKee and James's sister Elizabeth (MacMahon), Madeline, Kathleen and Margaret also joined the Sacred Heart order.[81] The MacMahon brothers all served mass in the Armagh convent over the years.[82] As a family, they were given a strong grounding in Catholicism, an integral part of their lives, which as previously stated fostered MacMahon's lifetime engagement with the Church.

The only extant record of James MacMahon's attendance at St Patrick's is for the school year of 1879-80.[83] He was enrolled as a day-boy. The cost for the two terms is noted in the school ledger as £5.14s, 3½ p. This sum included a charge of £2 for tuition, with the rest being billed for school supplies. The accounts show the following items were provided in the 'first session', a Latin grammar, Greek grammar, *Caesar*, arithmetic book, algebra book, exercise book, *Roscoe's chemistry,* and a lead pencil. In the second session he required a copy of *Xenophon*, the *Annals of England*, geometric drawing book, and an exercise book; the intermediate exam fee of two shillings and six pence and a further lead pencil were also charged.[84] These items were priced from seven and a half pence to three shillings and six pence. The lists are interesting on two levels. Firstly, they indicate that the school was fee paying, which was standard for the time and secondly give an overview of the subjects that MacMahon studied. In relation to school fees and extra charges, the Powis Commission of 1870 noted in its report that 'parents wishing to extend the education of their children should

---

[78] *Sacred Heart circular*, SHC/118 (8) [SHA].
[79] Ibid.
[80] Pauline Arthurs, family recollections.
[81] Ibid.
[82] SHC/118 (8).
[83] St Patrick's College, Armagh, archival records.
[84] Ibid.

do so on their own initiative; they have no claim upon the public for assistance'.[85]

The following school year of 1880-81, MacMahon's name was entered in the St Patrick's register but there are no details recorded. He did not return to the school although it might appear he was expected back. He moved to the French College, Blackrock, Co. Dublin. While the tuition fees were relatively low in St Patrick's, those in Blackrock at the time of the Powis Commission were up to £73 p.a. including extras such as gymnastics, drawing German and Italian.[86] In 1879, Thom's describes the school as providing an education embracing the entire course of classics and science: 'The college affords all the advantages of a French school, combined with a sound English education'.[87] The entry in Thom's also stated that 'there is a special department for the preparation for the higher branches of the civil service.[88]

The French School had opened in 1860 with 'two boarders and six day students ... in the beginning everything was in French'.[89] The combined continental and English ethos removed Blackrock to an extent from the English public school comparison, which saw a number of 'superior schools being labelled as the Eton of Ireland or the Irish Eton'.[90] One such school, Clongowes Wood, cited preparation for the Royal Military Colleges of Sandhurst and Woolwich, as well as the Indian civil service.[91] Conversely, St Vincent's College Castleknock was quick off the mark in 1879 to advertise that the 'course of education comprises all that is required for passing the examinations under the Intermediate Education Act'.[92] The perception of the French College was of a school for young gentlemen whose parents had aspirations of upward mobility for their offspring. This exposed the young MacMahon to a life-style that was distinct from the rougher environment Anderson encountered in George Watson's College.

---

[85] Royal commission of inquiry into primary education (Ireland) vol. 1, HC1870 [c.6] XXVIII pt.1,505.
[86] O'Neill, *Catholics of consequence*, p.33.
[87] *Thom's Dublin Directory*, 1879.
[88] Ibid.
[89] Seán P. Farragher, *The French College Blackrock, 1860-96* (Dublin, 2011), p. 24.
[90] O'Neill, *Catholics of consequence*, p.22.
[91] *Thom's Dublin Directory*, 1879.
[92] Ibid.

However, the pupils in Blackrock were not totally removed from the realities of Irish life and in particular the gradually changing political climate in Ireland. On St Patrick's Day 1866, a mere six years after the school was founded 'the boys procured the green flag, then recognised as the standard of the Republican movement and hoisted it on the roof of Castledawson House, the school building at the time'.[93]

MacMahon's academic ability seems to have been competent rather than exceptional. He was awarded a prize in the intermediate examinations, passing the junior grade with distinction while in St Patrick's in June 1880. He again merited an intermediate examination prize in 1881.[94] This was at middle grade level, which he took in Blackrock. In both years, MacMahon received third class prizes of books to the value of £2 each.[95] Whether under the direction of his parents, the school or his own inclinations, MacMahon studied at the Civil Service College in Blackrock for the year 1881-82. The college, which was founded in 1873, was situated in the 'Castle' in the school grounds.[96] According to Sean Farragher it 'facilitated an entrée for Catholic students into the most coveted posts in the civil service, which had previously gone to students from leading schools and universities in England'.[97] However, Mary E. Daly contended that inequalities in the educational system in Ireland combined with the Northcote-Trevelyan structure of the civil service, which emphasised an elite first division, left most Irish civil servants being designated as second division, despite increased access after the introduction of entry-level competitive examinations.[98] While these viewpoints are perhaps not totally incompatible, it could be hypothesised that the Civil Service Commission, acting under the recommendations of the Northcote-Trevelyan, did not actively discriminate against Irish Catholic candidates or other non-Oxbridge applicants, but assisted their entry to second division clerkship but not top tier positions.

Lack of empirical evidence makes it impossible to determine why MacMahon left St Patrick's after one year and enrolled in the French

---

93 Farragher, *The French College Blackrock*, 1860-96, p. 63.
94 James MacMahon, school record [BCA].
95 'Intermediate education board for Ireland, results of examinations 1880'.
96 Farragher, *The French College Blackrock, 1860-96*, p.49.
97 Ibid.
98 Mary E. Daly, 'The formation of an Irish nationalist elite?' pp. 281-301.

College. The only primary source indicating that it was perhaps an unplanned decision, was the entry in the St Patrick's College register. This ostensibly shows as mentioned, that the school expected him to return in September 1880. As he did not leave education after primary level there appears to have been no expectation that he would take up work immediately, perhaps in the family business or as a boy clerk. Conversely, the family prioritised secondary education for their eldest son. Success in the intermediate examination in 1880 may have turned his attention and that of his parents to a civil service career. There are no known sources to indicate that this was the case, or to provide details of what influences could have led to the decision. It could perhaps be hypothesised that given the very Catholic family in which he was reared that the initial purpose in sending him to St Patrick's was entry to the priesthood. If after a year he decided that was not for him, then Blackrock with its civil service college could have been regarded as a viable alternative.

James MacMahon's brother, Joseph Aloysius, who was born the year after MacMahon also attended the French College.[99] Joseph was a scholastic (student intending to join the priesthood), from 1880-83. He subsequently gave up whatever clerical aspirations he may have had and became a regular boarder from 1883-84.[100] His intermediate examination results indicate that he was perhaps more academic that his older brother James. However, this is not conclusive as he benefitted from four consecutive years boarding in Blackrock, as opposed to James's more disrupted secondary education. Joseph took the junior grade twice, achieving first class prizes of books, valued at £4 each in 1881 and the following year an exhibition valued at £15, tenable for three years. Taking the same grade twice could have been related to age or to an ambition to achieve higher marks and the possibility of winning an exhibition. At middle grade, he again won an exhibition this time valued at £25, tenable for two years. In 1884 he received a second class prize in the senior grade.[101] While James took Latin and French among other subjects in the middle grade, Joseph sat Latin, Greek, French and Italian and five other subjects.[102] Beyond academic endeavour and success, a photograph shows a Joseph MacMahon in the first senior cup team of 1887,

---

[99] Blackrock College, school register, 1880-83 [BCA].
[100] Ibid, 1883-84.
[101] Intermediate education board results 1880-84.
[102] Ibid.

but the date does not tally with the details recorded for his attendance at the school.[103]   Between 1884 and 1886 he was a university student at the Castle.[104] This may have qualified him to play on the team. Blackrock in common with other fee-paying schools, prepared students for the exams of the Royal University, Dublin, which examined extern students only. Joseph graduated and had a career as a school's inspector. A younger brother, Frank (Francis) attended the French School as a scholastic from 1882 until 1883, but the archival records do not show if he spent a longer period of time there, or if MacMahon's other brothers were pupils at the school.

David Neligan, a civil servant, who was born and grew up in Templeglantine, Co. Limerick and attended the local school, describes Joseph MacMahon from his early childhood memories as 'a stout fellow with a big head, loud voice and a hearty laugh'.[105]   Neligan recalls that Joseph managed to schedule his inspections for the days of the coursing meeting at Clounanna, and that he boasted of having lost a month's salary on dogs.[106] In what is likely to have been an exaggeration, Neligan claimed that on one occasion Joseph MacMahon, 'came in style in a chauffeur driven Model T Ford and gave a crowd of us a jaunt'.[107] Considering that Neligan claimed that the Rt. Hon. James MacMahon went to England after 1922 and died there, his facts do not always appear to be accurate.[108] It is a matter of record that after holding a number of executive roles in Ireland following the change in the Dublin Castle administration after 1922, James MacMahon died in Dublin in 1954.

Despite a relatively short time at Blackrock, MacMahon was to retain his links with the school throughout his life, as did John Anderson with his alma mater. Anderson was asked to be the orator at the first ever Watson's Founder's Day 1947. For fifty years, he was a member of the London Watsonian Club and president in 1925.[109]   MacMahon was likewise involved in his old school. He was president of the College Union in 1904-05.[110] A photograph from 1953, taken in Blackrock College just a short time

---

[103] Séan Farragher, *Blackrock College 1860-1995* (Dublin, 1995), p. 339.
[104] University College Blackrock, register [BCA].
[105] David Neligan, *The spy in the castle* (London, 1968), p.14.
[106] Ibid.
[107] Ibid.
[108] Ibid.
[109] R. Ogilvie MacKay, *The Watsonian*, 1958, vol 54.
[110] Farragher, *Blackrock College, 1860-1995*, p. 127.

before his death, shows him sitting next to Eamon de Valera with Cardinal D'Alton and 'his contemporaries'.[111] An obituary of MacMahon, details the fact that in 1881 Blackrock students won more distinctions than those of any two other schools or colleges in the country and went on to successful careers. 'James was one of many boys whose success was the glory of Blackrock …one of four Blackrock boys who entered the civil service in 1882 and reached first class rank in it'.[112] Like MacMahon, another of the four, Patrick Keawell, was to become Principal Clerk in the GPO.[113]

As previously mentioned John Anderson's early education was at the 'Wee School', the lower division of George Watson's, a Protestant/Church of Scotland school, located in Merchant Maiden Hospital, Archibald Place, Edinburgh.[114] He started in the school in 1888. Anderson himself confirmed the date of his enrolment at George Watson's in the details given in his civil service application.[115] Although Wheeler-Bennett contends that he entered at the age of seven years, given his birth in July 1882, he was only six. Anderson's father, David, was determined that his son should have the educational advantages which he himself was deprived of due to poverty.[116] He chose George Watson's for three reasons; the standard of education was of the highest in Scotland; it was near Livingstone Place, being situated just across the Meadows and at £7 per annum, it was affordable.[117] This fee of £7 for the lower division of Watson's, cited by Wheeler-Bennett, was not in fact correct. The elementary school had according to the school prospectus two levels of fees, both charged quarterly. The fees for the youngest pupils were twelve shillings and six pence per quarter and those for the older elementary children were fifteen shillings per quarter, the same as for the college.[118]

The Wee School, was housed in a four-storey building just separated from Royal Infirmary by a high wall. The classroom had a view of the

---

[111] Ibid, p. 288.

[112] *Blackrock College Yearbook*, 1954 'James MacMahon obituary' pp. 103-4.

[113] Ibid, p.104.

[114] Wheeler-Bennett, *John Anderson*, p.3.

[115] John Anderson civil service application, 1905 (TNA, records of the civil service commission, CSC 11/8).

[116] Wheeler-Bennett, *John Anderson*, p.4.

[117] Ibid.

[118] George Watson's College archives [GWCA], school prospectus, 1899-1900, by email from Fiona Hooper, archivist, 04 Oct. 2017.

infectious diseases department. The pupils found welcome relief from blackboard and abacus watching the nurses bustling around the wards.[119] George Watson's College was a former Hospital School, which had been set up in 1741 thanks to a legacy left by merchant banker George Watson, for the education of children from disadvantaged backgrounds.[120] In 1870, the Merchant Company, Archibald Place, under powers granted by parliament remodelled the hospital school into a day school.[121] Far from being a school for the aspiring middle classes, such as James MacMahon had experienced in the French College, the pupils at George Watson's were 'gathered from all parts of the city and country, owning no common traditions and animated by no espris (sic) de corps. Free fights were the order of the day'.[122] John Anderson entered the upper division of the school, George Watson's College, situated at the same address, in 1896. After he left three years later, the school was to remain at that location for over thirty years. In 1932, the boys' school moved to a new building on Colinton Road. On 1 October 1974, George Watson's College and George Watson's Ladies' College, which had been accommodated at 7 George Square, were amalgamated as a co-educational school on the current Colinton Road campus.

In a coincidence that in a minor way connected Arthur Conan's family in Dublin, with John Anderson's alma mater, Arthur Conan Doyle lived at 23 George Square across from Watson's Ladies' College in the Edinburgh Square; Anderson's sisters both attended the Ladies' College. They joined the school on 20 October 1896, when Catherine was aged ten and Janet seven years.[123] Catherine had previously been a pupil at Morningside Board School, near the family home on Braid Road. She left George Watson's Ladies College in 1904 and Janet's schooling ended in 1903, following the tragic accident already mentioned.

Anderson was fourteen years old when he was admitted into fifth year at the college. He completed his education at the school in the academic year between 1888 and 1899. Being a merit pupil, his fees at George Watson's College, were paid by a bursary.[124] In 1899, Anderson was in receipt of the

---

[119] *The Watsonian*, vol. xxiv, no. 1, Dec. 1927.

[120] George Watson's College, https://www.gwc.org.uk/our-school/our-heritage/school-history/ [accessed 17 May 2018].

[121] Ibid.

[122] *The Watsonian,* July 1920.

[123] Watson's Ladies' College, school register, [GWCA].

[124] Ibid.

Highland Bursary, which was only open to final year students. His academic results were outstanding. Class records, which only began in 1897-98 show that Anderson achieved 73% (8th in class) for French, 89% (6th in class) for Latin and 100% for Mathematics (1st place) in that year. During 1898-99, Anderson achieved 87% for English (5th in class), 4th in class for French, 98% for German (2nd in class), 92% for Latin (10th in class) and 99% for mathematics. Also in 1899, Anderson was made school Dux.[125] This distinction was awarded to the most outstanding pupil each year. He was the first mathematician and non-classicist to achieve the honour.[126] His achievement was notable given that 'the school year ended, as it does now, in the second half of July; as John Anderson was born on 8 July in 1882, he had virtually achieved the distinction of becoming Dux when he was only sixteen'.[127] Anderson also gained the Jenkins' Prize, the Lizars, and the Mathematical Medal in his final year at the school.[128]

Looking back to Anderson's time in George Watson's, a coincidence was to connect the school to the Irish administration, the first of two such occurrences. Two years older and probably not well known to Anderson at the time, a fellow pupil in George Watson's was also to be appointed to Dublin Castle in years to come. John James (Ian) MacPherson, was born at Strone, Kingussie, Scotland on 14 May 1880, to James MacPherson a farmer, and Anne MacPherson nee Stewart.[129] MacPherson's early education was at Newtonmore Public School (now Newtonmore Primary School) and Kingussie School, where he was enrolled aged eleven for secondary schooling.[130] MacPherson subsequently attended George Watson's in 1895, with the register showing his father's occupation as that of coal merchant. Known as J.J. at school, he attended the same maths and Latin classes as John Anderson, despite being older. Although his grades were good, he did not achieve the same academic heights as Anderson and was not a school Dux.[131].

---

[125] Ibid.
[126] Wheeler-Bennett, *John Anderson*, p.6.
[127] *The Watsonian*, 1905.
[128] Ibid.
[129] Scottish births register, 102/21, p.7.
[130] Kingussie School register 1891, archives [KSA], by email from Nicola Gow, administrative assistant, 14 Jan 2019.
[131] Annual results book, 1895, [GWCA].

Ian MacPherson graduated from Edinburgh University with an MA and LLB and was called to the bar in 1906. A Liberal MP, he was appointed Chief Secretary for Ireland on 13 January 1919, resigning in 1920.[132] MacPherson left Dublin Castle in April of that year, a month prior to the arrival of John Anderson and a British cohort. He had been on sick leave and while his illness may have been genuine, his time in Ireland was anything but a marked success. Perhaps his greatest failure was the 1919 Education Bill, which was withdrawn. MacPherson went on to assume the role of minister for pensions and 'his pensions act (1922) is considered his greatest political achievement'.[133] He died at the age of fifty-seven, having suffered a heart attack in a London restaurant on 14 August 1937.[134]

John Anderson continued his education in Edinburgh University after completion of his years in secondary school, setting him on a different path into the civil service to that of MacMahon. Following the introduction of the Scottish Leaving Certificate in 1888, a list of participating schools in 1891, the year that merit certificates were introduced, indicated that George Watson's Boys and Ladies' Colleges were entered for the examinations.[135] Higher level Leaving Certificate maths, Latin, English and German for Leaving Certificate are cited on Anderson's university degree details.[136] The list of students gaining bursaries in the first session in Edinburgh University 1899, showed George Robertson and J.H. MacLagan Wedderburn of George Watson's College taking the first two places with John Anderson coming eleventh, assuming the list was in merit order.[137] This seems an unlikely placing for Anderson.

During his time in Edinburgh University, Anderson gained ten medals and other prizes and certificates including the Hope Prize and the Vans Dunlop Scholarship in chemistry.[138] Wheeler-Bennet writes that in fact he won eleven medals.[139] Anderson left the university having been awarded a

---

[132] Patrick M. Geoghegan, 'MacPherson, (James) Ian (1880-1937)', *DIB*.

[133] Ibid.

[134] Ibid.

[135] https://digital.nls.uk/exams/browse/archive/129996597?mode=transcription, [accessed 24 Nov. 2018].

[136] John Anderson, Science degree, University of Edinburgh, special collections.

[137] George Watson's archives.

[138] *The Watsonian*, Dec. 1905.

[139] Wheeler-Bennett, *John Anderson,* p.9

BSc, with a special distinction in mathematics and an MA in Arts.[140] On strength of the Vans Dunlop scholarship, he went to Leipzig University for a year to study chemistry. While a career in science seemed assured, Anderson in fact chose to take the civil service examinations for a number of reasons.

Writing in the *University of Edinburgh Journal* following Anderson's death, his great friend, Alexander Gray, who sat the civil service entrance exams with him, said 'he never ceased to be a scientist but a change in his 'design for living' persuaded him that he ought to follow a less unworldly and possibly more remunerative calling'.[141] The fact that he wanted to marry Chrissie Mackenzie and the practicalities of doing so, allied with an expectation by Edinburgh University that its top students would take the civil service examinations, may have influenced him.[142] He returned to the university to take courses in economics and political science in preparation for the examinations.[143]

James MacMahon and John Anderson both married 'the girl next door'. MacMahon, with an address of 6 Clarinda Park West, Kingstown, Co. Dublin was married on 24 October 1892, approximately ten years after he returned to Ireland from the UK, to Mary Rochford, of 4 Clarinda Park West. Given that these houses, in what is now Dun Laoghaire, are large, it is possible that MacMahon had a flat in number six, while the Rochfords would most likely have been living in the entire property at number four. On the marriage certificate MacMahon's occupation was specified as 'clerk', his father's was given as 'merchant' and that of John Rochford, Mary's father, as 'civil engineer'.[144]

The MacMahons had three children, John (Jack) Rochford MacMahon, born on 27 August 1893 at 19 (Walton) Waltham Terrace, Blackrock, Co. Dublin.[145] Their eldest daughter, Mary McConnell MacMahon, was born on 18 March 1896. Her birth certificate shows that the family were still at the Waltham Terrace address.[146] Their youngest daughter, Margaret Mary,

---

[140] Ibid.
[141] Edinburgh University, special collections.
[142] Wheeler-Bennett, *John Anderson,* p.15.
[143] Ibid.
[144] CRS, ref. 2,174,749.
[145] John Rochford MacMahon, CRS, ref. 10516425.
[146] Mary McConnell MacMahon, CRS, ref. 9274099.

arrived on 19 September 1899. The family had now moved to 1 Neptune Terrace, Sandycove, Co. Dublin. From his appointment as Chief Clerk, GPO in 1913, MacMahon and his family lived at a number of different addresses, indicative of their rising position in society and established middle class status; Vernon House, 6 Summerville Road, Kingstown (1913-18), Under Secretary's Lodge, Phoenix Park (1918-22), Castlemont, Castleknock (1926-29) and St John's, Island Bridge (1930-54).[147]

The Censuses of 1901 and 1911 show the MacMahons as living in Neptune Terrace, Glasthule and number 6, Summerhill Road, Kingstown respectively.[148] The entire family and two servants were present on the night of the census of 31 March 1901, while just MacMahon, his wife, Mary, son John and one servant were registered as being together during the 2 April 1911 census. The census record for that year shows MacMahon's daughters to be among fifty-three girls with diverse home addresses in Ireland, England and India, living at '7.2, in Parkmore, Roscrea, Tipperary'.[149] This was described as being the residence for 'a Roman Catholic boarding school'.[150] Mary (Mollie or Molly[151]) and Margaret (Marjorie), were fourteen and eleven years old respectively at that time.

Like his father, John MacMahon, was educated at Blackrock College. He started in the school following some years at Presentation College, Glasthule, Co. Dublin. In 1912, again following his father's example, he joined the civil service and was posted to the Inland Revenue Department, Dublin. He spent five years in that position. In a minor connection, John Anderson was appointed Chairman of Inland Revenue in England just before his appointment to Dublin Castle. During his time in Revenue, John MacMahon studied law and was called to the Bar in 1916. He was auditor of the law students' debating society for the year 1916-17.[152] A member of the Volunteers, he left abruptly after the 1916 Easter Rising.[153] In 1917, he

---

[147] *Thom's Official Directory* for years 1913-1954.
[148] Census of Ireland 1901/1911, NAI.
[149] Ibid.
[150] Ibid, 1911.
[151] Name recorded as 'Mollie' in James MacMahon's will, 27 Jan. 1953 but elsewhere 'Molly' is used, such as in notes of conversation with León O'Broin, 21 Oct. 1974 (NLI, León O'Broin papers. Ms 31658 43 49).
[152] *Irish Independent* 9 Sept. 1941 'Jesuits' new provincial'.
[153] In conversation with Eilish Tennent, 2015.

entered the Jesuit novitiate at Tullabeg and was ordained a priest in 1926. MacMahon, despite his religious affiliations put his son on the train to Tullabeg with a heavy heart.[154] Fr MacMahon subsequently studied canon law at the Gregorian University in Rome and was awarded a doctorate.[155] In the early 1930s, he was chair of Canon Law at Milltown Park and was appointed provincial of the Jesuit order in September 1941.[156] Fr John Rochford MacMahon died on 22 October 1989.[157] A Jesuit obituary records his pride in the fact that he was descended from a Ballybay cadet family, nearly related to the last princes of Oriel.[158]

Both of MacMahon's daughters were educated in the Sacred Heart Convent, Roscrea. In keeping with the family's Catholic tradition, Mary (Molly) entered the Sacred Heart novitiate in Roehampton when she was sixteen. She left the order without being professed.[159] Molly married Walter Doolin, in 1923 and they had two children. Following an initial start to his career in the Public Record Office, as a first division clerk, Doolin became Private Secretary to MacMahon in Dublin Castle.[160] His appointment was jotted down in a brief sentence on a handwritten scrap of paper, found in a box of papers in the National Archives of Ireland.[161] Doolin's early life, education and career are outlined in 'The Old Castle Gang'. MacMahon's second daughter, Marjorie married Dermot Manning a bank official, who was a widower with two children, on 16 November 1938.[162] The marriage did not last.

John Anderson and Chrissie Mackenzie, his near neighbour in Eskbank, were married on 2 April 1907. The ceremony took place in St Andrew's Church, Drumsheugh, Edinburgh, with Anderson's friend Alexander Gray as best man. After their wedding John and Chrissie rented a small-furnished house on Throwley Rd, Sutton, Surrey.[163] John and his wife had two children, David born on 18 February 1911 and Mary Mackenzie Anderson

---

[154] According to Walter Doolin, grandson of Walter Doolin.
[155] 'Jesuit's new Provincial', *Irish Independent*, 9 Sept. 1941.
[156] Ibid.
[157] Proinsias ÓFionnagáin, SJ, *Irish Province News*, Jan. 1990.
[158] Ibid.
[159] Walter Doolin, family member.
[160] Ibid.
[161] NAI, CSORP 1918, 20502.
[162] CRS, ref. 1,331,991.
[163] Wheeler-Bennett, *John Anderson,* p.26.

born 3 February 1916.[164] Chrissie died tragically during an operation for cancer on 9 May 1920. After thirteen years of marriage, the loss was a huge blow to Anderson who was left a young widower.[165] At the time of her death, the children were nine and four years old.   Chrissie's sister Nellie Mackenzie, who had almost drowned with Nettie Anderson in 1903, gave up her nursing career and ran Anderson's household for the next twenty years.[166] The loss of his first wife at an early age and taking up a position in Ireland directly afterwards, provided a sharp contrast for Anderson to the stability of MacMahon's life. Molly Doolin recalled her parents entertaining the British cohort: 'They were glad to escape from the Castle atmosphere and let themselves go, singing around the piano. "Jonathan" Anderson rarely came. He was a bit of a stick. I never warmed to him'.[167] It is likely given his reticence, that she was unaware of his wife's death.

Anderson's son, David Alastair Pearson Anderson was educated at Malvern College, Pembroke College Cambridge, MA, MB, BChir and at St Thomas's Hospital.   His subsequent career showed that he shared his father's scientific ability. David became consultant physician to the Reading Group Hospitals, a Fellow of the Royal College of Physicians, London, F.R.C.P. and a Member of the Royal College of Surgeons (M.R.C.S.) England.[168] On the death of his father, he inherited the title, becoming second Viscount Waverley. David Anderson's sister, Brigadier Mary Pihl, née Mackenzie Anderson, attended Sutton High School, an independent day school for girls founded in 1884, and Brillantmont, Lausanne an international school that had been providing for foreign students since 1882. Mary was awarded the Order of the British Empire (M.B.E.) in 1958. She held the office of Aide-de-Camp to HM Queen Elizabeth II from 1967-1970 and was appointed Dame Commander (DBE) in 1970.[169]

The civil service careers James MacMahon and John Anderson differed greatly in terms of entry and early careers. From Blackrock College, James MacMahon was awarded a second-class clerkship in the civil service and

---

[164] http://www.cracroftspeerage.co.uk/online/content/waverley1952.htm [accessed 10 Jan 2019].
[165] Wheeler-Bennett, *John Anderson,* p. 47.
[166] Ibid, p. 48.
[167] Molly Doolin notes, 21 Oct. 1974 (NLI, papers of Sir James MacMahon as Under Secretary for Ireland 1918-1922, Ms 31658 43-49).
[168] *The Peerage,* [S37] BP2003 volume 3, page 4100.
[169] Ibid.

started work in the Post Office Savings Bank London in 1882. There is no record in the CSC files in the British Archives of his application form or place gained in the entrance examinations. Another Irishman, Michael Collins, who was to feature in MacMahon's future life and that of John Anderson, was likewise to take up a position in the Post Office Bank in London, twenty-four years later, as a temporary boy clerk/copyist at the age of fifteen and a half.[170] Collins, in what was most likely a prepared composition for the basic entrance level examination, wrote that without history 'we could not tell… how Great Britain came to be the greatest power on the face of the earth'.[171]

In respect of James MacMahon's appointment, his mother signed a solemn declaration on 24 June 1882 that said 'James MacMahon was born in 24 Fleet Street, Belfast on the 20th day of April 1865'.[172] This was pursuant to an act to abolish oaths and affirmations, substituting declarations in lieu thereof.[173] The list of principal officers in the post office in the 'Metropolitan and Provincial Establishments of Post Office Agencies Abroad' shows the following employment record for James Mac Mahon, who by 1918 was earning a salary of £1050 p.a.[174]

James MacMahon's post office positions up to 1918 [175]

Clk., 2nd Div., SBD, 8 Sept.1882; AO Dublin, 24 December 1882, Higher grade, 2 Mar. 1882; Cashier, 25 June 1897, Book-Keeper, 13 Aug. 1898; Examiner; 16 Jan. 1901; Acct. 31 Oct. 1906; Chief Clerk & Assist. Sec., 20 Sept. 1913; Sec., Dublin, 1 Jan. 1917.

---

[170] Michael Collins civil service application (TNA, CSC 11/63).
[171] Ibid.
[172] Civil service solemn declaration, 24 June 1882, accessed online at www.findmypast.ie on 15 Feb. 2016.
[173] 5 & 6 of William IV [c.62].
[174] 'Post offices and agencies abroad', 1 Jan 1917, BPM (formerly British Postal Museum and Archive).
[175] Ibid.

Post office salary scale [176]

PO Salary Scales: Sec: £1,000 by £50 to £1,200, **Chief Clerk**: £600 by £25 to £800; **Principal Clerk**; £400 by £20 to £540; **Clerk** 1st Class: £315 by 15 to £430, **Clerk** 2nd Div. £130 by 10 to £300. [177]

MacMahon returned from London within twelve months to the accounts branch of the GPO, Dublin. According to the above table he received regular promotions showing expanding professional skills, until he achieved the most senior position of GPO Secretary in late December 1916, commencing on 1 January 1917. It was claimed in an obituary that he was the first Catholic to hold the position.[178] This was not strictly accurate, as he was in fact the first Irish Catholic to be promoted to the role. His predecessor, Sir Reginald Egerton was also a Catholic, but an English convert to Catholicism.[179]

The resignation of Egerton in 1912, after serving in the position of Secretary since 1898, raised expectations that MacMahon would be promoted as his successor. However, once again the position went to an Englishman. On 30 September 1912, A.H. Norway, who had thirty years postal experience was offered the job by the Post Master General, Herbert Samuel.[180] Such a perceived injustice was reported as being 'one of the grossest jobs yet perpetrated and an insult to every Irishman in the Post Office'.[181] Tim Healy concluded that the appointment indicated that the Liberals did not believe that Home Rule would become law.[182] Healy also felt uneasy, as 'many of his friends in the Catholic Hierarchy and Cardinal Logue in particular, were close friends of MacMahon's'.[183] Members of the hierarchy including Dr Patrick O'Donnell, Bishop of Raphoe, wrote to John Redmond, who saw Samuel a number of times to no avail.[184]

---

[176] Ibid.

[173] Ibid.

[178] *Blackrock College Yearbook*, 1954, obituary, p.104.

[179] *The Tablet,* 22 Nov. 1930.

[180] BPM, 36/203, 1916-17.

[181] *Sinn Féin Weekly* 10 Aug. 1912.

[182] T.M. Healy, *Letters and leaders of my day* (London, 1928), p.508.

[183] McBride, *Greening of Dublin Castle*, p.164.

[184] Keith Jeffery, *The GPO and the Easter Rising* (Dublin, 2006), p.6.

D.P. Moran's newspaper the *Leader* used the promotion of Norway to highlight the blatant religious bias and pay-scale disparities that pertained in a number of departments, which it acknowledged were outside the remit of the office of the Chief Secretary in Dublin Castle. The paper emphasised the fact that eighty percent of the post office staff were Catholic and nationalist. However, it also pointed out that in relation to positions carrying higher level salaries there were sixteen Protestants and nine Catholics earning £5,300 and £2,700 respectively.[185] When assessed in the light of MacMahon's earnings as outlined, this was either a typographical error or somewhat of an exaggeration. Even the lower figure was in excess of what MacMahon earned as Secretary, the highest grade in the GPO. The newspaper concluded that in contrast, 'the permanent officials of Dublin Castle remain in their jobs whether a coercionist or a Home Rule government is in power'.[186] MacMahon was to see an improvement in his position on 20 September 1913, when he was appointed chief clerk.[187] He retained this role until the end of 1916. Norway was secretary throughout the Easter Rising and the occupation and destruction of the GPO. At the end of the year, on 18 December the following unsigned letter was sent to the Post Master General:

> Mr Norway's appointment as the Secretary to the Post Office in Ireland expires on the 31st instant. Mr Norway was originally appointed for two years from 30 Sept. 1912 and this appointment caused a considerable amount of protest on the ground that the post should be filled by an Irishman. Mr Norway's tenure of office was further extended for two years in 1914, pending the coming into operation of the Home Rule Bill ... to succeed him I recommend the appointment of Mr J. MacMahon at present Chief Clerk in the Dublin Office ... I understand he is a persona grata to both political parties in Ireland.[188]

A new post-master general, Charles Hobhouse had broken an agreement reached by John Redmond with Herbert Samuels in 1912, concerning the promotion of James MacMahon.[189] Hobhouse refused to honour the commitment of his predecessor Samuels despite repeated representations by

---

[185] *Leader*, 12 Oct. 1912.

[186] Ibid.

[187] 'Post offices and agencies abroad', 20 Sept. 1913, BPM.

[188] Ibid, 36/203, appointment of James MacMahon as secretary of GPO, 18 Dec. 1916.

[189] McBride, *Greening of Dublin Castle*, p.164.

John Redmond, John Dillon, Mathew Nathan, and Joseph Devlin. He decided that Norway should continue to hold the position until Home Rule was established whether that that 'took one, two or three years'.[190] The eventual departure of Norway in late December saw MacMahon promoted to Secretary, the position that many considered should have been his four years previously. Another Catholic, J.J. Coonan stepped into MacMahon's former job as Assistant Secretary. It was suspected that H.P. Pease, a Liberal and former postmaster-general was instrumental in securing MacMahon's and Coonan's promotions.[191]

Because of the destruction of the GPO in 1916, the first and most important consideration was that services continued uninterrupted. The Rotunda Hospital initially provided temporary accommodation for postal staff. GPO archivist, Stephen Ferguson contends that, 'the position was regularised a year later by James MacMahon, GPO Secretary. He signed an indenture between the governors of the Rotunda Hospital and the postmaster general, agreeing to pay £235 rent and carry on post office business in a manner that would do no injury to the health and comfort of the Rotunda's patients'.[192] It has been mooted that following the principle that when roots have been put down they are often left undisturbed, the GPO could still be in its emergency accommodation had the sorting office in the Rotunda Rink not been destroyed by anti-Treaty troops in 1922.[193]

James MacMahon's tenure as Secretary to the GPO lasted a mere eighteen months until mid-1918: 'His brilliant work in reconstructing the Post Office records and accounts after their destruction in the GPO in 1916', was highlighted after his death.[194] There are however, few extant examples of correspondence outlining his work as the senior postal official but a letter is on file in the British Postal Museum and Archives signed by MacMahon.[195] It recommended that established and auxiliary postmen (122 in all), be given additional leave in recognition of their contribution during the Rebellion of April 1916. MacMahon further wrote 'as regards the sub-postmistresses and scale payment sub-office assistants mentioned, I think

---

[190] Ibid, p.186.
[191] Ibid, p.225.
[192] Stephen Ferguson, *The GPO: 200 years of history* (Cork, 2014), p.159.
[193] Ibid p.159.
[194] G.C. Duggan, 'letter to the editor', *Irish Times*, 8 May 1954.
[195] *Irish Minutes of the British Postal Services*, BPM 36/202.

they are deserving of some mark of recognition of their services and suggest that the Controller be authorised to inform them that their loyalty to the Department during so trying a period is recognised and highly appreciated'.[196]

This concession may have resulted from the formation by female employees of their first civil servants trade union, the Federation of Women Civil Servants. It followed claims made to the *Royal Commission on the Civil Service (UK and Ireland) 1912-14*, which was set up to assess all branches of the service from Dublin Castle downwards. The commission was chaired by Sir Antony Patrick MacDonnell, a Catholic and former Under Secretary for Ireland, from 1902 to 1908. The particular claims to the commission were recorded as being from the 'most marginalised within the service, that is the temporary clerks and women clerks of the Post Office'.[197] McDonnell's report was subsequently described as 'the last insight into the civil service before war and rebellion swept over it'.[198] However, it was said that MacDonnell 'succeeded only in destroying the confidence of the ordinary civil servant'.[199]

James MacMahon's time as GPO Secretary was brief as a consequence of his being offered and accepting the promotion to Under Secretary to the Lord Lieutenant of Ireland in July 1918. Following his departure to Dublin Castle, his name is crossed out in the 1918 list of principal officers of the Post Office and that of 'Forsythe' is written in by hand.[200] Mr Forsythe's abilities and credentials are outlined in a letter from the Postmaster General of 17 July 1918, signed and agreed by 'AHI': 'Mr Forsythe is a native of the South of Ireland and he has filled the difficult posts of controller of the Dublin sorting office and postmaster of Belfast with marked success. I regard him as the most suitable officer to fill the vacant post'.[201] As was to be true of John Anderson two years later, James MacMahon had not sought the position of Under Secretary. It was an appointment that satisfied the Catholic hierarchy but at a cost to him personally. MacMahon wrote to his son John on 29 June 1918 informing him of the offer. The letter was

---

[196] Ibid.

[197] Maguire, *The civil service and the revolution in Ireland*, p.21.

[198] *Royal Commission on Civil Service, 1912-14, second appendix to the fourth report of the commissioners' minutes of evidence*, 9 Jan. 1913-20 June 1913, BPP

[199] Maguire, *The civil service and the revolution in Ireland*, p.24.

[200] 'List of principal officers', 1918, BPM 36/202.

[201] Ibid.

addressed to the Jesuit College, Tullabeg where John was then studying in the novitiate. It was brief and somewhat formal but conveyed not only the pressure MacMahon was under, but also gave an insight into the contacts and networks he had:

> I write this in train going to Newtown Forbes to spend weekend with Lord Granard. The Chief Secy. who is one of the party, sent for me today & formally offered me the appointment of Under Secretary – Vice Sir W. Byrne retiring to England. Though the job and work are not to my liking, I accepted on the advice of all my friends whom I consulted... for the present the affair is private. Pray for me.[202]

The change in his position was in fact to prove more fraught for MacMahon than he could have realised. It was of huge political sensitivity, as was shown in the reaction of press, which had been behind him in his advancement to the position of Secretary to the Post Office but now felt betrayed. The weekly *Leader,* which with other papers had supported MacMahon in relation to promotion in the post office, attacking the GPO for alleged masonic jobbery, used his departure to again highlight the issue of senior appointments of Catholics. According to Brian Maye, 'the readers of the Leader were mainly Roman Catholic, clerical and white-collar. They resented the domination of commerce and the upper reaches of the civil service by Protestants, who used patronage networks such as the Freemasons to keep their positions'.[203] However, the newspaper, which had championed MacMahon's appointment as Secretary of the GPO on the grounds of his being an Irish Catholic, showed a marked sense of grievance and even perhaps of betrayal by MacMahon, printing the following:

> Mac Mahon's gone from the G.P.O.,
> With the Longs and Shortts you'll find him.
> He took a hand in a bigger show
> And he left the grip behind him;
> 'G.P.O', cried MacMahon bold,
> 'I was your Papist warder,
> But once again is the post controlled
> By the square and compass order'.[204]

---

[202] James MacMahon to John Rochford MacMahon, 29 June 1918 (NLI, papers of Sir James MacMahon as Under Secretary for Ireland 1918-1922, MS 31658 43-49).
[203] Brian Maye, 'An Irishman's Diary', *The Irish Times,* 7 Jan 2002.
[204] *Leader,* 27 July 1918.

The words referred to Edward Shortt, then Chief Secretary, and Walter Long, ex Chief Secretary, who held the position briefly in 1905 under Balfour. Long was subsequently appointed by Lloyd George as Chair of the Cabinet's 'Long Committee on Ireland'.[205] A sketch of the restored GPO depicting it as a Masonic Lodge accompanied the above 'ditty'.[206]

The retirement or forced exit of Sir William Byrne had raised the possibility of MacMahon being appointed Under Secretary. That he should join the Castle administration was not a new idea. A few months earlier the Lord Lieutenant, John Denton, Viscount French had considered offering MacMahon the position of Assistant Under Secretary in place of Edward O'Farrell, but 'doubted that MacMahon could be induced to take the post'.[207] MacMahon accepted the higher position of Under Secretary for Ireland in July 1918, albeit as already said, with a certain reluctance.

> He can be seen as both exemplyfing the loyal Catholic meritocracy belatedly produced from the late 1870s by the Intermediate Education Act and the opening up of civil service positions to competitive examinations, and as an archtypical "Catholic Whig" – a pale green nationalist seeking advancement by administration rather than agitation and relying heavily on a Catholic hierarchy pursuing influence within the civil service apparatus.[208]

Maume's contentions in relation to meritocracy, the Intermediate Education (Ireland) Act, 1878 and the impact of competitive examinations on civil service positions are open to question. MacMahon's position in Dublin Castle was built on a career in the post office, through which he had a network of contacts across a broad Irish spectrum including but beyond the Catholic Church. Maume refers to 'his seeking advancement by administration' but fails to specify whether he meant on a personal or national level. Certainly it is contended by this study that MacMahon was in favour of administrative solutions as opposed to revolutionary action. It was that focus on the administration, as an avenue to independence that could be assumed to have been a deciding factor that led to MacMahon accepting the position of Under Secretary. While he shared a constitutional

---

[205] Richard Murphy, 'Walter Long and 'the making of the government of Ireland act', 1919-20', *Irish Historical Studies*, vol. 25, no. 97, (1986), pp. 82-96.
[206] *Leader*, 27 July 1918.
[207] French to Lloyd George, 30 May 1918 (PA, personal/political papers, LG F/48/6/13).
[208] Maume, 'MacMahon, James (1865-1954)', *DIB*.

nationalist perspective and a focus on dominion home rule with Stephen Gwynn and Horace Plunkett, he could not have agreed with Gwynn's support of the Government of Ireland Act, 1920, commonly referred to as the fourth Home Rule Bill or Act, with the inclusion of partition.

The protracted nature of Home Rule legislation had an impact that resonated within the administration. Although ostensibly political in appearance, according to Maguire, 'the Irish Home Rule bills, introduced by Gladstone in 1886 and 1893, were shaped to deliver administrative reform'.[209] Maguire contends that these reforms were primarily focused on the size and cost of the Irish administration, which was borne by the British Treasury and needed to be drastically cut.[210] The third Home Rule Bill, which was introduced on 11 April 1912, was enacted on 18 September 1914, but suspended on account of the First World War.[211] Maguire argues that the fact that 'Home Rule was not likely was never admitted and the Castle remained in the limbo of anticipated change that forever receded. As war transformed the British State, the Castle became anachronistic because it remained the same'.[212]

While it is appears apposite to describe MacMahon as a constitutional nationalist, albeit in a broad sense, this is not backed up by primary source evidence. It is however, a depiction that places MacMahon in a nationalist tradition, rooted in parliamentry democracy, and firmly against those who believed that Irish independence could not be achieved without the use of violence. Nonetheless, MacMahon was perceived by the unionist faction to be a nationalist with questionable loyalty to the Crown, and accusations of spying hung over him throughout his time as Under Secretary. It is argued that MacMahon was a committed civil servant, rooted in the administration, while embracing the strong Catholic faith of his background. Maume claims that he relied 'heavily on a Catholic hierarchy pursuing influence' will be interrogated within a framework of potential benefit to government and church, rather than MacMahon personally.[213] While a Catholic with many contacts in the hierarchy, MacMahon who had an established career in the

---

[209] Maguire, *The civil service and the revolution in Ireland,* p.8.
[210] Ibid.
[211] The Government of Ireland Act 1914, [H.C.] (4 & 5 Geo. 5 c. 90) (18 Sept. 1914).
[212] Maguire, *The civil service and the revolution in Ireland,* p.24.
[213] Maume, 'MacMahon, James', *DIB.*

post office, did not as highlighted, seek appointment as Under Secretary but undoubededly acquiesed to hierarchial influences, among others.

Lord French, however, had been firmly of the opinon that it was necessary to get into closer contact with the Catholic hierarchy: 'I believe they are the best representatives of really national aspirations of the country; the appointment of Catholic nationalists to bureaucratic and judicial positions would help to accomplish this task'.[214] Despite the purported expediency of the appointment, MacMahon had a proven record at senior level plus an extensive network built up over years; contacts that included not only the hierarchy but the Catholic upper classes in Ireland. Bernard Forbes, the 8th Earl of Granard, was prominent in this grouping and had been Assistant Postmaster General, 1906-09.[215] His influence may have been a factor in MacMahon's promotion and also in persuading him to accept the offer. The contact is also verification that MacMahon's network extended beyond 'every priest in Ireland'.[216]

The letter of his appointment is listed in the index to the records of the Chief Secretary's Office in the National Archives of Ireland but is not in the files.[217] However, a letter from Dublin Castle to the General Post Office relating to the cessation of MacMahon's GPO salary is in existence.[218] The appointment of MacMahon was a bitter blow to Assistant Under Secretary, Sir John Taylor, who had already seen the role of Under Secretary which he felt rightly was his under the Chief Secretaryship of Walter Long (12 March - 4 Dec. 1905), lost in a change of administration.[219] As serving Assistant Under Secretary in July 1918, he once again had expectations of promotion, only to see MacMahon assume the role. Rubbing salt into the wound it was his job as Assistant Under Secretary to write aletter to the GPO, in relation

---

[214] French to Lloyd George, May 19, 1918, MS F/48/6/12, cited in Mc Bride, *The greening of Dublin Castle*, p. 247.

[215] *Burke's peerage and gentry*, vol. II (107th ed.) (Oxford, 2003), p. 1629.

[216] León Ó'Broin, *W.E. Wylie and the Irish revolution 1916-1921* (Dublin, 1989), p.43.

[217] James MacMahon letter of appointment, NAI, CSORP, 18333, 18457.

[218] Letter from the Chief Secretary's Office Dublin Castle to the GPO, 20 July 1918, BMH, CD 104/4/1.

[219] George Chester Duggan, BMH, WS.1,091.

to MacMahon's acceptance of the position of Under Secretary, with a response from the GPO issuing to Taylor. [220]

In July 1918, MacMahon became the most senior member of the Irish civil service, a decision he may have regretted on many occasions. He faced political and sectarian bias and felt he was distrusted as a 'North of Ireland Catholic'.[221] However, for MacMahon despite the ill-feeling of the pro-unionist grouping led by J.J. Taylor, 'his loyalty to the crown went unquestioned (except perhaps when defined by Ulster unionists who were unhappy with an Armagh Catholic nationalist in the highest post in Dublin Castle) and his popularity made him something of an asset to the Irish Government'.[222] It was said that he had many friends from both the nationalist and unionist communities. The benefit for the hierarchy of having MacMahon in the Castle was equal to that accruing to the government. According to MacMahon's daughter Molly, 'Logue was a very close friend and often came to the Lodge and stayed there, as did Gilmartin and other bishops'.[223] Beyond the emphasis on MacMahon's religion and nationalism, Edward Shortt, Chief Secretary, considered the employment of MacMahon was a success. In a letter to Prime Minister Lloyd George, in early July, he wrote,'I hope you approved of the appointment of MacMahon as Under Secretary. He has impressed me greatly'.[224] Unfortunately for MacMahon, Shortt was recalled less than a year after he had taken position, being replaced by John James (Ian) MacPherson, a working relationship that was not to be mutually beneficial.

The Dublin Castle administration that MacMahon inherited was neglected in every way possible over the years. This was exacerbated by a lack of direction and support from a British government weakened by the First World War. However, the rise of Sinn Féin following its success in the general election of 1918, and the unrest that presaged the War of Independence brought a new governmental focus. While it was easy to blame inadequacies in the Castle administration for the unrest in the country, it was undeniable that the Cabinet had no coherent policy for Ireland. The

---

[220] BMH 104/4/1 Letter from J. Taylor Assistant Under Secretary to GPO, 20 July 1918.
[221] Joyce interview with James MacMahon, Stephen's Green Club, 18 Oct. 1949, BMH, S. 1374 J.V.
[222] McColgan, *British policy and the Irish administration,* p.7.
[223] Molly Doolin notes (NLI, MS 31658 43-49).
[224] Shortt to Lloyd George, 4 July 1918, Lloyd George Papers, PA, F/45/6/6.

fall-out from the Rising of 1916, led to an acceptance that 'the system of government in Ireland would have to be changed'.[225] The Government of Ireland Bill, 1919, was not a unifying measure, as the status quo of 'no policy at all' was essentially an option for many. MacMahon himself was opposed to the Bill, favouring a 'county option under a dominion home rule system with fiscal autonomy as advocated by Stephen Gwynn and without partition, by Horace Plunkett'.[226]

Plunkett, elected as a unionist MP in South County Dublin 1892, lost his seat in 1900 to J.J. Mooney, a nationalist.[227] His defeat combined with that of fellow Unionist MP, James Henry Mussen Campbell, 1st Baron Glenavy in the Stephen's Green electoral area, was to the detriment of southern Unionism. Following 1900, as noted by W.E.H. Lecky, 'Ulster unionism is the only form of Irish unionism which is likely to count as a serious political force'.[228] After his exit from politics, Plunkett 'gradually abandoned constructive unionism to become a dominion home ruler'.[229] He was elected chairman of the Irish Convention 1917, which ended inconclusively within twelve months. According to Trevor West, 'in 1919, Plunkett launched the Irish Dominion League, supported by the *Irish Statesman*, to emphasise the benefits of dominion home rule'.[230]

In 1918, MacMahon had joined an administration that was rendered ineffectual not only by British neglect, but by years of conflict and sectarian division in the Chief Secretary's office. This was to adversely affect his position in ways that even with his strongest doubts about the role, he could not have imagined. Having been appointed by Chief Secretary Edward Shortt, he found himself caught in the middle of an ongoing discord between Shortt and Lord French, who believed Shortt was working to undermine him. The antagonism between French and Shortt was political. According to G.C. Duggan, 'the Chief Secretary ardently supported Home Rule, while French 'though the Irish to be unfit for self-government and always likely

---

[225] Eunan O'Halpin, The *decline of the union: British government in Ireland 1892-1920* (Dublin, 1987), p.123.
[226] Maume 'MacMahon, James'.
[227] London Times, 11, 12 Oct. 1900.
[228] W.E.H. Lecky to Montgomery, 26 Nov. 1900, Hugh de Fellenberg Montgomery papers, P.R.O.N.I., T.1089/297.
[229] Trevor West, 'Plunkett, Sir Horace Curzon (1854-1932)', *DIB*.
[230] Ibid.

to be so'.[231] While French had initially supported MacMahon's appointment, he came to see him as taking sides with Shortt. Showing his typical inconsistency the Lord Lieutenant particularly objected to MacMahon's association with the hierarchy. He described MacMahon as 'simply the mouthpiece for the most rabid of Irish priests'.[232] This was despite his earlier contention that MacMahon's connections with the Church would serve as a means of improving communication with the clergy, which was very much to become part of his role in the years 1920 to 1922.

While MacMahon had arrived in the Castle with a reputation for having the ear of the Roman Catholic hierarchy, there is a common misapprehension that he was the first Catholic to be appointed to the position of Under Secretary. According to C.J. Woods 'the honours fell to Thomas Nicholas Redington, who was appointed on 11 July 1846 and was in office for the remainder of the famine period, until 1852; Thomas Henry Burke (Under Secretary from 1869 until 1882) and Sir Antony MacDonnell (1902-8), were also not only Catholics but like Redington, hailed from the west of Ireland'.[233] It was however, MacMahon's misfortune to take up the reins at a time when the Castle administration was struggling from the political turmoil without, and discord within the walls. With the Chief Secretary's tenure ending a bare six months after MacMahon took up his role, MacMahon came under pressure from Taylor who worked assiduously to undermine his position. This did not happen until the departure of Shortt at the beginning of 1919.[234] He wrote to MacMahon after leaving Dublin, 'the jealousy and stabs in the back all contribute to make the life of a Chief Secretary a rather heart-breaking business'.[235] He could have been holding up a mirror reflecting what was to be MacMahon's own experience as Under Secretary. Shortt went on to say, 'I am most grateful for the loyal help you invariably gave me'.[236]

In a reflection of the animosity between Shortt and French, MacMahon faced a strained atmosphere due to strong anti-nationalist feelings on behalf of pro-unionists, essentially driven by the bitter resentment of the Assistant

---

[231] Duggan.p.176.

[232] O'Halpin, *The decline of the union: British government in Ireland 1892-1920*, p.176-7.

[233] C.J. Woods, 'letters to the editor', *Irish Times*, 13 Feb. 1982.

[234] Duggan, p.176-177.

[235] Shortt to MacMahon, 12 Jan. 1919 (NLI, MS 31658 43-49).

[236] Ibid.

Under Secretary. Taylor blindly doubted both the new Under Secretary's ability and his loyalty. He created an impossible working environment, attempting to segregate the office into pro-Taylor and pro-MacMahon factions.[237] Apart from aspiring to MacMahon's job, any concession to a nationalist was considered by Taylor to be a weakness.[238] However, MacMahon had 'a high reputation from the Secretaryship of the Post Office in Ireland; he was known to be … easy to work with'.[239] As someone used to a senior position within the civil service MacMahon would have adhered to a workplace hierarchy in that Taylor, as his subordinate, would have been expected to take on much of the day-to-day running of the office. MacMahon had stated publically that 'everyone was anxious for a settlement'.[240] Alfred Cope, Assistant Under Secretatry 1920-22, was to say with regard to the Treaty settlement that MacMahon 'was working on it long before the English contingent was ever thought of and (you) took the guiding post on the peace side during the regime of that contingent'.[241]

Shortt's return to London and the arrival of a replacement Chief Secretary, Ian MacPherson, in January 1919 was to create further discord in the administration and consequently weaken MacMahon's position. The rift between himself and Taylor was escalated by what was to be the new Chief Secretary's unfortunate weakness in the position. MacPherson was out of his depth from the outset. He knew little of Ireland or the Dublin Castle administration and may have arrived with a preconceived bias. Among the correspondence he received after his appointment, a letter from Gen. Nevil Macready, dated 11 January 1919, was probably just one of a number which formed his opinions of Ireland.[242] It was blatantly anti-Irish and not likely to instil confidence in the presumptive Chief Secretary: 'I cannot say I envy you, for I loathe the country you are going to and its people with a depth

---

[237] G.C. Duggan, BMH, WS.1,099.

[238] O'Halpin, *The decline of the union*, p.177.

[239] Ó Broin, *W. E. Wylie and the Irish revolution*, p.43.

[240] Under Secretary's view', Nov. (NLI, newspaper clipping, date incomplete and newspaper unknown, MS 31658, 43-49).

[241] Ibid.

[242] Sir Cecil Macready, adjutant general, First World War and appointed commissioner of the London metropolitan police in 1918.

deeper than the sea, and more violent than that which I feel against the Boche'.[243]

MacPherson, a Presbyterian and supporter of Home Rule, was 'overwhelmed by the gradual collapse of the administrative system ... this was not helped by his ostracism of the Castle Under Secretary'.[244] Confirming the ill-feeling in the Chief Secretary's office, and how it affected not only the Under Secretary but the entire Castle personnel, civil servant G.C. Duggan claimed, 'Taylor had ousted his chief from all but the most routine tasks and in this he was supported by the Chief Secretary, Ian MacPherson and Lord French. As this de facto suppression was given official sanction by the Lord Lieutenant it was an unhappy time in the office, for Taylor's autocratic rule affected most of the staff'.[245] Taylor now had the Chief Secretary and Lord French united in supporting his divisive actions towards the Under Secretary and other Catholic nationalists, which impacted on the administration, to its detriment. Duggan however, noted that MacMahon's 'capacity for work was amazing, and his quickness of decision not the least admirable of his qualities'.[246] On the other hand Duggan regarded Taylor as 'cool, relentless, calculating – a man of narrow ideas but inflexible in carrying them out ...a machine, a car of Juggernaut that crushed the victims beneath its wheels'.[247]

William Evelyn Wylie, from Coleraine, who was Law Adviser to the Irish Government from 1919-21, was acutely aware of the need for a resolution to the issue of Taylor's disruptive actions and obstructionism. In his papers now archived in the National Archives, Kew, Wylie wrote of MacMahon, 'what a wonderful friend he has been to me ... his sanity and calm, his complete sincerity and his understanding of Irish problems has helped me time without number'.[248] Wylie couldn't tolerate Taylor and was acutely aware of the impact the Assistant Under Secretary's dominance was having, not only on MacMahon but on the functioning of the entire Chief

---

[243] Macready to MacPherson, 11 Jan. 1919 (OBL, Strath.papers, MS Eng. Hist. c490).

[244].Geoghegan, 'MacPherson, (James) Ian (1880-1937)', *DIB*.

[245] G.C.Duggan, letter to the *Irish Times* 5 May 1954, following the death of James MacMahon.

[246] Ibid.

[247] Duggan 'Periscope', *Blackwood's Magazine*, BMH, WS 1,099, Aug. 1922.

[248] W.E.Wylie 'Autobiographical memoir' (TNA, William Evelyn Wylie papers, 1839-1951, PRO 30/89-1).

Secretary's office. Wylie spoke of the matter to French, who wanted to know who he could trust in the Castle. Wylie told him to put his faith in MacMahon and not pay attention to what he had been told about him. He advised French to 'trust him and he won't let you down; he has forgotten more about Ireland than the rest of them will ever know'.[249] Perhaps in his usual habit of listening to the last person he spoke to, French agreed. According to Wylie, Taylor departed to England that night and he never saw him again.[250] It is debatable whether he resigned or was subject to 'French leave', a favourite ploy of the Lord Lieutenant. It was intended to force subordinates out, while giving them face-saving leave of absence, due to purported concern with their health or need for rest.

With French's full backing and Taylor out of the way, MacMahon was finally in a position to carry out the job for which he had been employed, in the pivotal postition in the Irish administration. French declared in a letter to Bonar Law, Lord Privy Seal, that he was 'reinstating MacMahon and making him responsible for everything that goes on in the Castle in the absence of the Chief Secretary'.[251] This absence was due to the fact that MacPherson had also been subjected to the 'French-leave treatment'. He left Ireland on 2 April 1920, ostensibly due to illness. With both Taylor and MacPherson gone from Dublin Castle, MacMahon was free to carry out his work as Under Secretary unimpeded and was effectively the de facto Chief Secretary. However, this new found equilibrium was to be short lived. Sir Warren Fisher, Alfred Cope and R.E. Harwood arrived in Dublin in early May 1920 to carry out an investigation into the Dublin Castle administration. This was once again to change MacMahon's position as he was to an extent side-lined by Fisher, with Sir John Anderson becoming joint Under Secretary.

According to Angus Calder, 'Sir John Anderson ... represented no section of the human race whatsoever, unless he can be seen as the epitome of the civil service where he made his career'.[252] Calder goes on to say that Anderson's 'rather formal and uncompromising manner has never infused into the machinery for which he is responsible any warmth, humour of

---

[249] Ibid.
[250] Ibid.
[251] Lord French to Bonar Law, 18 Apr. 1920PA, BL 103/2/11.
[252] Angus Calder, *The People's war* (London, 1971), pp. 119-20.

general sympathy… he was nicknamed 'pompous John or Jehovah'.[253] On the other hand, Mark Sturgis refers to him affectionately in his diaries as 'Jonathan'.'[254] Calder tells a story relayed to him by the Bishop of Winchester, which certainly demonstrates Anderson's lack of ready humour. He was talking to King George VI, on the subject of air raid shelters when he absent-mindedly replied to the King's remarks with, 'but my dear man'. The king roared with laughter but Anderson remained impassive.[255]

Anderson had an auspicious start to his civil service career taking first place in the Home Civil Service (HCS) and the Indian Civil Service Examinations (ICS), 1905.[256] His marks of 4566/7500 were the second highest ever recorded.[257] Asked by the family to write an official biography of Anderson, John Wheeler-Bennett wrote to the then British Public Record Office in January 1959.[258] He was looking for facts relating to Anderson's civil service career and particularly for confirmation that he had taken first place in 1905 and what subjects he took for the examination. A note in relation to the request states that 1905 was the last year in which a candidate was at liberty to present as many subjects as he pleased.[259] Wheeler-Bennett details fourteen, with the weakest being economics and political science, with a grade of 126/500.[260] Currently Anderson's file in the archives shows a number of his written examination papers although there are no individual grades. The examiner's remarks in relation to the political science paper included, according to Wheeler-Bennett, such comments as 'limited in scope and not clear in plan and does not know how to group and give points to his facts'.[261] Nothing appeared further from the truth in his future civil service career. Ironically, Wheeler-Bennett had written on the previous page that during his preparation year Anderson had studied economics and political science with his performance in both 'being well up to his usual

---

[253] Ibid.
[254] Mark Sturgis diaries (TNA, PRO 30/59/1/2/3/4/5).
[255] Calder, *The People's war,* pp. 119-20.
[256] Anderson civil service application (TNA, CSC 11/8).
[257] Wheeler-Bennett, *John Anderson,* p. 17.
[258] John Anderson file (TNA, CSC 11/8).
[259] Ibid.
[260] Wheeler-Bennett, *John Anderson,* p.15.
[261] Ibid p.17.

brilliant standard'.[262] Overall Edinburgh took the first three places in the examinations with Alexander Gray coming second to Anderson and a John Charles Hirschfeld Macnair third. Wheeler-Bennet noted that it was first of only three occasions 'during the present century' when a candidate from Oxford or Cambridge was not top of the list; Anderson was the second Watsonian to take first place, being preceded by John James Nairne in 1890.[263]

Following his success in the examinations, Anderson contributed an article called 'Side Lights on the Civil Service' to the 1905 winter edition of *The Watsonian.* According to Anderson, there were 'appointments and appointments', pointing out the huge differential between the positions of boy copyist (ironically the position later held by Michael Collins) and Under Secretary for State.[264] What he wrote next is perhaps most telling in terms of his own ambitions: 'Here it is the intention to deal only with the higher grades; that is with those positions which, so to speak, command a view of the top'.[265] The second point of interest is that Anderson who was considered, as mentioned, somewhat humourless in his future career, although Calder referred to his having 'a streak of dour humour'[266] presented an almost light-hearted view of the service when he wrote:

> The dignity of the public service must be allowed to count for something, although not, perhaps, for so much as some in high places would seem to suggest when proposals get on foot to dock salaries and curtail allowances. That however, is by the way; and for the comfort of the despondent it may be added that there is little prospect in the meantime of civil servants being required to live on dignity alone.[267]

In the article, Anderson gave an overview of the requirements for success in the competitive civil service examinations. He exhorted the Watson's pupil intending to go for the civil service to 'never neglect his school subjects', particularly recommending French, German, English and dynamics. With regard to modern languages, he wrote that for the Foreign Office 'a mastery of at least four' is essential. He further explained that when the prospective

---

[262] Wheeler-Bennett, *John Anderson,* p.16.
[263] Ibid, p.17.
[264] *The Watsonian,* 1905.
[265] Ibid.
[266] Calder, *The People's war,* pp. 119-20.
[267] *The Watsonian,* 1905.

candidates go to university, honours courses should be taken and if possible, a year should be spent abroad, which of course Anderson himself had done. Anderson concluded his article by stating 'meagre as the hints I have tried to give are, if they prove of any service to Watson's boys whose ambition leads them to look to the civil service, my object is attained'.[268]

Anderson was offered and accepted a second-class clerkship (a line was drawn through Class I in ink) in the Colonial Office by the Civil Service Commission in October 1905.[269] The salary scale was £200-500 rising by annual increments.[270] Anderson, who unlike MacMahon had applied for a first-class position in the Indian Civil Service and the Home Service, was effectively offered the same level of entry, although as a graduate his starting salary was possibly higher. However, as Anderson entered the civil service MacMahon had worked his way up to the position of accountant in the GPO in Dublin. In a 1912 application for the position of Principal Clerk in the National Insurance Commission, Anderson referred to his position in the Colonial Office, which had lasted approximately seven years, as being that of second-class clerk.[271] He had turned down an offer for the Indian Civil Service at first division level, which would customarily have been the optimum choice for leading candidates.

Given perhaps that he was about to marry and such a post would be more suited to a young bachelor, it was not attractive to Anderson, although he had taken the entry examination. From 1905 until 1912, Anderson worked in the Nigeria and West African departments. He was described as making a strong impression: 'From the first he displayed that maturity of judgement and gravity of outlook which was characteristic of him'.[272] The Head of the Nigeria Department said of Anderson while he was still at junior level, 'that he ought to be in his shoes as head of the department'.[273] During this period, Anderson was also secretary of a committee on West African currency.

---

[268] Ibid.

[269] The Civil Service Commission was established in 1855, following the publication of the Northcote-Trevelyan report to regulate recruitment to the civil service.

[270] Wheeler-Bennett, *John Anderson,* p.19.

[271] Anderson file (TNA, CSC 11/8).

[272] Edward Ettingdean Bridges, 'John Anderson, Viscount Waverley, 1882-1958, Obituary', *Biographical Memoirs of the Fellows of the Royal Society,* vol. 4, (1958).

[273] Ibid.

In the National Health Insurance Commission, he was one of a group of promising young civil servants from all departments gathered together under Sir Robert Morant to launch the National Health Insurance Scheme.[274] The World War and its unusual demands on personnel was to propel Anderson into promotional positions at a far more rapid pace than the earlier stages of MacMahon's career. For MacMahon advancement had seen a steady climb up the ladder with an almost annual progression from one grade to another within the GPO. Anderson was to be assigned to a variety of departments and higher roles as the need arose. In 1914, the supply of medicinal drugs from Germany was interrupted due to the war. Anderson was put in charge of dealing with the problem, which he did through the Medical Research Team. He encouraged cooperation between British drug companies in order to discover the composition of German drugs, including aspirin.[275] Anderson's role in the commission was considered to be of national importance and he was urged not to volunteer for military service.[276] Being handed a white feather, the sign of cowardice as he crossed Whitehall 'hurt him to the quick'. He volunteered for the Derby scheme of 1915, but was never called up.[277]

While neither Anderson nor MacMahon were involved directly with military service, Anderson in particular was engaged in work that was essential to the war effort, despite his conviction that he should play a more active role. There was however, no question of MacMahon volunteering for active service. Apart from circumstances such as contested conscription in Ireland, he was forty-nine years of age in 1914. As Secretary to the GPO in 1916, he had inherited the fall-out from another conflict, the Easter Rising of that year, in terms not only of overseeing the restoration of the post office building but maintaining essential services and the preservation of records. In 1917, Anderson was appointed Secretary to the newly formed Ministry of Shipping, a department designed to counter the German U-boat campaign, which was threatening Britain's food supplies. After the war, in March 1919, Anderson moved to the Local Government Board as an additional secretary. This was rapidly followed by an appointment as chairman of the Board of Inland Revenue.[278] When Warren Fisher offered

---

[274] Peden, Anderson, John', *ODNB*.
[275] *Ibid.*
[276] Ibid.
[277] Voluntary conscription scheme, 1915.
[278] Peden, 'Anderson, John', *ODNB*.

him the post of joint Under Secretary for Ireland, MacMahon had completed a total of thirty-eight years in the civil service, giving him an accumulative wealth of knowledge of Irish affairs. In an interesting juxtaposition of experience and age, Anderson was thirty-eight years old when he arrived in Dublin Castle in 1920.

Rt. Hon. James MacMahon (left) Image courtesy of Blackrock College Archives **and Sir John Anderson (right)** Image courtesy of the National Portrait Gallery, London.

The MacMahon family in 1887 showing James second from right at the back. Photograph courtesy of Eilish Tennent and Pauline Arthurs.

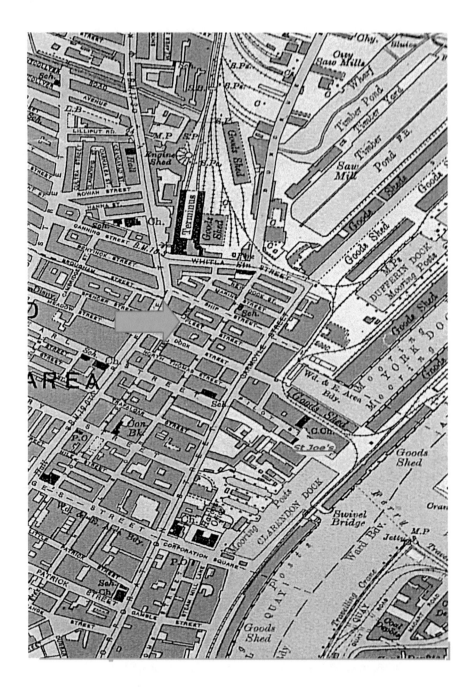

Map of Sailortown, Belfast – date unknown but later than 1865, the year of James MacMahon's birth. Fleet Street marked with blue arrow in centre of map. Courtesy of the Sailortown Regeneration, Belfast.

Rt. Hon. James MacMahon and his son Rev. John MacMahon (cut-outs c. 1920s). Private collection.

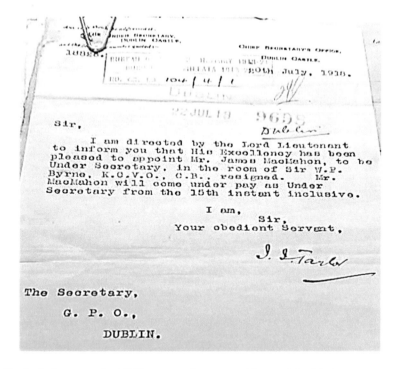

John Taylor's letter to the GPO re appointment of James MacMahon, BMH/CD 104/4/1, Military History Archives.

John Anderson's first home. 1 Livingstone Place, Marchmount, Edinburgh, with the Meadows to the left. Photographs by the author, July 2019.

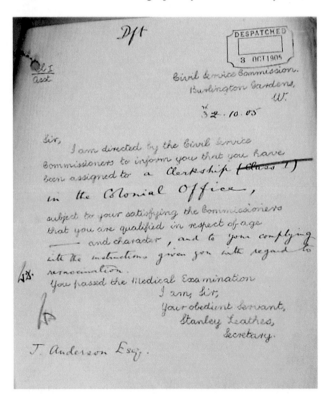

Civil Service first appointment of John Anderson, TNA, CSC 11/8.

PART FOUR

5

The Warren Fisher Report and the 1920-1922 administration

Impossible questions require impossible answers.

Plutarch, *Parallel Lives*

The findings of the Warren Fisher's report of 1920 into the Dublin Castle administration, led to the secondment of a British cohort under John Anderson, to work in tandem with the core Irish group. It also resulted in the creation of joint Under Secretaries. The investigation was driven by Lloyd George who 'coming into the British system from outside, had no respect for its traditions or accepted formalities... most of all, he distrusted the permanent officials'.[1] He relied heavily on the Garden Suburb[2] and what Milner described as his tendency 'to settle things that really mattered, or unsettle them, in his own favourite way, by devious methods and through anything but the regular agents'.[3] Was the investigation into the Castle an extension of a shake-up of the British civil service and a recognition of the need to initiate an Irish policy. Conversely, driven by a desire to find an answer to the 'Irish question', did Lloyd George, with the collusion of Sir Warren Fisher, set up a plan to discredit the Dublin Castle administration with a view to placing Whitehall civil servants at the coalface, so to speak?

While it would be relatively straight forward to take the Warren Fisher report at face value, the validity of the investigation into Dublin Castle and the impartiality of Fisher, must be broadly examined, given its impact. The reorganisation that followed the report was purportedly revolutionary in Dublin Castle administration and British policy. However, this argument ignores the initiatives of former Under Secretary, Antony MacDonnell (1902-1908), who had strong ideas on the need for reform of the Irish service. According to Maguire, 'his policy was not to abolish but rather to

---

[1] Eunan O'Halpin, Warren Fisher and the coalition, 1919-1922', *The Historical Journal*, vol. 24, (1981), pp. 907-927.

[2] In Jan. 1917, Lloyd George David Lloyd George formed what was the first prime-ministerial policy team, based in the garden of No 10 Downing Street.

[3] Alfred Milner note, 23 June 1921, Bodleian Library, Milner, MS dept. 1, fols.1-2.

strengthen the position of the Castle by giving it real control over the many boards and departments, with some independence from the Treasury'.[4] MacDonnell's predecessor as Under Secretary, David Harrel (1898-1902), had also advocated a similar approach.[5] Such initiatives point to the ongoing problems in the Irish administration, particularly in relation to the Treasury, rather than any new position.

Following the appointment of Sir Nevil Macready as G.O.C. in Ireland in March 1920, a string of his reports reached London on the 'administrative chaos that seems to reign here' where 'the machine was hopelessly out of gear'.[6] It has been recognised that 'Macready 's diagnosis of the ills of the Dublin Castle administration was largely correct, though he failed like so many others to see that his friend Lord French was the man primarily responsible for them, and he pressed for a committee of experienced administrators to examine the workings of the Irish administration'.[7] This tied in with post-war civil service reconstruction in Britain, and an investigation of the Dublin administration was instigated under the direction of Sir Warren Fisher, Head of the Civil Service, with the assistance of Alfred Cope of Pensions and R.E. Harwood, Treasury.[8]

Despite questions arising, the importance of the report cannot be overstated, leading as it did to the formation of the dynamic Dublin Castle administration, 1920-22. With Fisher responsible for the selection of personnel, biographical studies of the Irish and British cohorts of what was to be the final administration, would be lacking context and cohesion without a study of his own background and the changes he initiated in the Chief Secretary's office, Dublin Castle. Ostensibly, he not only changed the face of the Irish administration, but enabled a new direction in the course of Irish history through administrative input. Fisher was the official who

---

[4] Maguire, *The civil service and the revolution in Ireland* 1912-1938, p.18.
[5] Ibid.
[6] Geoffrey Sloan, 'Hide seek and negotiate: Alfred Cope and counter intelligence in Ireland 1919–1921', *Intelligence and National Security*, vol. 33, no. 2, (2018), pp. 176–195.
[7] O'Halpin, Warren Fisher and the coalition, 1919-1922.
[8] Fisher report into Dublin Castle administration carried out by A.W. Cope and R.E. Harwood, 12-15 May 1920 (TNA HO 317/50). According to section one of the report, the inspection was carried out from the 6-8 May 1920 but Alfred Cope and R.E.Harwood signed the report on 12 May 1920.

selected the civil servants for the Dublin administration of 1920 to 1922. This was a man at the height of his career, appointed Head of the Civil Service, or conversely nominated himself for that position, as discussed below. He directed the assessment of the Dublin Castle administration and subsequently assembled a British cohort to join existing civil servants in Dublin Castle, while maintaining an input into administrative regulation.

There is little in his early life to set Fisher apart from the stereotypical profile of an educated and privileged English civil servant. The son of Henry Warren Fisher, a gentleman of independent means, and Caroline Russell Fisher, late de Cardonnel Lawson, formerly Wilford, Norman Fenwick Fisher, was born on 22 September 1879, at 28 Weighton Road, Penge in the District of Croyden, Surrey.[9] He had one sister and a stepsister from his mother's first marriage. Fisher apparently did not enjoy a good relationship with his father.[10]

At prep school during the years 1887-1892, Fisher was a day-boy at the Dragon School in Oxford, where his family were then living. An obituary in the school magazine refers to Norman 'as he was called while a Dragon'.[11] It goes on to describe him as a young boy 'elegantly slender in figure and attractive in features, walking in Norham Road with his father and grown up stepsister, with a dog in attendance'.[12] Fisher was cited as being hard working while at the school. Then having then failed to gain entry to naval college on medical grounds, he went on to win tenth place on the roll in the scholarship entrance to Winchester College. Once again, the *Draconian* in an obituary referenced his appearance and work ethic, citing the fact that 'the combination of elegance and industry continued to mark Norman's career at Winchester'.[13]

There are no specific academic records for Fisher in the Winchester archives but his housemaster's record book shows that he made good academic progress at a time when pupils had to earn their promotion through the academic years. The Winchester scholars kept books known as 'chamber

---

[9] Norman Fenwick Fisher, GRO Croyden, vol. O2A, p.207.
[10] Eunan O'Halpin, *Head of the civil service: a study of Sir Warren Fisher* (London 1989), p.2.
[11] *The Draconian,* Christmas 1948, by email from Gay Sturt, archivist, 11 July 2018.
[12] Ibid.
[13] Ibid.

annals', in which they noted each other's characters. In 1894, Fisher was referred to as a 'painstaking second junior and valet (fag)'.[14] The annalist further stated that 'he was a solid mugster' (Winchester slang for someone who works hard) and had gained his promotion to a higher division.[15] It was recorded that Fisher played cricket 'with brilliance and dash'.[16] The 1895 annals referred to his being ·a charming little boy with attractive manners and a distinguished oar'.[17]   This reference by one boy about another's manners may not be quite as strange as it appears, with the Winchester motto being 'manners makyth man'. As a senior, Fisher, was in turn a school prefect. Demonstrating his drive to achieve, he won the English essay and the English historical essay prizes in 1898. Winchester College magazines show that Fisher rowed, primarily as stroke, and played cricket and football at inter house level.[18] He was in the college teams for Winchester's own game of football, which was played at six and fifteen a-side between the three different house teams and he also represented the home side in the college versus alumni matches.

Fisher's early interest in sport was to remain with him. Future colleagues however, regarded his enthusiastic promotion of the Civil Service Sports Council, which became the largest all-grade movement in the service, as somewhat strange and eccentric. He left Winchester having gained a scholarship to Hertford College, Oxford.[19] He graduated with a first class degree in Classical Moderations (Greek and Latin) in 1900 and achieved a second in Greats (classical literature) in 1902.[20] Following the tradition of Winchester, Fisher committed to a public service career. He failed the examination for the Indian Civil Service in 1901, which was not in itself remarkable given the numbers who did so. He sat the examinations again in 1902 without success. Subsequently he applied for the home civil service,

---

[14] Warren Fisher, Winchester College, *Chamber annals,* summer of 1894, by email on 17 July 2018 from Suzanne Foster, archivist.
[15] Ibid.
[16] Ibid
.
[17] *Chamber annals,* spring 1895.
[18] *The Wykehamist,* 28 July 1895.
[19] Ibid, 1897. 'We congratulate ... and N.F.W. Fisher on his election to a scholarship at Hertford College, Oxford'.
[20] Geoffrey K. Fry, 'Fisher, Sir (Norman Fenwick) Warren (1879-1948)', *ODNB.*

coming fifteenth in the examination in 1903 and achieving a first class clerkship in the Board of Inland Revenue.[21] Nonetheless, his exam placing was much below the achievement of his near contemporary John Anderson, who as shown in the previous chapter took first place in the entrance examination and was an academic powerhouse.

On 24 April 1906, Fisher married Mary Ann Lucy (Maysie) Thomas.[22] They had two sons. However, the marriage did not last. While they separated in 1921, there was no formal divorce as Maysie was a Roman Catholic. He rarely saw her again and had little to do with his sons.[23] Predeceasing his wife, Fisher made no provision for her in his will and she was to die virtually penniless.[24] Despite a reputation for being a 'ladies' man', his relationships with women after the separation do not appear to have been anything other than platonic. According to O'Halpin, the novelist Ann Bridge with whom he spent a lot of time in the late 1920s stated empathetically that 'he never made a pass at me ... at any point'.[25] Nonetheless, Fisher's personal life and his career were at times interlinked. It was through the tearful entreaties of Ann, that Fisher declared her husband Sir Owen O'Malley innocent of charges that saw his colleagues in the Foreign Office dismissed for currency speculation.[26] Whether there were other specific incidents of Fisher allowing friendship to influence his judgement is not obvious.

Fisher's civil service career began as stated, in the Board of Inland Revenue where he worked his way up to the position of private secretary to the chairman of the board, Sir Robert Chalmers in 1908. He himself was appointed chairman ten years later in 1918. Sixteen years after Fisher started in the service he became permanent secretary to the Treasury and after 1919 was de facto Head of the Civil Service. Was Fisher responsible for giving himself the title? Marking his retirement, the *Draconian* stated that he was 'the first Permanent Secretary to the Treasury to bear the title of head of the civil service'.[27] His obituary in the same publication amended this to 'he

---

[21] Warren Fisher civil service application, 1903 (TNA CSC 11/95).
[22] O'Halpin, *Head of the civil service*, p.9.
[23] Ibid p.10.
[24] Ibid.
[25] Ibid, p.12
[26] Ibid.
[27] *The Draconian*, Apr. 1939.

revived and held the position and style of head of the civil service'.[28] Whatever the course of events that led to the designation, a Treasury minute issued in 1919 announcing his appointment, stated that 'the permanent secretary would act as head of the civil service'. This was further expanded in a minute of 4 September 1919 and another of 15 September, the same year.[29] A House of Lords debate on the headship of the civil service in 1942 centred on a question by the Earl of Perth on when and by what instrument the title of 'Head of the Civil Service' was first bestowed.[30] The official reply indicated that this went back to 1867 and had been reaffirmed by the government in 1919.

The title of head of the civil service gave Fisher considerable influence in the making and unmaking of the careers of higher civil servants. In this regard, he wielded absolute power, with consequences for Ireland in terms of the reorganisation of the Dublin Castle administration. Nonetheless, with Ian MacPherson and John Taylor having already gone back to London, the only one in a senior position to be forced out by Fisher in May 1920 was Maurice Headlam, the Treasury Remembrancer, who finished his career in London in an obscure department in the Treasury. Fisher was not only responsible for recommendations to the prime minister regarding promotions to senior level posts but as auditor of the civil list, the awarding of honours.[31] This is of particular relevance to the current publication, not least in the matter of the conferral of honours in the wake of the British withdrawal in 1922.

Fisher's public school background marked him out as relatively different from some of his British colleagues and certainly from Irish civil servants. It would have given him an authority and remove, most likely eliciting a certain deference, when he arrived in Dublin Castle. Nothing in Irish educational provision in the post 1878 years could compare to the sheer weight of history and tradition of an English public school. Winchester, founded in 1382, was the oldest of the seven leading public schools reviewed by the Clarendon Commission commencing in 1861. However, as the commission was mainly concerned with financial management and the structure of the schools, it is unlikely that it addressed the purported

---

[28] Ibid, Christmas 1948.

[29] Treasury announcements 4 Sept. and 15 Sept 1919 (TNA, PRO T199/50b).

[30] *Hansard Parliamentary Debates*, HL deb., 25 Nov. 1942, vol. 125 cc 224-72.

[31] O'Halpin, *Head of the civil service*, p.61.

unsavoury practices of those institutions. 'English public schools in the last part of the nineteenth century tolerated if they did not actually encourage the development of strong homoerotic friendships between students'.[32] Whether as a graduate of such a system or due to specific matters relating to his lifestyle, suggestions of homosexuality were made in relation to Fisher throughout his career. These have been described as far-fetched.[33] This is despite Fisher's unusual penchant for calling men love and darling. Given that very little is known of Fisher's private life, it is difficult to dismiss the rumours entirely, just as it is impossible to prove their veracity. Such speculation could be treated as irrelevant to his work and achievements in the civil service. That is of course to ignore the potential danger to his reputation and the possibility of blackmail.

Warren Fisher's career could not have been totally described as coming under Martin Maguire's description of members of the 'Junta' 'fading into obscurity'.[34] While not a member of the seconded cohort he was the driving force behind its establishment and kept a certain control over it. According to Sir James Grigg, while Sir Warren Fisher was held in high esteem up to 1930, after that his reputation was diminished.[35] It seems if he could write his own obituary it might say ambition spent, he chose obscurity. For what reason he did so is unclear.[36] After his retirement, one of Fisher's successors at the Treasury, Sir Edward Bridges, described him as a 'distinctly controversial figure'.[37] He was certainly a complex character with accolades such as being the greatest civil servant of his time balanced by accusations of being rather mad.[38] He died in 1948, a few days after his sixty-ninth birthday. In a eulogy in *The Times*, Sir Noel Curtis-Bennett, a member of the Olympic committee, wrote, 'in his passing the nation loses not only a great

---

[32] Venn Bullough and Bonnie Bullough, 'Homosexuality in nineteenth century English public schools', *International Review of Modern Sociology*, vol 9, (1979), pp. 261-69.

[33] O'Halpin, *Head of the civil service*, p.12.

[34] G.C. Duggan, 'Last days of Dublin Castle', 1922, no. 128 p.150. Duggan coined the now much used term 'the Junta' to describe the British cohort. *The Encyclopaedia Britannica* defines 'Junta' as

[35] Fry, 'Fisher', Fisher, (1879-1948)' *ODNB*.

[36] O'Halpin, *Head of the civil service* p.294.

[37] Fry, 'Fisher', *ODNB*.

[38] Ibid.

and distinguished public servant, but a very simple and true English gentleman who loved his fellow-men and was not afraid to show it'.[39]

Prior to the Fisher investigation, the Dublin Castle administration included, Viscount French, the Lord Lieutenant, Sir Hamar Greenwood officially appointed Chief Secretary, James MacMahon, Under Secretary, John Taylor, Assistant Under Secretary, Maurice Headlam, Treasury Remembrancer, W.E. Wylie, Law Adviser, and senior personnel, G.C. Duggan, Joseph Brennan and Walter Doolin among others. According to O'Halpin, 'John Dillon maintained that any one of five, the lord lieutenant, chief secretary, attorney general, lord chancellor or under secretary, could dominate by dint of personality or ability but even the strongest figures could not control the whole apparatus.[40] In the case of Dublin Castle in 1920, the lack of a strong figure at the top was the greatest weakness of the administration, with French however putting the blame for his administration's failings on MacPherson.[41] However, from April 1920, French lost his residual influence over Irish policy.[42] O'Halpin describes his becoming 'irrelevant to the administration of which he was technically still head'.[43] According to Maume, 'French was replaced by Viscount FitzAlan at the end of April 1921, as part of the preparation for the final peace initiative'.[44] In what could be seen as further weakness in the administration, MacMahon had allowed his position of Under Secretary to be undermined by Taylor to the extent, that prior to the Assistant Under Secretary's departure, he had ostensibly ceded authority to his subordinate.

However, there was short-lived respite in April 1920 when MacMahon was effectively acting as Chief Secretary on foot of the departure of the Chief Secretary, the Assistant Under Secretary and the firing or resignation of Lord French's private secretary, the unionist die-hard Edward Saunderson and the departure to London of John Taylor.[45] The administration in Dublin Castle had an appearance of stability. O'Halpin cites MacPherson as telling French

---

[39] *The Times*, 8 Oct. 1948.
[40] Ibid, p. 7.
[41] Ibid, p201.
[42] Patrick Maume, 'French, Sir John Denton Pinkstone (1852–1925)', *DIB*.
[43] O'Halpin, *The decline of the union*, pp.206-7.
[44] Maume, 'French, Sir John Denton', *DIB*.
[45] O'Halpin, *The decline of the union*, p.205.

that 'my disloyal colleagues and their satellites have triumphed and I wish them joy'.[46]

The new found equanimity was to end a month later with the arrival in Dublin of Sir Warren Fisher, Alfred Cope, of Pensions and R.E. Harwood, Treasury, to examine the workings of the Under Secretary's office. Investigation was also focussed on the offices of the Inspector General of the Royal Irish Constabulary and the General Headquarters of the Irish Command. The work of Cope and Harwood was carried out over a three-day period from 6 May to 8 May 1920. The main points of the report as outlined by the two civil servants, acting for and under the direction of Sir Warren Fisher, were presented in sixteen sections primarily concerning the administrative and financial divisions of the Under Secretary's office.[47] The report recommended the restoration of the judicial branch in the Castle, due to prevailing disturbed conditions. It looked at the roles of the Royal Irish Constabulary, the military authorities and questioned the need for 'five separate and distinct systems of intelligence working with the same object, each under a different control, viz., the military, naval, two police forces and Scotland Yard'.[48]

Accompanying the report to the Cabinet was a memorandum by Warren Fisher in ten sections, four of which concerned a description of what Fisher saw as the weaknesses of the Under Secretary, James MacMahon but recommending his retention. Fisher stated that that Sir John Anderson, at that time Chairman of the Board of Inland Revenue, would be an admirable choice as an additional Under Secretary and 'would rapidly acquire the real control'.[49] Fisher also recommended that Sir John Taylor 'ought not return to the Castle'.[50] One of the main thrusts of Fisher's correspondence was the need for new personnel.[51] The final report into the investigation was dated 12 May, as was the accompanying memorandum. However, before the official submission Lloyd George wrote as follows to Churchill, Secretary of State for War, on 10 May 1920:

---

[46] Ibid. p.200.
[47] Fisher report (TNA HO 317/50).
[48] Ibid.
[49] Warren Fisher to the Prime Minister, Chancellor of the Exchequer and Lord Privy Seal and Prime Minister, 12 May 1920 (TNA HO317/60).
[50] Ibid.
[51] Ibid.

> My dear Winston, I am very anxious about Ireland, and I want you to help. We cannot leave things as they are … I understand from Bonar (Law) that there will be an important conference tomorrow to discuss the situation. Macready has certain proposals, which he is bringing over from Ireland. I am very anxious you should see him before the conference.[52]

The letter puts the emphasis on Macready with no mention of the Fisher report. This appears strange as Macready was to the forefront in pushing Lloyd George and the cabinet to sanction an investigation. Lloyd George did not attend the meeting on account of illness, with the chair being taken by Bonar Law. According to Ronan Fanning, the ministers decided that 'all requirements of the Irish executive should be promptly met'.[53] In an outline of the meeting given by Fanning, it seems that again the Fisher report was not mentioned.[54] Approximately twenty-four hours later, Warren Fisher presented his report to the Chancellor of the Exchequer. Fanning describes it as 'a devastating indictment of Dublin Castle, whose requirements he (Austen Chamberlain) and his ministerial colleagues had endorsed only the day before'.[55] While Macready was to the forefront in pressurising the Cabinet to investigate the Dublin Castle administration, Fanning contends he was operating at a higher level. Prior to taking up the position of General Officer Commanding British forces in Ireland in 1920, the King asked him 'to write personally on the state of Ireland, establishing a channel of communication so secret that even the prime minster seems to have been unaware of its existence'.[56]

In relation to the instigation of the Dublin Castle assessment, Macready raised the issue of administrative chaos and in his first communication with George V on 27 April 1920 he complained that, 'the official machine at Dublin Castle was largely in the hands of one man, the arch unionist, John Taylor'.[57] However, from the perspective of the Fisher report, his assessment of the situation was on the grounds of very limited experience of the workings of the Castle as he was only is his position for a matter of weeks

---

[52] Francis Costello 'Lloyd George and Ireland, 1919-1921: an uncertain policy', *The Canadian Journal of Irish Studies*, (1988), vol. 14, no. 1, pp. 5-16.
[53] Ronan Fanning, *Fatal path: British government and Irish revolution 1910-1922* (London, 2013), p.226.
[54] Ibid.
[55] Ibid.
[56] Ibid, p.223.
[57] Ibid.

before the arrival of Fisher. According to O'Halpin 'Macready pressed for a committee of experienced administrators to examine the workings of Dublin Castle, a suggestion that was well received in London'.[58] However, O'Halpin does not mention that Fisher was in fact the fourth person approached to undertake a review of the Irish administration. McBride claimed that Winston Churchill, Sir Herbert Creedy and David Harrel, former Under Secretary for Ireland, all 'declined to undertake the task'.[59] It seems strange that Fisher was not considered earlier, given that he was at that time, according to Maguire, 'deeply engaged in the most far reaching reforms of the British civil service'.[60] Maguire went on to say that 'the entire civil service in Britain, from the senior to the most junior ranks, through the departmental Whitley Councils, was now engaged in thinking about the problems of reorganisation and reform as part of post-war reconstruction. It was inevitable that such thinking would influence policy on Ireland'.[61]

Civil service restructuring in Britain and pressure from Macready, combined with the removal of General Sir Joseph Byrne, head of the Royal Irish Constabulary in 1920, were factors that led to an appraisal of the Dublin administration.[62] Following remarks made in the Kildare Street Club by Byrne in relation to the Lord Lieutenant's policy on the closing of small police stations, Lord French reacted by enforcing his signature response of indefinite leave. The Chief Secretary Ian MacPherson stated in the House of Commons on the 12 February that 'Sir Joseph Byrne had been granted three months leave pending a reply to a request that he should avail himself of an opportunity to send in his resignation'.[63] Byrne's anomalous position, which saw him removed from his job on what appeared to be baseless grounds, had far-reaching consequences. It is ironic that Byrne, a Roman Catholic effectively turned the attention of the British government to the purported shortcomings of the Irish executive, ultimately affecting the position of the Under Secretary, James MacMahon, a fellow Catholic. Byrne's initial reaction to his dismissal was to submit a string of reports directed against the administration. Coupled with the overarching reforms of the civil service

---

[58] O'Halpin, *Head of the civil service*, p.85.

[59] McBride, *The greening of Dublin castle*, p.279.

[60] Maguire, *The civil service and the revolution in Ireland*, p.69.

[61] Ibid.

[62] O'Halpin, *Head of the civil service*, p.83.

[63] *Hansard Parliamentary Debates*, HC, 12 Feb. 1920, vol. 125 c196, oral answers to questions on Ireland, Sir Joseph Byrne's dismissal;

carried out by Warren Fisher in Britain under the Whitley councils, there are adequate grounds for assuming changes in the Irish administration were regarded as necessary. The British government insisted that the Fisher investigation was merely to prepare for the recently approved recommendations of the National Whitley Council on reorganisation.[64] However, as early as 1 April 1920, Ulster Unionist leaders became aware of imminent changes in the Castle.[65] It has been asserted 'that from some highly official source, the *Belfast News Letter's* London correspondent continued to elicit leaks about changes at Dublin Castle, a weeding out as it were of permanent officials, which he claimed had already begun with John Taylor's holiday'.[66] The paper's correspondent went on to state in early May that the 'change in policy now in operation, which was also forecasted, had been determined'.[67]

The findings of Cope and Harwood were submitted to Warren Fisher on 12 May 1920. The opening sentence of the report stated: 'In accordance with your instructions we made an inspection of the Under Secretary's Office at Dublin Castle'.[68] Within the three days allotted for their investigation, Cope and Harwood came to emphatic conclusions on the Dublin administration. Strong criticisms of the Under Secretary, James MacMahon, the Assistant Under Secretary, Sir John Taylor and the workings and deficiencies of the Dublin Castle office were made. The interviews conducted with members of the existing Dublin Castle administration were integral to the report, but no comprehensive record of them was produced.[69] The ability of British civil servants to come into a strange environment and accurately gauge the situation in a very short period is questionable. McColgan quotes a Castle official as saying 'in the twinkling of an eye … they had settled the office reorganisation, even those portions of it which [they] had not seen, much less grasped'.[70] Was their assessment impartial or were they there to make certain findings to fit in with a formulated proposal, following a pre-arrival briefing in London?

---

[64] Maguire, *The civil service and the revolution in Ireland*, p.70.
[65] McColgan, *British policy and the Irish administration*, p.23.
[66] Ibid.
[67] *Belfast News Letter*, 25 May 1920.
[68] Fisher report (TNA HO 317/50).
[69] Ibid.
[70] McColgan, *British policy and the Irish administration*, p.5.

The investigation by Cope and Harwood was a major undertaking in a short time by officials with little knowledge of Ireland. According to O'Halpin, Fisher had a half-Irish Roman Catholic wife, a number of Irish friends and was 'a life-long Home Ruler'.[71] It could therefore be assumed that he had a certain conception of the country, although he was not actively involved in the investigation, with Cope and Harwood acting under his instructions. Conversely, neither Cope nor Harwood appear to have had any previous knowledge of Ireland or its people. McBride erroneously claimed that Cope was Irish but this was not the case.[72] He was born and raised in Kennington, London.[73]

The report delivered an assessment of the two divisions of the Under Secretary's office, that is Administration and Finance. This was inclusive of names, positions held and salaries of a number of civil servants. It noted that the administration division was subdivided into two sections, one dealing with the appointment and control of public officials, parliamentary and Irish Privy Council work, while the other primarily related to law and order and the supervision of the Royal Irish Constabulary and the Dublin Metropolitan Police.[74] The financial division was noted as dealing with general public expenditure and the operation of acts of parliament.[75] The report recommended the restoration of the judicial branch to deal with the maintenance of law and order.[76]

In relation to James MacMahon, it was stated that he 'falls considerably short of the requirements now generally demanded of a permanent head of an important department'.[77] Apart from judgements on MacMahon's general ability to carry out the job of Under Secretary, section nine stated that 'the Under Secretary and his subordinate, the Inspector General of the Royal Irish Constabulary, appear to be uncertain as to whether they or the military authorities are in control'.[78] The report went on to note that MacMahon's failure to assert authority over subordinates showed him to be lacking in character and general ability. However, while the Under Secretary was

---

[71] O'Halpin, *Head of the civil service*, p.84.
[72] McBride, *The greening of Dublin Castle*, p.279.
[73] Eunan O'Halpin, 'Cope, Sir Alfred William (1877-1954)', *ODNB*.
[74] Fisher report, (2).
[75] Ibid.
[76] Ibid, (3).
[77] Ibid, (5).
[78] Ibid, (9).

described as a weak official, it was noted that 'Mr MacMahon is a man of strong political opinions and he seems to have escaped all share of the disfavour with which the Castle administration is regarded'.[79] While it is not specified who exactly regarded the Castle administration with disfavour, the report stated that MacMahon attributed his immunity to 'his well known nationalist sympathies and frankly admits that he had numerous friends who are avowed Sinn Féiners'.[80] This led to a short discussion on MacMahon's association with anti-government circles but it was noted that he was in no way disloyal to his duties as a civil servant. Overall, the report noted that MacMahon's popularity was probably an asset to the administration and that it 'would be impolitic to remove him'.[81]

While MacMahon's contacts with the clergy are most often cited, it was found that he also had an accord with influential figures, who were over the course of his four years in the Castle, of benefit to himself, his colleagues and superiors in the administration. These networks were based on his northern background, education, post office career, particularly as Secretary of the GPO and on the social side, his membership of the Stephen's Green Club and others. Of utmost importance to MacMahon were his fellow alumni of Blackrock College. While beneficial in the main, such associations also highlighted what was an almost naive trust in those with whom he considered he shared a common bond. This was one of the factors that led to suspicions being raised in relation to spying for the nationalist cause.

It has been demonstrated that the virulent unionist antagonism towards Irish nationalists that was rife in the internal politics of the Castle administration and the personal jealousy and bias which were directed towards MacMahon in his first two years, created an erroneous perception of his ability that still exists. Available material confirms that MacMahon did make an important contribution to the foundation of the State, despite the misconceptions that have tainted his 'legacy'. It has been shown that his commitment as a civil servant was driven by his loyalty and dedication to his country and to the position of Under-Secretary. Through his work in that capacity he brought the unique perspective of a Catholic nationalist with a commitment to the constitutional movement and a belief in the possibility of achieving settlement through administrative measures. Sources show that he

---

[79] Ibid.
[80] Ibid.
[81] Ibid.

had no sympathy for physical force activists and was in no way a revolutionary, or spy. MacMahon's complete loyalty to his position as Under-Secretary and a senior civil servant, was an essential part of who he was, during his years in Dublin Castle and throughout his future lifetime. He was the consummate civil servant; a constitutionalist who never shared the ideals of the physical force elements, whose primary aims were the same as his, but whose methods were vastly different.

Beyond the role of the Under Secretary and others, the Fisher report further discussed the weaknesses of Mr Connolly, Chief Clerk, who was considered to bring nothing to his role in the department and was overpaid. Both he and Sir John Taylor were recommended for retirement. Although Taylor was in London, the report relied heavily on evidence gathered from other personnel, as outlined in sections six and seven. It is perhaps in section ten that one of the driving forces behind the report was to be found. It stated that 'if the government of the country is to be exercised through civil power, a drastic re-organisation of the administrative division of the Chief Secretary's Office is required and ... the introduction of new and additional, personnel into the department is urgently necessary'.[82]

Fisher sent a covering memorandum to Whitehall with the formal report.[83] It was dated 12 May 1920, as was the report carried out by Cope and Harwood. The supplementary memorandum was addressed to the Chancellor of Exchequer, Lord Privy Seal, and the Prime Minister in that order. This seems unusual given that the office of the Prime Minister is senior to the other two positions. Was there a set precedence used in correspondence which was ignored, or was the order merely a random one? Could it be that Lloyd George already knew what the letter was likely to contain and his briefing was just a formality? Both the Warren Fisher report of 1920 and the accompanying memorandum written by Fisher are key to the subsequent changes to the Irish administrative modus operandi. A review of Fisher's letter or supplement to the report to the Prime Minister, David Lloyd George shows that he went much further than the findings by Cope and Harwood with a strong denunciation of the administration and the Under Secretary's office in particular.[84] 'Fisher claimed that in relation to policy or

---

[82] Ibid (10).
[83] Fisher to the Prime Minister, Chancellor of the Exchequer and Lord Privy Seal, 12 May 1920 (TNA, HO317/60).
[84] Fisher memorandum, 12 May 1920 (TNA, HO317/60).

the application of policy 'it simply has no existence'.[85] While writing that the attached report by Cope and Harwood discusses the castle in detail, Fisher expanded and highlighted certain points, particularly in relation to the work of the Under Secretary.

The letter has the appearance of a document written in frustration that the report, in the writer's opinion, failed to deliver the necessary coup de grace. Fisher's letter is in marked contrast to the relative restraint of the report. He focussed on the post of Under Secretary, contending that the prevailing conception is that the holder of the position is a routine clerk. Fisher then attributed this to 'the personality of some of the occupants of the post and the attitude of some chief secretaries'.[86] It could be argued that he was citing material, which may have been discussed prior to arrival in Dublin, in an attempt replace the Under Secretary, James MacMahon or at the least diminish his role. Fisher stated in his memorandum that MacMahon who had a distinguished career in the Post Office, rising to the position of chief secretary, 'is not devoid of brains, but lacks initiative, force and driving power. Neither by temperament nor training is he ready for responsibility'.[87] This showed a lack of knowledge of MacMahon's work as Secretary to the GPO in the politically sensitive months following the Easter Rising and the problem solving initiatives he brought to that position, demonstrating his administrative strengths.

Fisher further compounded his own ignorance of MacMahon by writing that 'his conception of his function conforms to the traditional Irish limits, and he has no experience of running a big show or shaping policy'.[88] While Fisher's statement on 'traditional Irish limits', has the appearance of being deliberately derogatory or a cultural dichotomy, his contention that MacMahon had no experience in 'running a big show or shaping policy' in not only negated by the aforementioned work MacMahon carried out in the GPO, but by a letter of 18 April 1920 from French to Law. The date of this letter is important. As previously stated, MacMahon had been entrusted with control of the Castle prior to Fisher's arrival, making the attack on MacMahon's ability more open to question. Not only had French written that he was reinstating the Under Secretary and making him responsible for

---

[85] Ibid (1).
[86] Ibid (2).
[87] Ibid (5).
[88] Ibid.

running the Castle, but he also completely removed himself from any blame for actions against him: 'MacPherson completely ostracised the Under Secretary, MacMahon and would not permit him to fulfil his proper functions'.[89] However, French's assessment in relation to fulfilling proper functions, ostensibly shows a weakness in MacMahon's leadership or even a dereliction of his duties, independent of Fisher's arguments. In contrast to his opinion of MacMahon, Fisher had great praise for General Nevil Macready, whom he claimed was shoring up the administration. He quoted Macready's negative assessment of the Irish administration, and seems to have been strongly influenced by his viewpoint.

The roles played by the Lord Lieutenant and the Chief Secretary, as political appointments outside the administration, did not form an integral part of the investigation. This prevented a comprehensive overview of the Dublin Castle chain of command. Cope and Harwood mentioned neither French nor MacPherson. While it would be difficult for civil servants to criticise senior political appointments, it was in fact, most likely unknown to Cope and Harwood, that the inconsistency of Lord French in relation to the Under Secretary increased the discord that existed between MacMahon and the Assistant Under Secretary, John Taylor. However, Fisher did not hold back in alluding to the Chief Secretary, writing that when he 'skied on Olympus, and his top permanent official hewed wood in the remotest valley, the natural expectation is that essentials must suffer'.[90] It is questionable which Chief Secretary Fisher is referring to, as MacPherson had resigned on 2 April 1920 and Greenwood's appointment had only been made on 12 April 1920.

Fisher again referencing the Chief Secretary, presumably MacPherson, wrote that he 'appears to be under the illusion that a civil servant, even though he has the position and emoluments of permanent head of the Irish administration, is entirely unconcerned with the exploration or settlement of the problems which the Irish administration exists to solve'.[91] If Fisher was referring to MacPherson would it not have been more logical to have used the past tense? Although appointed to the position on 12 April, Hamar Greenwood was unlikely to have come under censure for the problems in the Castle administration of the past two years. Furthermore, according to

---

[89] French to Law, PA, 18 Apr. 1920, BL 103/2/11.
[90] Fisher memorandum (TNA, HO317/60).
[91] Ibid, section 2.

O'Halpin, Fisher was amazed that the administration 'has since the start of 1919 been dominated by a unionist clique, incompetent as it was extreme'.[92] In his view, 'they were successful only in one respect, squeezing Roman Catholics, who had become objects of suspicion, out of positions of power'.[93] However as mentioned, there is a case to be made that MacMahon as Under Secretary, did not enforce his authority and seniority in respect of his dealings with Taylor, or in relation to any divisive action by the Assistant Under Secretary. On the face of it, for whatever his reason, he allowed his subordinate to dominate and effectively usurp his role.

The Fisher report and memorandum recommended the retirement of Taylor, the leader of the unionist faction, but that MacMahon be retained, albeit in a reduced capacity. MacMahon was most likely expected to make the transition a smooth one for the British cohort, led by Sir John Anderson, with Mark Sturgis, Alfred Cope, A.P. Waterfield, Geoffrey Whiskard among the group of nine members. However, the arrival of the seconded personnel caused problems, which were to resonate within a section of the existing administration. Martin Maguire referred to them as the 'suave and sophisticated Englishmen with neither careers nor commitments in Ireland'.[94] He further stated that the fact they were 'cosseted and believed to be receiving huge salaries. Regarding the impact of the report, the primary consideration centres around whether it should be accepted as a genuine assessment of the Dublin Castle administration in May 1920, or a pretext to effect changes in personnel, particularly with regard to the 'loan' of Whitehall civil servants. It is open to question as stated previously, whether the recommendations made by Fisher, Cope and Harwood were based on directions and proposals put in place before they left London.

The recommendation for new personnel led to the formation of what was in essence a dual Dublin Castle administration comprised of the 'Old Castle Gang', that is the Irish group which was already in place in the Chief Secretary's office and a British cohort seconded from Whitehall. While it goes without saying that each group was likely to have entered the new look administration with different outlooks and directions, to assess their roles within the complex and changing political developments in Ireland from 1920 to 1922, could in fact form the basis of separate research. While their

---

[92] O'Halpin, *Head of the civil service,* p.87.

[93] G.C. Duggan, 'The life of a civil servant', unpublished memoir.

[94] Maguire, *The civil service and the revolution in Ireland,* p.73.

individual actions as integral parts of the administration will be profiled, the emphasis will be on comparative biographies from an educational and career perspective. The focus on the British cohort as assembled by Fisher puts an emphasis on what was essentially one part of the whole, in terms of the Dublin Castle administration, 1920-22. They may have perceived themselves as 'conquerors' but for most of the next two years their lives and work were interwoven with those of the 'Old Castle Gang', or existing cohort in the Chief Secretary's Office. While the biographical studies of the Irish group will be limited to those who had worked directly with James MacMahon from 1918-20, the British grouping is somewhat larger. It extends across a number of departments and while providing a basis for comparison with Irish colleagues, is also a microcosm of Whitehall civil servants with a diversity of backgrounds and experiences.

John Anderson's group of British civil servants had set up their 'mess' in the Royal Marine Hotel in Kingstown, on what was to be a temporary basis.[95] Courtesy of Anderson, extra provisions were nodded through for his British officials, in terms of first class travel and other special allowances.[96] Less than a month later, they packed their bags and moved into Upper Castle Yard.[97] Given the attempted murder of Lord French in an ambush at Ashtown six months earlier on 19 December 1919 and the murder of RIC Lieutenant Colonel Gerald Bryce Smyth on 17 July 1920 in the Country Club, South Mall, Cork, just days after their arrival, the group of British civil servants were assessed by Fisher as being potential targets.

Fisher wrote a four-page memorandum on the perceived dangers, which the group were facing.[98] This document was circulated to members of the Cabinet and discussed at a meeting on 13 August 1920.[99] R.P.M. Gower wrote to Sir Maurice Hankey, Cabinet Secretary, in a memo regarding the circulation of the paper, 'that for your private ears some of the most important of the officials concerned i.e. Sir John Anderson are now in this country, and may have to return to Ireland in the next two or three days'.[100]

---

[95] Sturgis diaries, 15 July 1920 (TNA, PRO 30/59/1).

[96] Parl. papers 1920, (TNA, Treasury conference on special allowances 11 Sept 1920, T 158/1).

[97] Ibid.

[98] Warren Fisher, 'Position of English Civil Servants in Ireland', 7 Aug. 1920 (TNA, CAB 21/207).

[99] Ibid.

[100] Ibid.

This may have added urgency to Fisher's request. Had Anderson spoken to Fisher of concerns regarding himself or the group? Fisher wrote to the Chancellor of the Exchequer that, 'it is my duty as permanent head of the civil service to represent through you to the Cabinet the situation in which the small band of picked civil servants on temporary duty in Dublin may find themselves at almost any moment'.[101] Why was this becoming apparent less than a month after the cohort arrived but not realised before they were deployed in July?

While Fisher concluded that the group could no longer reside in safety in the Marine Hotel, Kingstown, the alternative of moving them into the Castle could he claimed 'accelerate the total paralysis of the machinery of civil government'.[102] There was also the issue noted by Fisher that providing police protection could expose 'the protége', which was almost certainly a reference to Alfred Cope, ostensibly charged with making contact with Sinn Féin by Lloyd George. Despite the Chancellor's fear that the newly passed Restoration of Order in Ireland Act, 1920 could exacerbate Sinn Féin attacks, the Cabinet decided the group should stay in Ireland and reside in Dublin Castle.[103]

However, the situation was far from clear-cut as a memo from Sir Malcolm Ramsey to C. Longhurst showed.[104] Ramsey stated that the Chancellor was concerned that the minute was so worded to 'admit of the interpretation that the civil servants concerned had expressed a fear as to their safety ... but the men concerned never made any suggestion that they might be in personal danger'.[105] The Chancellor felt, 'it would be most unfortunate if a record stood which conveyed any possible reflection on the men concerned'.[106] From the correspondence, it appears that Fisher or others overly emphasised the situation with regard to the safety of the British cohort. The course of Irish history would have been changed had Fisher succeeded in his proposed recall of the British civil servants on perhaps exaggerated safety fears. However, far from worrying about their position,

---

[101] Ibid.

[102] Ibid.

[103] Ibid. Cabinet response to Warren Fisher, 13 Aug. 1920 (TNA, 48.20).

[104] Ibid, 26 Aug. 1920, Sir Malcolm Ramsey, permanent secretary, controller of establishments.

[105] Ibid.

[106] Ibid.

Mark Sturgis noted that very day in his diary, 'I lunched with MacMahon and Jonathan (John Anderson) at the St Stephen's Green Club, of which I shall shortly I believe become a member, proposed by Wylie and seconded by MacMahon'.[107]

---

[107] Sturgis diaries, 13 Aug. 1920, PRO 30/59/1.

URGENT-

<u>Chancellor of the Exchequer</u>.

It is my duty as Permanent Head of the Civil Service to represent through you to the Cabinet the situation in which the small band of picked English Civil Servants on temporary duty in Dublin may find themselves at almost any moment.

You will remember that for a period of several months (ending some time last April) the acting permanent head of the Irish Executive - with several others - immured himself in the Castle. The corollary of this was a natural demoralisation of the various agents constituting the machinery of Civil Government throughout the Country upon whom depended the execution of the orders of the central authority.

In May the Cabinet decided upon a change in the personnel of the Administrative Headquarters and there have accordingly been seconded for service in Ireland Sir John Anderson and ten or eleven specially selected men from London Departments.

Sir John and his colleagues have been clear from the start that it would be fatal to any prospect of success either in restoring the Civil machinery or in influencing public opinion if they allowed themselves to be besieged in the Castle. Not merely would such a course have rendered impossible any live contact with the actualities of the situation (and therefore proper opportunity for informing the Cabinet); but also the more fact that the Permanent Executive thus avowed a presumption that they were

in

Memorandum from Warren Fisher to Andrew Bonar Law, Chancellor of the Exchequer, 1920, TNA CAB 21/207.

in danger would have reacted disadvantageously on the already impaired morale of the Government agents throughout the Country, while at the same time it would have been received as an encouraging sign by the partisans of physical force and, so far as the majority of the population was concerned, would have been interpreted as a continuation of the "keeping at arm's length" attitude.

Accordingly since landing in Ireland these English Civil Servants have for these reasons deliberately proceeded about their business as free men. I do not mean to say that they have wandered about the slums of Dublin at midnight any more than they would commit a similar folly in the East End of London; but they have lived together at Kingstown, gone out to lunch from the Castle and generally have declined to allow their sphere of utility to be restricted by being "caged in". (The two regular Chiefs of the Police who live cooped up in the Castle - a phenomenon not unnoticed by, and not without effect upon, the officers and rank and file of the two forces - have frequently placed on record their opinion that these officials should be given "police protection". They have done this, not because they are ignorant that it is no protection at all in the present condition of Ireland, but simply in order to be absolved of technical responsibility if anything untoward were to happen.

The only effect of "police protection" is to advertise the movements of the protégé and to destroy his necessary liberty of action.)

The public attitude towards these English Civil

Servants

Memorandum from Warren Fisher to Andrew Bonar Law, Chancellor of the Exchequer, 1920 (2), TNA CAB 21/207.

Servants has been one of benevolent neutrality - a striking contrast to the positive hostility displayed towards some of their immediate predecessors. The cause of this improvement was twofold; In the first place the Irish majority interpreted the substitution of personnel as evidence of a new orientation of British thought; and, secondly, the personality, training, outlook and capacity of these very able Englishmen commanded not unsympathetic recognition. Under these circumstances this handful of men has so far been immune from virulent criticism in the press and generally, nor has there been any attempt, or suggestion of an attempt, to interfere with them or intimidate them, still less to imperil their lives. But there are signs that the period of immunity is unlikely to continue; the situation is hardening and for reasons (unconnected with the men themselves) - which may be good or bad, but in any event are outside my province - these men are on the point of coming under the ban.

It follows that the lives of these men will henceforth no longer be safe.

Two alternatives - and two alone - present themselves (1) that they should be ordered by the Government into the Castle or (2) that they should resume their duties in London.

(1) If Sir John Anderson and his colleagues have to take up their quarters in the Castle, they at once become prisoners. They will never be able to go out except under armed escort (for the same reason that caused their removal into the Castle). They will be marooned, out of touch, deprived of the liberty of action and movement without which real direction and

real

Memorandum from Warren Fisher to Andrew Bonar Law, Chancellor of the Exchequer, 1920 (3), TNA CAB 21/207.

real knowledge are alike impossible. And with their disappearance into the Castle the creaking machinery of Civil Government must come to a standstill.

It is true, of course, that they will be able to think and write in personal safety within the walls of the Castle; but when their thinking and writing have issued in the form of orders, who is going to carry out these orders? Certainly not the ordinary civilian agents of Government outside the Castle and isolated from protection, in Dublin or anywhere else; for these men will have seen the danger signal in the removal to the Castle of the central executive and they could not be expected to function at the peril of their lives in order to carry out orders given by men whom the Government has removed to the Castle because of the prevailing danger.

It must be remembered that there is all the difference in the world between a military machine and a civil machine in circumstances such as now obtain in Ireland.

G.H.Q. issues its orders and those orders are executed by a machine which is outside and independent of the civil population and which by its very character, arrangement and dispositions is not paralysed by intimidation.

The Castle issues its orders and the execution of those orders depends upon individual members of the civilian population - often working in ones and twos and always entirely at the mercy of violence which can be sufficiently organised because of the apathy or

hostility

Memorandum from Warren Fisher to Andrew Bonar Law, Chancellor of the Exchequer, 1920 (4), TNA CAB 21/207.

hostility of public opinion towards the central Government. Once the heads of the Civil Executive are removed into the Castle for their safety, the natural instinct of the civilian agents outside is to follow the example and themselves play for safety, that is, no longer even to try and give effect to the orders of the Castle.

It, therefore, seems to me that if the Government direct Sir John Anderson and his colleagues to retire into the Castle, they will thereby ensure their personal safety but at the same time accelerate the total paralysis of the machinery of Civil Government.

(2) If this be right, and Sir John Anderson once in the Castle becomes impotent, it is a matter for consideration whether he and his colleagues should not resume their duties in their respective London Departments where they are badly needed and could be effectively employed. This involves issues outside my competence; but I may perhaps be allowed to remark that, as soon as the Civil Executive is unable any longer to function effectively, the only resort is the military machine.

In conclusion, may I just say that a decision in regard to this little band of English Civil Servants may well be a matter of great urgency, for the agents of murder may now at any time proceed to extremes against any one or all of them.

(Intld.) N.F.W.F.

7/8/20.

Memorandum from Warren Fisher to Andrew Bonar Law, Chancellor of the Exchequer, 1920 (5), TNA CAB 21/207.

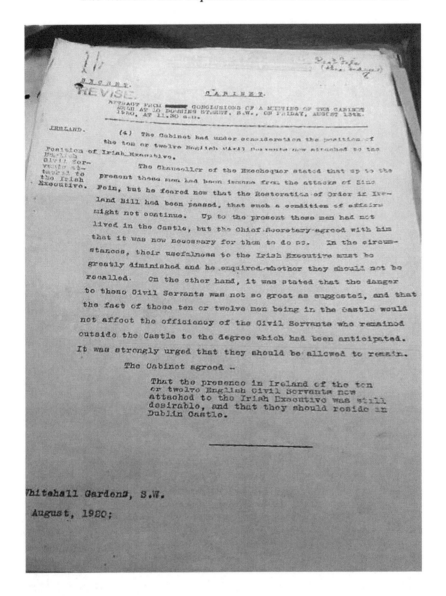

Response from the Cabinet to Warren Fisher, 13 Aug. 1920, TNA, 22/E CAB 48.20.

PART FIVE

6

The 'Old Castle Gang': Core Irish group in the Castle

For it is not histories that I am writing, but lives; and in the most glorious deeds there is not always an indication of virtue or vice.

Plutarch, *The Life of Alexander the Great*

Working under James MacMahon, the core Irish group in the Dublin Castle administration of 1920-22, was part of the pre-1920 Chief Secretary's office. They were ostracised by the unionist clique, which had divided the office into pro-Taylor and pro-MacMahon factions and to an extent dominated, until the removal of its most divisive member, the Assistant Under Secretary. Sir John Taylor had departed for England prior to recommendations of the Fisher report, which endorsed his removal. Within the parameters of the 'Old Castle Gang' the role of James MacMahon, now designated as joint Under-Secretary and an integral part of the newly merged Irish and British administration, is paramount. Aside from MacMahon, who were the members of the Irish cohort, what were their career and educational backgrounds? What benefit, if any, had they gained from increased educational provision in Ireland resulting from the Intermediate Act of 1878?

Among the 'Old Castle Gang', James MacMahon and key personnel, W.E Wylie, G.C. Duggan, Joseph Brennan and Walter Doolin, survived the coup engendered by Warren Fisher in 1920. In tandem with the British team, the Irish group formed the nucleus of the last British administration in Ireland. While considering the Irish senior level members of the Dublin Castle civil service during the period 1920-22, there are pairings that immediately spring to mind for different reasons. G.C. Duggan and Joseph Brennan were colleagues in the finance division and Brennan and Doolin were not only colleagues but lifelong friends. Both Doolin and his fellow Clongownian, Brennan took up positions in Dublin Castle prior to the changes brought to the administration by the Fisher report of 1920. Joseph Brennan and Walter Doolin were 'inseparable', according to Molly Doolin.[1]

---

[1] Molly Doolin notes NLI, MS 31658 43-49.

Apart from the fact that both attended Clongowes Wood, albeit with a gap of three years, with Brennan being the elder, they entered the civil service as Irish Catholics who benefitted from a first class secondary and university education. While in college in Dublin, Brennan often 'digged' with Walter Doolin's family as following the death of Walter's father, Mrs Doolin had been left in difficult financial circumstances.[2] They were part of the 'Old Castle Gang' and very much senior Irish Catholic civil servants in the new era of competitive examinations and university education. W. E.Wylie and the Rt. Hon. James MacMahon were colleagues and friends since 1918. Wylie and Duggan shared the similar background of an Irish Protestant education. The most obvious connection within the group was that they were all Irish. While they were part of the 1920-22 administration they had also been in the Chief Secretary's office in the two previous years of MacMahon's tenure as Under Secretary. In the case of Wylie this was not as a civil servant but as the law adviser to the government.

James MacMahon, with whom Sir John Anderson was to share the position of Under Secretary from 1920, was the most prominent member of the 'Old Castle Gang'. MacMahon and Anderson had similar early lives. They had experienced upward mobility from relatively humble origins. Both benefitted from educational advantages, which influenced their civil service careers. Nonetheless, this was to be an unequal partnership. For the Irish officials and general public MacMahon was the established figure, the face of the Castle administration. Effectively on home ground he had the upper hand on Irish matters, played in his usual urbane, quiet manner. For two years, he had lived with his family in the Under Secretary's Lodge in the Phoenix Park, an outward manifestation of his position, which he did not vacate for the newcomer. However, following the announcement of the appointment of Anderson, MacMahon , courteous as always, sent him a telegram of welcome.

MacMahon had a unique understanding of Ireland. According to W.E.Wylie, he had forgotten more about Ireland than the rest knew.[3] MacMahon's contacts ranged across the spectrum of Irish society and among the Catholic hierarchy, a network that Anderson could not hope to match. He was in touch with the people of Dublin and had a social conscience developed through membership of the St Vincent de Paul

---

[2] Ibid.
[3] Ó Broin, *W.E. Wylie and the Irish revolution*, p.52.

Society, which he had joined while still in Blackrock College. He assumed full control of Dublin Castle following MacPherson's departure. On the other hand, Anderson came to Dublin with the imprimatur of Warren Fisher and Lloyd George and was not perceived as tainted by being a member of the 'Old Castle Gang'. From a British perspective, his was the definitive position. G.C Peden makes two unsubstantiated claims from a British viewpoint in the *DNB*. He writes that Anderson 'was in effect the senior Under Secretary' and that 'he established a good rapport with the IRA commander, Michael Collins during discussion on how to hand over the administration to the provisional government of the Irish Free State'.[4] While the first assertion is relative, the second is somewhat speculative as Collins dealt primarily with Cope.

MacMahon was involved in what could be seen as a forced common purpose with the British cohort. Despite personal feelings, an ever-present sense of duty to the civil service would have been paramount for him. Cementing his position in 1920 he was sworn in to 'His Majesty's most honourable privy council in Ireland'.[5] MacMahon's modus operandi, which was developed in the two years of association with Taylor, was of quiet behind the scenes networking and constant work towards peace; but 'never seeking public acclaim, his work went largely unnoticed'.[6] Nonetheless, by 1921, MacMahon was being portrayed as playing a very active role in seeking conciliation. Sturgis, in what he refers to as the 'peace stakes' noted 'Andy is good and strong right out in front by himself. MacMahon, who was nowhere early on, has come through and lies second'.[7] Sturgis was of course accentuating the work of his English colleague and arguably not as informed as he believed himself to be.

Perhaps the most notable Whitehall/Dublin co-operation was in fact between MacMahon and his subordinate, Cope. What Sturgis did not know was that Cope was according to himself, acting under the direction and support of MacMahon, his superior. While Cope is widely credited with facilitating the Anglo-Irish Treaty, he himself recognised the immense input of MacMahon. He was also to tell MacMahon's son in the 1950s that 'he had worked under MacMahon's leadership and could have done nothing

---

[4] Peden, Anderson, *ODNB*.
[5] 'Privy Councillors (Ireland)', *London Gazette*, supplement 1 Jan. 1920.
[6] *Irish Independent*, 3 May 1954.
[7] Sturgis diaries, 19 May 1921 (TNA, PRO 30/59/5).

without him'.[8] In recognition of MacMahon's efforts for settlement, he wrote in 1922, 'you were working on it long before the English contingent was ever thought of and you took the guiding part on the peace side during the regime of that contingent'.[9]

As had occurred in his earlier years in Dublin Castle, MacMahon again came under suspicion of spying while on a family holiday in Portrush with Wylie and his family in 1920. The reaction of Anderson in a letter to Andrew Bonar Law is one of the few primary source indications of the working relationship between the two men:

> I really want to say that so far as that conversation related to MacMahon, I am quite sure the information that has reached you is absolutely baseless. MacMahon has been staying en famille at Portrush and except for one visit to Cardinal Logue, (which resulted in the publication of the strongest statement in denunciation of outrage that has as yet emanated from the hierarchy), one visit to Belfast to attend the funeral of an official, has spent his holiday in a peaceful normal way in and around Portrush.[10]

However, their differing viewpoints in relation to concilation is shown in a letter from Anderson to MacMahon following an announcement by the Prime Minister on dominion home rule:'I understand your disappointment with the Prime Minister's statement on the ground that it falls short of your hopes ... England has gone a long way to meet Ireland and if the one real bar to peace is that Ireland won't go one step to meet England, one can only say, the pity of it'.[11] However, demonstrating the strength of MacMahon's standing with regard to settlement, Sturgis notes on 17 August 1921 that Anderson asked MacMahon's view for ministers, who were meeting on that day at 5pm.[12] As noted by Sturgis 'it remains unchanged and MacMahon interpreted the Sinn Féin speech that day as meaning that they will not accept the offer as settlement but as a basis of discussion it will not be rejected'.[13]

MacMahon continued to maintain a constitutional nationalistic stance, as a counter to revolutionary methods and physical force. Sean T. O'Kelly

---

[8] Ó'Broin, *W.E. Wylie and the Irish revolution.* p.140.

[9] Alfred Cope to James MacMahon, 27 Dec. 1922 (NLI, MS 31658 43-49).

[10] John Anderson to Andrew Bonar Law, 2 Sept. 1920 (PA, Ireland, Sir John Anderson, BL102/7/2).

[11] Anderson to Sir (sic) James MacMahon, 18 Aug. 1920 (NLI, Joseph Brennan Papers, MS 31,701).

[12] Sturgis diaries, 17 Aug. 1921, (TNA, PRO 30/59/5).

[13] Ibid.

recognised this in 1949, when he said that MacMahon 'had no sympathy with the physical force movement'.[14] As a nationalist, the Ulster unionists were reluctant to see him in a position of power in Dublin Castle. On a visit to Derry, MacMahon, Anderson, Tudor (Major-General Hugh Tudor, RIC) and Wylie were perceived as representing Dublin Castle. MacMahon was singled out by the *Belfast News-Letter* for his comment that 'a peace based on force would not be a lasting one'.[15] Sir James Craig made a strong attack on MacMahon and less strongly on Macready and Anderson.[16] Following a raid on MacMahon's mother's hotel in Armagh, Sturgis summed up the northern feeling about MacMahon in a somewhat muddled diary entry:'What a country! Belfast doesn't admire MacMahon and Armagh is in Ulster'.[17] Sturgis, albeit with a tendency to exaggeration and an obvious bias towards his British colleagues, provided a vivid, albeit unofficial record of the work of MacMahon and Anderson and the Irish and British cohorts in Dublin Castle. While his information was not always correct he managed to portray the day-to-day working of the Castle administration, and the highs and lows of MacMahon and Anderson among others in a highly volatile situation, as work progressed towards settlement.

Despite Mark Hopkinson's contention in the the Introduction to *The Last Days of Dublin Castle,* that MacMahon was 'a somewhat shadowy personality in the Diaries', his edited version contains numerous references to the Under Secretary. The original volumes confirm that Sturgis repeatedly referred to MacMahon as a pro-active member of the administration, particularly throughout 1921. In doing so he provides a valuable and in fact the only primary source record of the Under Secretary's efforts towards peace and settlement, prior to the establishment of the Free State. One of Sturgis's first diary entries writen shortly after his arrival in Ireland on 14 July 1920, highlights the Freemans Journal's sensational account of a speech purportedly delivered by Col. Smyth, Divisional Commissioner for Munster. What is of note is that Sturgis pinpoints MacMahon's involvement with the official reaction to the event. A meeting was held on 15 July in London between 'the Chief Secretary, Jonathan, MacMahon etc. at which Col. Smyth explained himself and which resulted in a denial in the House

---

[14] Sean T. O'Kelly to Col. Dan Bryan, 25 Jan 1949, BMH, S.1374.

[15] McColgan, *British policy and the Irish administration*, p.24.

[16] Ibid, p.26.

[17] PRO 30/59/2, 21 Oct. 1920.

of Commons of the accuracy of the Freeman's account by the Chief Secretary'.[18] The Journal in response to the official reaction published the following:

> The Government of funk is on the run.
> Greenwood gathered the gang and held a hurried investigation.
> He sent for Smyth.
> Then he made up his mind.
> He packed his grip and fled to Downing Street.
> In his wake his shivering subordinates followed.
> Sir John Anderson went.
> The Rt. Hon. James MacMahon went.
> Mr Smyth the bellicose orator of Listowel went to complete the party.
> The more the merrier…'[19]

Three days later on 18 July 1920, Smyth was shot dead in Cork. According to the diary of 20 July the Prime Minister summoned Macready, Tudor, Cope, MacMahon and Wylie to London, at Lady Greenwood's suggestion.[20]

Sturgis was not however above criticism of MacMahon and indeed other members of the administration. Later in 1920 he remarked in a strange entry to his diary that MacMahon was unusually pessimistic. He claimed on 7 December he wanted to quit but did not want to lose his pension. 'He covets Wrench's job as Estates Commissioner and thinks Wrench might make way for him at the price of a baronetcy'.[21] A week later the matter of MacMahon 'resignation' took a strange turn. It was claimed that the Chief Secretary said that MacMahon was to go at once and wanted to know the best way to do it, with MacMahon perhaps being seconded from the Castle to the Wrench job. There is little about this that rings true and the proof is that nothing happened, other than a loose remark of MacMahon's in a gloomy moment being spun by Sturgis into something more than it was. It is also noted on the same day that MacMahon was 'less than sanguine regarding the Archbishop … (also) the Chief Secretary was distinctly peeved at the Prime Minister sending over a direct envoy to treat with the enemy'.[22] This refers to the Australian Archbishop Clune. While it was perhaps a strange decision on the part of Lloyd George to send an Australian priest as an informal

---

[18] Ibid, p.12.
[19] *Freeman's Journal,* 15 July 1920.
[20] PRO 30/59/1, 20 July 1920.
[21] PRO 30/59/3, 7 Dec. 1920.
[22] Ibid.

intermediary without informing Greenwood, it is perhaps not unexpected when taken in tandem with the Prime Minister placing Cope in the Castle to make contact with Michael Collins, a fact also unknown to the Chief Secretary.

On 14 January 1921 Sturgis lunched with MacMahon and Wylie in the Stephen's Green Club. He subsequently remarked that it was curious, that MacMahon is completely left out of the peace plots, despite the fact that he was supposed to be the main link with the RC Church. 'Some go to Andy, some to Jonathan, some approach Macready, none, so far as I know to MacMahon'.[23] The words 'as far as I know' are key, as will be shown. However his next sentence is pure vitriol. 'Perhaps this is by his own act and he has announced his aloofness too loudly to be taken up to the neck in anything'.[24] A few days later, Sturgis seems back on good terms with MacMahon. He was concerned about MacMahon's wife and how weak she was after an operation the previous day. On 18 January he lunched with MacMahon, one of his daughters and Andy Cope. Again referring to the operation, he says that Mrs MacMahon 'is not better but holding her own'.[25]

On 4 April 1921, Sturgis writes, 'MacMahon wanted me to dine tonight to meet Logue and Gilmartin (Archbishop of Tuam). The presence of Hamar and Jonathan in Ireland was said to make this impossible, as there might be feelings. Hope to see them however somehow'.[26] The followng day Sturgis without thought or rationalisation, completely contradicted his comment on MacMahon and the hierarchy of 14 January. Jonathan and Sturgis went to the Viceregal Lodge, where Cardinal Logue and Archbishop Fogarty were staying. 'On being introduced to Logue, Sturgis remarked: 'He is a wonderful old man … he said there was no tyranny like the tyranny of a republic'. The Cardinal added that the 'bar to negotiation was pride on both sides'.

The next day Sturgis notes that he spoke to MacMahon. 'He tells me that the clericals are really pressing hard for peace and are inclined to confidence. It is arranged for Jonathan to see Fogarty tonight or tomorrow'.[27] It would appear that MacMahon was still very much in touch with the hierarchy, with

---

[23] PRO 30/59/3, 14 Jan 1921.
[24] Ibid.
[25] PRO 30/59/4, 18 Feb. 1921.
[26] Ibid, 4 Apr. 1921.
[27] Ibid, 6 Apr. 1921.

Fr Fogarty being a prominent intermediary. The diary entry continues, illustrating the ongoing part played by MacMahon in efforts to engender a settlement and his contacts beyond the clergy: 'MacMahon got hold of an out and out Shinner this morning – probably a gunman, to arrange for him to see de Valera himself tomorrow, which he is confident will be arranged.

Highlighting the social side of Castle life, Sturgis records on 8 April 1921, that there was 'a very grand dinner last night at the CS Lodge. Eighteen people : Mrs Howard, Royal Hospital party, PS Lodge party - Jonathan, MacMahon etc.[28] On Saturday it was business as usual with the diary entry stating that MacMahon had a meeting with de Valera at 7pm. The entry for the following day is interesting, not least as it contains another admission by Sturgis that he is not kept informed of all that was going on:

> I am as usual completely at sea as to what is happening, am not sure whether MacMahon actually saw de Valera yesterday or not. I think he did but whether he did or not, de V declined to discuss anything political at all. The natural supposition is that the strike in England has made SF sufficiently bobbery to sit tight and make no move of any sort till they see what way the cat jumps t'other side. Andy on the other hand had a story from MacMahon that they won't touch us because L.G. is in direct communication.[29]

By 14 April, Sturgis had concluded that MacMahon did not have a meeting with de Valera, but spoke to him on the phone. Apparently de Valera was willing to see his old friend but with no talk of politics. [30] 'On this MacMahon did not go. I would have gone anyway and seen what came out of it but perhaps M. was right – it might have looked like running after them'.[31] Sturgis records that on the following day MacMahon picked up Cardinal Logue at the Gresham and drove him back to the Park. 'The old Cardinal was very pleasant and asked me with a prying finger stuck in my side, did I wear a tin waistcoat!'[32]

On 25 April MacMahon was recorded as being in fair spirits, as Lord Derby had a long meeting with Cardinal Logue. While he didn't meet de

---

[28] Ibid, 8 Apr. 1921.

[29] Ibid, 10 April, 1920.

[30] This would most likely refer to both being alumni of Blackrock College and members of the St Vincent de Paul Society. It could also be a reference to Lord Derby, as according to the diary of 25 April a potential meeting which MacMahon was trying to broker on his behalf did not take place.

[31] PRO 30/59/4, 14 Apr. 1921.

[32] Ibid, 15 April 1921.

Valera, he had meetings with some influential Sinn Fein members and according to Sturgis's account, may have had a letter from de Valera. Sturgis then asserts in relation to Derby that 'MacMahon is told that he has gone back to England with a clear assurance from Sinn Fein that they will accept less than a Republic if Lloyd George will make them an offer, but that they will not say this openly or put it in writing until they have the PM nailed. It remains to be seen what my Lord Derby can do with this in England'.[33] The talk of his involvement is very much indicative of the role that MacMahon played in facilitating negotiations for potential settlement. He subsequently confirmed a meeting between de Valera and Lord Derby did take place.[34]

A light hearted diary entry of the 29 April 1921 refers to MacMahon refusing to go to the Depot with Sturgis, Cope, Whiskers and Clark, for what is described as the 'inspection', as he 'wouldn't been seen on the same grounds as the Black and Tans'. He followed on later for lunch and was most disappointed that the expected salmon was not served, despite it being Friday. 'We put an auxiliary bonnet on him after lunch to give him the atmosphere and he looked very fine'.[35] Three days later Sturgis relates that he asked MacMahon to tell him the stories of Lord Derby's visit to the Cardinal in Armagh and how on a walk in the Cardinal's grounds, a curate was hoodwinked into believing that Derby was a Mr Edmunds. The curate unwittingly told him the best apple in that part of the country was the Lord Derby.[36]

Both the clerical and political connections of MacMahon were again highlighted on 19 May when Sturgis writes that MacMahon and Cope went to Greystones to lunch with the Church and to meet 'Gawd knows who'. He also notes that MacMahon had produced evidence on the previous day that the 'Craig Agenda'[37] was being favourably considered by Sinn Fein leaders. MacMahon was now overtly being portrayed as playing a very active role in seeking conciliation. Sturgis, in what he refers to as the 'Peace Stakes', could not miss an opportunity however, to highlight one of his group. As previously mentioned he noted that 'Andy is good and strong right out in

---

[33] PRO 30/59/4, 25 Apr. 1921.

[34] Ibid 27 Apr. 1921.

[35] PRO 30/59/4, 29 April 1921. Sturgis uses the general army term 'bonnet. But there was a distinction between the headgear of the Auxiliaries who wore 'a caubeen' and the 'Glengarry cap' of the Black and Tans.

[36] Ibid, 2 May 1921.

[37] James Craig, Viscount Craigavon, First Prime Minister of Northern Ireland.

front by himself. MacMahon, who was nowhere early on, has come through and lies second'.[38] Furthering their efforts 'Andy and MacMahon spent yesterday visiting the Cardinal and urging a second meeting at once between de Valera and Craig, without waiting for the not forthcoming representative of the Prime Minister'.[39] On 6 June Sturgis writes that matters concerning de Valera and Craig are basically in a stalemate position, with de Valera seeing no point in meeting again with Craig or Cope. He says that Andy is 'much depressed'. On the other hand he ascribes undue optimism to McMahon, just back from 'his Cardinal' and states that MacMahon overestimates the influence of the Church at that time.[40]

In late June it was reported that Cope had talked to MacMahon on the wire from London and says all was going well in terms of potential talks. MacMahon says for certain that de Valera will go.[41] On 28 June, the diary records that MacMahon and Andy have been in and out all day – what Macready calls 'down the main drain' - pushing for the Shinn reply and trying to persuade them to refrain from spoiling it.[42] An entry of 2 July references the senior position of MacMahon. In the diary Sturgis notes that he went out with Andy soon after 11am. Cope had a letter in his pocket from Smuts (Gen. Jan Christian Smuts, South African and British Commonwealth Statesman, whom Cope met in London and subsequently invited to Dublin), which Andy 'handed over to MacMahon'[43]

Sturgis had the following entry in his diary just four days before de Valera was to write accepting a meeting with Lloyd George regarding a truce. 'Mansion House Meeting yesterday. Protestant Churches had special prayers for peace by order of Gregg, Archbishop of Dublin. No similar steps seem to have been taken by RCs which seems strange in view of the united view of their bishops as reported by MacMahon'.[44] The next day Sturgis notes that he talked to MacMahon who remained calm; MacMahon was of the opinion that it didn't matter if Ulster made trouble and Sinn Fein knew it. In fact he felt that this was a positive as they could blame Ulster if thing went wrong. Sturgis further hypothesises that 'if once they get to London

---

[38] Ibid, 19 May 1921.
[39] PRO 30/59/4, Fri. 3 June 1921.
[40] Ibid, 6 June 1921.
[41] PRO 30/59/4, 27 June 1921.
[42] Ibid, 28 June 1921.
[43] PRO 30/59/4, 2 July 1921.
[44] PRO 30/59/4, 4 July 1921.

and MacMahon is sure they will go, they have ipso facto given up the 'Republic' as the only solution'.[45] On 8 July, MacMahon was proven correct, as a letter from Eamon de Valera to Lloyd George shows, '... I am ready to meet and discuss with you on what bases such a conference as that proposed, can reasonably hope to achieve the object desired'.[46]

On 5 July as pre-Truce fever was mounting; Sturgis gives comprehensive details of Mac Mahon and Cope being out, as Smuts was in Dublin. By 6pm he records that they had returned and that the 'mountebank Shinns' have wasted their day talking about a Republic with them and Smuts. Deferring to the Under-Secretary's opinion, as MacMahon is shown to be more and more to the fore in facilitating the official ending of the war, he gives MacMahon's reading of the situation. 'They don't want to tell anybody who comes from London that they will take less than a Republic, so that when they get to L.G., as they mean to, they can start with that and come down, instead of starting with Dominion Home Rule and coming down from that. Very ingenious'.[47]

The Truce was signed on 11 July 1921 and the settlement initiatives continued. In an entry of 26 July, Sturgis recorded that there was no news from London until after 6pm, when Cope 'ordered 'the instant attendance of Commandant Duggan TD, to get the PM's reply to de V[alera]'. With regard to the reply from Lloyd George, Sturgis notes that MacMahon was quite pleased with it. The following month Sturgis gave his opinion of Duggan, 'MacMahon introduced me to Duggan when he arrived, a pleasant little man with no obvious appearance of distinction. In normal times a little middle class solicitor with a poor practice'.[48]

Throughout August the tension between Catholics and Protestants in the North is barely concealed. On this and other issues MacMahon is more cheerful than Cope and told Sturgis that the Sinn Fein people he has seen, say 'Lloyd George has some private bargain with de Valera and neither will precipitate a crisis'.[49] Demonstrating the lead that MacMahon had assumed in relation to settlement, Sturgis notes on 17 August 1921 that Anderson

---

[45] Ibid, 5 July 1921.
[46] No. 138, Irish Foreign Policy, *Official correspondence relating to the peace negotiations June-September 1921* (Dublin, 1921).
[47] PRO 30/59/4, 5 July 1921.
[48] PRO 30/59/5, 26 Aug. 1921.
[49] Ibid, 13 Aug 1921.

asked MacMahon's view for Ministers, who were meeting on that day at 5pm. Sturgis noted that 'it remains unchanged and MacMahon interpreted the Sinn Fein speech that day as meaning that they will not accept the offer as settlement but as a basis of discussion it will not be rejected'. MacMahon further said that he was told the object was to send away a happy Dail content to leave further negotiations in the hands of the Cabinet.[50]

Three weeks later Plunkett writes that he met MacMahon who told him the diehards in the Cabinet are getting sorry for their concessions to the Irish. The latter, he said 'have accepted the invitation to send plenipotentiaries. MacMahon seemed to fear a dangerous hitch. I don't'.[51] Again on 5 October, pressure seems to be making MacMahon unusually 'direct'. The entry in Sturgis's diary notes that MacMahon says 'S.F.'s opening oration at the conference will be full of tripe; will probably start with Ireland's claim in 1100 and get down to 1921 in about two days'. However, he didn't have to attend. 'Mac Mahon's old father-in-law died so he wasn't there'.[52]

The Gresham was a centre of activity for MacMahon and Sturgis on 12 October, with most of the day spent there. When they were leaving MacMahon met Fr Fogarty and introduced him to Sturgis. The diary entry notes, this 'sinister priest' turns out to be a genial middle aged gentleman inclining to stoutness. He was very pleasant and agreeable. Of a meeting the same day with Fintan Murphy, Sturgis records that MacMahon was extremely interested to discover that Murphy was with the Volunteers in the GPO in 1916, at the time 'MacMahon was head of it'. This is of course factually incorrect as Norway was the secretary during the Rising.

On 6 December 1921, the Treaty was signed. This was noted in letters and telegrams of congratulation to the Prime Minister and others, from all over the world. An effusive message was sent to Sir Hamar Greenwood. The message from John Ross, Lord Chancellor read: 'I take off my hat to you as the most intrepid figure I have ever seen in public life. Your name will go down in history. I congratulate Lady Greenwood on having a real hero for a husband'.[53] Although MacMahon was not in receipt of such excessive praise, a letter from Lord French at the Hôtel de Crillon, Place de la

---

[50] Ibid, 17 Aug. 1921.
[51] NLI, Horace Plunkett diaries, 12 Sept 1921.
[52] PRO 30/59/5, 5 Oct. 1921.
[53] John Ross to Hamar Greenwood, 7 Dec. 1921 (PA, personal/political papers, F/20/1/2).

Concorde, Paris, concerned the 'turn of events' in relation to the Treaty and highlighted MacMahon's input: 'You were always right in the way you gauged the situation'.[54] This may have caused MacMahon a wry smile considering French's past attitude towards him.

Two days after the Treaty signing, the committee charged with the transfer of civil service functions to Northern Ireland met, with MacMahon taking an active role. The Truce of 11 July 1921, following the War of Independence had raised question in relation to the partition of the civil service. With the start of the Treaty negotiations on 9 November the British Government had announced the moving of services to Northern Ireland. While Craig wanted a transfer of functions he stated emphatically that he didn't want a transfer of staff. The Civil Service Committee set up as a consequence of the Government of Ireland Act, 1920 was regarded as very much a partition committee. Prior to its inaugural meeting the lack of a southern representative was seen as a potential stumbling block. Rather than dissolve the Southern Parliament, Lord FitzAlan appointed MacMahon to the committee.[55] Its first meeting was held on 8 December with MacMahon representing the southern government. Sam Sloan and Michael Gallagher on behalf of the existing Irish officers, challenged the appointment of MacMahon, as being contrary to the 1920 Act. They also stipulated that the proceedings would be provisional until ratified under the terms of the Act.[56] There were to be further consequences for the committee early in the New Year.

On 20 December Sturgis notes that the Collin's crowd was in the depth of depression. It was thought that the de Valera lot had made great headway and might reject the Treaty by a majority of two. 'MacMahon this morning is sure that this is nonsense and that the ratification is safe tho the expected majority may be smaller than he expected'.[57]Cope had sent a telegram to Hemming in the Irish Office in London on 18 December in respect of meeting Michael Collins that morning, who was not expecting an imminent decision. Cope noted that the ratification party was not having an easy time

---

[54] Lord French to James MacMahon, 12 Dec. 1921 (NLI, MS 31658).
[55] NAI, CSORP, 1921-22, 2429/156, Order-in-Council to create a temporary Civil Service Committee, 9 Nov. 1921.
[56] Martin Maguire, the civil service and the revolution in Ireland, 1912-38 (Manchester, 2008), p.115.
[57] PRO 30/59/5, 20 Dec. 1921.

with the extremists, despite support in the press and country and that it would not be desirable to rush matters. Clarke (presumably Basil Clarke) had likewise telegraphed Street of the London Office, stating that he felt the oppostion such as the communists, academic socialists and the 'black women, whose political development ceased the day they bacame widows' were unlikely to upset the ratification.[58] The Treaty was finally ratified on 7 January, 1922.

In perhaps a tacit recognition of MacMahon's right to 'full honours' as Under Secretary since 1918 and a member of the 'Old Castle Gang', John Anderson was not present at the historic handing over of Dublin Castle on Monday 16 January 1922. This saw the Lord Lieutenant, Lord FitzAlan, the first Catholic to hold the office, relinquish the machinery of government and the Castle itself to Michael Collins, Chairman of the Provisional Government, as British administrative and military personnel withdrew from Ireland. A photograph of the Lord Lieutenant and Under Secretatry is hugely significant. There is a sense that a relaxed MacMahon is escorting a disgruntled Lord FitzAlan out of the Castle and symbolically out of Ireland, when the Free State formally came into existence and the office of Lord Lieutenant was abolished.[59]

For MacMahon the photo could be regarded as a justification of his role in the administration. From the outset, he was focused on the hope that by accepting the position of Under Secretary he could contribute to a peaceful solution to the situation in Ireland. MacMahon had publically stated, 'everyone was anxious for a settlement and if he, was able to do anything to help in that direction it would be the greatest day of his existence'.[60] A conversation with Horace Plunkett appears to show that MacMahon felt that this could be achieved despite British ineptitude. In what can be regarded as strangely outspoken even to someone he felt he could trust, MacMahon confided in Plunkett that 'FitzAlan is a fool; honest, ultra-Tory, stupid, Macready dishonest and the military mostly longing for renewal of

---

[58] TA LG/F/20/1/10, Clarke to Street.
[59] Image, *The Graphic*, 21 Jan. 1922.
[60] 'Under Secretary's view', Nov. { } (NLI, clipping from an untitled newspaper, date incomplete, MS 31658 43-49).

hostilities'.[61] Plunkett noted in his diary 'thank God MacMahon is certain there will be peace'.[62]

On 18 January, Sturgis with his superior attitude visible to the end, lamented the newspaper announcements of the 'surrender of Dublin Castle' the phrase used by Sinn Féin saying, 'it leaves a nasty taste in the mouth; it is so caddish'.[63] Another news report of 21 January highlighted the removal of important documents which saw anything of importance shipped to London.[64]

> The departments centred in Dublin Castle were packed on Saturday and ready to go as soon as they get orders from the Provisional Government, which was set up on that day in the Mansion House. In the corridors and rooms of the Castle big stacks of documents and records, all neatly arranged in bundles and parcels duly docketed, labelled and catalogued. A huge bonfire of 'wastepaper' blazed all the morning and afternoon in the courtyard beyond the Upper Castle Yard.[65]

With little regard for his years as the senior civil servant in Dublin Castle, Maguire contended that 'MacMahon, who had smoothed the waters for the transfer of authority, was given two weeks to clear out of the Under Secretary's lodge in the Phoenix Park'.[66] At the end of his career in the Irish administration he nominally remained a Privy Councillor, although the council ceased to function after 1922. As well as the destruction of his Dublin Castle papers, he refused to engage with any requests to share his experiences. MacMahon responded to such a request during a phone conversation with Col. Joyce from the Bureau of Military History saying, 'it would be a breach of confidence on his part to disclose confidential information, which he might have elicited while in the service of the British Government'.[67]

MacMahon further said that 'he had already been approached by several people, who had asked him to record his experiences in Dublin Castle during

---

[61] MacMahon to Plunkett, 21 Aug. 1921 (NLI, Horace Plunkett diaries, 1854-1932, MS 42,222/41).

[62] Ibid.

[63] Sturgis diaries, 18 Jan 1921 (TNA, PRO 30/59/5).

[64] *Anglo Celt*, 21 Jan. 1922.

[65] Ibid.

[66] Maguire, *The civil service and the revolution in Ireland,* p.155.

[67] Col. J.V. Joyce memo re phone conversation with James MacMahon, 13 Oct. 1949, BMH, S.1374.

the British regime'.[68] Expanding on this when he met Col. Joyce in the Stephen's Green Club, MacMahon stressed that he was not confident 'that any guarantee given would be honoured by a succeeding Government and he felt that anything he might consent to say now, might be published long before he could ever agree to have any publication made'.[69] During this off the record talk with Col. Joyce, MacMahon referred back to the requests made to him for information saying 'he was very friendly personally with T.M.Healy, Governor General, Irish Free State and his intimate friend, Lord Beaverbrook. The latter was a newspaper magnate who continually offered him substantial inducement to write his reminiscences for the press, but he consistently refused'.[70]

According to G.C. Duggan, MacMahon 'preserved the discretion of the civil servant, but it is a loss that he never wrote his memoirs. His sense of humour and his understanding of human character would have alleviated some of the shadows of the times in which he lived; and the fact that he was an Ulsterman and could appreciate those with whom his childhood was spent would have added piquancy to the story that he might have written'.[71] A letter from Sean T. O'Kelly, Uachtarán na hÉireann to the Bureau of Military History states that in 1949, 'he met the Rt. Hon. James MacMahon, who was Under Secretary of State for Ireland in Dublin Castle at a very critical stage in the struggle for Irish independence and had many contacts with the Irish leaders including Michael Collins'.[72] According to O'Kelly the meeting took place 'in the Priory of Adam and Eve's after the ceremony of consecration of the Rt. Rev. J.M. McBride as Archbishop'.[73] O'Kelly mentioned the work of the Bureau of Military History to MacMahon and asked if he would provide a statement. MacMahon's response was that 'the matters with which he was most closely associated were in general things which should not be published, at least not yet'.[74] O'Kelly further wrote: 'James MacMahon is a very important witness and a contribution from him would be of very great historic value. In dealing with him it will be

---

[68] Ibid.

[69] Col J.V. Joyce meeting with James MacMahon, 18 Oct. 1949, BMH, WS.947.

[70] Ibid.

[71] G.C. Duggan 'Letters to the editor', *Irish Times*, 5 May 1954.

[72] Sean T. O'Kelly to Col. Dan Bryan, 25 Jan 1949, BMH, WS 1374. Forwarded to Col. Joyce on 25 July 1949.

[73] Ibid.

[74] Ibid.

necessary to use infinite tact and to bear in mind that from a national point of view his leanings were entirely with the constitutional movement as represented by Mr John Redmond MP'.[75] There is unfortunately nothing in the Bureau's administrative file on MacMahon to indicate that he changed his mind on giving an official statement, even with a long-term embargo.

Although he was then fifty-seven years old, MacMahon did not retire in 1922; in fact, he did not leave employment until four months before his death at the age of eighty-nine, when he officially retired as director of the Allied Dublin Gas Company on 2 January 1954. Under the new Irish government MacMahon held a senior position in a number of state and private enterprises. His many directorships included the Great Southern Railways of which he was chairman. He lived in the railway's official residence, St John's, Islandbridge until his death and frequently holidayed in the GSR hotel in Parknasilla.

MacMahon was also involved with the Fishguard and Rosslare Railway and Harbours, the Dublin United Transport Company and the Insurance Corporation of Ireland, the Congested Districts Board and was a member of the Local Government Board. He was an active member of the St Vincent de Paul Society, the Ancient Order of Hibernians, the Catholic Truth Society and perhaps the Knights of Columbanus, although this is not possible to clarify as the list of members is secret. In terms of the social and sporting life of Dublin before and after the foundation of the State, MacMahon enjoyed membership of the Stephen's Green Club, Royal Irish Yacht Club, Portmarnock Golf Club and the Royal Irish Automobile Club.[76] He was elected president of the Royal Dublin Society for 1947. He was also a member of the Royal Irish Yacht Club in Dun Laoghaire, which mainly counted not only established Catholic 'gentry' but the Catholic middle classes, upper level civil servants and professionals among its members. This was a similar membership to the Stephen's Green Club, which was included in data by Fergus Campbell but without any attempt to discuss this aspect of social advancement.[77]

James MacMahon continued his social work with the poor of Dublin and retained his strong links with the Catholic Church. On 14 January 1927 he was received by the Pope (Pius XI). He was accompanied by the daughter

---

[75] Ibid.
[76] *Blackrock College Yearbook*, 1954, pp. 103-05.
[77] Campbell, *The Irish establishment,* p.71.

and niece of his friend T.M. Healy, Governor General of Ireland.[78] While this was reported in Ireland it would have been a semi private visit. Nonetheless it was a tacit acknowledgement of MacMahon's contribution to the Catholic Church over many years. Two days after his death on Saturday, 1 May 1954, on the eve of the Spring Show the flag over the RDS flew at half-mast. It mourned a remarkable man who in the RDS, as in countless other fields of Irish Public Service had made an enduring mark.[79] Formal recognition of his role on a national level has however been denied to MacMahon, both in terms of honours from the British and Irish sides. Whether he would have accepted a knighthood if offered, is open to conjecture. Following the ratification of the Treaty in 1922 the only 'heroes' that the British lauded were those on their side of the administration. As demonstrated by the New Year Honours list for 1923, the Whitehall group were not short-changed.

Prominent among the Irish cohort were Joseph Brennan and Walter Doolin. As members of established Catholic merchant and professional families with access to established schools, they did not benefit directly from the Intermediate Education (Ireland) Act, 1878 in terms of educational provision, but they were in many ways the realisation of the aspirations of the legislation. Personally, the spur of competitive examinations with the recognition and rewards in their years at secondary school and university, provided an access to upper level administrative positions. They competed for entry to the civil service and both achieved first division clerkships. This entry level had previously been denied to Irish Catholics due to a lack of university education or access to patronage, which had opened doors for well-connected British applicants. This was particularly prevalent prior to the introduction of civil service competitive examinations. The entrance system, recommended by the Northcote-Trevelyan report, which stated that 'a central board should be constituted for conducting the examination of all candidates for the public service, was based on meritocracy and sought to eliminate patronage.[80]

---

[78] *Cork Examiner*, 15 Jan. 1927.
[79] *Irish Times*, 3 May 1954.
[80] Recommendation regarding competitive examinations to replace patronage, by the *Northcote-Trevelyan report on civil service reform*, submitted to both Houses of Parliament, Feb. 1854 (paper 1713).

However, for Catholic students in Ireland, such progression was hampered by the lack of effective denominational university provision. It was over twenty years after increased secondary school provision before Irish Catholics, deprived for so long of a full collegiate university experience had access to a vibrant denominational university education, with the foundation of University College Dublin in 1908. The previous provision had seen the private Catholic University (formally established in 1854) and some secondary schools prepare students for the non-denominational Royal University of Ireland (1879) external examinations. This had no built environment and no provision for accommodation, lecture halls, or teaching for students. Research indicates that changes to entrance criteria were slow to impact on the Irish administration. A hierarchical structure under English dominance, it historically presented few opportunities for first division postings or advancement to senior level positions for Irish Catholics up to the foundation of the Free State. As has been shown, certain historians such as Lawrence McBride disputed any such 'blocked mobility'.

Joseph Francis Brennan was born on 18 November 1887, in South Main Street, Bandon, Co. Cork to a merchant father, Joseph Brennan and Mary Brennan, née Hickey.[81] Brennan Snr. was a successful businessman whose interests included Brennan Ltd. (general store and bakery), Bandon Milling Co., Bantry Woollen Mills, and West Cork Bottling. Exemplifying the expanding Catholic middle classes, the Brennans moved from Main Street to Hill Terrace and then to Kilbrogan House, a double-fronted mansion, near the northern edge of Bandon.[82] While the Brennan family could in some ways be compared to that of James MacMahon and John Anderson, the extent of the business portfolio of Joseph Brennan Snr. was far greater. They had an established social status and any upward mobility was relative. Although the Brennans were part of the evolving Catholic middle class, their status was cemented prior to the Intermediate Education (Ireland) Act, 1878, as was the case with the Conan family.

Brennan's father was highlighted in an article 'Our Manufacturers' in the *Clongownian,* which cites him as being a past pupil of St Stanislaus College, Tullabeg, which amalgamated with Clongowes Wood College in 1886.[83] Coming from a Catholic family with no lack of social or financial standing,

[81] Joseph Francis Brennan, GRO, reg. 11820598, Bandon, Co. Cork.
[82] León Ó Broin, *No man's man* (Dublin, 1982) p.12.
[83] 'Our manufacturers', *The Clongownian*, 1905-07, p. 295.

education was prioritised for young Joseph Brennan also. From 1899-1905, he was a pupil at Clongowes Wood College, considered the leading Catholic school in Ireland. Looking through the *Clongownian*, Brennan's name features prominently. His younger brother Jeremiah was also a student at the school, attending from 1899-1908. At the time of their registration, the family was living at 1 Hill Terrace, Bandon. This address is given in the *Dictionary of Irish Biography* as that of Joseph's birth, but according to his official birth certificate, that was not the case. The two brothers achieved remarkable academic records in Clongowes. They both featured strongly in the intermediate examination results, with Joseph and Jeremiah being exhibitioners in 1905.

After leaving Clongowes, Brennan attended University College. He was not happy with the college; 'the teaching was poor, study facilities were very restricted and generally he felt he was wasting his time there'.[84] It was unfortunate for Brennan that his entrance to university just preceded the Universities Act, 1908, which saw University College Dublin (UCD) become a constituent college of the National University of Ireland and the demise of the Royal University and University College. Although he could have chosen to finish his studies in UCD, he transferred to Christ's College Cambridge in 1909, where he was enrolled until 1911.

Joseph Brennan's papers in the NLI contain examples of essays and notes from his time in Clongowes and university in Dublin and Cambridge, with the bulk being from the English university.[85] He was awarded a first in the classical tripos there in 1911.[86] Brennan then applied to the civil service in the same year. Having obviously done well in the examinations (not all results are available in the British archives), he started his career as a first division clerk, defying the odds against Irish Catholics gaining entry at that level. However, his success must be counted among the numbers at Cambridge to gain such entry, thirty that year as opposed to two in Dublin, one of whom was his friend Walter Doolin.[87]

For a brief period, Brennan worked with the Board of Customs and Excise and the Port of London. In a link to a future association, Alfred Cope,

---

[84] Ó Broin, *No man's man*, p.95.
[85] Essays and notes (NLI, Joseph Brennan papers, **MSS 25,,075-25,116** and **MS 26,000-26,437**).
[86] Sean Cromien, 'Brennan, Joseph (1887-1976)', *DIB*.
[87] *Royal commission on the civil service* (TNA, CSC 5/57).

English civil servant and member of the seconded British cohort to the 1920 administration, was employed as a Customs and Excise inspector at that time. It is not likely that they would have met in London but Cope was to state in the 1920 Fisher report on the Dublin administration that Mr Duggan and Mr Brennan (who do the work of the finance division) impressed us favourably'.[88] There is perhaps a touch of irony in the less educated Cope being in a position to judge the work of Brennan and G.C. Duggan. Although they were not recommended for promotion, Fisher retained both of them. Brennan had moved from London to a position in the Chief Secretary's Office in Dublin on 1 June 1912.[89] A friend wrote to congratulate him; 'I feel certain that in the New Ireland we are anticipating you will do a man's share of the guiding and directing of her civil service'.[90] Brennan was to excel in his role in the administration both pre and post 1922, combining duty with a non-revolutionary patriotic zeal, as will be shown. Having started but not completed studies for the bar at the Inner Temple in London, Brennan was briefly assigned to the convicts' office in 1913, where much of his worked involved dealing with the suffragettes. This posting was followed in quick succession by appointments as secretary to a Viceregal committee of inquiry into pay and conditions of the police, and an Irish War Savings Committee.[91] Settled in Ireland Brennan married Evelyn Simcox, a university graduate and daughter of another Cork merchant on 25 September 1918. They had two daughters and a son.[92]

Like MacMahon, Brennan had been the subject of Sir John Taylor's anti-Catholic bias. G.C. Duggan wrote that on being appointed superintending clerk in the finance section a position for which Duggan described himself as being 'supremely ignorant', he was however assisted by 'the unselfish help given to me by Joseph Brennan ... who now found himself superseded'.[93] However, Taylor objected to Duggan sharing an office with Brennan, although according to Duggan he was working as his assistant, 'because in his [Taylor's] view Brennan was suspect'.[94] This suspicion was ostensibly based on Taylor's hatred of those he perceived to be Catholic

---

[88] Fisher report (TNA, HO 317/50).
[89] T .K. Whitaker, 'Brennan, Joseph (1887-1976)', *ODNB*.
[90] Ó Broin, *No man's man*, p.8.
[91] Sean Cromien, 'Brennan, Joseph', *DIB*.
[92] Ibid.
[93] Duggan, BMH, WS 1,099.
[94] Ibid.

nationalists. It was to cause Brennan to lose an appointment in 1918, as Edward Shortt's private secretary.[95] It was just one of the disappointments that Brennan faced. He had been consistently disillusioned with Dublin Castle since 1916 and by 1920, he was considering his future, not only in the Castle but the civil service.[96] On the verge of leaving, an unexpected intervention by an old Clongownian contemporary, Patrick McGilligan led to clandestine meetings with Michael Collins providing 'a fulfilling if dangerous' outlet for Brennan's patriotism.[97] Much is made of Alfred Cope's communication and interaction with Michael Collins and others in Sinn Féin. Not highlighted to anywhere near the same extent, are the briefings organised by Brennan for Collins, on the financial aspects of the treaty negotiations in 1921. Operating within the constraints of his position in the British civil service, Brennan nonetheless assisted the Irish treaty delegation in drawing up the financial clauses of the Anglo-Irish treaty. Not only was this adding 'excitement' to Bennan's role but by default cementing his future career.

Brennan's work prior to the foundation of the Free State, unlike that of MacMahon, was recognised by the new government. He was given a free hand by Collins to set up an Irish exchequer based on the British model in 1922. However, like MacMahon he did not receive British honours. As Secretary of the Department of Finance, Brennan became head of the Irish civil service in 1923 and established the office of comptroller and auditor general.[98] Brennan remained in the position of secretary until 1927 when he retired from the civil service. He was appointed chairman of the Currency Commission, 1927-43 and first Governor of the Central Bank in 1943.

Walter Doolin was born on 13 April 1890, in 20 Ely Place, Dublin to architect, Walter Doolin and his wife Marion Doolin, née Creedon.[99] He attended Clongowes Wood College between 1903 and 1907. His two brothers were also at the school, William from 1903 to 1904 and Daniel from 1903 to 1906. Walter's father died in 1902 a year prior to his entry to

---

[95] Ibid.

[96] Cromien, 'Brennan, Joseph', *DIB*.

[97] Whitaker, 'Brennan, Joseph', *ODNB*.

[98] Cromien, 'Brennan', *DIB*.

[99] Walter Doolin, GRO, reg. 9576424, Dublin South City no. 4.

Clongowes.[100] It has been suggested that Walter and his brothers would have been given financial assistance due to the loss of their father.[101] Nonetheless given the middle-class lifestyle the family enjoyed, Doolin like Brennan cannot be considered to have benefitted from upward social mobility. During his time at the school, Doolin was described as 'a brilliant student of Clongowes Wood College'.[102] He was part of a class that were referred to as, 'the nation builders of the future'.[103] Walter took a high place in the intermediate lists in what was considered by many to be a peak period for Clongowes in the examination results.

According to the school yearbook, 'the class in which Doolin found himself was of an exceptionally high standard and Walter was among the best, if not the very best of that group'.[104] He won school prizes and exhibitions for French, German and the Keogh National Irish History prize, examined by Padraig Pearse. Doolin excelled not only academically but also at sport, playing three-quarters in the football team in his final term at the school and was one of the best batsmen on the cricket eleven. He was subsequently 'a prominent member of the Pembroke Cricket Club and of Lansdowne rugby club'.[105] Doolin was awarded first place in French and German graduating with an MA degree from University College Dublin.[106] He subsequently won an appointment to the higher division of the civil service. In 1911, Dublin universities achieved two first class clerkships with the number increasing to five in 1912. This compares with thirty for Cambridge in 1911 and thirty-four in 1912 and fifty-eight for Oxford in 1911, with forty-eight in 1912.[107]

Doolin started his civil service career in the Records Office, Dublin. As previously stated he then took up the position as personal secretary to the Under Secretary, James MacMahon. According to Molly Doolin née MacMahon, whom Doolin married in 1923, Walter was Brennan's

---

[100] 'Doolin, Walter Glynn (1850-1902)' *Dictionary of Irish Architects 1720- 1940,* https://www.dia.ie/architects/view/1575/DOOLIN,+WALTER+GLYNN [accessed 26 May 2019].
[101] Ibid.
[102] *The Clongownian,* June 1940, vo. 3, p.56.
[103] *The Clongownian,* 1907, p.225.
[104] Ibid.
[105] Walter Doolin obituary, *Irish Independent,* 23 June 1939.
[106] Ibid.
[107] *Royal commission on the civil service,* 1912-1914 (TNA, CSC 5/57).

successor in the role.[108] However, any time spent by Brennan in the position would have been brief as Doolin's appointment in the Under Secretary's office was from 1 August 1918, shortly after MacMahon arrived in the Castle.[109] Doolin had a wealth of experience of both MacMahon's work and the general running of the Chief Secretary's office and the broader Dublin Castle administration. Had he not died at the early age of fifty in 1940, which was almost a decade before statements were taken by the Bureau of Military History, he would likely have been, to use the general words of the bureau, 'a valuable witness'. But would he have been prepared to give a statement? Just as MacMahon refused to cooperate, it can be hypothesised so too would Doolin, particularly in relation to his work with MacMahon. A move to the Free State administration would not presumably have removed his obligation of confidentiality to the British civil service.

On the other hand, G.C. Duggan as will be shown, gave a detailed account of his time in the British service particularly with regard to his colleagues. The only statement given by Joseph Brennan for example, was in relation to written questions from the Bureau of Military History concerning the British Oath of Allegiance 1918.[110] The Bureau wrote to Brennan stating that 'the director understands that at that time you were close to the centre of administration and it has occurred to him that you may be in a position to throw some light on this development'.[111] In response Brennan briefly quoted sections two and nine of the Promissory Oaths Act 1868 concerning exemptions from taking the oath and his own experience of this in 1918.[112]

In 1922, after the foundation of the Free State, Doolin continued his civil service career under the new government. Both he and his colleague and friend Joseph Brennan made the transition from the Dublin Castle administration to that of the New Ireland with ease. They were the young successful Irish Catholic middle-class of the Free State. Like Brennan, Doolin transferred to the Department of Finance, firstly as a principal officer and ultimately rising to the position of assistant secretary. According to an obituary, Walter Doolin 'enjoyed the complete trust of ministerial chiefs

---

[108] Molly Doolin notes (NLI, MS 31658 43-49).
[109] Chief Secretary's Office 1918, office keepers records, NAI, CSORP no 20502.
[110] Joseph Brennan, BMH, WS 468.
[111] Ibid, 19 Dec. 1950.
[112] Ibid, 17 Jan. 1951.

under British and Irish rule, from whom he received many personal commendations'.[113] Doolin, who had been perhaps in the shadow of MacMahon and without the pre-1922 profile and associations of Brennan, did not reach the same heights in the new administration. That he did not achieved a higher profile in the Irish administration was of course also influenced by his premature death.

If Joseph Brennan and Walter Doolin epitomised a fully emergent educated, Catholic middle class at the heart of Dublin Castle administration, W.E. Wylie and G.C. Duggan were from a Protestant background that had the advantage of assumed progression from established secondary schools to Trinity College Dublin or other universities denied to Catholic students by the Catholic Church. It was not an accident that the Fisher report noted a 'flexibility' in both Wylie and Duggan.[114] Both of these men attended Church of Ireland schools and were inherently different from their Catholic colleagues. Nonetheless MacMahon and Wylie had a strong bond from the period 1918-20, which continued long after 1922.

William Evelyn Wylie was born in Kenilworth House, Kenilworth Square, Rathmines, Co. Dublin on 6 June 1881, to Robert Beatty Wylie, Presbyterian clergyman and Marion Wylie, formerly Drury.[115] It is uncertain if the family were living in Dublin at the time of Wylie's birth or just there temporarily, as his father's address was given as Eden Vale, Coleraine. There was no 'Wylie' recorded as living in Kenilworth Square in 1881. However, a Mr John Girdwood Drury and his wife lived in number three.[116] This most likely indicates that baby William Evelyn was born in his maternal grandparents' house. Wylie, known as Lyn in school was educated at Coleraine Academical Institution (CAI), locally known as Coleraine Inst. A voluntary grammar school for boys it was founded in 1860 on Castlerock Road as a boarding school, which changed to day-only in 1999. Following his schooling in Coleraine of which there is little record, Wylie attended Trinity College, Dublin, studying law. During this period, he was a distinguished racing cyclist. Wylie was called to the Irish bar in 1905, taking silk as a King's Counsel in 1914. He served as a lieutenant in the Territorial Army, with the Trinity College Officer Training Corps in Dublin. He did

---

[113] *Irish Independent*, 23 June 1939.
[88] Fisher report (TNA HO 317/50).
[115] William Evelyn Wylie, GRO, reg. 10721394, Rathmines, Co. Dublin.
[116] *Thom's Dublin Street Directory,* 1881, p.1571.

not however take part in the defence of the college during the 1916 Dublin rising, being 'far away from Dublin on that fine Easter Monday afternoon'.[117] He was subsequently appointed prosecuting officer at the trial of the leaders of the rising and law adviser to the Irish government from 1919 to 1920.

Although Wylie was not the beneficiary of the additional educational provision after 1878, he was very much influenced by attending an established school and university in Ireland, building a network of contacts, as had MacMahon. His position as law adviser to the Irish government and his acceptance by the Irish and British civil servants and political appointees made him a strong force within Dublin Castle. He worked very much in tandem with the administration until he was appointed a judge of the Supreme Court of Judicature of Ireland in 1920. Prior to his judicial appointment Sturgis remarked, 'W[ylie] very jumpy today because he hasn't heard about his judgeship ... he thinks he may get assassinated on the brink of safety though I don't see why the Shinns should necessarily 'forgive him his sins just because he takes a judgeship as a reward of em'.[118] Sturgis notes a few days later that 'Jonathan wires that he comes tomorrow with Wylie's judgeship in his pocket'.[119] The following day when 'the PM's letter appointing Wylie as a judge of the Supreme Court and commissioner of the Land Commission arrived, they had a celebratory lunch with his uncle, the retiring judge; ' a most splendid looking old fellow'.[120] While he did not to spend much time in Dublin Castle after this, his appointment to the bench did not stop Wylie from giving his views on the 'Irish question'. He took the lead in preparing a declaration, which was delivered to Lord FitzAlan, successor to Lord French, in June 1921.[121] The statement contained the following list of perceived failures in policy implementation:

> The restoration of order in Ireland has utterly failed.
> The Government of Ireland Act has failed in Southern Ireland.
> The hostility between North and South is intensified.
> The Ulster Parliament will find itself unable to cope with the situation even within the borders of the six counties.

---

[117] Ó Broin, *W.E. Wylie and the Irish revolution,* p. 6.
[118] Sturgis diaries, Oct. 1920 (TNA, PRO 30/59/4).
[119] Ibid, 3 Nov. 1920.
[120] Ibid, 4 Nov. 1920.
[121] Edmund Bernard FitzAlan-Howard, 1st Viscount FitzAlan of Derwent, Conservative, a Catholic.

> Murder and outrage had increased fourfold in the past few months.
> Imperial interest and foreign relationships are jeopardised.[122]

Wylie remained a judge of the High Court in the Irish Free State. He served as a judicial commissioner to the Irish Land Commission until his retirement in 1936.[123] According to León Ó Broin, de Valera, with whom Wylie had often disagreed on policy, was to say how much he appreciated his great work for Ireland. Wylie kept up his friendship with James MacMahon, with the ex Under Secretary being the only outsider at a private funeral service for Wylie's wife, Ida. Wylie himself died in 1964, at the age of eighty-three. He was buried with Ida in the non-denominational graveyard beside the gates of their house in Clonskeagh.[124]

While James MacMahon and E.T. Crutchley were conscious of an obligation to keep details of work undertaken with the British administration confidential, the same cannot be said of G.C. Duggan, superintending clerk of the Chief Secretary's Office, 1920. It was a case of some observed confidentiality, some didn't. He gave an extensive statement to the Bureau of Military History, based on the manuscript of his unpublished memoir, *The life of a civil servant*. He also published under the pseudonym Periscope and contributed articles to the *Irish Times* on his time with the Northern Ireland service.[125] It was in a *Periscope* article that Duggan coined the now much used term 'the Junta' to describe the British cohort.[126] Whether his actions in 'telling all', could be considered unprincipled, his writings leave valuable primary source insights into the Castle administration between 1918 and 1922. Like Sturgis and E.T. Crutchley (to a far lesser extent), he left a record that helps define the lives of the personnel of the pre-1922 administration.

The second of four sons, George Chester Duggan, was born on 5 February 1885, in Parsonstown, King's County (Offaly) to George Duggan, a banker and Emily Duggan, née Grant.[127] At the time, Duggan's father was most probably working with the Provincial Bank in Parsonstown. In 1890, Thom's Directory shows George Duggan to be an inspector with the

---

[122] Ó Broin, *W.E. Wylie and the Irish revolution*, p. 124.
[123] Ibid p.140.
[124] Ibid, p.144.
[125] G.C. Duggan, 'Northern Ireland, success or failure', *Irish Times* 19 Apr. 1950.
[126] Hopkinson, *The last days of Dublin Castle; The diaries of Mark Sturgis*, p.150.
[127] George Chester Duggan, GRO, reg. 10579918, Parsonstown, King's County.

Provincial Bank and living at 88 Marlborough Road, Donnybrook. Six years later, his address was given as 54 Morehampton Road, Donnybrook. G.C. Duggan refers in a BMH statement to a property in Greystones as 'a house my father owned to which he and my mother usually went for week-ends and holidays'.[128] This was a lifestyle not dissimilar to that of Geoffrey Whiskard, albeit without the English public school background.[129] Duggan was educated at the High School Dublin, as were his three brothers. Their religion was noted as Church of Ireland. The school register recorded two addresses for the family at firstly 5 College Street Dublin (Provincial Bank of Ireland's Head Office, now the Westin Hotel). Given that Duggan Snr. did not become manager of the head office of the Provincial Bank in College Street until 1908, this address must have been added to the school file after initial registration.[130] The second, Eversley House, Military Road, Killiney, most likely lived in by G.C. Duggan and his wife and family, as noted in Duggan's statement to the BMH, 1954/5.

Enrolled for his first term on 1 September 1896, Duggan left on 30 June 1903.[131] Publication of the school magazine started in 1899 and Duggan's brother G.G., George Grant Duggan, was treasurer for subscriptions until 1904. There are a number of references to Duggan's academic achievements over his years at the school. In terms of sport, Duggan was credited with coming second in the egg and spoon race (100 yards, 26 competed).[132] In 1903, he was mentioned in a football report as 'another hard worker, who would be very good with a little more weight'.[133] However, Duggan does not seem to have been a sportsman of note. The results of the Christmas examinations in 1900 show that Duggan was awarded the French prize in form V.[134] The same year he achieved a total score of 2604 (third in his class), in the intermediate middle grade with seven subjects taken.[135] In 1901, it was noted that Duggan failed English in the intermediate

---

[128] Duggan, BMH, WS 1,099.

[129] Geoffrey Whiskard, a member of the British cohort was educated at St Paul's School, London.

[130] *Thom's Dublin Street Directory*, 1908.

[131] High School Dublin archives [HSD], by email from Alan Phelan, archivist, 06 Feb. 2019.

[132] *The Erasmian*, Sept. 1901, no 10.

[133] Ibid, June 1903, no 17, p.12.

[134] Ibid. Mar. 1900, no 4, p. 96.

[135] Ibid, Sept. 1900, no 6, p.38.

examination senior grade by not sitting the test.[136] He was to go on to take first place in English literature in the Trinity College entrance examinations, and second in French and modern history, gaining an entrance prize.[137] Born seven years after the Intermediate Education Act 1878, Duggan did not receive an education beyond what would have been his 'heritage' without the legislation. Given his background and his father's promotion within the Provincial Bank, it is almost certain that Duggan would have gone to a good Protestant school and on to Trinity regardless.

On the 23 December 1914, Duggan, who had been working in the Chief Secretary's Office in Dublin, returned to his previous posting in the transport department of the Admiralty in London, where he had started his civil service career in 1908.[138] He was to remain there for the duration of the First World War, returning to the Dublin administration four and a half years later. His war years like those of John Anderson were spent in London in an administrative role, although there is no record of whether he wished to enlist. Two of his brothers were killed in action in Gallipoli on the same day, 16 August 1915.[139]

Post war, Duggan was assigned again to the Chief Secretary's Office as superintending clerk in the finance division. On his return, he was to suffer what he described as the worst twelve months of his civil service career working under Sir John Taylor.[140] His description of Taylor and his modus operandi is revealing.[141] He wrote of Taylor a being 'cool, relentless, calculating, a man of narrow ideas, but inflexible in carrying them out … had he been a leader of men, which he was not, he might have been a born general, ruthless in carrying out a plan'.[142] With Taylor having gone back to London just prior to the changes in the administration in 1920, Duggan's work primarily involved analysing the legal effects of the financial clauses of the Government of Ireland Act 1920.[143]

---

[136] Ibid, Sept. 1901, no 10, p.52.
[137] Ibid, Dec.1903, No19.
[138] Pauric J. Dempsey and Shaun Boylan, 'Duggan, G.C. (1885-1969)', *DIB*.
[139] *Erasmian* 2013-14, two poems written by G.C. Duggan in memory of his brothers, HSDA.
[140] Duggan, BMH, WS, 1,099.
[141] Ibid.
[142] Ibid.
[143] Pauric J. Dempsey and Shaun Boylan, 'Duggan, G.C.'.

However, aside from his official role, his character sketches and assessments of the British cohort are unique, particularly his summing up of their 'mission'. He stated 'they carried matters to the appointed end which was to extricate England from Ireland; they did not bring peace to Ireland for their orders were to stop short of complete autonomy, but at any rate, England could wash her hands. This phenomenon of almost autocratic power in the hands of civil servants struck me so forcibly'.[144] After 1922, Duggan left Dublin for the newly formed civil service of Northern Ireland. Sir John Anderson said that 'someone from the senior staff in the Chief Secretary's Office must go to Belfast to help in the establishment of the administration'.[145] Duggan and Brennan both had experience of finance but Brennan wished to stay in Dublin, so Duggan went to the Ministry of Finance in Belfast.[146] Brennan subsequently sought his advice in relation to reform of the public accounting system in the early days of the Free State.[147] Like all of the Irish civil servants, Duggan did not receive any honour in 1923, although he had been created an OBE in 1918, after the war and in 1930 received a CB.

After 1878 with intermediate education providing a new era of education for Irish Catholics some parents still chose to send their children to schools abroad, such as the prominent Bonaparte Wyse family from Waterford. The Bonaparte connection originated with the marriage of Sir Thomas Wyse, politician and educationalist[148] to Princess Letizia Bonaparte, a great-niece of Napoleon Bonaparte.[149] His grandson Andrew Bonaparte Wyse, schools' inspector, civil servant, scholar, and permanent secretary with the Northern Ireland Ministry of Education was a remarkable figure in both education and the civil service. While he was not directly involved with the Dublin Castle civil service in 1920-22, the combination of education and administration in Bonaparte Wyse's career ties in with the overarching theme of this study.

---

[144] Duggan, BMH, WS, 1,099.

[145] Duggan witness statement incorporating unpublished manuscript 'Life of a Civil Servant', BMH, WS 1,099.

[146] Ibid.

[147] Sean Cromien, 'Joseph Brennan', *DIB*.

[148] Thomas Wyse presented a memorial on primary, intermediate and university education to the British Prime Minister, Earl Grey at the end of 1830. While this was to be influential in the setting up of the national school system the following year, there was no provision for intermediate and university levels.

[149] Bridget Hourican, 'Wyse, Andrew Reginald Nicholas Gerald Bonaparte' (1870-1940)', *DIB*.

Two other schools inspectors have been mentioned previously, Joseph MacMahon, brother of the Dublin Castle Under Secretary and James W. Greer, father of intermediate certificate student, Peter Paul Greer. Due to his input to the position, Bonaparte Wyse was to play an influential role in the developing education system in both the north and south of Ireland, beyond that of schools' inspector.

Andrew Reginald Nicholas Gerald Bonaparte Wyse was born on 1 November 1870, in Limerick, the second of four sons of William Charles Bonaparte Wyse, a gentleman of 'Cecil Street at present' and Ellen Linzee Wyse née Prout.[150] With regard to his own schooling, Bonaparte Wyse was not a beneficiary of educational provision in Ireland. He was sent to public school in England, albeit it a Catholic establishment, the Benedictine, Downside School, Bath. Wyse attended the school from May 1880- July 1885, initially in the prep school.[151] His registration details and academic records are unavailable as pre-1920 registers or files are not extant in the Downside archives.[152] Conversely, according to other information provided by the Downside archives 'the most complete and reliable data on pupils at Downside runs from the year 1856 to 1886, aided by a handwritten register containing the addresses, date of entry and date of birth of the majority of students between those years'.[153]

Irish born students at Downside from 1 Jan. to 31 Dec. 1899. The figures show that the numbers peaked in 1870-79 and declined from 1880 following the introduction of the Intermediate Education (Ireland) Act of 1878.[154]

Decade	1850-59	1860-69	1870-79	1880-89	1890-99
Total pupils	152	184	28	251	261
Total Irish	36	65	82	65	61
Total % Irish	24%	35%	36%	26%	23%

---

[150] Andrew Bonaparte Wyse, GRO birth reg: 8257692.
[151] 'Register of students at Downside School,' DSA, C/S2IH.
[152] Ibid.
[153] Downside Abbey Archives [DAA], C/S2IH.
[154] O'Neill, 'Rule Etonia', p.187.

The midsummer prize list in the *Downside Review* of 1883, his third year at the school noted that Andrew Bonaparte Wyse was overall first in his class (Lower Syntax), with first place in classics, mathematics, history, and English, showing early promise of the remarkable scholar and public servant he was to become. A teacher at Downside remarked 'Andrew Wyse, under a shy, cold, and reserved exterior, concealed a sensitive and impassioned heart, and his uncommon abilities and learning at the age of 13 were by no means his only claim to admiration'.[155] Wyse was part of a new era at Downside, which saw 'a period of modernisation in the early 1880s including the introduction of public examinations.[156] According to Ciaran O'Neill, these examinations were qualifying rather than competitive and therefore had 'a decided advantage over the Irish Intermediate examinations, as being less calculated to promote cram'.[157] While this is a valid point, it could be argued that they did not accord with the new era of competitive entry to the civil service and other positions and even encouraged the continuation of patronage. Why Bonaparte Wyse left Downside at fifteen is unknown. According to O'Neill, Downside students studied for their BA and matriculation externally with the University of London, which like the Royal University of Ireland was an examining and degree awarding body only. If Wyse left Downside after matriculation to London University, it was at a relatively young age. He subsequently took an external London University degree in French in 1890 and an MA in classics in 1894; between degrees, he worked as a teacher in a school near Chester.

On 16 September 1896, Wyse married Mariya Dmitryevna, daughter of Count Dmitry de Chiripunov of Oryol.[158] According to an American weekly gossip magazine, 'the wedding was a society event at Moscow'.[159] He was appointed an inspector of schools at the young age of twenty-four.[160] Given that he was effectively out of Ireland from the age of ten years, the possibility that nepotism played a part in his advancement, cannot be discounted. As a member of the Waterford landed gentry and in consideration of his father's work for educational reform it is possible.

---

[155] Augustine Watts, 'My Class at Downside,' *Downside Review,* vol. IX, Mar. 1890, pp. 37-38.
[156] O'Neill, 'Rule Etonia', p.192.
[157] Ibid, p.193.
[158] *Truth,* 7 Jan. 1897.
[159] Ibid.
[160] Bridget Hourican, 'Wyse, Andrew', *DIB*.

However, from that point he excelled in a manner beyond the normal expectations of the role. In 1897, possibly due to the strength of his linguistic ability, he was sent to France and Belgium on a fact-finding mission for the Belmore commission's inquiry into the Irish primary school curriculum.[161] In 1919, in a direct tie-in with the pre 1920 administration, he advised the then Chief Secretary Ian MacPherson on the ill-fated Intermediate Education Bill of that year. Subsequently, Bonaparte Wyse was the only Catholic on the Lynn committee set up in 1921 to draft proposals for education in Northern Ireland. In an effort to placate the hierarchy who had opposed MacPherson's bill, Lord Londonderry appointed Bonaparte Wyse as vice-chairman. This totally overlooked the fact that he was a liberal free thinker and a supporter of non-denominational education.[162] This might be considered to have been at odds with 'placating the hierarchy'.

In 1922, Bonaparte Wyse transferred to the new Ministry for Education in Northern Ireland. However, he never settled in Belfast and commuted each week from his home in Blackrock, Co. Dublin.[163] As permanent secretary to the Ministry of Education from 1927 to 1939, he was the only Catholic to have charge of a civil service department in Stormont'.[164] While he cannot be categorised as educated in Ireland, a product of social mobility or even a member of the Catholic middle class, Bonaparte Wyse reached a unique level of distinction for an Irish Catholic in the Dublin and Northern Ireland administrations. Furthermore, in recognition of his ability as a scholar, he was elected a member of the Royal Irish Academy and awarded a CB in 1939.[165] Not being among the British cohort in Dublin Castle in 1922, his contribution to education was apparently not considered for honours at that time.[166]

Highlighting the faces and personal lives behind a number of senior level civil servants in the Irish cohort, their backgrounds have shown a strong correlation between educational access and the Dublin Castle administration of 1920-1922. Research has indicated that without the benefit of secondary school and university provision, they were unlikely to have been in pivotal

---

[161] Ibid.
[162] Ibid.
[163] Ibid.
[164] Ibid.
[165] Ibid.
[166] Arthur Green, 'Wyse, Andrew Reginald Nicholas Gerald Bonaparte (1870-1940)', *ODNB*.

positions in the civil service, in what was to prove to be the final administration. However, advancement of the Irish personnel could not be said to have benefitted to a marked degree from the expanded secondary provision of the Intermediate Act of 1878. Senior civil servants such as Brennan and Doolin, who came from established merchant and professional Catholic backgrounds were ostensibly privileged and outside the normal. Social position and family tradition saw them enrolled in one of the top Catholic schools in Ireland. Likewise, Duggan and Wylie had a middle class upbringing and attended established Protestant schools. Nonetheless, the competitive spur of the Intermediate examinations, combined with university access, meant they were well prepared for entry to the civil service.

Comparing the civil service careers of Brennan and Doolin with that of James MacMahon, all of whom sat the intermediate examinations, a real difference is highlighted. The disparity is focused on university provision available to Brennan and Doolin and access to expanded first division entry. MacMahon despite his education at a leading Catholic school did not attend university and worked his way up from a second-class clerkship. However, what is also apparent is that none of those profiled could be said to have benefitted from social mobility, with the exception of MacMahon. If his appointment as Under Secretary was pushed by his connections both within the Catholic Church and beyond, MacMahon himself did not seek such advancement and had progressed through the post office ranks to the top position. His immediate subordinates in the Chief Secretary's office in Dublin Castle came from established families; they went to established schools and universities and were part of an Irish establishment that owed little to legislative enactment. While those from established families within the general population were to the fore in intermediate results, there were also some signs of upward mobility. This increased exponentially over a relatively short time from the first examinations following the Intermediate Education (Ireland) Act, 1878.

Indications exist in primary sources that MacMahon played a decisive role in the 1920-22 administration. However, it is difficult to assess the individual contributions of the Irish cohort given the burning of official documents relating to 1922.[167] Brennan's meetings with Michael Collins,

---

[167] As previously referenced, the Sturgis diaries, letters, witness statement etc.

while perhaps assuaging his nationalistic fervour within the bounds of professional constraints were on the face of it, covert. However, like the other members of the cohorts, he would have mainly come under the direction of the joint Under Secretaries, if not the Lord Lieutenant and Chief Secretary.

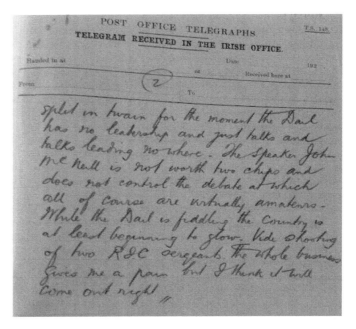

Page two of telegram from Clarke to Street re Dail Treaty discussions. TNA LG/F/20/1/10

Lord FitzAlan leaving Dublin Castle with the Rt. Hon. James MacMahon (not cited in original caption) on 16 January 1922, *The Graphic, 21 Jan. 1922.*

James MacMahon in his later years, with his brother Captain MacMahon 1930s (left, location unknown) and with Mrs MacMahon and their grandaughter at the Great Southern Hotel Parknasilla (1934). Private collection.

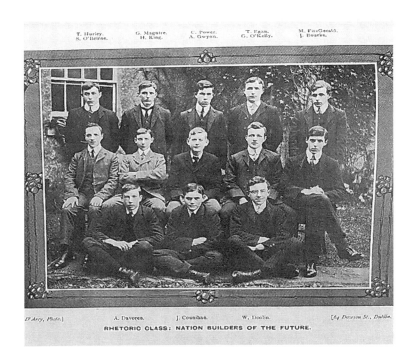

Walter Doolin (front right). *The Clongownian 1905-07.*

Joseph Brennan (middle second from right). *The Clongownian 1905-07.*

197

7

A seconded British Cohort 1920-1922

The future bears down upon each one of us with all the hazards of the unknown ... thus ambitious spirits in a commonwealth, when they transgress their bounds are apt to do more harm than good.

Plutarch's Lives.

The 'Junta' or British cohort arrived in Dublin on 15 July 1920, headed by Sir John Anderson. They were ostensibly emissaries of Empire, assured, and entitled for the most part. They had King and country behind them and came 'to occupy Dublin Castle'.[1] Accompanying Sir John Anderson were Alfred W. Cope, A.P. Waterfield, Mark Sturgis, G.W Whiskard, L.N. Blake Odgers, N.G. Loughnane, T. D. Fairgrieve and E.T. Crutchley. Lionel Curtis and Sir Ernest Clark (later Under Secretary in Belfast) were also part of the group. Their remit from a British perspective was to shore up the existing administration according to the recommendations of the Fisher report.[2]

The British cohort provides an opportunity not only for a general interrogation of educational opportunities and civil service careers but also as a comparative study with the core Irish group. Allied with an assessment of the legislative provision for education in Ireland, Scotland and England, the effects of such enactments on the administration from an Irish perspective have been assessed. The current chapter looks at the faces behind the names of the British cohort under Sir John Anderson, investigating who they were and what they contributed to the final Dublin Castle administration. While the dual or comparative biography of the Rt. Hon. James MacMahon and Sir John Anderson covered MacMahon's time as sole Under Secretary from 1918-1920, it did not encompass the years 1920-22, when as joint holders of the position of Under Secretary both himself and John Anderson brought their own unique talents to the new look administration. Together they headed a team of Irish and British civil servants in Dublin Castle. In this chapter John Anderson's role in the Irish administration is assessed along with the other members of the British cohort, just as MacMahon's 1920-22 tenure was profiled in the previous one.

---

[1] Sturgis diaries, 15 July 1920, PRO 30/59/1.
[2] Fisher report (TNA, HO 317/50).

The overall emphasis was on discovering who exactly the individual members of the British team were and how educational provision and career advancement put them in line for secondment to Ireland in a combined British/Irish administration

According to John McColgan 'the administration of Ireland through the Chief Secretary's office at Dublin Castle ground to a halt in 1920'.[3] He appears to have taken his cue from the Warren Fisher report of 12 May 1920, which he cites extensively. In effect, was the Chief Secretary's office in Dublin Castle actually in urgent need of reform and if so what effect did the British cohort have on it? John McColgan's book published in the early 1980s, ahead of those of O'Halpin and McBride when little had been written on the administration, broke new ground in administrative history. While O'Halpin's focus is ostensibly on the British government in Ireland, he provides a comprehensive overview of the Irish administration as a whole, questioning the inherent weaknesses of Dublin Castle, but firmly shifting blame away from the ranks of the civil service. He concluded that the problems with the Irish administration lay with Westminster and not 'with the embattled officials of Dublin Castle'.[4] In this regard, it could be claimed that the British cohort arrived to fix an historic problem of Whitehall's own making, particularly in relation to the Treasury, which had failed to sufficiently fund the Dublin administration.

Inevitably, studies of the British civil servants will show comparisons with others from within their own group, as well as with Irish senior personnel already working in the Castle administration. The divergence of experience between the members of the British cohort seconded from Whitehall and those from the Dublin base cannot be discounted in the overall piecing together of a profile of the administration. Did differing exposure to education particularly at secondary and university levels shape the administration? Irish personnel at senior level in the 1920-22 administration came from established families and availed of first class Irish education. However, given that superior schools were colloquially described as 'the Eton of Ireland' and many were advertised as providing a sound English education, were the copies up to comparison with the real thing?

---

[3] McColgan, *British policy and the Irish administration, 1920-22*, p.14.
[4] O'Halpin, *The decline of the union*, p.217.

Did the level of educational provision and civil service advancement that most of the English cohort enjoyed and which was much sought after in Ireland, overshadow that of the existing 'Old Castle Gang'? While these questions are pertinent,even among the British cohort, there were educational and social divisions. When W.E. Wylie asked how Anderson, Cope and Sturgis attained such high positions, Sturgis replied, 'Anderson came in through the front door, Cope via the back door and himself through the drawing-room window'.[5] According to Wylie this was understood to mean that Anderson had got in through high marks in the home and Indian civil service examinations, Cope as a second division clerk and Sturgis through his association with the former Prime Minster, H.H. Asquith.[6] Although the analogy is much quoted and seemingly trite in its depiction of the three men, it is of paramount importance in so far as it highlights patronage versus meritocracy and raises interesting questions in relation to Alfred Cope in particular.

Increased educational provision had seen changes to the profile of the senior Irish personnel. That in the main had brought the most noticeable advantages to the younger members of the service particularly in relation to university attendance, which among most of the upper level of British administrative personnel was the norm, but was not readily available to Irish Catholics until the late nineteenth and early twentieth centuries. Historians have carried out very little investigation into key civil service personnel, particularly the British in Dublin Castle in the years 1920-22, beyond their names and positions; that is with the exception of Sir John Anderson and Warren Fisher. Even in relation to these two senior officials, much of the research into biographies by Wheeler-Bennett on Anderson and O'Halpin in respect of Fisher, concentrated on the totality of their careers rather than the two years in Dublin..

Just as Plutarch wrote of ambitious spirits in a commonwealth and the outcomes of their actions, focus is on the collective and individual initiatives and ambitions of the British cohort and their bearing on the events of 1922. However, it should not be overlooked that these were career civil servants assigned to Dublin. Their ambitions may not have been any less, but in some cases even more than if, they were still in Whitehall or the Scottish Office. On a personal level, it has been contended that 'apart from Anderson

---

[5] W.E.Wylie 'memoir' (TNA, PRO 30/89-1).
[6] Ó'Broin, *W.E. Wylie and the Irish revolution*, p.65.

himself, their work in extracting Britain from Ireland was not the launch of a brilliant career for the civil servants and the members of Anderson's 'Junta' faded into obscurity.'[7] However, these postings to Dublin were temporary and for most, not career defining.

In profiling the members of the British cohort, the focus could have been solely on the type of schools they attended and their seniority within the group. However, themes emerged based not only on schooling but on a similarity of background and perceptions of patronage. Such themes indicated for example that John Anderson and T.D. Fairgrieve shared a similar background and attended the same school and university in Edinburgh, although they ultimately had very difference civil service careers. Mark Sturgis and Alfred Cope, albeit from different social strata, may both have benefitted from patronage as opposed to meritocracy. A.P. Waterfield and G.G. Whiskard shared a social and educational background. Basil Clarke and E.T. Crutchley were successful despite a lack of third level education, while Loughnane and Blake Odgers were the least visible and ostensibly least effective members of the cohort.

Two of the British group, Sir John Anderson and Thomas Dalgleish Fairgrieve, attended George Watson's College in Edinburgh. Likewise, although outside the cohort, Chief Secretary Ian MacPherson was also a pupil. Anderson differed from most of the senior level of the British cohort in so far as he did not come from a public school background, but this did not detract from his later position. He was the main figure in the British cohort, not only by virtue of being the joint Under Secretary but also by seniority within Whitehall. Anderson's role in the 1920-22 administration was on the 'political' side, almost on par with that of the Chief Secretary.

Unlike MacMahon, who had his finger on the pulse of the Irish side in Dublin, Anderson spent much of his time in London, meeting with the Prime Minister and with Greenwood among others on the political spectrum, when attending his Whitehall office. The *DNB* claims that he was the 'senior Under Secretary'.[8] This may have been the viewpoint from the British perspective but the reality was both men had different strengths and carried out very different roles. For Anderson the move to Dublin was stepping away from the familiar and came at a time of great personal grief, following as it

---

[7] Maguire, *The civil service and the revolution in Ireland,* p.128.
[8] Peden, 'Anderson, John', *ODNB.*

did his wife's death only a week earlier. He also had to leave his young family who had suffered the loss of their mother. However, it may have provided a welcome distraction, as Warren Fisher had considered when persuading Anderson to take up the position.

Anderson's academic brilliance and rapid advancement through the ranks of the civil service had provided proof not only of his ability but of the effectiveness of competitive entrance to the service as outlined by Northcote and Trevelyan. He commanded respect by his administrative strength. However, Molly Doolin noted that while the British cohort would sing around the piano in the Under Secretary's Lodge, Anderson rarely came. She also said that 'she could never warm to him'.[9] Looking at the photograph of the 'Junta' he is by no means casual or relaxed, sitting almost like a schoolboy in a class photograph. His hands are in fists on his thighs in contrast to the casual pose of the other three in the front row. Nonetheless, not even a year later, G.C. Duggan was to stumble across a very different Anderson. Summoned to London on 17 March 1921 to deliver the Irish estimates, Duggan described a rare visit to the House of Commons. He wrote that 'I was introduced for the first time to Sir Hamar Greenwood, the Chief Secretary in his room at Westminster. To my surprise, Lady Greenwood was also in attendance. While reclining full length on a settee, Sir John Anderson was in a negligent attitude, more concerned I thought with light (for him) conversation with her ladyship than with weightier matters of state'.[10] This incident highlights not only another side of Anderson's personality but a sense of the ease with which, as a Whitehall civil servant he moved between Dublin and London.

In the almost two years he spent in Dublin Castle he was the strong link with Warren Fisher and the main policy makers in the upper echelons of parliament. In terms of his overall impact in Dublin, Duggan was to write of Anderson, 'no civil servant has ever wielded, or is ever likely to wield such power as he did'.[11] Duggan was further to say that from an official perspective he found 'the one and a half years in the chief Secretary's Office under the rule of John Anderson exhilarating'.[12] As head of Treasury (Ireland) with the day-to-day running of the department delegated to

---

[9] Molly Doolin notes (NLI, MS 31658 43-49).
[10] Duggan, BMH, WS.1,099.
[11] Ibid.
[12] Ibid.

Waterfield, Anderson's power was indeed unlimited: 'He had a mind of very great grasp and reach'.[13] Duggan ascribed Anderson's selection for the post in Ireland to his outstanding capabilities, as 'the Government knew that the cumbersome machinery of the Government of Ireland Act would need a deft organiser to set each several part in motion'.[14] Recognised as that organiser, Anderson was given a free hand. With the British government determined to take action on Ireland: 'The Anderson team constituted from the day of their arrival until the creation of the provisional government under the Treaty, a "super bureaucracy" of competent and trustworthy civil servants in Ireland'.[15]

Anderson and Warren Fisher had agreed a new policy for Ireland, an immediate offer of dominion home rule with protection for Ulster and British defence interests allied with unflinching coercion. They brought this to Cabinet in July 1920 where, as noted in a memo by Wylie, disagreement led to support for more coercion as advocated by Tudor and Churchill.[16] While the British cohort was very much part of the administration, according to Maguire 'the role of the Anderson team was clearly political in the sense that they responded to the crumbling of British political supremacy in Ireland'.[17] Wylie communicated with Anderson on 2 August, writing, 'since my return from London I have made enquiries from everyone as to the prospect of a dominion home rule scheme being acceptable to the country. I have not heard one dissenting voice'.[18] Wylie went on to say that unionists, nationalists, and Sinn Féiners all agreed that the scheme would be eagerly accepted but the government 'would not have the good sense or good sportsmanship to put it in force'.[19]

In January 1922 with the withdrawal from Ireland underway, Anderson tendered his resignation as joint Under Secretary to the Lord Lieutenant, FitzAlan, who received it with regret.[20] Throughout his time in Ireland,

---

[13] Ibid.

[14] Duggan, BMH, WS.1,099.

[15] Martin Maguire, 'The civil service, the state and the Irish revolution'
1886-1938' (PhD, University of Dublin, Trinity College, 2005).p.143.

[16] Wylie to Anderson, 30 July 1920 (TNA, Anderson papers, CO/904/188/449).

[17] Maguire, *The civil service and the revolution in Ireland,* p.75.

[18] Ibid, 2 Aug. 1920.

[19] Ibid.

[20] Lord FitzAlan to John Anderson, 31 Jan. 1922 (TNA, papers relating to Ireland, 1917-1923, HO 317/65).

Anderson had continued to be nominally chairman of the Board of Inland Revenue and it was to that post that he returned in January 1922. Two months later aged forty he was appointed permanent Under Secretary at the Home Office, where he remained for ten years.[21] According to G.C. Peden, 'in 1931 Anderson was asked to become governor of Bengal, a province of India troubled by terrorism directed at the British authorities'.[22] During the Second World War Anderson, then an Independent MP became home secretary and minister of home security. It was in this role that perhaps his outstanding claim to fame evolved, that is the creation of the 'Anderson shelters'. Anderson was regarded in Whitehall as 'the greatest administrator of his age, perhaps of any age'.[23] A few days before his death in 1958, the Order of Merit was conferred on him in hospital. He perhaps wryly remarked, 'the civil service will be pleased about this'.[24]

Based on the fact that both John Fairgrieve and David Anderson were stationers and likely to have known to each other in Edinburgh, a check was made with John Anderson's alma mater, George Watson's College, regarding the possible attendance of another member of the British cohort. It was confirmed that Thomas Dalgleish Fairgrieve, born on 3 February 1892,[25] at Park Road, Edinburgh was a pupil at the school. Fairgrieve attended George Watson's from October 1897 to July 1909. In the school register, the family address was given as 1 Savile Terrace, Edinburgh.[26] The Fairgrieves were still living there in 1911 according to the census of that year. On finishing school, Fairgrieve joined McAdams civil service classes.[27] Subsequently like Anderson, he attended Edinburgh University, 1910-14. He was awarded an MA (Hons) in history.

From October 1914, Fairgrieve joined the Royal Fleet Auxiliary as a 2nd Lieutenant and was promoted to major in April 1917. He served in France from 1915-17 and Salonika from 1918-19. His older brother John (twenty-five years old at the time of the 1911 census), was killed in the war.[28] Given

---

[21] Peden, 'Anderson', *ODNB*.

[22] Ibid.

[23] Ibid.

[24] Keith Laybourn, 'Anderson Sir John, Viscount Waverley (1882-158)', *British political leaders: A biographical dictionary* (Oxford, 2001).

[25] Thomas Dalgleish Fairgrieve, NRS, 685/5 155.

[26] School register, 1897, GWCA.

[27] Ibid.

[28] *First World War book*, George Watson's College archives.

an association, perhaps even a friendship between their fathers and being past pupils of the same school, although not of similar age, it is perhaps likely that Anderson played a part in Fairgrieve's secondment to the Dublin administration. However, little is known of Fairgrieve's contribution to the administration during his two years there. In a rare reference to him Maguire writes that as an economic frenzy swept through Whitehall, Fairgrieve had 'airily dismissed a Treasury demand for reductions in staff' ... ordinary conditions applicable to Great Britain are not possible as regards Ireland just yet'.[29]

In matters relating to the Castle British cohort, T.D. Fairgrieve was not described as anything other than 'of the Scottish Office'. His initials gave away nothing about his forenames. Preliminary research failed to shed much light on his origins. However, a search of the National Records of Scotland (NRS) produced two possibilities, both with the name Thomas Darling Fairgrieve, with birth dates of 1884 and 1888. Looking at his photograph among the 'Junta' in Dublin Castle, these dates were while possible, unlikely. Following up with a check of the census they were ruled out, as by 1911 both men were working in manual positions. Another search produced a 'Thomas Dalgleish Fairgrieve', born in 1892, which would have made him twenty-eight in 1920, a seemingly perfect match. The census of 1911 however was somewhat misleading, noting the right family but with a description of Thomas D. Fairgrieve as an art student, which was in fact to prove incorrect. A newspaper photograph of Fairgrieve in the George Watson's archive has a caption stating that Lieut. Thomas D. Fairgrieve, who was wounded in the field, was awarded the Military Cross. His parents' address was given as Cockburn Street. This was in fact the shop address for Fairgrieve's father who by that time was running a post office, perhaps in conjunction with his earlier stationery business.[30]

Fairgrieve with Crutchley and Blake Odgers were the only members of the British cohort known to have been on active service during the First World War. The three of them were also the only ones to receive no recognition for their work in the Dublin administration in the 1923 New Year's Honours list. Alfred Cope, while not mentioned in the 1923 list, had already received a KCB in 1922. After 1922, Fairgrieve returned to Scotland. A minute on housing attributed to T.D. Fairgrieve, Principal is noted in a

---

[29] Maguire, *The civil service and the revolution in Ireland*, p.73.

[30] John Fairgrieve, *Edinburgh, and Leith post office directory*, 1911-12.

history of the Scottish Office but the book contains no further reference to him.[31] On the basis of available evidence it appears that Fairgrieve, while making an impact during the war, was not a prominent member of the seconded British cohort and did not advance to the upper echelons of the civil service. At the time of his death on 23 January 1952, at fifty-nine years of age, Fairgrieve had risen to the position of Assistant Secretary at the Scottish Home Office.

Among the group of senior civil servants seconded to Dublin Castle, a number were educated at English public schools. What is particularly interesting is the fact that although from comfortable and in some cases affluent backgrounds, most of them entered secondary schools on foot of scholarships and likewise went on the gain university exhibitions, primarily to Oxbridge. It was an almost certain progression to university, that saw British candidates for the civil service starting in many cases with first class clerkships, positions which came much later for Irish Catholics. Certain appointments to the British cohort ostensibly show that patronage was still likely to have been a feature of civil service selection in the early part of the twentieth century. This is perhaps evident in the inclusion of Mark Beresford Russell Sturgis. He was related to Fisher by marriage through Fisher's mother, Caroline Russell Fisher. What influence, if any, that had on Sturgis' early civil service advancement is unknown. However, Fisher may have been behind his secondment to Dublin Castle in 1920.

Mark Beresford Russell Sturgis was born into an affluent family on 10 July 1884, at 17 Carlton House Terrace, St James's London.[32] Although his father, Julian Sturgis gave his occupation as 'barrister', he had embarked on a writing career as a novelist, poet, playwright and librettist ten years before Mark's birth. Born in the US, Russell Sturgis took British citizenship in 1877. He attended Eton and Balliol College, Oxford. As an amateur association football player, he was the first non-British player in an FA cup final. Mark followed his father into Eton attending from the Lent Term (Spring) of 1898 to the Lent term of 1903. His younger brothers Gerald Boit Sturgis and Roland Josslyn Russell Sturgis were also pupils, with Gerald being at the school during the same timescale as Mark. In 1898 when Sturgis entered the college there were over 1,000 boys on the register of which 200

[31] Ian Levitt (ed.) *The Scottish office, depression and reconstruction 1919-1959* (Edinburgh, 1992), p.68.

[32] Mark Beresford Russell Sturgis, GRO, Strand, reg. OB 646.

would have been in his year.[33] Unlike his father, Sturgis does not seem to have had a particularly distinguished career at Eton and again unlike his father is not mentioned in the list of notable old boys. There are some references to 'Sturgis' in the *Eton Chronicle* but with the exception of one entry, initials are not given. Therefore, it is not possible to distinguish between Mark and his brother Gerald, although the latter is cited in a section on rowing as a 'cox'.

The *Dictionary of Irish Biography* and the *Oxford Dictionary of National Biography* differ as to whether Mark Sturgis went up to Oxford. However, Oxford's archives show no record of his having attended. The university archivist checked the card register that lists all those who matriculated between 1891 and 1932 but found no reference to Mark Beresford Russell Sturgis (or any other Sturgis with similar forenames). The archivist stated that 'it would therefore appear that he was not a student here'.[34] Whether he attended any other university or went straight into the civil service after leaving Eton is unknown. While the elimination of patronage was the driving force behind the Northcote-Trevelyan report, it was, as mentioned previously strongly resisted by British society and this may have helped Sturgis in his civil service career.

As the National Archives in Kew do not keep records of all civil servants as previously mentioned and details of Sturgis' application and exam results are not available, it is impossible to know what his level of attainment was. He became assistant private secretary to Rt. Hon. H.H. Asquith from 1906-08 and one of his private secretaries when he became prime minister (1908-10). He was appointed special commissioner of income tax in 1910.[35] Was it a coincidence that he was seconded to Dublin Castle from the Board of Inland Revenue, where Fisher started his own career? On the face of it, such advancement seems strange for a young civil servant who had moderate academic success in Eton and did not attend Oxford, or perhaps any other university. Did his connections through not only Fisher, but also his wider family help Sturgis to rapid advancement?

---

[33] Eton College archives, school register 1898, by email from Georgina Robinson, archivist, 04 Oct. 2017.

[34] Oxford University archives, by email from Simon Bailey, archivist, 24 June 2019.

[35] Martin F. Seedorf, 'Sturgis, Sir Mark Beresford Russell Grant (1884-1949), *ODNB*.

While Sturgis made no marked contribution to the 1920-22 administration, he created a valuable historical record for future generations. At the instigation of Fisher, Sturgis kept a diary of the day-to-day activities of the Castle, which provides a rare insight into personalities and matters of political and social importance. While naturally biased towards himself and the British cohort, the diaries surveyed the actions of the administration and the two political appointments, that is, the Lord Lieutenant and Chief Secretary.

Cementing his social position Sturgis married Lady Rachel Montagu-Stuart-Wortley, daughter of the 2nd Earl of Wharncliffe and Ellen Gallwey in 1914. They had three children. While it could be said that the facts speak for themselves, there is no proof that Sturgis did in fact benefit from his societal connections. Nonetheless, his subsequent appointment by Fisher to Dublin Castle cannot be overlooked or deflect accusations of nepotism. Despite such perceived advantages, Sturgis arrived in Dublin as a member of the British cohort with no defined role, although it was mooted that he was to be an Assistant Under Secretary, which did not initially happen. Prior to leaving London, Sturgis was briefed about the Dublin administration or 'the Old Castle Gang'. He wrote in his diary, 'for several days I have been … talking Ireland and trying to learn'.[36]

Although primed for a role in the administration Sturgis, in what was to prove to be his main task, wrote his extensive diaries during his time in the Dublin administration and Fisher had them typed up in the Treasury. Ironically, Fisher was placing a spy in the Castle, within an administration that was considered by Lord French to be 'honeycombed with spies and informers and men who cannot be trusted'.[37] By this of course he meant Catholic nationalists. In essence, Sturgis was spying on British and Irish colleagues alike. While ostensibly driven by a desire on the part of Fisher to avail of frequent information updates on every possible detail of an administration, which he had essentially created, the historiographical value of the diaries is immeasurable.

As for Sturgis, his self-seeking, self-promotional references in the diaries show a dilettante, a man about town enjoying what entertainment Dublin had to offer, from private clubs and dining, to theatre and riding in the Phoenix

---

[36] Sturgis diaries, 14 July 1920, PRO 30/59/1.
[37] French to MacPherson, 11 Dec 1919 (Strath papers, OBL, MS c.490, f. 173).

Park, where he taught John Anderson to ride.[38] Although his charm made him many friends in the Castle and on the Dublin social scene, his feelings on the general population were not always benign. Sturgis' contempt for the Irish at large is apparent in an outrageous outburst: 'I almost begin to believe that those mean, dishonest, insufferably conceited Irishmen are an inferior race'.[39]

Despite the rancour conveyed by such a claim, Sturgis was in essence 'an amiable man and a dashing huntsman, who brought a rare quality of gaiety to the dismal surroundings of the Castle'.[40] The discrepancy between the 'civil service uniform' worn by the group in the photograph inside Dublin Castle in 1920 shown at the start of this chapter and the casually elegant attire favoured by Sturgis is indicative of his flamboyance. As an observer through his diaries his role was remarkable but otherwise is difficult to see what he contributed to the cohort. Sturgis noted that when Hamar Greenwood remarked that Anderson was a real civil servant, Andy Cope asked 'what about Mark?' Greenwood replied, 'oh, he never was one'.[41]

Until he was eventually given the title of Assistant Under Secretary, Sturgis had no official role in the administration: 'French told MacMahon yesterday that he thought he must have a new PS, if only a part-time one. He said he would like to have Sturgis if that were possible and asked if he was "too big".[42] MacMahon told me he said he thought not – that a lesser light would not be sufficiently au fait with events to fulfil his "Ex's" main requirement, which is to be kept posted on what goes forward'.[43] Sturgis was unofficially appointed as a secretary to Lord French, commuting daily between the Castle and the Vice-Regal Lodge. He noted in a diary entry in December 1921: 'I am to be made a full-blown Assistant Under Secretary tomorrow ... before the attacks on Andy make it look as though they had something to do with my appointment to share his job'.[44] The Chief Secretary could be said to have needed an efficient secretary given his

---

[38] Marie Coleman, 'Sturgis, Sir Mark Beresford Russell Grant (1884-1949)', *DIB*.

[39] Sturgis diaries, 3 Sept. 1920, PRO 30/59/2.

[40] Charles Townshend, *The British campaign in Ireland 1919-1921* (Oxford, 1975), p.80.

[41] Sturgis diaries, 6 May 1921 (TNA PRO 30/59/5).

[42] Ibid, 30/59/4, 5 Nov. 1920.

[43] Ibid.

[44] Sturgis diaries, 2 Dec. 1921, PRO 30/59/5, (referencing accusations of spying made against Cope).

correspondence with Lloyd George the following month. Greenwood wrote to the Prime Minister from the Vice Regal Lodge, 'am having a good rest here, Dublin suits me and Lady G. blossoms as the rose here'.[45] In response Lloyd George ends a four page official communication by saying 'I trust you and Lady Greenwood are enjoying your Irish rest cure'.[46]

Sturgis was awarded a KCB in 1923 for 'services to Ireland'. Cope later remarked in a letter to MacMahon in 1922 in relation to the New Year honours list: 'For the life of me, I can't see what Sturgis did either for coercion or peace'.[47] Sturgis left Ireland in 1924, having been Assistant Under Secretary of State for Irish services under the Colonial Office in London since March 1922, effectively succeeding both his former superiors, Sir Hamar Greenwood and Sir John Anderson.[48] He returned to the Treasury and remained a civil servant for many years.

In keeping with his flamboyant persona, on inheriting the Hillersdon Estate in Devon in 1935 from a relative, Johnnie Grant, Sturgis changed his name to Grant-Sturgis.[49] Whether based on deep conviction or not, Sturgis became a member of the Eugenics Society of Great Britain in 1936 but resigned in 1939, after the start of the Second World War. He died in London in 1949.[50]

The status of Alfred 'Andy' Cope, a senior member of the British cohort was in sharp contrast to the social, familial, and educational advantages enjoyed by Mark Sturgis. In comparison to the legal and literary background of Julian Russell Sturgis, Cope's father was a bottle merchant. The family lived in disadvantaged circumstance in a working class environment. Cope was an enigma within the British cohort, uneducated among the highly educated, unsocial among the highly social. For lower middle or working classes of the late nineteenth and early twentieth century England, progression beyond primary school was exceptional.

T.J. McElligott claimed that the inherited notion that secondary education was the exclusive privilege of children of higher social position prevailed in

---

[45] Greenwood to LG, 2 Dec. 1920 (PA, personal/political papers, LG F/19/2/24).

[46] LG to Greenwood, 2 Dec 192 (PA, personal/political papers, LG F/19/2/26).

[47] Cope to MacMahon, 27 Dec. 1922 (NLI., MS 31658).

[48] Martin F. Seedorf, 'Sturgis, Sir Mark, *ODNB*.

[49] Marie Coleman, 'Sturgis, Sir Mark', *DIB*.

[50] *The Times*, 30 Apr. 1949.

England as well as Ireland.[51] The Education Act for England and Wales, 1870 legislated only for elementary provision. Conversely, both the Intermediate Education (Ireland) Act, 1878 and the Education (Scotland) Act 1872, which were ostensibly based on the English legislation, extended the parameters to secondary education. While equating patronage with Sturgis, to suggest the same in relation to Alfred Cope is to consider the matter in a different light, focused on work-based assistance rather than family or social connections.

While it is possible to accept that Mark Sturgis benefitted from patronage, a privileged rise to a senior position within the civil service without the advantage of educational provision, social status, or family connections, as in the case of Alfred Cope is questionable. Given purported links between education and the administration what influences, if any, led to the advancement of Cope who fell outside the sphere of secondary or university level provision. The common denominator in the advancement of Sturgis and Cope could be argued to be Warren Fisher. As head of the civil service and author of the report into the Dublin Castle administration, he was responsible for the secondment of both Sturgis and Cope. Given that is understandable why he would include a family member in the cohort, it is difficult to rationalise Cope's place among the group, especially as referenced by Fisher, as 'the protégé'.[52]

Who was the man who essentially hid behind a mask of secrecy in Dublin Castle: what was his family background, and what experiences led to his appointment to the Irish administration? With there being little evidence of Cope having attended even the early years of secondary education, the emphasis of a biographical study is placed on his background prior to secondment to Dublin Castle and on his perceived contribution to the administration. Questions centre on how Cope's career prior to taking up a role in the Dublin administration in 1920 led to his inclusion in the cohort and involvement in covert operations in Dublin, that were so secret that even the Lord Lieutenant was unaware of them.

Alfred William Cope entered the world in London on 14 January 1877, in his parents' home at 192 Kennington Park Road, Lambeth, London.[53] His father, also named Alfred Cope, was described on the birth certificate as a

---

[51] McElligott, *Secondary education in Ireland,* p.30.
[52] 'Position of English civil servants in Ireland' (TNA, CAB 21/207).
[53] Alfred William Cope, GRO Vol O1D, pg. 485.

cooper or a bottle merchant. His mother's name was given as Margaret Elizabeth Cope, formerly Dallimore.[54] The census for 1881 recorded that Alfred (4) and his family (he had one sister of three years of age), were still living at the above address. They were the only inhabitants of the property, with a fifteen-year old domestic servant.[55] This was also the business address given for 'Alfred Cope, cooper and bottle merchant'.[56] On either side of number 192, were a postal telegraph office and a tobacconist. It is likely that there was a shop or office for businesses on the ground floor of each house, with living accommodation overhead.[57] The property on Kennington Park Road was between Ravensdon Street and Kennington Road.[58] Some years prior to Cope's birth, 'dense building and the carving-up of large houses for multiple occupation caused Kennington to be very seriously over-populated'.[59] According to the same report, this led to an outbreak of diphtheria.

By 1891, the family of then fourteen-year-old Alfred William Cope (clerk), his sister Florence E. (13) and a younger sister Sarah (3) were living with his mother's father, Edward G. Dallimore (90) widower, bootmaker, and employer, at 28 Methley Street, Lambeth.[60] Moving from Kennington Road may have been indicative of financial difficulties or an employment setback for Cope Snr. All brief biographies of Cope, including that of the *ODNB* state that he was the oldest of eleven siblings. This seems unlikely given that the 1881 census records two children, with that of 1891 naming three. With a gap of ten years between the second and third child, it seems unlikely that eight others had died or were living elsewhere on the night of 1891. The subsequent census of 1911 shows no other offspring. Also living in the house in Methley Street were Hugh C. Dallimore (28) Civil Service GPO, Henry C. Dallimore (23) bootmaker, sons of Edward Dallimore and Henry G. White (25) lodger plus three others. Alfred Cope Senior was recorded at this time as being a wine cooper.[61] Methley Street was a mix of

---

[54] Ibid.

[55] England and Wales Census 1881, London, Lambeth, Kennington first, district 5.

[56] *The Commercial Gazette*, 26 Feb. 1889, p.8 of 26.

[57] Lambeth Archives, London Borough of Lambeth, by email from Susan Shanks, archivist, 08 Oct. 2018.

[58] Ibid.

[59] Karl Marx, *Das Kapital* (Berlin, 1867).

[60] England and Wales Census 1891, London, Lambeth, Kennington 1st district 04.

[61] Ibid.

tenements, pickle factories and slaughter houses. Probably its greatest claim to fame was that Charlie Chaplin lived for a time at number thirty-nine.[62]

Cope was baptised in St Philip Church, Kennington Road, which was founded in 1863 and closed in 1973.[63] No extant record of his schooling was found during research. As the census shows, he was working at fourteen, so he could not have gone into full time education beyond primary level. Either St Philip's or St Mark's primary schools, Kennington Road would most likely have been attended by Cope but investigation in the London Metropolitan Archives, failed to show his name on a register. One box contained records that were in such bad condition that it was not open for viewing, preventing conclusive research.[64] This effectively ended any evidence of Cope's primary schooling. However, while he was outside the scope of investigation into educational advancement leading to the Castle administration of 1920-22, he was nonetheless a senior member of the British cohort. As such, he is included in biographical studies in tandem with his colleagues, although with a different focus beyond educational influence, to that of career progression.

While Cope was noted as employed as a clerk in the 1891 census, in that of 1901 he was cited as a civil servant in the Inland Revenue Office, with the family living at 8 Sharsted Street, Kennington. If this appointment were in the civil service like his uncle according to the 1891 census, primary level education would have been sufficient for the entrance examination. His early years of employment would have been on par with cohort member E.T. Crutchley and civil servant and Irish revolutionary, Michael Collins, with whom he was to become familiar in 1920. They were on opposite sides of the 'Irish Question' but seeking a solution to it for very different reasons. Advancement by Cope to second division clerk would have required additional examinations, which may have necessitated further education.

The census of 1911 indicates a certain upward mobility for the Cope family. They were shown to be in possibly better circumstances, living in

---

[62] *London Standard*, 21 July 1909.

[63] Church of England births and baptisms, parish of St Philip, Lambeth, reg.no. 588.

[64] Records of St Mark's School, Kennington, LMA, A/KNS/046.

'Roseneath', 30 Langham Court Drive, Leigh-on-Sea, Essex.[65] For the family, Leigh-on-Sea, a fishing village must have seemed distant from the socially deprived area of Lambeth. At the time of the 1911 census, Alfred Cope is recorded as being 'single, a civil servant and a customs and excise inspector'.[66] The position of inspector has a more official resonance and more in line with the civil service than the description of detective, which was commonly used to describe Cope's early career.

A newspaper report on proceedings relating to the 'Discovery of Saccharin' by Cope and two officers also cited him as an inspector.[67] This case while not related to Cope's time in the Dublin administration, is one of the few indications of his possible early personality and his modus operandi. Cope appeared as a witness involved in the finding of twenty-nine tins of saccharin, each containing five pounds in weight. The trial further included evidence that saccharin had been smuggled into Russia. When Cope testified that the defendant, Hausmann had done his best to mislead him, Hausmann rose and excitedly exclaimed 'he is telling lies'.[68] This in itself is not remarkable, as it is impossible to know if the defendant was telling the truth. However, as an indication of the lengths that Cope might have been prepared to go to get a job done, it is worth noting and does in fact tie in with other instances of potential deception by him.

In 1919, Cope was appointed second secretary at the Ministry of Pensions, a year before his secondment to Dublin Castle. This appears to be a huge leap from customs detective or inspector. As described by Eunan O'Halpin it was 'a remarkable achievement for a man of modest origins and limited education who entered the civil service at the humblest rank'.[69] Can this promotion be ascribed to patronage or can Cope be considered to have worked his way up to a senior position? Was Warren Fisher responsible for his promotion in his capacity as head of the civil service? Without a recorded increase in educational attainment or relevant experience, Cope was 'tasked with bringing order to a department on the verge of collapse'.[70] According

---

[65] England and Wales Census 1911, Essex, Leigh, 04, Newington Folio 22 p.35 and *Kelly's Directory of Essex, Hertfordshire and Middlesex*, Essex only from a collective volume (1914, London).

[66] Ibid.

[67] 'Discovery of Saccharin' *London Standard*, 21 July 1909.

[68] Ibid.

[69] Eunan O'Halpin, 'Cope, Sir Alfred William', *ODNB*.

[70] Ibid.

to the official line, he was successful in doing so, being awarded a CB, Companion of the Order of the Bath, in the New Year honours list in 1920 in respect of his work. However, in a further indication of how he operated, a letter containing a report obtained by Michael Collins and sent to Desmond FitzGerald, painted an entirely different picture, that of a man who was totally out of his depth.[71]

The report by C.E. O'Leary claimed that reforms to the P.I.O. have not yet been put in train due to the fact that, 'Mr Cope is totally unfit for such a task both by his lack of training, capacity and character'.[72] His lack of organisational skills rebounded on colleagues and subordinates. According to the report, one such colleague, 'Shannon, overwhelmed, repeatedly appealed for staff without success'.[73] O'Leary stated that Shannon subsequently committed suicide.[74] Not only was Cope's inability to carry out the work questioned by the writer but his honesty and integrity. C.E. O'Leary spoke of raising the matter of fraud with Cope and being met with the response 'what do I care if the tax payer is being robbed of millions – all we have to do is get the work up to date'.[75] Again according to O'Leary, 'in his capacity of D.G.O he is held in ridicule and contempt throughout the Ministry; it is impossible, should we differ in any way from his preconceived views to enter into any reasonable discussion with him and his dishonesty in argument is notorious'.[76] Is this report to be taken at face value or perhaps to be ascribed to black propaganda?

Cope was the most controversial member of the British cohort of 1920-22. Within the Anderson led group, he was reputedly looked down upon as being 'not of the same class'.[77] From his arrival in the Dublin administration his perceived differences, his personality, and his work methods were subject to keen observation by his colleagues. However, his background was ostensibly to provide a reason for his inclusion within the cohort. Among the

---

[71] Michael Collins to Desmond FitzGerald (NLI, a report on Cope to a Mr G. Chrystal referencing minute of 21/4/20 (re lack of progress on reforms to P.I.O – sent by C.E. O'Leary (P.I.O Regents Park), 28 Sept. 1920, MS 22,766).

[72] Report enclosed with note from Collins to Desmond FitzGerald (NLI, MS 22,766).

[73] Ibid.

[74] Ibid.

[75] Ibid.

[76] Ibid.

[77] Molly Doolin notes (NLI, MS 31658, 43-49).

group, which was mainly made up of civil servants from leading public and independent grammar schools, Cope was conspicuously different from the rest of the bevy. He was not only from a different background but unknown to his colleagues had what was to prove to be a 'secret mission' to contact Irish revolutionaries.

Far from rising above his origins as had John Anderson and James MacMahon before him, lack of education and social stigma ostensibly marred Cope's temperament, and affected those around him. That he was a product of his environment and family circumstances is undoubted. Cope's ostensible lack of secondary education would have been particularly marked among his well-educated colleagues in Dublin Castle, not only on the British side but also among the Irish civil servants. This would most likely have affected his interaction with them and perhaps his ability to perform certain tasks. From the beginning, he appears to have been not only a misfit but a puzzle to the 'Junta'. Most members of the group found initial impressions of Cope hard to overcome. Sturgis wrote that he had given 'Whiskers' the early part of his diary to read and that he made a valid criticism, that nearly all references to Andy (Alfred Cope) although often affectionate, were at the same time critical.[78] This is not surprising given that Sturgis, an Old Etonian, came across in his diaries as a consummate snob. What is notable is reading in his later entries how his acceptance of his colleague grew and he developed an almost affectionate attitude towards him.

Cope had been included by Warren Fisher as part of the investigation into the administration in Dublin Castle in May 1920. He was as stated, also a member of the subsequent British cohort seconded to Dublin Castle, led by John Anderson. According to Eunan O'Halpin, 'his main task was to develop lines of communication to the Irish separatist leadership in order to explore opportunities for a settlement'.[79] What O'Halpin does not stress was the supposition that Lloyd George himself had instructed Cope to make contact with Sinn Féin, a fact unknown to his colleagues at the Castle. This contention is supported, among others by Charles Townshend who was of the opinion that, 'working to secret instructions from Lloyd George, who often disowned his moves in Cabinet, Cope tirelessly struggled to establish common ground for negotiations'.[80] Pauric Dempsey and Richard Hawkins

---

[78] Sturgis diaries, 2 Apr. 1921, PRO 30/59/4.

[79] Eunan O'Halpin, 'Cope, Sir Alfred William', *ODNB*.

[80] Townshend, *British campaign in Ireland,* p.80.

likewise support the theory that Cope was acting on secret instructions from the Prime Minister: 'With Lloyd George's covert encouragement, he sought contact with the Sinn Féin leadership despite an explicit ban by the cabinet, growing distrust by the military and police authorities, and personal danger'.[81] Ronan Fanning contends that following Bloody Sunday the government policy of pushing through the Government of Ireland Bill and establishing a parliament in Belfast was continued but 'henceforth coercion was diluted with the prospect of negotiation; the doves in Dublin Castle, notably Andy Cope, sought not to crush Sinn Fein but to talk to them'.[82]

There appears to be no documentation or correspondence between Lloyd George and Cope to confirm that any arrangement existed with Cope prior to his secondment to Dublin Castle. Perhaps the fact that Cope received a KCB in the 19 October, 1922 Dissolution Honours, which are given at the personal behest of the outgoing prime minister, whereas the other members of the cohort had to wait until the New Year's list of 1923, indicated a connection. Nonetheless, the issue of honours was very much the preserve of Fisher, who undoubtedly influenced the prime minister. Cope told MacMahon that he had great difficulty getting a KCB. 'They wanted me to take a KBE'.[83]

According to George C. Duggan, 'the new Assistant Under Secretary, Mr A.W. Cope was a strange personality. A detective by his training in the customs, he seemed at first sight a curious choice for the post'.[84] He went on to describe Cope as having 'a lean face, a large mouth, a ponderous jaw, hard eyes and capacious brow. At first glance, there seemed something cruel and fierce, until a mischievous smile lit up his face, a ready laugh would ring out and a gleam come across the eyes'.[85] Sir John Lavery in his portrait of Cope, which was included in a collection of thirty-four paintings given to the Hugh Lane Gallery in 1935,[86] captures Duggan's description, in fact it mirrors it. The painting is superb but there is little benign about the face that stares out from the canvas other than the slight hint of a smile as noted by Duggan.

---

[81] Pauric J. Dempsey and Richard Hawkins, 'Cope, Sir Alfred William ('Andy') (1877–1954)', *DIB*.

[82] Fanning, *Fatal path*, p.245.

[83] Cope to Mac Mahon, 27 Dec. 1922 (NLI, MS 31658).

[84] Duggan, BMH, WS 1,099.

[85] Ibid.

[86] Logan Sisley, Acting Head of Collections, Hugh Lane Gallery 21 Oct. 1919, by email.

Duggan also stated that when Cope met views that did not correspond with his own 'his choice of language was something not often heard in the passionless calm of government offices'.[87] Yet those who knew him best say that he craved sympathy and that he felt deeply the isolation in which he lived. Not that he was a total recluse: 'His boyish temper could enter with zest into a set of rackets, or a game of vingt-et-un with high stakes, and he took an immense delight in a stage-like rehearsal of the swearing-in of the new Viceroy, in which as clerk of the council he played a leading role'.[88] W.E. Wylie considered Cope to be 'a grand fellow but completely different from Anderson'.[89] Cope's nervous disposition and depressive moments, were frequently referred to by Mark Sturgis in his diaries.[90] How secure he actually was in his position is open to question. In terms of physical safety, Molly Doolin recalled that when he came to stay in the Under Secretary's Lodge, he carried a gun, but that all the British cohort did.[91]

If the accusations contained in the report by C.E. O'Leary were in fact true, was it considered necessary to cover up his failure by awarding him a CB? Assuming that Lloyd George made a secret request for Cope to contact Sinn Féin leaders, as mentioned previously, then he was being asked to revert to investigative undercover work that carried not only physical danger but was open to suspicion by all sides. Sturgis referred to what he considered strange behaviour by Cope that was not in keeping with his position: He goes 'down the drain' not only for business but for pleasure, spends most of his evenings with Shinns of various sorts and seems to dislike all other society. *They* remember if he seems to forget sometimes, that he is a highly placed British official with much of the dignity of England in his hands and I worry sometimes that his sympathy will encourage them to think they can get through him all they ask.[92] It appears that Cope forged a strong relationship with Michael Collins. This was to the extent that he wrote to Lionel Curtis in relation to attending the funeral, stating that Free State ministers 'know I was on intimate terms with MC'[93]

---

[87] Duggan, BMH, WS 1,099.

[88] Ibid.

[89] O'Broin, *W.E. Wylie and the Irish revolution,* p.66.

[90] Sturgis diaries (TNA, PRO 30/59/1-5).

[91] Molly Doolin notes (NLI, MS 31658 43-49).

[92] Hopkinson, *The last days of Dublin Castle: The diaries of Mark Sturgis,* p.213.

[93] Cope to Curtis, 16 Aug. 1922 (TNA CO 739/6).

The appointment of Cope as Assistant Under Secretary and Clerk of the Privy Council (Ireland) was commensurate with his seniority in Pensions. However, the work took its toll and Cope was frequently depressed and unable to function as noted by Sturgis and confirmed by Cope himself to James MacMahon: 'Without your advice and helpfulness in my too frequent periods of depression and your friendship to me I should have thrown in the sponge in the early days'.[94] Cope had a strong working relationship and friendship with MacMahon, his superior and acknowledged his gratitude on a number of occasions, both to MacMahon himself and to others. According to solicitor James J. O'Connor, James MacMahon's advice saved Cope from being arrested by Gen Macready as a traitor. O'Connor stated that Cope took out a staff car to pick up three members of the Republican Army at the request of Eamon Duggan, solicitor and later politician. The following day Cope told MacMahon that he was very worried as he did not know the officer who drove the car and was afraid he'd report him. MacMahon told him to take out another car and go to see French in the Vice Regal Lodge and explain that he was associating with Duggan for the purpose of getting information. Cope told French that the matter was secret but that he would be sending a report to the prime minister. Macready subsequently informed French that he was going to arrest Cope as a traitor. French told him to do no such thing as Cope had risked his life to get important information and that he had just dictated a letter to the prime minister recommending that a suitable honour be conferred on Cope.[95]

MacMahon's seniority and leading role was definitively stated by Cope in 1922, as previously mentioned.[96] Cope would most certainly have relied on MacMahon's contacts, particularly within Sinn Féin. He would undoubtedly have used MacMahon's own admission during the interviews held for the compilation of the Fisher report, that he had numerous friends who were Sinn Féiners.[97] While he may have drawn on his network to set up meetings for Cope, MacMahon would not consent to meet with Collins. According to Sturgis, MacMahon was asked if would he see Michael Collins and he said 'indeed he would not, that if Michael was arrested when he was

---

[94] Cope to Mac Mahon, 27 Dec. 1922 (NLI, MS 31658).
[95] WS 1,214, statement by James J. O'Connor, solicitor.
[96] Ibid.
[97] Fisher report (TNA HO 317/50.5).

with him both sides would call him a traitor'.[98] This not to say that MacMahon never met Collins. Such an acquaintance was for example highlighted in a newspaper article in 1996. It concerns MacMahon's membership of the Dublin Blue Terrier Club and refers to a breed show on 16 October 1920.[99]

> Secretary Oliver St John Gogarty and Michael Collins were members ... so too was the Under for Ireland, Sir (sic) James MacMahon and a Capt. Wyndham Quinn from the Vice Regal Lodge'.[100] Mr O'Neill, secretary of the Club was adamant 'that Collins, MacMahon and Wyndham Quinn knew who each other were, and out of respect as dogs' men, never let politics interfere with their participation in the club.[101]

A witness statement to the Bureau of Military History gave an insight into the work of MacMahon and Cope, within what MacMahon would most likely have regarded as acceptable parameters. Charles J. MacAuley arranged a meeting with James MacNeill, who had served with the Indian Civil service and was subsequently to become Governor General of the Free State: Shortly before the Truce, at James MacNeill's request, a secret meeting was held in my house, 22 Lower Fitzwilliam Street. To the best of my knowledge, in addition to James MacNeill, Cope and James MacMahon were there ... I could only guess at the subject for discussion, which I took to be some form of secret peace negotiations.[102]

Duggan noted that Cope had an insatiable appetite for taking on multiple tasks. Because of this, 'the work in some directions was bound to suffer'.[103] In this, Duggan had unwittingly affirmed the assessment of Cope by C.E. O'Leary of Pensions, by highlight a lack of organisational skills. According to Duggan 'his driving power was immense, but it dispersed itself in too many directions, and had a further disadvantage in that it weakened the sense of responsibility in subordinates'.[104] In a further reference to Cope's disorganisation, Duggan wrote 'when Alfred Cope went to London on a prolonged visit after the signing of the Treaty, MacMahon descended on his

---

[98] Sturgis diaries, 6 Apr. 1921 (TNA, PRO 30/59/4).
[99] Justin Comiskey, 'An Irishman's Diary' *Irish Times*, 12 Nov. 1996.
[100] Ibid.
[101] Ibid.
[102] Charles J. MacAuley, M.B., F.R.C.S., Joseph Plunkett's medical attendant, 1916, member of Prisoners' Aid Association, BMH, WS.325.
[103] G.C. Duggan, BMH, WS 1,099.
[104] Ibid.

room in the Castle where files undealt with lay in heaps, and in three weeks had swept away the logs that had jammed the flow of administration, for six months'.[105]

Cope was credited as having worked to develop his own contacts with Sinn Féin. This was despite the cabinet decision that no authority existed for any person serving the Irish government to contact Sinn Féin except to convey government policy.[106] Cope however continued in isolation. In one instance he insisted that Anderson sanction the release from Mountjoy prison of Arthur Griffith, Eoin MacNeill, Eamonn Duggan and Michael Staines. Although unaware of what was going on, Anderson agreed to the release of all four convicted Republicans. Anderson then wrote to the Chief Secretary to officially record for the first time the extent that Cope was acting far beyond his remit: 'Cope is working for himself'.[107]

There is in fact no evidence that the purported arrangement between Cope and Lloyd George existed. Cope was ostensibly unknown to the prime minister at the time of the assessment of the Dublin Castle administration. Fisher seemed to confirm this when he wrote in the letter that accompanied the report, 'John Taylor ought not to return to the Castle. To fill the post of Assistant Under Secretary I would suggest the loan of Mr A.W. Cope, now Second Secretary of the Ministry for Pensions'.[108] This communication suggested that any arrangement may have been between Fisher and Cope in an effort to facilitate Lloyd George's objective of contacting the Sinn Féin leaders.

Cope was certainly at ease with groups that would have been perceived as revolutionary or violent, perhaps due to his role as a customs inspector. Fisher may have assumed that this would give him the ability to set up channels of communication with members of Sinn Féin, which Sturgis and the other 'public schoolboys' of the cohort would have been possibly unable to do and unwilling to try. That Cope was prepared to go beyond the limits of his position and in doing so showed extreme hubris, was demonstrated in

---

[105] G.C. Duggan, 'Letter to the editor' *Irish Times*, 5 May 1954, following MacMahon's death.
[106] 'Irish situation committee', 8 July 1920 (TNA, Anderson Papers, CO/904/188/447).
[107] Sir John Anderson to the Chief Secretary of Ireland, 30 June 1921 (PA, Lloyd George papers, LF/19/5/8).
[108] Fisher memorandum (TNA, HO317/60).

the recollections of Patrick Moylett, of Sinn Féin, in relation to a meeting with Cope.[109] He claimed that Cope made it clear that he had superseded both the Lord Lieutenant and the Chief Secretary. According to Moylett Cope also claimed that although he was only an ordinary civil servant, he was there to make peace.[110] While demonstrating the lengths that Cope went to in order to achieve his ends, Moylett's statement could be taken as proof that Cope was acting on his own. It also indicated that the Lord Lieutenant and Chief Secretary were most likely unaware of what was happening.

The honours list of October 1922 was an indication that the British regarded Alfred Cope as a driving force behind the Anglo-Irish Treaty of 1921. On the other hand, he was shortly to come under suspicion of handing over important documentation and providing other assistance to Sinn Féin. The Castle administration that had encouraged accusations of spying against MacMahon by Taylor and French, now saw another civil servant targeted. Cope although not publically named, was to be on the receiving end of a similar accusation on 3 November 1921, based on a matter raised in the House of Commons.[111] According to Sturgis he was 'charged almost by name in the House with stealing the Government cipher book and giving it to the Shinns, and also with having a safe conduct from them during the war'.[112] No action was taken against Cope and he remained in his position in Dublin Castle.

However, the issue of Cope's actions was again referenced on 5 March 1924 in the House of Lords, with Hansard recording it as having been raised by Lord Muskerry. Unlike the news story of 1921, Cope was actually named. His colleague, Thomas Jones defended him, but may have little knowledge of Cope outside the Whitehall box. His defence was not in parliament but in a diary entry. Nonetheless Jones pointed out that 'the trouble about this sort of attack is that some people will say there is no smoke without a fire but no-one who knew and worked with Cope could doubt his essential loyalty throughout all infinitely difficult dangerous negotiations which he put through'.[113] Jones saw Cope as a fellow civil servant in Whitehall, but it is

---

[109] Patrick Moylett, Sinn Féin's interlocutor with Lloyd George, BMH, WS 767.
[110] Ibid.
[111] *Hansard Parliamentary Debates*, HC deb., 3 Nov. 1921, vol. 147 Col 1900.
[112] Hopkinson, *The last days of Dublin Castle: The diaries of Mark Sturgis*, pp. 221-2.
[113] Jones, *Whitehall diary*, p.227.

unlikely that he had any idea of his entanglement with Sinn Féin in Ireland. However, the matter was to come to an end. Following a notice on the order paper by Viscount FitzAlan of Derwent (ex-Lord Lieutenant of Ireland), Lord Muskerry withdrew his statement.[114] While such an outcome would on the face of it exonerate Cope, the parliamentary issue seems to have hinged more on an abuse of privilege due to the matter being raised in the House of Lords. Lord Curzon summed it up by saying: 'What I have to consider, at any rate what I do consider, is the manner in which we discharge our obligation as members of the House of Lords and the manner in which we use, or, as it seems to me in this case abuse the privilege which we enjoy'.[115] The issue was in fact a grey area, with Cope's purported actions being lost in parliamentary procedure.

The main consideration was not whether Cope was culpable, but the fact that it was not regarded as appropriate to criticise civil servants, but rather their superiors were expected to support them. Lord FitzAlan rushed to confirm that, 'I take full responsibility for every action that Sir Alfred Cope took during the time that I was Lord Lieutenant of Ireland'.[116] This is ironic, as neither the Lord Lieutenant nor the Chief Secretary were apparently aware of what the administration was doing in the eighteen months prior to the setting up of the Free State. James MacMahon was to say in 1949, that 'he came in constant contact with the Lord Lieutenant of the time and he said that very often this individual did not know what was happening. In the case of Lord Fitzalan, the last of the Lords Lieutenant, he said this was particularly noticeable'.[117]

While there is no definitive proof of treasonable actions, Sinn Féin may have known what they could get from Cope and how to play him. Nonetheless, no matter how rogue he went it was the relationship that Cope built up with Michael Collins that was credited by some on the British side with being an important contribution to the Truce of 1921 and the subsequent British withdrawal in 1922. If Cope went to the 'dark side' as it were and fed important information to Collins that lead to deaths of British personnel, then far from being a hero, he was a traitor and culpable of treason. It is questionable why he was never accused in civil court, rather than in

---

[114] *Hansard Parliamentary Debates*, HL deb., 19 Mar. 1924 vol. 56 cc914-24.
[115] Ibid.
[116] Ibid.
[117] Col J.V. Joyce meeting with James MacMahon, 18 Oct. 1949, BMH, WS.947.

parliament. That the British government should have worked to cover up such accusations both pre and post 1922 is understandable in political terms. However, as has been shown, Cope was not above using suspect methods. Nonetheless, his involvement with matters of betrayal was unproven and open to suspicions of propaganda.

Cope left the civil service after his time in Ireland having briefly returned to the Ministry of Pensions. He did not go on to achieve the high civil service rank or a political profile that he might have expected. Following his brief return to Pensions, 'he became general secretary of the National Liberal Party but found his hero Lloyd George a difficult employer and in 1924, he resigned'.[118] He then took up commercial appointments in Amalgamated Anthracite Colliers Ltd and W. Abbotts and Sons Ltd.

A request for a statement from the Bureau of Military History was sent to Cope via the Irish Embassy, London in November 1950.[119] His response in early January the following year was an attack on Ireland. He asserted that he regarded 'the period (and that following the Treaty) to be the most discredible of your country's history, it is preferable to forget it; to let sleeping dogs lie'.[120] He quoted commonly held views on the travesty of historical bias and the place of the IRA as 'national heroes' and the British as 'brutal oppressors'.[121] His final words in a rant against self-seeking politicians, focused on love not hate being the only password to earthly happiness and the heavenly kingdom.[122] How much do these sentiments highlight his own regret for his part in Ireland's history? He would perhaps have been better served to have said that his work as a civil servant was confidential and that it could not be discussed, as MacMahon had done.

In a comparison that resonates in many ways with Irish civil servants, Walter Doolin and Joseph Brennan, G.G. Whiskard and A.P. Waterfield came from similar backgrounds and were model civil servants. Although they did not attend the same school they were both educated at public schools; their fathers were upper-middle class professionals and outside the

---

[118] O'Halpin, 'Cope, Sir Alfred William (1877-1954), *ODNB*.

[119] M. McDunphy to John W. Dulanty, Irish Embassy, London, regarding Sir Alfred Cope, 18 Nov. 1950, BMH, WS 469.

[120] Reply from Sir Alfred Cope to Elizabeth Foxe, Private Secretary, Irish Embassy, 3 Jan. 1951, WS. 469.

[121] Ibid.

[122] Ibid.

designation of upwardly mobile, with Ernest Whiskard being a banker and William Waterfield retired, Bengal Civil Service. The Whiskards availed of ease of living, their home being situated near the Beckenham Junction Railway Station, which was opened by the Mid-Kent Railway (MKR) on 1 January 1857.[123] Just as John Anderson's family moved to Eskbank on the outskirts of Edinburgh which was facilitated by the extension of the railway line, so too the Whiskards benefitted from the Victorian suburban growth and substantial housing outside of London. For the Andersons the new address would have seen the family move from the lower middle classes to a more established status, whereas the Whiskards at the time of Geoffrey's birth were positioned firmly in the upper middle class of the professionals. Shortly afterwards, the family moved to Kensington as his father was appointed manager of the Capital and Counties Bank's local branch.[124]

The only son and second of three children Geoffrey Granville Whiskard was born on 19 August 1886, at 3 Hartington Villas, Penge Road, Beckenham, Kent.[125] Coming from an ostensibly middle class background, Whiskard or 'Whiskers' would have had a certain status through his father's position as a bank manager, further enhanced by his own educational opportunities. Whiskard entered St Paul's School in London as an exhibitioner in 1898.[126] However, strangely for a scholar his academic career was according to school records, a series of highs and lows. Despite this, he gained Oxford and Cambridge school certificates in 1902 and again in 1903.[127] As an all-rounder Whiskard actively participated in sport and extra-curricular activities. He was recognised in the *Pauline*, the school magazine for his contribution to House rugby and was a member of the St Paul's 2nd XV winning teams against Merchant Taylor's School and Leys School'.[128] He was involved in the Cadet Corps and was beaten by only one point in the

---

[123] *Morning Post,* 5 Jan 1857.

[124] C.J. Wright 'Whiskard, Sir Geoffrey Granville (1886-1957)', *ODNB*.

[125] Geoffrey Granville Whiskard, GRO, Bromley, vol: 02A p.429. 'Hartington Villas' illegible on birth certificate – confirmed in the Beckenham directory for 1887.

[126] St Paul's School, Kayton Library, register for 1898, 22 Nov. 2018 sent by email by Hilary Cummings, librarian.

[127] Ibid.

[128] *The Pauline,* Dec.1903.

Eastbourne Cadet Trophy in his third year at the school. He was also a member of the team, which won the inter-house competition in 1903.[129]

An active contributor to the Union, Whiskard was commended for an excellent speech in 1903 'clearly thought out and clearly and unfalteringly delivered'.[130] As Treasurer of the Union in 1903, he persuaded his father to present a presidential chair. Although Whiskard lamented the almost empty coffers at the fiftieth anniversary meeting of the Union in the same year, he 'rejoiced over the new furniture'.[131] A beneficiary of what could be said to have been the best of English educational provision, Whiskard was set on the path to potential career success. Following his time in St Paul's he was awarded a scholarship to Wadham College, Oxford in 1904. With continued ambition and application, he graduated with a first in 'Mods' in 1907 and 'Greats' in 1909. Having applied for the civil service Whiskard entered the Home Office in 1911 as a first class clerk according to his file in the British archives.[132] He married Cynthia Salome Caroline Reeves in 1915. They had three children Richard, Mary, and John. On the 30 July 1940, Cynthia died of heart failure brought on by a severe asthma attack whist visiting Sydney. Geoffrey remarried in 1946.[133]

Following his secondment to the Irish administration in 1920, James MacMahon's daughter Molly Doolin had a strong recollection of Whiskard when he arrived in Dublin. 'We did not like Whiskard; he was a funny sort of Englishman, impudent and uppish'.[134] Whether such a comment reflected Doolin's own prejudice is impossible to say, but to an extent it mirrored another assessment. Duggan described him in his statement for the Bureau of Military History, as 'the unemotional pale-faced blue-eyed Englishman whose part it was to bring into the office the scientific outlook of the Home

---

[129] Ibid, July 1903.

[130] *The Pauline,* Dec. 1903.

[131] Ibid.

[132] Geoffrey Whiskard, letter of appointment to first division clerkship, 21 Jan. 1911, (TNA, HO 45/19942).

[133] Whiskard, Sir Geoffrey (Granville), *Who Was Who*, A & C Black, 1920–2015; online edn, Oxford University Press, 2014.

[134] Molly Doolin notes (NLI, MS 31658).

Office on crime.'[135] Conversely, Mark Sturgis, with perhaps the insight of a fellow Englishman notes that 'W[iskard] is a very nice serious fellow who expands under treatment. I like him very much. I am sure he is a very good young man and a pattern civil servant'.[136] Within the cohort, Whiskard's main role was as assistant secretary to the chief secretary for Ireland, Sir Hamar Greenwood (MP for Sunderland). He was in fact, seconded to the Irish administration from the Home Office to co-ordinate civil and military forces. His arrival in Ireland found him thrown in at the deep end with the hunger strike of the Lord Major of Cork and others. According to Sturgis writing in his diary about Whiskard 'these hunger strikers give him a big job but he never seems to get rattled or lose his sense of proportion'.[137]

Whiskard was knighted (Companion of the Order of the Bath) in the 1923 honours list. Although commended by Sturgis who indicated throughout the diaries that he was a visible and hard-working member of the administration, Cope as previously stated wrote to MacMahon that he didn't object to the awards to the members of the cohort but the list if properly labelled should be headed 'honours for failures'.[138] Far from being a failure, Whiskard joined the Colonial Office after leaving Ireland with official consent for the necessary transfer stating 'it will be a very serious loss to the Home Office'. Adding the position of diplomat to his career trajectory Whiskard was subsequently appointed as the First British High Commissioner to Australia (1936-41). He died in 1957.

A.P. Waterfield was not among the 'Junta' photographed at Dublin Castle shortly after their arrival from Whitehall. However, he was to prove one of the most influential of the cohort. Apart from missing the group photograph and being in the main ignored by Sturgis in his diaries, Waterfield was far from being in the background of the British group. He effectively took over the day-to-day Treasury role of John Anderson, as Martin Maguire highlighted: 'Waterfield, as Assistant Under Secretary at Treasury (Ireland), was now head of the Irish civil service answering only to Anderson himself'.[139] Within the administration, Waterfield as the new Treasury

---

[135] Duggan, BMH, WS, 1,099.
[136] Sturgis diaries, 25 July 1920 (TNA, PRO 30/59/1).
[137] Ibid,, 28 Aug. 1920 (TNA, PRO 30/59/1).
[138] Cope to Mac Mahon, 27 Dec. 1922
(NLI, MS 31658).
[139] Maguire, *The civil service and the revolution in Ireland* p.76.

Remembrancer and acting principal assistant-secretary under John Anderson, was a key figure in the Castle. Ronan Fanning emphasises Waterfield's position as head of the Irish civil service under Anderson's direction.[140] This was ignoring the fact that James MacMahon was joint Under Secretary and the role carried the designation of head of the civil service in Ireland.

Alexander Percival Waterfield was born on 15 May 1888, at 9 St Leonard Road, Exeter, two years after Whiskard.[141] His father was named as William Waterfield and his mother, Matilda Rose Waterfield, formerly Herschel.[142] Waterfield had three brothers, two of whom were from his father's previous marriage. He noted on his application form for the civil service that his father was born in the Cloisters, Westminster Abbey.[143] In fact his father's family home was at 6, Dean's Yard, part of the terrace on which Church House was later built in 1896 (rebuilt 1940).[144] Waterfield's first school was that of Mr Frank Townsend, Barnstaple, Devon, later Bexhill-on-Sea, Sussex from September 1896 to July 1901. He then attended St Peter's College, Westminster (otherwise Westminster School) from 1901 to 1907.[145] Not only did Waterfield's three brothers and father also attend the school but his uncles, grandfather, grandmother's brother, his nephew, his niece's husband, cousins and cousin's sons.[146]

Like his father before him, Waterfield was Captain of Westminster. He wrote in 1906 'I shall always look back upon it with pleasure, not unmixed with pride that I have been deemed worthy of holding so high an office as that of Captain of Westminster'.[147] He also succeeded his brother as honorary secretary of the debating society in 1905. Adding sports to his list of achievement, Waterfield played football for the school's second XI. In an obituary in the school magazine, he was described as 'a distinguished

---

[140] Ronan Fanning, *The Irish department of finance, 1922-1958* (Dublin 1978), p.12.

[141] Alexander Percival Waterfield, GRO, Exeter, vol. O5B p.92.

[142] Second wife of William Waterfield.

[143] Waterfield (TNA, CSC 11/260).

[144] Mathew Payne, keeper of muniments, Westminster Abbey, by email 02 July 2018.

[145] 'Record of Old Westminsters', Westminster School archives [WSA], by email from Charlotte Robinson, archivist, 15 Nov. 2017.

[146] *The Elizabethan*, Dec. 1965 [WSA].

[147] *The Captain's Book*, [WSA], p. 182.

member of a distinguished Westminster family'.[148] The records of Old
Westminsters (alumni of Westminster School), show that Alexander
Percival Waterfield entered the school as a King's Scholar on 26 September
1901. He subsequently gained a Mure Scholarship in 1904.[149] Following
Westminster, Waterfield was elected to Christ Church Oxford in 1907. He
was awarded a first Classics (Mods.) in 1909; Hertford Scholar 1909; Craven
Scholar 1909 and first class literae humaniores in 1911.[150] He applied for the
civil service on 18 June the same year and was offered a second-class
clerkship in the Treasury on 3 October 1911.[151] That this was not a first
division position is strange, considering his academic achievements.
However, although his application to the civil service is available in the
British national archives there are no examination results included in his file.

Waterfield was seconded to Dublin Castle in 1920. If the viewpoint that
an administrative apparatus on the verge of collapse was thoroughly
modernised within eighteen months is to be accepted, Waterfield's
achievements in Ireland deserve recognition. While ruthless in the carrying
out of his reforms, he was nonetheless considered by the civil service
associations as 'being an improvement on Headlam'.[152] With an ambitious
zeal, Waterfield embarked on change across the board of all the departments
under the administration. It is probable that he was following a personal
directive from Anderson. Reorganisation was an opportunity to simplify and
reduce the cost of the Irish administrative machine, the same task that
Warren Fisher was pursuing in Whitehall.[153] For example, Waterfield with
blunt incisiveness informed the Intermediate Education Office that their
work was inferior and quasi-routine, suitable for writing assistants rather
than clerical grades, with overly generous salary scales.[154] At one stage,
Waterfield under pressure to employ First World War veterans was willing

---

[148] *The Elizabethan*, Dec. 1965 [WSA].

[149] Ibid.

[150] Record of Old Westminsters,
[WSA].

[151] A.P. Waterfield, civil service letter of appointment to second-class clerkship, 3
Oct. 1911 (TNA, CSC 11/26).

[152] M.J. Gallagher, 'Memoirs of a civil servant 1895-1974' (unpublished, private
collection), p5.

[153] O'Halpin, *Head of the civil service*, pp 46-67.

[154] Waterfield to Butler, 24 Feb. and 23 Mar. 1921 (TNA, Treasury: Dublin Office
and Treasury Remembrancer in Ireland: out-letter books, T158/2).

to force departmental heads to dismiss women in temporary posts and employ ex-servicemen in their positions.[155]

If order and well-run departments contributed to the Irish Free State, then Waterfield more than did his share. He ostensibly left behind a legacy for the new state in terms of a first class civil service machine. However, as well as providing a certain stability for the new government, it has been argued that administrative continuity impeded innovation.[156] On a personal level, far from falling victim to Maguire's contention in relation to future obscurity, Waterfield pursuing an ambitious path that had marked his time in Dublin, went on to become the First Civil Service Commissioner, 1939-51.[157] However, it was due to his contribution to the war effort in the Ministry of Information that his name is perhaps best remembered. This is in relation to a Second World War morale-boosting home publicity poster campaign. Rebecca Lewis writes, 'A. P. Waterfield came up with the slogan, Your Courage, 'as a rallying war-cry that will bring out the best in every one of us and put us in an offensive mood at once'.[158]

In linking Basil Clarke and E.T. Crutchley, the common denominator is the fact that neither of them was university educated. Perhaps their most obvious connections lie in public relations, diaries, and memoirs and the First World War. Crutchley saw active service while Clarke was a colourful war correspondent. Both however had wartime experience in common with L.N. Blake Odgers and T.D. Fairgrieve. Crutchley, like Sturgis was also a diarist who left some insights into the Castle administration. However, these were on a far lesser scale than those written by Sturgis. Basil Clarke's inclusion among the group seconded to Dublin Castle in 1920 was contentious. His role was officially head of publicity. However, Martin Maguire claimed that, 'as a propagandist he has had greater success with later historians than he had with his contemporaries'.[159] Certainly, Clarke's time in Dublin and in particular his response to Bloody Sunday in November

---

[155] Waterfield to Patterson and Waterfield to Cope, 8 Nov. 1921 (TNA, T158/5).

[156] J.J. Lee, *Ireland 1912-1985: Politics and society* (Cambridge 1989) and David Fitzpatrick, *Two Irelands: 1912*-1939 (Oxford, 1998).

[157] *Who Was Who* [accessed online 02 July 2018].

[158] Rebecca, Lewis, 'Keep Calm and Carry on' and other Second World War Posters: British Home Front Propaganda Posters of the Second World War', (PhD, University of Winchester, 2004).

[159] Maguire, *The civil service and the revolution in Ireland*, p.72.

1920 was not without controversy but Clarke was far from being a failure. His journalistic background enabled the establishment of a strong news or propaganda unit, working within set parameters. It has been suggested, that while some of the statements issued by Clarke's office at the twice-daily press briefing at Dublin Castle were incorrect, there is no strong evidence this was done deliberately.[160]

Wilfrid Ewart, novelist and journalist, referred to Mr Basil Clarke on his secondment to Dublin Castle, as 'the mouthpiece of the Irish Government through the sieve of whose intelligence all Irish news and all propaganda passed'.[161] It was during this period that Clarke developed his views on propaganda by news, managing the media through the routine issue of news stories and photographs, all of which had 'the key quality of verisimilitude, the air of truth'.[162] David Miller and William Dinan argue that with its colonial past, Britain was one of the foremost exponents of propaganda and that the government was quick to use this particular skill both during the Great War and afterwards in the battle against the Irish republican movement, counteracting its propaganda machine. They also claim that British intelligence officers pioneered the use of what they called 'black propaganda' in the battle against the Irish republicans during the 1920s.[163]

Thomas Basil Clarke was born on 11 August 1879, at 14 Ashley Road, Altrincham, to James Thomas Clarke, a chemist and druggist and Sarah Clarke, formerly Ely.[164] From 1890 to 1895 Clarke attended the independent Manchester Grammar School, having previously been a pupil at Altrincham Grammar School.[165] After a short career in banking Clarke who had an early interest in a music career, spent most of 1903 travelling, teaching English and playing the piano in an orchestra.[166] In Germany, he wrote a series of articles that brought him to the attention of the *Manchester Guardian*.

---

[160] Alan Clarke. 'The life & times of Sir Basil Clarke – PR pioneer', *Public Relations*, 1969, vol. 22, no. 2, pp. 8–13.

[161] Wilfrid Ewart, *Journey in Ireland 1921* (London, 1922), p.8.

[162] David Miller and William Dinan, *A century of spin: how public relations became the cutting edge of corporate power* (London, 2008).

[163] Ibid.

[164] Thomas Basil Clarke, GRO, Altricham, 08A 169.

[165] Manchester Grammar School archives, by email from Rachel Kneale, archives assistant, 13 Sep. 2019.

[166] Richard, Evans. *From the frontline: The extraordinary life of Sir Basil Clarke* (Gloucestershire, 2013).

Subsequently Clarke reported from Europe during the First World War and on the 1916 Easter Rising in Dublin, for the *Daily Mail*. He was known as 'the Mail man who went to the trenches in a bowler hat and Burberry coat; eccentric, rebellious and breathtakingly brave'.[167]

In 1918, Clarke entered the civil service as Director of Special Intelligence at the Ministry of Reconstruction. He then moved to the Ministry for Health 'becoming established as a civil servant.[168] While the Dublin Castle pressmen reputedly went on to have chequered careers, Basil Clarke's was largely successful. Having returned to the Ministry for Health after the Treaty, he received a knighthood for his services in Ireland in the New Year Honours list in 1923. Clarke was the only member of the cohort to be appointed a baronet at this time, indicating the importance placed on his contribution to the Irish administration. The following year he founded what was considered the first public relations company in Britain, Editorial Services Ltd. Clarke was credited with being the man who invented public relations. According to Michael Barry, he also developed 'the first code of conduct for the public relations industry'.[169]

Although he was a member of the British cohort in Chief Secretary's office, Ernest Tristram Crutchley was very much a blank face in the Dublin administration. There was even a lack of awareness of his correct name. He was cited as G.N. Crutchely in the caption to the photograph of the 'Junta' at Dublin Castle. Sturgis did not mention him; at least not in Hopkinson's edited *Last Days of Dublin Castle* and G.C. Duggan or Martin Maguire did not refer to him. However, while perhaps lacking a very visible or dynamic presence, Crutchley, as will be shown, was an interesting observer within the group. The son of a naval officer, Crutchley was born in 1878.[170] Both he and his brother, Arthur attended Emanuel School, Battersea, south-west London, endowed by Anne Sackville, Lady Dacre in 1594.[171]

---

[167] Richard Evans, 'Mail man who went to the trenches in a bowler hat and Burberry coat', *Daily Mail*, 15 Jan. 2014.

[168] Ibid.

[169] Michael B. Barry 'How the British faked 'battles' during the War of Independence', *Irish Times*, 20 June 2019.

[170] Entry book, 1890, Emanuel School, London.

[171] Jan Broadway, 'Fiennes [née Sackville], Anne, Lady Dacre (d. 1595)', *ODNB*. Lady Dacre made provision for the erection of an alms-house for twenty poor persons, ten of each sex, and a school for twenty poor children in her will of 20 Dec 1594.

The school entry books gave the brothers' address as 124, Tuffnell Park Road, London.[172] As fees were paid for Crutchley from 1890 to 1893, this period is taken by the school archivist to be his years of attendance. Crutchley played on the 'Fives' team and won a number of academic prizes. While there are no records of his yearly academic results, he is noted as passing the Junior Cambridge local examination.[173] This was approximately equivalent to the junior level of the Intermediate examination in Ireland, in terms of age groupings. While benefitting from four years at a good school Crutchley left at the age of fifteen, whether due to family difficulties or other reasons is not known Crutchley's departure from the Emanuel School was confirmed by the school journal. 'A few weeks before the close of the term, the magazine was deprived of its editor, E.T. Crutchley'.[174]

Although like Clarke, he lacked a public school background or a university education, Crutchley likewise defied the stereotypical view of senior-level British civil servants.. In 1893, Crutchley entered the civil service at the lowest level as a boy clerk. He was appointed to the post office, which was a similar start to Michael Collins. Crutchley was rapidly promoted to assistant surveyor, 'upon a special recommendation from the Post-Master General'.[175] Was this another incidence of patronage or a well-earned promotion? During the First World War Crutchley organised the army postal service and was commissioned as a captain in the Royal Engineers. Finishing the war as an acting Lieutenant Colonel, he received an OBE in 1919.[176] Immediately after the war Crutchley served in the Ministry of Transport; then in 1920 he was seconded to Dublin Castle. While Crutchley's Dublin posting does not appear to have contributed to the administration to any marked degree, nonetheless his future in the service defied any assertion that the British civil servants in Ireland did not go on to have brilliant careers. Crutchley rose to become the representative of the UK Government in the Commonwealth of Australia in 1931. He did so pending the appointment of the first High Commissioner who was in fact as stated

---

[172] Emanuel School, London, archives, by email from Tony Jones, archivist, 21 July 2019.

[173] The University of Cambridge local examinations, introduced in 1858, with a junior grade for students under 16 years and senior, under 18 years.

[174] *Emanuel School magazine*, no 1 Easter 1893.

[175] *The London Gazette,* 24 Sept. 1909. p. 7126.

[176] *Who Was Who*, A & C Black, 1920–2016.

earlier in the chapter another member of the cohort, Geoffrey Whiskard. An Adelaide newspaper reported in 1935 that Crutchley was returning to London and would be succeeding Sir Stephen Tallents as public relations officer to the post office.[177]

From his early start as a founding editor of the Emanuel School magazine to this position in public relations, Crutchley had an obvious talent for literary pursuits. Unique among the cohort, with the exception of Sturgis, he describes in autobiographical writings based on his diary, the circumstances that led to his appointment to the Dublin administration. Following the war, Crutchley was attached to the parliamentary branch at the Ministry for Transport. Asked to suggest a response to a difficult and long-winded parliamentary question, which was causing a problem for his colleagues, he impressed with his reply.[178] When it was made known that John Anderson wanted someone adept in the art of replying to parliamentary questions to go to Dublin immediately, Crutchley was proposed for the job. A few weeks later 'he was steaming into Kingstown Harbour to take up the position as a principal officer in the Chief Secretary's office'.[179]

While answering PQs, no matter how well the replies were written, was a routine civil service task and not likely to have contributed much towards the events of 1920-1922, Crutchley did make a unique contribution to the understanding of the make-up of the British cohort in terms of his diary. In what is primarily autobiographical writing on his time in Australia, Crutchley gave a brief description of four of the team or 'the Saxon Invasion, as I heard it called by an Irish civil servant'.[180] Crutchley described 'being in daily touch with a great administrator, John Anderson'; he referred to Andy Cope as 'a big-hearted passionate, reckless reformer and Geoffrey Whiskard is described as 'another fine administrator with a fine knack for getting things done'.[181] Crutchley depicted Mark Sturgis as, 'a kindly, light hearted, but deeply intelligent flâneur'.[182] In one word, he summed up a picture of the almost Parisian colour and gaiety that Sturgis brought to the

---

[177] *The Advertiser* ((Adelaide SA) 15 Aug. 1935 p.8.
[178] Papers of Ernest Tristram Crutchley [microfilm] 1928-1940/Series 1/autobiography.
[179] Ibid.
[180] Ibid.
[181] Ibid.
[182] Ibid.

greyness and routine of Castle life. Crutchley mentioned Loughnane, whom he wrote was from the Ministry for Labour, confusing the issue of Loughnane's Whitehall base. He also referenced Fairgrieve, Clarke and 'young Blake Odgers', but only gave their job titles and which departments they purportedly came from. Unlike Sturgis, he made no mention of the Irish civil servants. In another insight into the lives of the cohort, he stated that the British messed together in a house in the Upper Castle yard with Whiskard as mess president. Creating a distinction between the society entertainment that Anderson, Sturgis and Cope and perhaps Waterfield whom he didn't mention at all would also have been part of, he wrote that the mess group 'played poker every evening when we had finished work which was usually about ten'.[183] As a typical civil servant he did not elaborate further saying, 'over the rest of our life I must draw a veil'.[184]

Crutchley in later years also wrote a history of the UK GPO, which did not mention his work in Ireland. He did say in the *Preface* (1935) that he was returning to the post office after an absence of twenty-one years, confirming that his early civil service posting prior to the First World War was in the postal service. Strangely, given the time he spent there, he made only one reference to Ireland. He may not have known that James MacMahon, his superior in Dublin Castle had started in the GPO in London and was appointed to the top position in the Irish post office prior to taking up his role as Under Secretary. He noted however that the GPO had employed at least two famous men, one being W.W. Jacobs, an English author and the other the Sinn Féin leader, Michael Collins.[185]

Two of the cohort were effectively invisible in the administration. Although they were both university educated, with one attending public school, they appeared to have little prominence in the group. The son of a successful barrister, William Blake Odgers, KC (Recorder of Bristol), Lindsey Noel Blake Odgers was born on 21 December 1892, in Altrincham, Chester.[186] His mother was named as Frances Odgers, née Hudson with no 'Blake'. This could indicate that the surname may not have been Blake Odgers, but rather that 'Blake' was a Christian name that had passed from father to son. Blake Odgers was educated at Rugby School. He was noted in

---

[183] Ibid.
[184] Ibid.
[185] E.T. Crutchley, *GPO* (Cambridge, 1938), p.195.
[186] Lindsey Noel Blake Odgers, GRO, Hampstead, 01A 672.

the school register as entering the school in 1907, leaving in 1911/12. The school magazine for the years Blake Odgers spent in Rugby has according to the archivist, not yet been digitised, so there is no readily available record of his academic or sporting achievements. However, Odgers was subsequently a scholar of St. John's College, Cambridge, gaining a BA in 1914.[187]

As career civil servants the majority of those seconded to the Chief Secretary's Office, Dublin Castle had not seen active service in First World War, either for health reasons or as in the case of John Anderson because of his value to the administration. While no record of his application to the civil service exists in the national archives, there are two files on a Captain Lindsey Blake Odgers M.C., the Duke of Cambridge's Own (Middlesex Regiment) 1914-19. The record shows that: 'He led his company in the attack with great courage and determination … he commanded the front line of the battalion, organized its defence and consolidated the ground'.[188] His bravery resulted the award of a Military Cross. Following the war Odgers joined the civil service in 1919 as an assistant principal in the Home Office. He was seconded to Chief Secretary's Office, Dublin Castle from 1920 until 1922. Research sourced little information in respect of Odgers' time in Dublin. Certainly, there is no indication that he played any major role in the administration. It can perhaps be assumed that he worked in a routine relatively junior capacity. His subsequent career does not show much ambition beyond standard civil service promotion, without remarkable achievement. Following his secondment to Dublin, Odgers returned to the Home Office, where he is recorded as being a principle in 1926; assistant secretary, 1937 and Assistant under secretary of state, Home Office, 1949–54. His recreation was gardening.[189] Perhaps more than any other member of the British cohort, he was not only a lower level member of the administration but was to fade into the reputed obscurity of those seconded to Dublin Castle. Odgers died on 19 Nov. 1979.

According to G.C. Duggan, a member of the British cohort, N.G. Loughnane had Irish antecedents, which were thought likely to make him a

---

[187] School register, 1907, Rugby School archives, by email from Jonathan Smith, archivist, 11 July 2018.
[188] Captain Lindsey Blake Odgers (TNA, WO 339/1009).
[189] *Who Was Who* [accessed online 02 July 2018].

sympathetic press officer.[190] His role in the administration was as Hamar Greenwood's press secretary. What his Irish connections were is unknown. Likewise, what department he was seconded from is also uncertain. While Martin Maguire references him as a Treasury principal, Duggan claimed in his BMH witness statement that he was from the Ministry of Pensions and Sturgis wrote 'Loughnane who used to be '...' summing up the lack of information on his career prior to Dublin Castle. Norman Gerald Loughnane, was the son of an Inland Revenue officer, Denies I. Loughnane. He was born on 4 April 1883 in Lochcarron, Scotland. Although his father's name and occupation are clearly visible on the birth certificate, his mother's details are illegible.[191] No details of his early education were sourced but he subsequently attended London University.[192] Although there was confusion among his colleagues in relation to his earlier civil service background, his record after 1922 is clear. Loughnane became a colonial office representative in the Irish Free State 1923-24. He died in 1954.[193]

Cope claimed that Loughnane had been awarded a CB or CBE in the 1923 New Year's honours list.[194] However, there appears to be no record of his having received either. Cope goes on to claim in relation to those who been honoured, 'they were 'a very motley crowd and all coming out of the Treaty, which (except Loughnane) they did so much to bring about!!'.[195] It is difficult to interpret whether given the exclamation marks he was being sarcastic and felt none of them had done anything except Loughnane, or if he meant that Loughnane did nothing. However, Thomas Jones, English civil servant described Loughnane as Cope's assistant.[196] Therefore, it is likely that Cope knowing his contribution, would most likely have singled Loughnane out as deserving of an honour.

Jones who was in Dublin for Arthur Griffith's funeral, paints an interesting picture of Dublin Castle; 'this is an immense dull barracks, with

---

[190] Duggan, BMH, WS, 1,099.

[191] NRS, ref. 076/20 p.7.

[192] Charles Kevin Matthews, 'The Irish boundary crisis and the reshaping of British politics: 1920- ..*01925*' (PhD, London School of Economics and Political Science, 2000).

[193] Jones, *Whitehall diary*, p.214.

[194] Cope to MacMahon, 27 Dec. 1922 (NLI, MS 31658 43-49).

[195] Ibid.

[196] Thomas Jones, letter to his wife, 17 Aug. 1922, *Whitehall Diary*, p.214.

huge private rooms and no trace of a woman's presence anywhere. Cope and Loughnane are pigging it here, with a Kathleen coming in at 8 am to make their breakfast and beds etc'.[197] Jones also referred to having gone 'with James MacMahon (Rt. Hon. and formerly Under Secretary) to O'Connell's Bridge and watched the procession, much more impressive than the service and *most* representative'.[198]

Biographical studies of the British cohort have shown that a variety of backgrounds, educational provision, and life experiences coalesced into a certain unity, not only among themselves but also of necessity with their Irish colleagues. To a greater extent than the core Irish group, the British cohort came from diverse educational backgrounds. While public school attendance is evident, independent, merchant and grammar school backgrounds were likewise represented. The correlation between education and senior level positions in the civil service is strongly supported by research into the British cohort. With the exceptions of Clarke, Crutchley and Cope, they all attended university. While there is little evidence of patronage, except perhaps in the cases of Sturgis or Cope, an assumption of education by right comes through strongly, with meritocracy and university level education being the accepted avenue into the civil service.

The early career trajectory of even the older members of the cohort, such as John Anderson could be said to prove the rule. Such advancement was contrary to the experience of the Irish Catholic personnel. The colour that Sturgis brought to the British cohort was not a common feature of the group, which overall was marked by seriousness. This is not remarkable given that three of the nine men had been in the First World War and others such as Anderson had contributed to the war effort in demanding roles within the civil service. The cohort as a whole would have been aware that Dublin Castle was a temporary posting. However at a pivotal point for the administration and Irish history, it seemed that Fisher had been determined that the group would be withdrawn.

Given the distribution of honours in 1923, it can be concluded that the British government were confident that the seconded cohort, which despite Fisher's reservations remained in Dublin, had carried out their allotted role within the administration and had contributed to the withdrawal of Britain

---

[197] Ibid.
[198] Ibid.

from Ireland. In saying that, some more than others were actively involved in the process while mostly operating within the bounds of their civil service roles. This chapter stepped outside the structure of the influence of educational provision on the members of the Castle cohorts, to engage by way of contrast and in the interest of parity, with a biographical study of one of the group who appears to have had very little formal education. It is considered valid to have include Alfred Cope in the studies as key a member of the cohort. In doing so, it was necessary to place the focus primarily on his early life and his contribution to the Dublin Castle administration. A picture emerges of a complex man out of his depth in some situations and totally at ease in others, particularly those beyond the normal remit of a civil servant. That he contributed to the Treaty negotiations is generally accepted by contemporaries and historians. How that contribution was made and at what human cost is unknown.

The British 'Junta'. Seated, from left - Geoffrey Whiskard; Alfred W. (Andy) Cope; Sir John Anderson; Mark Sturgis Standing from left - Basil Clarke; 'G.N.'(Errnest Tristram) Crutchley; L.N (Lindsey Noel) Blake-Odgers; Norman (Gerald) Loughnane; 'J.P'.(Thomas Dalgleish) Fairgrieve (source unknown)

Wedding of Mark Beresford Russell Sturgis and Rachel Montagu-Stuart-Wortley, 1914.

Tatler, 15 July 1914.

Alfred William Cope, a controversial member of the British cohort (John Lavery). Reproduction courtesy of collection & image © Hugh Lane Gallery, Dublin

Epilogue

Following the handover of Dublin Castle to Michael Collins on 16 January 1922, the final administration dispersed.

All that remained of the civil service bustle and daily routine, was an echo of voices throughout the offices and living quarters, which had held the administrative workforce that effectively brokered a 'New Ireland'. While the British civil servants in the main returned to their previous postings, Irish personnel came under new directives. The Provisional Government swiftly issued a decree, which restricted the movement of the majority of civil servants without the permission of the government. This resulted in the Civil Service Committee, which had last met on 8 December 1921, adjourning indefinitely on 19 January 1922.[1]

---

[1] Ernest Clarke Papers, D1022/2/18, PRONI, Civil Service Committee meeting minutes, 17 Jan. 1922.

Bibliography

Bibliography

Primary Sources:

Manuscripts:

National Archives of Ireland:

CSO/RP Registered Papers of the Chief Secretary's Office.

CSORP 31765 3/695/13 Report of attack on Lord French, 20 Dec. 1919.

The National Archives (UK):

CSC 11 Civil Service Commission.

CSC 5/57 Royal commission on civil service, 1912-1914.

CSC 11/95 Sir Warren Fisher, recruitment and establishment, individual cases.

CAB 21/207 Position of English Civil Servants in Ireland, 1921.

CO 739/6) Cope to Curtis, 16 Aug. 1922.

CO/904/188/447 Anderson Papers, 'Note by Irish Situation Committee 8 July 1920'.

LG/F/20/1/17 Archbishop Byrne to James MacMahon, 29 Jan. 1922.

LG/F/20/1/17 (b) FitzAlan to Archbishop Byrne, 29 Jan. 1922.

HO 313/50 Cope and Harwood to Fisher, 12-15 May 1920.

HO 45/19942 Appointment of G.G. Whiskard, Home Office, registered papers.

HO 317/50 Warren Fisher report, 12-15 May 1920.

HO 317/65 Lord FitzAlan to John Anderson, 31 Jan. 1922.

HO 317/60 Fisher to Chamberlain, Bonar Law, and Lloyd George, 12 May 1920.

PRO 30/59/1/2/3/4/5 Mark Sturgis Diaries, 5 July 1920-20 Jan. 1922.

T158/2 Waterfield to Butler, Treasury Remembrancer in Ireland, 1 Dec. 1920-31 Mar. 1921.

T158/5 Waterfield to Patterson and Waterfield to Cope, 8 Nov. 1921.

TI/125/92 Irish Question – urgency of treatment 13 & 16 May 1920.

Parliamentary Archives Westminster:

BL102/7/2, Anderson to Bonar Law, 2 Sept. 1920.

BL103/5/2 Long to Law, 1920.

BL103/2/11 French to Law, 18 Apr. 1920.

F/48/6/13 French to Lloyd George May 30, 1918.

F/45/6/6 Edward Shortt to Lloyd George, 4 July 1918.

F/19/5/7 Lloyd George papers, 25 June 1921.

London Metropolitan Archives:

A/KNS/046 Roll, St Mark's School, Kennington.

Military Archives of Ireland:

CD 104/4/1 GPO to J.J. Taylor and J.J.Taylor to GPO, 20 & 22 July 1918.

Witness statements (consulted variously at Cathal Brugha Barracks and online at http//www.bureauofmilitary-history.ie

WS 325, Charles J. MacAuley, M.B., F.R.C.S., Joseph Plunkett's Medical Attendant, 1916, member of Prisoners' Aid Association.

WS 468, Joseph Brennan, letter 17 Jan. 1951.

WS 469, Sir Alfred Cope, correspondence 1950-51.

WS 687, Rt. Rev. Monsignor M. Curran.

WS 731, Mrs. Katherine Barry-Maloney, sister of Kevin Barry.

WS 767, Patrick Moylett, Sinn Féin's interlocutor with Lloyd George.

WS 947, Col Dan Bryan, correspondence 1954.

WS 1,099, Extract from 'Periscope', G.C. Duggan, Blackwood's Magazine, Aug. 1922.

WS 1,214, statement by James J. O'Connor, solicitor.

WS. 1374 Col. J.V. Joyce, telephone conversation with Rt. Hon. James MacMahon, 18 Oct. 1949.

WS 1374, Statement by Col. Dan Bryan, J.V. Joyce interview with James MacMahon, Stephen's Green Club, 18 Oct. 1949.

WS 1374, Sean T. O'Kelly to Col Dan Bryan, 25 Jan. 1949. WS 1716, General Sean MacEoin.

British Postal Museum (formerly British Postal Museum and Archive)**:**
Post offices and agencies abroad, appointment of James MacMahon as chief clerk GPO, Dublin, 20 Sept. 1913.

36/203 Appointment of James MacMahon as secretary, GPO, Dublin.

36/202 James MacMahon's recommendation re additional leave for GPO staff.

University Archives:

Bodleian Library, Oxford.

Edinburgh University Special Collections.

National University of Galway (NUIG).

National University of Ireland (NUI).

Queen's University, Belfast (QUB).

Trinity College Dublin (TCD).

University College Dublin (UCD).

School Archives:

Alexandra College, Dublin:

Archival research relating to Kathleen Morrow, Hannah Moylan, Jeanette, and Florence Conan.

Belvedere College, Dublin:

General intermediate examination queries.

Blackrock College (The French College) Dublin:

Archival research relating to James MacMahon, Joseph MacMahon, Arthur Conan, and Walter Conan.

Castleknock College, Dublin:

General intermediate examination queries.

St Stanislaus College, Tullabeg, (now Clongowes Wood College):

Archival research relating to Peter Paul Greer.

Clongowes Wood College, Kildare:

Archival research relating to Joseph Brennan and Walter Doolin.

Coleraine Academical Institute, (now Coleraine Grammar School, Co. Londonderry):

Archival research relating to William Evelyn Wylie.

Downside School, Bath, Somerset:

Archival research relating to Andrew Bonaparte Wyse.

Dragon School, Oxford:

Archival research relating to Norman Fenwick Warren Fisher.

Emanuel School, London:

Archival research relating to Ernest Tristram Crutchley.

Eton College, Windsor:

Archival research relating to Mark Beresford Russell Sturgis.

Foyle College, Londonderry:

Archival research relating to William Andrew Russell.

George Watson's, Edinburgh:

Archival research relating to John Anderson, John James (Ian) MacPherson and

Thomas Dalgleish Fairgrieve.

Kingussie High School, Kingussie:

Archival research relating to James John (Ian) MacPherson.

Manchester Grammar School, Manchester:

Archival research relating to Thomas Basil Clarke.

North London Collegiate School:

Archival research relating to Agnes and Josephine Conan.

Oscott College, Birmingham:

Archival research relating to T.H. Burke.

Sacred Heart Convent, Dublin:

Archival research relating to Mary MacMahon, her sisters and daughters (Sacred Heart Convent, Armagh and Mary and Marjorie MacMahon ((Sacred Heart Convent, Roscrea).

Sacred Heart College, Limerick (now Crescent College Comprehensive):

Archival research relating to Charles Doyle.

St Patrick's College Armagh/Armagh CBS (St Patrick's Grammar School):

Archival research relating to James MacMahon.

St Malachy's College Belfast:

Archival research relating to James MacMahon.

Rugby School, Rugby:

Archival research relating to Lindsey Noel Blake Odgers.

St Paul's School, London:

Archival research relating to George Granville Whiskard.

Summerhill College, Sligo:

Archival research relating to Sir Antony MacDonnell.

Victoria College, Belfast:

Archival research relating to Alice Mary Baxter and Lucy Moore.

Westminster School, London:

Archival research relating to A.P. Waterfield.

Winchester College, Winchester:

Archival research relating to Norman Fenwick
Warren Fisher.

National Library of Ireland:

Kildare Street Club, List of Members.

MS. C. 490, f.173, French to MacPherson, Dec. 11, 1919.

MS 22,766, Michael Collins to Desmond FitzGerald, 28 Sept. 1920.

MS 22,766, report enclosed with note from Michael Collins to Desmond FitzGerald.

MS 2269 John French Diaries, June 1919-Aug. 1920.

MS 28, 812 (2) Letter from William Lawson Micks to James MacMahon with MacMahon's reply, 21 May 1920.

MS 31,658 43-49, Alfred Cope to James MacMahon, 27 Dec. 1922.

MS 31,658. James Mac Mahon. Documents re career of James MacMahon as Under- Secretary for Ireland.

MS 31,701 Sir John Anderson to James MacMahon 18 Aug. 1920.

MS 35,294/5 Correspondence between Laurence O'Neill, Lord Mayor of Dublin, Ian Macpherson, Chief Secretary and James MacMahon Under Secretary, 25 Mar –Apr. 1919.

MS 42,222/7 Plunkett, Horace Curzon Diaries, 1854-1932.

British Library:

MS. 44291 ff. 93–103, W.E. Gladstone to Lord John Russell, Jan. 1854.

The Bodleian Library Oxford:

MS Eng. Hist. 491 Strathcarron Papers.

MSS. ppc/75, Disraeli to Hicks-Beach, 17 Dec. 1874.

MS Eng. Hist. e. 216 MacDonnell Papers, fo.16^{r-v}. Antony MacDonnell to his wife, 18 Nov. 1902.

TCD Collections:

Dillon papers, MS 6801/167, 'meeting 5 Mar. 1915'.

UCD Collections:

Curran Collection, 'Minutes of the Catholic Graduates & Undergraduates Association'.

Church Records:

Cardinal Tomás Ó'Fiaich Memorial Library and Archive.

Jesuit Archives, Dublin.

Galleries:

National Gallery of Ireland, Dublin.

The Hugh Lane, Dublin.

The National Portrait Gallery, London.

The National Gallery, London.

The National Galleries of Scotland, Edinburgh.

Official Publications:

Ireland:

Intermediate Education (Ireland)Act, 1878, 46 & 47 *Vict. c.* 39

Intermediate Education (Ireland) Act, 1900, Edw. 7c. 49.

Education (Ireland) Bill 1919 (proposed but withdrawn).

Government of Ireland Act 1920, *10 & 11 George 5, ch. 67.*

Scotland:

Education (Scotland) Act, 1872, 35 & 36 Vict. c. 62.

Education Scotland Act 1918, 6 Edw. 7.c. 57.

England:

Elementary Education Act for England and Wales 1870, 33 & 34 Vict. c. 75.

The Education Act 1918, *8 & 9 Geo. V c. 39.*

Public Schools Acts, 1868-73, 31 & 32 Vict. c. 118.

Hansard: House of Commons Debates:

01 Apr. 1870, vol 200 cc 1090-146, W.E. Gladstone, Prime Minister

28 June 1878, vol 241 cc 415-46, Intermediate Education (Ireland).

12 Feb. 1920, Oral Answer to Questions on Ireland: Sir Joseph Byrne's Dismissal.

Hansard: House of Lords Debates:

01 Apr. 1870, vol. 200 cc 1090-146.

21 June 1878, vol 241 cc7-19.

3 Nov. 1921, vol 147 Col 1900.

19 Mar.1924 vol. 56 cc 914-24.

Civil Service Commissions:

Commission on the Civil Service (UK and Ireland) 1912-14.

Civil Service Commission Reports:

Annual reports of the Civil Service Commission Census of Population, 1901, 1911, vol II.

Thirty-fourth report of the Civil service Commissioners, 1890 [c.6142] XXVI.

Royal Commission on Civil Service, 1912-14, second appendix to the fourth report of the commissioners' minutes of evidence, 9 Jan. 1913-20 June 1913.

The Northcote-Trevelyan report on Civil Service Reform submitted to both Houses of Parliament, Feb. 1854, paper 1713.

Education Commissions:

Clarendon Commission on Public Schools, 1861-1864.

Belmore Commission on Irish Primary Schools Curriculum, 1897.

Taunton Commission on Grammar Schools, 1868.

Vice Regal Commission on Intermediate Education (Maloney), 1919.

Education Commission Reports:

Final report of the Dublin commissioners, appointed by the Universities Act [CD. 5877] vol. 21, 1911.

Royal Commission of Inquiry into Primary Education (Ireland) vol. 1, Powis report HC1870 [c.6] XXVIII, 1911.

Report of Her Majesty's Commissioners appointed to inquire into the revenues and management of certain colleges and schools, and the studies pursued and instruction given therein. Presented to both Houses of Parliament by Command of Her Majesty, vol 1, 1864.

Board of Intermediate Education:

Results of Examinations 1879 – 1902 being list of Successful Candidates (Nat. Library). The board published the results up to and including the 1921 examinations, but changes such as candidate names replaced by anonymous numbers were introduced in 1902.

Report of the Intermediate Board for Ireland for 1879 [c.2600], H.C. 1880.

Report of the Intermediate Board for Ireland for 1880 [c.2919], H.C. 1881.

Report of the Intermediate Board for Ireland for 1881 [c.3176], H.C. 1882.

Report of the Intermediate Board for Ireland for the year 1882 [c.3580], H.C. 1883.

Report of the Intermediate Board for Ireland for the year 1883 [c.3990], H.C. 1884.

Report of the Intermediate Board for Ireland for the year 1884 [c.4464], H.C. 1885.

Report of the Intermediate Board for Ireland for the year 1885 [c.4688], H.C. 1886.

Report of the Intermediate Board for Ireland for the year 1886 [c.5032], H.C. 1887.

Report of the Intermediate Board for Ireland for the year 1887 [c.5333], H.C. 1888.

Report of the Intermediate Board for Ireland for the year 1889 [c.6001], H.C. 1890.

Report of the Intermediate Board for Ireland for the year 1890 [c.6324], H.C. 1891.

Report of the Intermediate Board for Ireland for the year 1891 [c.6619], H.C. 1892.

Report of the Intermediate Board for Ireland for the year 1892 [c.7040], H.C. 1893.

Report of the Intermediate Board for Ireland for the year 1893 [c.7403], H.C. 1894.

Report of the Intermediate Board for Ireland for the year 1894 [c.7677], H.C. 1895.

Report of the Intermediate Board for Ireland for the year 1895 [c.8044], H.C. 1896.

Report of the Intermediate Board for Ireland for the year 1896 [c.8405], H.C. 1897.

Report of the Intermediate Board for Ireland for the year 1897 [c.8798], H.C. 1898.

Report of the Intermediate Board for Ireland for the year 1898 [c.9294], H.C. 1899.

Report of the Intermediate Board for Ireland for the year 1899 [cd.172], H.C.1900.

Report of the Intermediate Board for Ireland for the year 1900 [cd.588], H.C. 1901.

Report of the Intermediate Board for Ireland for the year 1901 [cd.1092], H.C.1902.

Report of the Intermediate Board for Ireland for the year 1919, [cd. 904], H.C. 1920.

Censuses:

Census of Ireland 1901 and 1911, National Archives, Dublin.

Census UK 1841-19 – 1911, National Archives, Kew.

Registration of Births, Deaths, and Marriages:
GRO Ireland:

Reg. 11820598, Brennan, Joseph.

Reg. 9576424, Doolin, Walter.

Reg. 10579918, Duggan, George Chester.

Reg. 10721394, Wylie, William Evelyn.

Reg. 8257692, Wyse, Andrew Bonaparte.

PRONI Belfast:

Reg. F 4838 IED, MacMahon, James Stanislaus.

National Records of Scotland:

Reg. 685/5 966, Anderson, John.

Reg. 685/5 155, Fairgrieve, Thomas Dalgleish.

Reg. 076/20, Loughnane, Thomas Gerald.

Reg. 102/21, MacPherson, John James (Ian).

GRO: England:

Reg. O1B 646, Beresford Russell, Mark.

Reg. O1A 672, Blake Odgers, Lindsey Noel.

Reg. 08A 169, Clarke, Thomas Basil.

Reg. vol. O1D, p.485, Cope, Alfred.

Reg. vol. 02A p.207, Fisher, Norman Fenwick Warren.

Reg. vol. 05B, p.92, Waterfield, Alexander Percival.

Reg. vol.02A, p.429, Whiskard, Geoffrey Granville.

Current Regulations Ireland:

General Data Protection Regulations 2016/679, EU.

Printed Primary Sources:

Catholic Headmasters of Ireland: *Memorial to the Board of Intermediate Education, 1879.*

Crutchley, E.T. *GPO* (Cambridge, 1938).

Duggan G.C. 'The last days of Dublin Castle', *Blackwood's Magazine 212:1 282* (Aug. 1922).

Graduates of the Royal University. *The present provision for higher education in Ireland plainly stated,* (London, 1890).

Hennessy, John Pope. *Lord Beaconsfield's Irish policy: two essays on Ireland* (London, 1885).

Hennessy, Peter. Founder's Day address, Hawarden Castle 8 July 1999, paper 03/49, cited in 'Whither the civil service', House of Commons Library.

Jones, Thomas. *Whitehall Diary* (Oxford, 1971).

Leebody J.R. 'The Irish universities question': by an Irish graduate', *Fraser's Magazine, vol. 5*, (1872).

Marx, Karl. *Das Kapital*. (Berlin, 1867).

Mitchell, Arthur and Ó'Snodaigh, Pádraig (eds.) *Irish political documents 1916-1949* (Dublin, 1985).

Peter, R.M. *The Origins and development of football in Ireland*, being a reprint of Irish football annual of 1880.

'Records of the central association of the graduates of the Royal University, UCD roll book 1886-1889'.

Remonstrance of the headmasters of Ireland against the financial changes made by the Board of Intermediate Education in their rules for 1882 (Dublin 1882). *Royal University Calendars, 1898-1908. Fourth report of the Royal University of Ireland*, (Dublin, 1886).

Strong, John. *A history of secondary education in Scotland* (Oxford, 1909).

Walsh, W.J. 'Statement of the chief grievances of Irish Catholics, in the matter of education, primary, Intermediate and university', *The Irish ecclesiastical record: a monthly journal under episcopal sanction*, Ser. 3, Vol. XI, (Sept. 1890), pp. 859-863.

Wilson, Trevor (ed.) *The political diaries of C.P.Scott 1911-1928* (London, 1970).

Memoirs:

Bridges, Edward Ettingdean. 'John Anderson, Viscount Waverley, 1882-1958,

Biographical memoirs of the fellows of the Royal Society, vol. 4, (1958).

Gallagher, M.J. *Memoirs of a civil servant 1895-1974* (private collection).

Headlam, M.F. *Irish reminiscences* (London, 1947).

Microfilm:

Crutchley, Ernest Tristram. Papers [microfilm] 1928-1940/Series 1/autobiography.

Newspapers:

Anglo Celt.

Belfast Morning News.

Belfast News Letter

Daily Mail.

Dublin Evening Mail.

Freeman's Journal.

Irish Times.

Irish Weekly Times.

Irish Independent.

London Gazette.

New Zealand Tablet.

Sinn Fein Weekly.

The Advertiser.

The Leader.

The Limerick Chronicle.

The London Gazette.

The Graphic.

The London Standard.

The Morning Post.

The Tablet.

Magazines:

Blackwood's Magazine.

Tatler.

Truth.

School Publications:

The Alexandran (Alexandra College, Dublin).

Blackrock College Yearbook.

The Clongownian (Clongowes Wood College).

Downside Review (Downside School)..

Emanuel Magazine (Emanuel School).

The Elizabethan (Westminster School).

Limerick Jesuit Centenary Record, 1859-1959.

The Meteor (Rugby School).

NLCS School Magazines, 1879-1882 (North London Collegiate School).

The Pauline Magazine (St. Paul's School).

The Watsonian (George Watson's College).

Wesley College Quarterly (Wesley College, Dublin).

Sacred Heart Circular.

The Spectrum, (Eton College, Eton/Windsor)

Conference Papers:

Ainsworth, John. 'British Security in Ireland, 1920-1921: A desperate attempt by the Crown to maintain Anglo-Irish unity by force', *11th Irish-Australian Conference*, Perth Western Australia.

On-line Resources:

http://www.ancestry.com/search/places/europe/ireland/

https://books.google.com/ngrams/

http://www.census.nationalarchives.ie/

https://heartheboatsing.com/2016/04/24/a-shadow-of-cloud-on-the-stream/

https://www.corkpastandpresent.ie/mapsimages/corkphotographs/

https://www.dia.ie/architects/view/1575/DOOLIN,+WALTER+GLYNN

https://www.gwc.org.uk/our-school/our-heritage/school-history/

https://www.libraryireland.com/UlsterDirectory1910/Armagh.php

https://www.midlothian.gov.uk/

https://www.militaryarchives.ie/collections/online-collections/bureau-of-military-history-1913-1921

http://rbai.org.uk/

www.cracroftspeerage.co.uk

www.digital.nls.uk/exams/browse/archive/129996597?mode=transcription

www.findmypast.ie/

www.limerickcity.ie/media/Media,9269,en.pdf

www.libraryireland.com/UlsterDirectory1910/Armagh

Secondary Sources:

Books:

Anderson, Robert, Freeman, Mark and Paterson, Lindsay (eds.), *The Edinburgh history of education in Scotland* (Edinburgh, 2015).

Arnold, Mathew. R.H. Super (ed.). *Schools and universities on the continent* (Michigan, 1990).

Atkinson, Norman. *Irish education: a history of educational institutions* (Dublin, 1969).

Baguley, Margaret (ed.). *World War 1 and the question of Ulster: the correspondence of Lilian and Wilfrid Spender* (Dublin, 2009).

Barrington, T.J. *The Irish administrative system* (Dublin, 1980).

Bassett, George Henry. *The book of County Armagh* (Dublin, 1888).

Battersby, William John. *History of the Institute of the Brothers of the Christian Schools in the nineteenth century* (London, 1963).

Bourdieu, Pierre. *The logic of practice* (Cambridge, 1990).

Bourne, J.M. *Patronage and society in nineteenth century England* (London, 1986).

Breathnach, Eileen. 'Women in higher education in Ireland' in *Women's history reader,* Alan Hayes and Diana Urqhart (eds.) (London, 2001).

Brown, W.J. *The civil service clerical association, its achievements, and its plans for the future* (London, 1925).

Bullock, Alan. *Hitler and Stalin, Parallel Lives* (London, 1991).

Calder, Angus. *The people's war* (London, 1971).

Campbell, Fergus. *The Irish establishment 1879-1914* (Oxford, 2009).

Coldrey, Barry M. *Faith, and fatherland: The Christian Brothers and the development of Irish nationalism 1838-1921* (Dublin, 1988).

Coogan, Tim Pat. *The man who made Ireland: the life and death of Michael Collins* (1993).

Cook, Chris, Jones, Philip, Sinclair, Josephine, Weeks, Jeffrey. *Sources in British history* vols 1-6 (London, 1975).

Coolahan, John. *Irish education, history, and structure* (Dublin, 1981).

Coolahan, John & O'Donovan, Patrick F.A. *History of Ireland's school inspectorate, 1831-2008* (Dublin 2009).

Comerford, R.V. *Inventing the nation: Ireland* (London, 2003).

Corcoran, Timothy Joseph. *The Clongowes Record 1814-1932* (Dublin, 1932).

Curran, Joseph M. *The birth of the Irish Free State* (Alabama, 1980).

Douglas, David Charles and Handcock, W.D. (eds.), *English historical documents* 1833-1914, 'Ireland and Irish affairs, 1833-1914' (London, 1977).

Dowling, P.J. *A history of Irish education: a study in conflicting loyalties* (Cork, 1971).

Dunne, Tom, Coolahan, John, Manning, Maurice, Ó Tuathaigh, Gearóid (eds.). *The National University of Ireland, 1908-2008: centenary essays* (Dublin, 2008).

Dwyer, T. Ryle. *The Squad: and the intelligence operations of Michael Collins* (Cork, 2005).

Elliot, Marianne. *The Catholics of Ulster: a history* (London, 2000).

Evans, Richard. *From the frontline: the extraordinary life of Sir Basil Clarke* (Gloucestershire, 2013).

Fanning, Ronan. *Fatal path: British government and Irish revolution 1910-1922* (London, 2013);

_____ *The Irish department of finance, 1922-1958* (Dublin, 1978).

Farmar, Tony. *Privileged lives: a social history of the Irish middle class 1882-1989* (Dublin, 2012).

Farragher, Sean. *Blackrock College 1860-1995* (Dublin, 1995).

Farren, Sean. *The politics of Irish education 1920-65* ((Belfast, 1995).

Ferguson, Stephen. *The GPO, 200 years of history* (Cork, 2014).

FitzAlan Howard, Alathea. *The Windsor diaries 1940-45* (London, 2020).

Fitzpatrick, David. *Politics and Irish life 1913-1921: Provincial experience of war and revolution* (Dublin, 1977);

_____ *The two Irelands, 1912-1939* (Oxford, 1998).

Foster, Gavin M. *The Irish civil war and society: politics, class, and conflict* (London, 2015).

Foster, R.F. *Vivid faces* (New York, 2015): *Modern Ireland 1600 -1972* (London, 1988).

Gray, Peter and Perdue, Olwen (eds.). *The Irish lord lieutenancy c.1541-1922* (Dublin, 2012).

Handcock, W.D. (ed.). 'Ireland and Irish affairs, 1833-1914', *English historical documents* (London, 1977).

Harte, N.B. and North, John. *The world of University College, London, 1828-1990,* (London, 1991).

Hatfield, Mary. *Growing up in nineteenth century Ireland: a cultural history of middle-class childhood and gender* (Oxford, 2019).

Healy, T.M. *Letters and leaders of my day* (London, 1928).

Hittle, J.B.E. *Michael Collins and the Anglo-Irish war* (Washington, 2011).

Hopkinson, Michael *Irish war of independence: the definitive account of the Anglo Irish War* (Dublin, 2002).

_____ (ed.).*The last days of Dublin Castle: the diaries of Mark Sturgis* (Dublin, 1999).

Horowitz Murray, Janet, Stark Myra (eds.). *The Englishwoman's review of social and industrial questions: 1883* (Oxford, 2017).

Howe, Stephen. *Ireland and empire* (Oxford, 2000).

Hutchinson, John. *The dynamics of cultural nationalism: The Gaelic revival and the creation of the Irish nation state* (London, 1987).

Jackson, Alvin, *Judging Redmond & Carson: comparative Irish lives* (Dublin. 2018).

Jeffery, Keith. *The GPO and the Easter Rising* (Dublin, 2006).

Keenan, Desmond. *Ireland within the union 1800-1921* (Philadelphia, 2008).

Kennedy, Conan. *Grandfather's house* (Mayo, 2008).

Keogh, Dermot. *The Vatican, the bishops, and Irish politics 1919-39* (Cambridge, 1986).

Laffan, Michael. *The resurrection of Ireland: the Sinn Féin party 1916-1923* (Cambridge, 1999).

Larkin, Emmet J. *The historical dimensions of Irish Catholicism* (Dublin 1997).

Lavery, John. *The life of a painter* (London, 1940).

Lawlor, Sheila. *Britain and Ireland 1914-1923* (Dublin, 1983).

Laybourn, Keith. *British political leaders: a biographical dictionary* (Oxford, 2001).

Lee, J.J. *Ireland 1912-1985: politics and society* (Cambridge 1989).

Lee, Joseph. *The modernisation of Irish society 1848-1918* (Dublin, 1973).

Levitt, Ian (ed.) *The Scottish office, depression and reconstruction 1919-1959* (Edinburgh, 1992).

Mackay, James. *Michael Collins: a life* (Edinburgh, 1996).

McBride, Lawrence W. *The greening of Dublin Castle: the transformation of bureaucratic and judicial personnel in Ireland 1892-1922* (Washington, 1991).

McCartney, Donal. *UCD: A national idea: The history of University College Dublin* (Dublin, 1999).

McColgan, John. *British policy and the Irish administration 1920-22* (London, 1983).

McDowell, R.B. *The Irish administration 1801-1914* (London, 1964).

McElligott T.J. *Secondary education in Ireland 1870-1921* (Dublin, 1981).

McKinney, Stephen J. and McCluskey, Raymond (eds.). *A history of Catholic education and schooling in Scotland: new perspectives* (London, 2019).

McMahon, Paul. *British spies and Irish rebels: British intelligence in Ireland, Part I* (Suffolk, 2008). Mansergh, Nicholas. *Nationalism and independence* (Cork, 1997).

Maguire, Martin. *The civil service and the revolution in Ireland 1912-1938: shaking the blood-stained hand of Mr Collins* (Manchester, 2008).

Murphy, Brian P. *Patrick Pearse and the lost republican ideal* (Dublin, 1991).

_____ *The origins and British propaganda in Ireland and its significance today* (Cork, 2006).

Murphy, James H. *Nos Autem: Castleknock College and its contribution* (Dublin, 1996).

Neligan, David. *The spy in the castle* (London, 1968).

Newman, Kate. *Dictionary of Ulster Biography* (Belfast, 1993).

O'Broin, León. *The Chief Secretary, Augustine Burrell in Ireland* (London, 1969): *W.E. Wylie, the Irish revolution 1916-1921*, (Dublin 1989).

O'Halpin, Eunan. *The decline of the union: British government in Ireland 1892-1920* (Dublin, 1987):

____ *Head of the civil service, a study of Sir Warren Fisher* (London, 1989).

O'Neill, Ciaran, *Catholics of consequence* (Oxford, 2014).

Pašeta, Senia. *Before the revolution: nationalism, social change, and Ireland's Catholic elite, 1879-1922* (Cork, 1999).

Privilege, John. *Michael Logue and the Catholic church in Ireland, 1879-1925* (Manchester, 2009).

Rafter, Kevin (ed.) *Irish journalism before independence* (Manchester, 2011).

Raftery, Deirdre and Fischer, Karin (eds.). *Educating Ireland: schooling and social change 1700-2000* (Dublin, 2014).

Raftery, Deirdre, and Parkes, Susan M. *Female education in Ireland 1700-1900: Minerva or Madonna* (Dublin, 2007).

Ruane, Joseph and Todd, Jennifer. 'The role of the middle classes in twentieth-century Ireland' in Biagini, E. and Daly, M. (eds.) *The Cambridge Social History of Modern Ireland* (Cambridge, 2017).

Scotland, James. *A history of Scottish education* (London, 1969).

Searle, G. R. *A new England? Peace and war 1886-1918* (Oxford, 2005).

Shrosbree, Colin. *Public school and private education: The Clarendon commission 1861-1864 and the Public Schools Acts* (Manchester, 1988).Titley, E. Brian. *Church, state, and the control of schooling in Ireland 1900-1944* (Dublin, 1983).

Townshend, Charles. *British campaign in Ireland, 1919-1921: The development of political and military policies* (Oxford, 1975).

Truscot, Bruce. *Red brick university* (London, 1951).

Wheeler-Bennett, John W. *John Anderson, Viscount Waverley* (London, 1962).

Wilkinson, Rupert. *The prefects: British leadership and the public school tradition* (London, 1964).

Winter, Ormonde de L'Épée. *Winter's tale* (London, 1955).

Book Reviews:

Atkinson, Norman. Review of T.J. McElligott, *Education in Ireland* (Dublin, 1966) in *Comparative Education Review* 11, no. 3, Oct. 1967, pp. 390-391.

Canning, Paul M. Review of Eunan O'Halpin, *The decline of the union: British government in Ireland 1892-1920* (Dublin, 1987) in *The American Historical Review,* vol. 94, issue 3, June 1989, pp. 779-780.

Coleman, Marie. Review of Martin Maguire, *The civil service and the revolution in Ireland, 1912-38: shaking the blood-stained hand of Mr Collins* (Manchester, 2008) in *Irish Historical Studies*, vol. 36, no. 144, Nov. 2009, pp. 664-666.

Flanagan, Kieran. Review of Lawrence W. McBride, *The greening of Dublin Castle: The transformation of bureaucratic and judicial personnel in Ireland, 1892–1922* (Washington, 1991) in *Irish Historical Studies*, Vol. 29, Issue 113, May 1994, pp. 131-133.

Knirck, Jason. Review of Fergus Campbell, *The Irish establishment, 1879–1914* (Oxford, 2009) T*he American Historical Review*, vol. 115, Issue 2, Apr. 2010, pp. 611-612.

Lowe, W.J. Review of Fergus Campbell, *The Irish establishment, 1879-1914* (Oxford, 2009) *Journal of British Studies*, vol. 49, No. 3, July, 2010, pp. 717-719.

McConnel, James. Review of Fergus Campbell, *The Irish establishment* (Oxford, 2009) by Fergus Campbell, Irish Historical Studies, vol 37, issue 145, May 2010, pp. 156-157.

Journals/Reviews:

Berry, Edmund G. 'The De Liberis Educandis of Pseudo-Plutarch', *Harvard Studies in Classical Philology,* vol. 63, (1958), pp. 387-399.

Bullough, Venn and Bonnie. 'Homosexuality in nineteenth century English public schools', *International Review of Modern Sociology*, vol 9, (1979), pp. 261-269.

Byrne, Peter C.M. 'The Irish Education Act, 1878: before and after', *The Irish Ecclesiastical Record*, vol. V, (Jan, Feb. 1915), pp. 16-27 and 126-144.

Daly, Mary E. 'The formation of an Irish nationalist elite? Recruitment to the Irish civil service in the decades prior to independence 1870-1920', *Paedegogia, Historica* vol. 30:1, (1994), pp. 281-301.

Drake, Frederick and Soderlund, Richard. 'In memoriam: Lawrence W. McBride (1945-2004), *Perspectives on history, American Historical Association*, vol. 42:8, (2004).

Ellis, Heather. 'Efficiency and counter-revolution: connecting university and civil service reform in the 1850s', *History of Education*, vol. 42, no. 1, (2013), pp. 23-44.

Fahy, Tony. 'State, family and compulsory schooling in Ireland', *The Economic and Social Review*, vol. 23, (1992), pp. 369-395.

Greenaway, John. 'Celebrating Northcote–Trevelyan: dispelling the myths', *Public Policy and Administration,* vol. 19, no.1, (2004), pp. 1-14.

Harford, Judith. 'An Experiment in the Development of Social Networks for Women: Women's Colleges in Ireland in the Nineteenth Century', *Paedagogica Historica*, 43:3, (2007), pp. 365-381.

Hatfield, Mary and O'Neill, Ciaran. 'Education and empowerment: cosmopolitan education and Irish women in the early nineteenth century' *Gender & History*, vol.30, no.1, (2018), pp. 93-109.

Healy, John. 'University education in Ireland', *Dublin Review*, vol. xxiii, (1890), p. 26.

Hughes, Edward. 'Sir Charles Trevelyan and Civil Service Reform, 1853–5', *The English Historical Review* vol. 64, no. 250 (1949) p.72.

Lucey, John. 'Hannah Moylan (1867-1902): 'Educationist who was first woman Bachelor of Science in Ireland', *Irish Journal of Education,* vol. 41, (2016), pp. 61-77.

Middleton, Nigel. 'The Education Act of 1870 as the start of the modern concept of the Child', *British Journal of Educational Studies,* vol. 18, no. 2, (1970), pp. 166-179.

Moody, T.W. 'The Irish university question of the nineteenth century', *History,* vol. 43 no. 148, (1958), pp. 90-109.

Murphy, Richard. 'Walter Long and 'the making of the Government of Ireland Act', 1919-20', *Irish Historical Studies*, vol. 25, no. 97, (1986), pp. 82-96.

O'Connor, Anne V. 'Influences affecting girls' secondary education in Ireland', *Archivium Hibernicum,* vol. 41, (1986), 83-98.

O'Donovan, Patrick F. 'Ireland's national school system in the time of the Great Famine: an overview', *History of Education*, (2021), https://doi.org/10.1080/0046760X.2021.1906455 [accessed 29 Jan. 2021].

O'Halpin, Eunan. Warren Fisher and the coalition, 1919-1922' *The Historical Journal*, vol. 24, (I98I), pp. 907-927.

Raftery, Deirdre, Harford, Judith and Susan M. Parkes. 'Mapping the terrain of female education in Ireland, 1830-1910'. *Gender and Education*, vol. 22 no. 5, (2010), pp. 561-578.

Warren, Allen. 'Disraeli, the conservatives and the government of Ireland: Part 1, 1837-1868', *Parliamentary History,* vol 18, (1999), pp. 45-64.

Biographies:

***Dictionary of Irish Biography*:**

Andrews, Helen. 'Ball, Thomas John (1815-1898)'.

Coleman, Marie. 'Sturgis, Sir Mark Beresford Russell Grant-Sturgis (1884-1949)'.

Cromien, Sean. 'Brennan, Joseph (1887-1976)'.

Dempsey, Pauric J. and Boylan, Shaun. 'Duggan G.C. (1885-1969)'.

Dempsey, Pauric J. and Hawkins, Richard. 'Cope, Sir Alfred William 'Andy' (1877-1954)'.

Geoghegan, Patrick M. 'MacPherson, (James) Ian (1880-1937)'; 'O'Hagan, Thomas (1812-85), Lord Chancellor of Ireland, and 1st Baron O'Hagan'; 'Morris, Sir Michael (1826-1901) 1st Baron Morris and Killanin'.

Gow, Roderick. 'Salmon, George (1819-1904)'.

Hawkins, Richard. 'Cairns, Hugh McCalmont (1819–85), 1st Earl Cairns'.

Hourican, Bridget. 'Wyse, Andrew Reginald Nicholas Gerald Bonaparte (1870-1940)'.

Leaney, Enda and Byrne, Patricia M. 'Maunder, Annie Scott Dill Russell (1868–1947)'.

Maume, Patrick. 'MacMahon, James (1865-1954)'.

_____ 'Anderson, John (1882-1958), 1ˢᵗ Viscount Waverley', *DIB*.

_____ 'French, Sir John Denton Pinkstone (1852–1925)'.

Osborough, W.N. 'Palles, Christopher 1831-1920'.

Quinn, James. 'Burke, Thomas Henry (1829–82)'.

Oxford Dictionary of National Biography:

Broadway, Jan. 'Fiennes, [née Sackville], Anne, Lady Dacre (d. 1595).

Dudley Edwards, Owen. 'Doyle, Sir Arthur Ignatius Conan (1859-1930)'.

Fry, Fisher, 'Sir Norman Fenwick Warren (1879-1948)'.O'Halpin, Eunan. 'Cope, Sir Alfred William (1877-1954)'.

Paz, D. G. 'Wyse, Thomas. (1791–1862)'.

Peden, G.C. 'Anderson, John, first Viscount Waverley (1882-1958),

Seedorf, Martin F. 'Sturgis, Sir Mark Beresford Russell Grant (1884-1949),

Whitaker, T.K. 'Brennan, Joseph (1887-1976)'.

Wright, C.J. 'Whiskard, Sir Geoffrey Granville (1886-1957)'.

Unpublished Theses:

Clarke, Mary. 'The origins and impact of the Northcote-Trevelyan report on civil service reform in Britain', (PhD, Queen's University, Belfast, 2010).

Flanagan, Kieran. 'The rise and fall of the Celtic ineligibles: competitive examinations for the Irish and Indian civil services in relation to the educational and occupational structure of Ireland, 1853-1921', (D.Phil. University of Sussex, 1978).

Hyland, Aine. 'An analysis of the administration and financing of national and secondary education in Ireland, 1850-1922' (PhD, University of Dublin, Trinity College, 1982).

O'Halpin, Eunan. 'The Irish administration in crisis 1916-20 (MA, University College, Dublin, 1978).

O'Neill, Ciaran. 'Rule Etonia: educating the Irish Catholic elite 1850-1900' (PhD, University of Liverpool, 2010).

Lewis, Rebecca, 'Keep calm and carry on and other Second World war posters: British home front propaganda posters of the Second World war', (PhD, University of Winchester, 2004).

Maguire, Martin. 'The civil service, the state and the Irish revolution 1886-1938' (PhD, University of Dublin, Trinity College, 2005).

Matthews, Charles Kevin. 'The Irish boundary crisis and the reshaping of British politics: 1920- 1925' (PhD, London School of Economics and Political Science, 2000).

Rush, Claire Elizabeth. Girls' secondary education in the north of Ireland, 1867-1947, (PhD, Queen's University, Belfast, 2010).

Works of Reference:

Belfast and Province of Ulster Directory for the year 1865.

Burke's peerage and gentry, vol. II (107th ed.) (Oxford, 2003).

Cracroft Peerage. Cracroft-Brennan, Patrick (ed.), 2002.

Dictionary of Irish Architects 1720- 1940.

Dictionary of Irish Biography, 9 vols, (Dublin and Cambridge: Royal Irish Academy and Cambridge University Press, 2009), McGuire, James, and James Quinn (eds.).

Ellis, W.E. *Irish Education Dictionary, and Scholastic Guide* (Dublin, 1887).

Irish Statute Book.

Kelly's Directory of Essex, Hertfordshire and Middlesex (1914, London).

McCarthy, John P. *Ireland: A Reference Guide from the Renaissance to the Present.*

Oxford Dictionary of National Biography, 60 vols. (Oxford, 2004), Leslie Stephen, Sidney Lee, Christine Nicholls (eds.).

Strabane and Lifford Trades Directory, 1880.

Thom's Dublin Directory, for the years 1879-1920.

Index

Act of Union (1800) 82
Ainsworth, John 5
Alexandra College, Dublin 9, *61*, 74, 76, 77, 78
Alexandra University College 77
Alison, John 92
Allied Dublin Gas Company 176
Altrincham Grammar School 231
Amalgamated Anthracite Colliers Ltd 224
Ancient Order of Hibernians 176
Anderson, Catherine B. (Katie) 90, 100
Anderson, Charles 90
Anderson, Chrissie (*née* Mackenzie) 91–2, 103, 105–6
Anderson, David Alastair Pearson (2nd Viscount Waverley) 105, 106
Anderson, David Alexander Parsons 90, 91, 99, 204
Anderson, Janet J.P. (Nettie) 90, 92, 100, 106
Anderson, Janet Kilgour (*née* Bregelmann) 90
Anderson, Sir John (1st Viscount Waverley) 15, 81, *127*, 234, *240*
   academic awards 101, 102–3
   arrival in Dublin 201–2
   biography 84, 85, 91, 92, 99, 122–3, 200
   Board of Inland Revenue, chairman of 125, 140, 204
   Bonar Law, letter to 163
   children 105–6
   civil service career 83, 85, 104, 106, 122–3, 124–5, 202
   civil service examinations 103, 122, 123, 136, 200, 202
   Collins and 162
   Colonial Office, position in 124, *130*
   death of wife 106, 202
   dominion home rule and 203
   education 91, 92, 93, 95, 98, 99–101, 102–3, 200, 201
   family background 89–91, 92, 225
   family home, Edinburgh 89–90, 99, *130*
   Fisher's recommendation of 140, 202
   Highland Bursary awarded to 100–1
   Home Office, Under Secretary at 204
   impact of 202
   MacMahon and 84, 163
   marriage 92, 103, 105, 124
   Medical Research Team and 125
   Ministry of Shipping 125
   National Health Insurance Commission 124, 125
   obituaries 91, 103
   Order of Merit conferred on 204
   personality 86, 121–2, 202
   political aspects of role 201, 203
   Presbyterian religion 86, 93
   Republican prisoners, release of 221
   resignation 203–4
   siblings 90, 100
   'Side Lights on the Civil Service' 123–4
   Under Secretary (joint) (1920–22) 60, 85–6, 121–2, 126, 132, 149, 161, 162, 198–9, 201, 203
   Vans Dunlop scholarship 103
   Whitehall and 83, 125, 201, 202, 204
   see also British cohort; Dublin Castle administration (1920–22)
Anderson, Mary Mackenzie (*later* Pihl) 105–6
Anderson shelters 91, 204
Anglo-Irish Treaty 5, 16, 119, 203

Clarke's telegram to Street 173, *195*
Cope and 119, 162–3, 222, 237, 239
financial clauses 181
MacMahon and 119, 162–3, 172
negotiations 171, 172, 181
ratification of 172, 173, 177
signing of 171–2, 220
Asquith, H.H. 200, 207
Assembly College, Belfast 12
Assistant Under Secretary
MacMahon and 113
see also Cope, Alfred William; Sturgis, Mark Beresford Russell; Taylor, Sir John
astronomers 65
Australia
Archbishop Clune 165–6
British High Commissioner 227
Commonwealth of 233

Balfour Act (1902) 25
Balfour, A.J. 25–6, 113
Ball, John Thomas (Lord Chancellor) *52*, 53
Bandon Milling Company 178
Bantry Woollen Mills 178
Baptists 26
Barry, Michael B. 232
Baxter, Alice Mary *61*, 75
Beaverbrook, William Maxwell Aitken, 1st Baron 175
Belfast
linen industry 86, 87
Sailortown 86, 87, *128*
Belfast News Letter 143
Bell, Barbara 75
Belmore Commission 192
Belmore, Somerset Richard Lowry-Corry, 4th Earl 36, *52*, 54, 192
Belvedere College, Dublin 12
Benedict XV, Pope 16
Benedictine Order 190

Downside School, Bath 53, *190*, 191
Berry, Edmund G. 44
Bigger, Mr 65
Birmingham University 24
Black and Tans 168, 168n35
Blackrock College, Dublin 12, 30
see also French College
Blackrock College Yearbook, 1914 67
Blake Odgers, Lindsey Noel *see* Odgers, Lindsey Noel Blake
Bloody Sunday (1920) 217, 230–1
Board of Customs and Excise 179, 180
Board of Inland Revenue 125, 136, 140, 204, 207
Board of National Education (1831) 25, 28, 29, 33
Boer War 67, 88
Bohan, Edmond *64*
Bonaparte, Napoleon 189
Bonaparte, Princess Letizia 189
Bonaparte Wyse family 189–92
see also Wyse, Andrew Reginald Nicholas Gerald Bonaparte; Wyse, Sir Thomas Bonaparte
Bonar Law, Andrew (Chancellor of the Exchequer) 121, 141
Anderson's letter to 163
Fisher's memorandum to *153–7*
French's letter to 147
Bourdieu, Pierre 14
Boyle, Revd Patrick, CM 93
Bregelmann, Charles 90
Bregelmann, Janet Kilgour (*later* Anderson) 90
Brennan, Evelyn (*née* Simcox) 180
Brennan, Jeremiah 179
Brennan, Joseph Francis *197*
Board of Customs and Excise 179
civil service career 179–81, 193
Collins and 181, 193–4

Currency Commission, chairman
of 181
Department of Finance,
Secretary of 181
Doolin, friendship with 160–1
Dublin Castle and 139, 160,
177, 180–1, 183
education 161, 179
family background 178, 193,
224
Governor of the Central Bank
181
Irish Exchequer and 181
legal studies 180
marriage 180
NLI, papers in 179
Oath of Allegiance and 183
patriotism 181
Port of London 179
Taylor's anti-Catholic bias and
180–1
Brennan, Joseph, Snr 178
Brennan Ltd 178
Brennan, Mary (*née* Hickey) 178
Bridge, Ann 136
Bridges, Sir Edward Ettingdean 138
Brillantmont, Lausanne 106
British cohort (Junta) 149–52, *240*
arrival of 149, 198
Dissolution Honours list (1922)
217, 222
dominion home rule and 203
Dublin Castle, residence in 151
Dublin posting, perception of
200–1
Duggan's assessment of 189,
202–3, 226–7, 236
educational backgrounds 27,
137, 199–200, 201, 204,
206, 238
educational divisions among
200, 233
English public schools and 27
First World War, active service
in 205

Fisher's concerns for 150–1,
153–7
guns carried by 218
'Junta', use of term 186
New Year Honours List (1923)
177, 217, 227, 232, 237
perception of 15, 189, 203, 226–
7, 236
personnel 198
political role 203
remit 198
Royal Marine Hotel, temporary
mess in 150, 151
secondment of 3, 5, 132, 134
social divisions among 200, 201,
208, 210, 215–16, 235
Whitehall and 3, 5, 150
see also Anderson, Sir John;
Clark, Sir Ernest; Cope,
Alfred William;
Crutchley, Ernest
Tristram; Curtis, Lionel;
Fairgrieve, Thomas
Dalgliesh; Loughnane,
Norman Gerald; Odgers,
Lindsey Noel Blake;
Sturgis, Mark Beresford
Russell; Waterfield,
Alexander Percival;
Whiskard, Geoffrey
Granville
British Postal Museum and Archives
110
British Public Record Office 122
Bryant, Sophie (*née* Willock) 69, 70
Bureau of Military History 174, 183,
186, 187, 224, 226–7
Burke, Thomas Henry (Under
Secretary 1869–82) 82–3, 118
Butt, Isaac, MP 38
Byrne, Edward J., Archbishop of
Dublin 16
Byrne, General Sir Joseph 142–3
Byrne, Revd Peter, C.M. 78
Byrne, Sir William 112, 113

Cairns, Hugh McCalmont, 1st Earl
25, 28, 30
Calder, Angus 121–2, 123
Cambridge University Act (1856) 22
Campbell, Fergus 81–2, 83, 176
Carlingford, Samuel Parkinson-
Fortescue, Baron 33, 39–40
Carrigan, Adam 86
Carson, Sir Edward 80, 81
Castledawson House, Dublin 96
Castleknock College, Dublin 12, 57,
60, 95
Catholic Church
Free State and 16
girls' education, attitude towards
37, 38, 47, 74
MacMahon's links with 84, 89,
94, 113, 114, 176, 177,
193
MacPherson Bill (1919), views
on 41
in Scotland 26, 33
universities and 10, 184
see also religious orders
Catholic convents 9, 47, 64, 94, 105
examination results 74–5
French educational methods 9
Catholic Emancipation Act (1829) 18
Catholic hierarchy
education of girls, views on 48
FitzAlan, views on 16
inspection of schools, opposition
to 39
MacMahon and 108, 111, 114–
15, 116, 118, 145, 161,
163, 166–7
Queen's Colleges and 10
university education and 9–10,
12, 42–3
Catholic schools
continental 47
English 53, 190–1
fee-paying schools 46
Scottish 26–7

success in examinations 59, *60*,
74
superior Catholic schools 7, 45,
46, 71, 199
un-endowed 59, 71
versus Protestant schools 45, 58,
59, 71, 74
see also Catholic convents;
religious orders
Catholic Truth Society 176
Catholic University of Ireland 10, 11,
42, 57, 78, 93, 178
Catholic University Medical School
10–11
Catholics
civil service and 96, 108, 109–
10, 177, 178, 192, 192–3,
238
education, access to 8, 45, 70–1,
93, 178
headmasters 55–6
landed gentry 83
middle class 3, 44, 45, 46, 57–8,
66, 70–1
mixed marriages 66, 70n109
percentage of the population 10
professional class 44, 45
sectarian tension and 170
university education and 9–10,
42–3, 78, 178
upward mobility 3, 8, 13, 44,
57–8
Census (1881) 74, 212
Census (1891) 212, 213
Census (1901) 63, 70, 76, 104
Census (1911) 104, 204, 212, 213
Central Bank of Ireland 181
Chadwick, Edwin 13
Chalmers, Sir Robert 136
Chamberlain, Austen 141
Chaplin, Charlie 213
Cheltenham Ladies College 75
Chief Secretary
abolition of office 16
role of 16, 148

see also Forster, William
    Edward; Greenwood, Sir
    Hamar; Hicks-Beach, Sir
    Michael; Long, Walter;
    MacPherson, Ian (John
    James); Shortt, Edward
Chief Secretary's Office 2, 15, 83,
    115
    abolition of 16
    conflict and division in 117, 120
    employment of women 48
    re-organisation of 133–4, 146
    see also British cohort; Dublin
        Castle; Dublin Castle
        administration (1918–20);
        Dublin Castle
        administration (1920–22);
        Old Castle Gang
Christian Brothers
    boy clerkship examinations 73
    examination success 72, 73
    industrial schools 72
    orphanages 72
    schools 71, 72, 73, 74, 93
Christian Brothers Schools, Armagh
    93
Christian Schools, Belfast 72–3
Chrystal, G. 215n71
Church of England 34, 213n63
Church of Ireland
    disestablishment of 11, 34, 53
    schools 76, 184, 187
Church of Scotland 26, 33, 99
    see also George Watson's
        College; George Watson's
        Ladies' College
Churchill, Winston 140–1, 142, 203
civic colleges 24
Civil Service
    Board of Customs and Excise
        179, 180
    Board of Inland Revenue 125,
        136, 140, 204, 207
    boy clerkships 73, 107, 233
    Cambridge and *20*, 22, 23, 123,

        179, 182, 236
    candidates, Class 1 positions
        (1877–86) *20*
    Catholics and 96, 108, 109–10,
        177, 178, 192, 192–3, 238
    clerkships, first division 73–4,
        96, 178, 206
    clerkships, second division 73,
        96, 106–7, 124, 200, 213
Colonial Office 124, *130*, 210,
    227
competitive examinations 5–6,
    19–20, 21, 42, 113, 177,
    202
Dissolution Honours list (1922)
    217, 222
education and 3, 5–6, 7, 13, 27,
    58, 60, 73, 74, 137, 177
entrance examinations 13, 103
Foreign Office 123, 136
hierarchical structure of 178
Home Civil Service (HCS)
    examinations 122, 123,
    135–6
Home Office 204, 226, 236
Indian Civil Service 95, 122,
    124
Inland Revenue Office 213
Irish applicants, disadvantaged
    position of 21, 73–4
Irish Catholic advancement
    within 6, 7
Irish Office, London 172
Medical Research Team 125
meritocracy 3, 6, 13, 19, 20, 42,
    74, 113, 177, 200, 201,
    238
Ministry of Pensions 214, 224
National Health Insurance
    Commission 124, 125
New Year Honours list (1920)
    215
New Year Honours list (1922)
    210
New Year Honours list (1923)

177, 217, 227, 232, 237
Oxford and 13, *20*, 20n7, 21, 23,
    42, 123, 182
partition of 172
patronage 20, 177, 206, 207,
    211, 238
patronage versus meritocracy
    200, 201
Port of London 179
post-war reconstruction in
    Britain 133
Protestants, over representation
    of 14, 112
reform of 21, 142
*Royal Commission on the Civil
    Service (UK and Ireland)
    1912–14* 111
trade union 111
Treasury 136, 137, 199, 210,
    229
Treasury (Ireland) 202–3, 227–8
university education and 13, *20*,
    22, 24, 124, 192–3
Whitley Councils 142, 143
women, employment of 39, 48,
    111
see also Fisher Report;
    Northcote-Trevelyn
    Report
Civil Service College, Blackrock 96
Civil Service Commission 96, 124,
    124n269
Civil Service Commissioners 58, 230
Civil Service Committee 172, 242
Civil Service Sports Council 135
Clarendon Commission (1861–64)
    27, 137–8
Clark, Sir Ernest 198
Clarke, James Thomas 231
Clarke, Mary 58
Clarke, Mathew John *64*
Clarke, Sarah (*née* Ely) 231
Clarke, Thomas Basil 168, 201, 235,
    240
    civil service career 230–1, 232

Director of Special Intelligence
    232
Dublin Castle, secondment to
    230–1
Editorial Services Ltd founded
    by 232
education 201, 230, 231, 238
family background 231
head of publicity 230–1
journalism 231–2
knighthood 232
Ministry of Reconstruction 232
propaganda and 231
public relations and 232
telegram to Street 173, *195*
war correspondent 230, 232
Clongowes Wood College, County
    Kildare 12, 46, 52, 161, 179,
    181–2
    amalgamation with St Stanislaus
        College 178
    'Eton of Ireland' 27, 95
    Royal Military Colleges,
        preparation for 95
    see also St Stanislaus College
Clongownian 178, 179, *197*
Clune, Patrick Joseph, Archbishop of
    Perth 165–6
Coldrey, Barry M. 71–2
Coleraine Academical Institution
    (CAI) 59, *60*, 184
Collège Chaptal 68
Collins, Michael 16, 175
    Brennan, meetings with 181,
        193–4
    civil service examination 107
    civil service position 107, 123,
        213, 233, 235
    Cope and 162, 166, 172–3, 213,
        215, 218, 223
    Dublin Castle, handover of 162,
        173, 242
    funeral 218
    Irish exchequer 181
    MacMahon and 219–20

Provisional Government and 173

Treaty negotiations 181

Collins, Thomas, MP 33

Colonial Office 124, *130*, 210, 227

Commissioners of Church Temporalities in Ireland 34

Conan, Agnes 66, 70

Conan, Agnes (*later* Lady Hamer) 69–70

Conan, Alexander 68–9, 70

Conan, Arthur 66–7, 68, 70, 78, 100

Conan family business 68, 69

Conan, Florence 70

Conan fuse 68

Conan, Jeanette 70

Conan, Joseph 66, 67, 68, 69, 70

Conan, Josephine 69–70

Conan, Robert 68

Conan, Walter 66, 68, 70

Congested Districts Board 176

Connolly, Mr (Chief Clerk) 146

Conroy, Bishop 39

conscription 4, 125

Conservatives 26, 28, 33, 35, 53, 54, 82

constitutional nationalism, MacMahon and 113–14, 145, 146, 163–4, 176

Coolahan, John 58

Coonan, J.J. 110

Cope, Alfred, Snr 211–12

Cope, Alfred William (Andy) (Assistant Under Secretary) *240, 241*

Anglo-Irish Treaty and 119, 162–3, 222, 237, 239

arrival in Dublin 149, 198

Bureau of Military History, request from 224

CB awarded to 215, 218

civil service career 180, 200, 201, 211, 213, 214, 219

colleagues' perception of 215, 216, 218, 219

Collins and 166, 172–3, 213, 215, 218, 223

commercial appointments 224

concerns for safety 151

court case ('Discovery of Saccharin') 214

Customs and Excise inspector 180, 214

deception and 214, 215

Dublin Castle, secondment to 15, 149, 211, 219, 221

Duggan's perception of 217, 218, 220–1

education 213, 216, 238

family background 210, 211–12, 213

Fisher Report and 121, 133, 140, 143–4, 146, 216

House of Lords, referenced in 222–3

KCB awarded to 205, 217

Lloyd George and 165, 216, 217, 218, 221, 224

MacMahon and 162–3, 219

Macready's plans to arrest 219

Ministry of Pensions and 214, 219, 224

New Year's Honours list (1923), view on 237

organisational shortcomings 215, 221

patronage 238

perception of 218, 219, 222

personality 217, 234

Privy Council (Ireland), Clerk of 219

'the protége' 151, 211

Republican prisoners, release of 221

second division clerkship 200

siblings 212

Sinn Féin and 216, 217, 218, 219, 221–2, 223

Smuts, meeting with 169

treason, allegations of 222–4

undercover work 216, 217, 218, 219, 221
Whiskard, views on 227
Whitehall and 222–3
Cope, Florence E. 212
Cope, Margaret Elizabeth (*née* Dallimore) 212
Cope, Sarah 212
Corish, Patrick J. 71–2
Corry, Sir James Porter *52*, 53–4
Craig, Sir James 164, 168, 169, 171
Creedon, Marion (*later* Doolin) 181
Creedy, Sir Herbert 142
Crescent College *see* Sacred Heart College
Cromie, James 89
Cromie, John 89
Cromie, Mary (*née* MacMahon) 89
Crutchley, Arthur 232
Crutchley, Ernest Tristram 186, 198, 201, *240*
    army postal service organised by 233
    civil service career 233–5
    colleagues, assessment of 234–5
    Commonwealth of Australia 233–4
    diaries 230, 232
    Dublin Castle, secondment to 234
    education 232–3, 238
    family background 232
    First World War and 205, 230, 233, 235
    Ministry of Transport 233, 234
    OBE awarded to 233
    parliamentary questions, answering 234
    public relations 234
    Royal Engineers and 233
    UK GPO, history of 235
Cullen, Paul, Cardinal 45
    Hicks-Beach, correspondence with 47n12, 47–8, 48n13–14

Currency Commission 181
Curtis, Lionel 198, 218
Curtis-Bennett, Sir Noel 138–9
Curzon of Kedleston, George Nathaniel, Earl 223

Dacre, Anne Fiennes (*née* Sackville) Baroness 232, 232n171
Dáil Éireann 171
Daily Mail 232
Dallimore, Edward G. 212
Dallimore, Henry C. 212
Dallimore, Hugh C. 212
Dallimore, Margaret Elizabeth (*later* Cope) 212
D'Alton, John Francis, Cardinal 99
Daly, Mary E. 6–7, 73, 96
de Chiripunov of Oryol, Dmitry, Count 191
De Selby Mining Company, Tallaght 68
de Valera, Éamon 99, 167, 168, 172, 186
    Craig and 169
    Lloyd George and 169, 170
Dempsey, Pauric J. and Hawkins, Richard 216–17
Department of Finance 181, 183–4
Derby, Edward George Villiers Stanley, 17th Earl 167, 168
Devlin, Joseph 110
Dictionary of Irish Biography (DIB) 85, 179, 207
Dictionary of National Biography (DNB) 162, 201
Dillon, John 110, 139
Disraeli, Benjamin 28, 53
Dissolution Honours list (1922) 217, 222
Dmitryevna, Mariya (*later* Wyse) 191
Dominican Order 9
    Dominican College, Eccles Street 12, 74, 75, 77
dominion home rule 5, 114, 117, 163, 170, 203

Doolin, Daniel 181
Doolin, Marion (*née* Creedon) 181
Doolin, Mary McConnell (Molly)
    (*née* MacMahon) 105, 116,
    160, 182
    Anderson, perception of 106,
        202
    Cope, perception of 218
    Whiskard, perception of 226
Doolin, Walter *197*
    Brennan, friendship with 160–1
    civil service career 182–3, 193
    death 183
    Department of Finance and 183–
        4
    Dublin Castle and 105, 139,
        160, 177
    education 161, 181–2
    exhibitions and prizes 182
    family background 181, 193,
        224
    Keogh National Irish History
        prize 182
    Lansdowne Rugby Club 182
    MacMahon, personal secretary to
        182, 183
    marriage 105, 182
    obituary 183–4
    Pembroke Cricket Club 182
Doolin, Walter, Snr 181
Doolin, William 181
Dougherty, Sir James Brown (Under
    Secretary 1908–14) 48
Downing, Timothy McCarthy, MP
    18–19
Downside Review 191
Downside School, Bath 53, *190*, 191
Doyle, Charles Francis *61*, 62, 63, 78
Doyle, Daniel 62
Doyle, Eliza Lily 63
Doyle, James 63
Doyle, Sir Arthur Conan 22, 23, 67,
    100
    Sherlock Holmes 67
Draconian 134, 136–7

Dragon School, Oxford 134
Drennan, William 30
Drury, John Girdwood 184
Drury, Marion (*later* Wylie) 184
Dublin Castle 237–8
    Catholics and 83, 109
    handover 16, 173–4, 242
    Irish history, boycott of 28
Dublin Castle administration (1918–
    20) 198
    atmosphere of suspicion and
        espionage 82, 180–1
    boycott of Irish history teaching
        28
    Catholic landed gentry in 83
    Catholic middle class and 184
    contemporary perceptions of 82
    criticism of administration 133,
        143, 147–9
    divisions within 117, 118–19,
        120–1
    funding 199
    inadequacies in 116–17, 199
    judicial division 16
    reform, need for 132–3
    unionist clique, domination of
        149
Dublin Castle administration (1920–
    22) 2–3
    Anderson, British perception of
        role of 162
    Anderson, impact of 202
    Anderson's defence of
        MacMahon 163
    civil division 16
    conciliation/settlement,
        MacMahon and 163–4,
        168–9, 170–1
    dual administration 149–50
    espionage, allegations of 163,
        208
    Irish-born Catholics and
        nationalists 82
    Lloyd George and 165–6
    military division 16

official documents, burning of
193
social life 167
Treasury (Ireland) 202–3
Ulster Unionists and 164
see also Anderson, Sir John;
British cohort; Fisher
Report; MacMahon,
James Stanislaus; Old
Castle Gang
Dublin Evening Mail 57
Dublin Irish Blue Terrier Club 220
Dublin Metropolitan Police (DMP)
144
Dublin Metropolitan School of Art 70
Dublin United Transport Company
176
Duffy, Brigid J. 75
Duggan, Eamonn Seán 170, 219, 221
Duggan, Emily (*née* Grant) 186
Duggan, George Chester
Anderson, perception of 202–3
British cohort, assessment of
189, 202–3, 226–7, 236
Bureau of Military History and
186, 187, 237
civil service career 188–9
Cope, perception of 217, 218,
220–1
death of brothers at Gallipoli
188
Dublin Castle and 117–18, 120,
139, 160, 161, 175, 180,
183, 188
education 184, 187–8
family background 186–7, 193
honours received by 189
House of Commons, visit to 202
'Junta', use of term 186
memoir (unpublished) 186
Northern Ireland civil service
189
pseudonym (Periscope) 186
Taylor, assessment of 188
Whiskard, assessment of 226–7

Duggan, George Grant 187
Duggan, George, Snr 186–7
Duggan, Brother J.B. 72
Durham University 20n7, 22, 24

Easter Rising (1916) 104, 109, 117,
232
GPO and 109, 110, 125, 147,
171
trial of the leaders 185
École Turgot 68
Edinburgh University 22, 91, 102–3,
204
Hope Prize 102
University of Edinburgh Journal
103
Vans Dunlop Scholarship 102,
103
Editorial Services Ltd 232
education
Catholics and 8, 45, 70–1, 93,
178
civil servants and 3, 5–6
cramming, issue of 39, 62–3
foreign education 45, 47, 66, 69,
189
girls' secondary education,
nineteenth century 8–9
governesses, contribution of 9
Irish system, changes within 6
Killanin report 40, 40n107
legislation 25–8
post-war spending cuts 40
social class and 29–30, 70–1,
210–11
social equality and 58
see also Education Acts; girls;
headmasters; Intermediate
Education (Ireland) Act
(1878); Intermediate
Education (Ireland) Bill
(1878); national school
system; schools
Education Act (1918) 40
Education Bill (1918) 40

Education (England and Wales) Act (1902) 25–6
Education (Ireland) Bill (1919) 40–1, 42, 102, 192
Education Office (London) 42
Education (Scotland) Act (1872) 25, 26, 33, 81, 93, 211
Education (Scotland) Bill (1872) 40
Egerton, Sir Reginald 108
Elementary Education Act (1870) 25, 28, 81, 211
elite (term), use of 7–8, *8*
Elizabeth II, Queen 106
Ellis, Heather 20, 21
Emanuel School, London 232–3, 234
Endowed Schools Act (1869) 27
Endowed Schools Commission 72
English public schools 7, 23, 137–8
    see also Eton College; Rugby School; St Paul's School; Winchester College
Episcopalians 26, 33, 55–6
Eton Chronicle 207
Eton College 27, 54, 56, 206–7
Eugenics Society of Great Britain 210
Ewart, Wilfrid 231

Fairgrieve, John, Snr 204, 205
Fairgrieve, John 204
Fairgrieve, Thomas Dalgleish 198, 201, 235, *240*
    civil service career 205–6
    Dublin Castle, secondment to 205
    education 204
    family background 204, 205
    First World War service 204, 205, 230
    Military Cross awarded to 204
    Royal Auxiliary Fleet and 204
    Scottish Home Office and 206
Faithful Companions of Jesus 9
    Laurel Hill Convent 64
Fanning, Ronan 141, 217, 228
Farmar, Tony 14

Farragher, Sean 96
Farren, Sean 41
Federation of Women Civil Servants 111
First World War (1914–18) 116, 205
    army postal service 233
    civil service, war effort and 238
    Conan fuse, depth charge and 68
    Derby Scheme (1915) 125
    Duke of Cambridge's Own (Middlesex Regiment) 236
    Gallipoli 188
    Home Rule Bill, suspension of 114
    medicinal drugs, shortage of 125
    Royal Engineers 233
    Royal Fleet Auxiliary 204
    veterans, employment of 229–30
    war correspondent 230, 232
Fisher Bill (1918) 40
Fisher, Caroline Russell 134, 206
Fisher, Henry Warren 134
Fisher, Herbert Albert Laurens 40
Fisher, Mary Ann Lucy (Maysie) (*née* Thomas) 136
Fisher, Sir Norman Fenwick Warren
    Anderson and 140, 202, 203
    arrival in Dublin 121
    biography 136, 142, 144, 149, 200
    Board of Inland Revenue 136, 207
    British civil servants and 5, 150–1, *153–7*
    children 136
    civil service career 135–7
    Civil Service Sports Council 135
    Cope and 211, 214
    death 138–9
    dominion home rule policy 203
    Dublin Castle administration, investigation of 133–4, 140

education 134–5, 137
eulogy 138–9
family background 134
Head of the Civil Service 136–7
homosexuality, rumours of 138
MacMahon and 121, 125–6, 140
marriage 136
memorandum to Bonar Law
153–7
memorandum to Cabinet 140,
146, 147
obituary 134, 135–6
perception of 138
response from Cabinet *158*
Sturgis, secondment of 206
Taylor and 146, 149, 221
Treasury, permanent secretary to
136, 137
unionist clique, Dublin Castle
and 149
Whitehall, reorganisation of 229
Fisher Report 6, 15, 84, 132, 141,
143–8, 160, 211
Administration division 144
Chief Secretary's Office 146,
199
Connolly (Chief Clerk),
assessment of 146
Cope and 121, 133, 140, 143–4,
146, 216
Finance Division 144
Irish civil servants, retention of
180, 184
MacMahon, assessment of 140,
143, 144–5, 147
recommendation for new
personnel, effect of 149–
50
Taylor, assessment of 146, 149
Fishguard and Rosslare Railway and
Harbours 176
FitzAlan of Derwent, Edmund
Bernard FitzAlan-Howard, 1st
Viscount 139, 172, 203, 223

Catholic hierarchy's perception
of 16
Dublin Castle, departure from
195
Dublin Castle handover 173
MacMahon's perception of 173
memorial mass for Pope
Benedict XV 16
policy implementation, Wylie's
statement on 185–6
FitzGerald, Desmond 215, 215n71
Flanagan, Kieran 6
Fogarty, Michael, Archbishop of
Killaloe 166, 167, 171
Foreign Office 123, 136
Forster, William Edward (Chief
Secretary 1880–82) 25, 57
Forsythe, Mr 111
Foster, R.F., *Vivid faces* 80
Foyle College, Londonderry 64
France, Irish students educated in 66,
68
Free Church of Scotland 26, 33
Free State 2, 40, 173
administration, handover of 162
Catholic Church and 16
Governor General 175
Freeman's Journal 164, 165
Freemasons 112
French College, Blackrock (Blackrock
College) 30, 46, 59, *60*, 66, 67,
95–8
ethos 95
foundation of 95
MacMahon and 88–9, 92, 93,
95, 96–7, 145
perception of 95, 96
St Patrick's Day (1866) 96
students, distinctions won by 99
French leave ix, 121
French, Sir John Denton (1st Earl of
Ypres) 16, 41, 115, 120, 121,
139
attempted murder of 150
Cope and 219

Dublin Castle administration,
 views on 208
Home Rule, views on 117–18
letter to MacMahon 171–2
MacMahon and 118, 147–8,
 172, 222

Gallagher, Michael 172
General Election (1918) 4, 116
General Post Office (GPO)
 Easter Rising (1916) and 109,
  110, 125, 147, 171
 MacMahon and 104, 108, 109,
  110–11, 112
 restoration of 125, 147
George V, King 141
George VI, King 122
George Watson's College, Edinburgh
 102, 123, 124
 Anderson and 91, 92, 95, 98, 99,
  101, 102, 123, 201, 204
 Fairgrieve and 201, 204, 205
 fees 99
 Founder's Day 98
 London Watsonian Club 98
 MacPherson and 101
 Watsonian, The 123–4
 Wee School (lower division) 92,
  99–100
George Watson's Ladies' College
 100, 102
Gilmartin, Thomas Patrick,
 Archbishop of Tuam 116, 166
girls
 Celtic studied by 75
 education, Catholic hierarchy's
  views on 48, 74
 education on the continent 47
 English utilitarian education 8, 9
 examination results (1879) *61*,
  75
 French educational methods 8, 9
 Greek studied by 74, 75
 intermediate education and 37–8
 Intermediate Education (Ireland)
  Act (1878) 8, 38, 47–8
 Latin studied by 74
 secondary education in Ireland
  8–9
 subjects studied by 74, 75
 see also suffragettes; women
Gladstone, William Ewart 37, 38, 53
 civil service reforms 21
 Home Rule Bills 114
 Northcote-Trevelyan report
  commissioned by 19
 University Bill (1873) 11, 28
Glenavy, James Henry Mussen
 Campbell, 1st Baron 117
Gogarty, Oliver St John 220
Goubaux, Prosper 68
Governess Association of Ireland
 (GAI) 9
governesses 9
Government of Ireland Act (1920) 5,
 114, 172, 203
 Civil Service Committee and
  172
 financial clauses 188
 making of 5
Government of Ireland Bill (1919) 5,
 117
Gower, R.P.M. 150
grammar schools 27, 93, 216, 238
 Altrincham Grammar School
  231
 Coleraine Academical Institution
  (CAI) 59, *60*, 184
 Grammar School, Galway *64*
 Londonderry Academical
  Institution (Foyle College)
  61, 64, 65, 66
 Manchester Grammar School
  231
 Royal Belfast Academical
  Institution (RBAI) 29n44,
  30, 53, *60*
Granard, Bernard Forbes, 8th Earl of
 10, 112, 115
Grant, Emily (*later* Duggan) 186

Grant, Johnnie 210
Grant-Sturgis, Mark Beresford Russell
    see Sturgis, Mark Beresford
    Russell
Granville, George Leveson-Gower,
    2nd Earl 37
Graphic, The **195**
Gray, Alexander 103, 105, 123
Gray's Inns, London 52
Great Southern Hotel **186**
Great Southern Railways (GSR) 176
Green Party 69
Greenwood, Sir Hamar (Chief
    Secretary 1920–22) 165, 166,
    171, 201, 202
  appointment as Chief Secretary
    16, 139, 148
  Chief Secretary, perception of
    his role as 210
  Loughnane as press secretary
    237
  Sturgis as unofficial secretary
    209
  Whiskard as assistant secretary
    227
Greenwood, Margery (*née* Spencer),
    Lady 165, 171, 202, 210
Greer, James W. 64, 190
Greer, Peter Paul **61**, 64, **64**, 190
Gregg, John Allen Fitzgerald,
    Archbishop of Dublin 169
Gresham Hotel, Dublin 167, 171
Grey, Charles Grey, 2nd Earl 18,
    189n148
Griffith, Arthur 24, 221, 237
Grigg, Sir James 138
Gwynn, Stephen 114, 117

Hamblin and Porter's School, Cork
    53
Hankey, Sir Maurice 150
Harford, Judith 75–6
Harrel, David (Under Secretary 1898–
    1902) 133, 142
Harwood, R.E. 121, 133, 140, 143–4,

146, 147, 148, 149
Hatfield, Mary 9
Headlam, Maurice 40n107, 137, 139,
    229
headmasters
  girls' education, monetary
    rewards and 8, 38, 57
  grievances 8, 35, 38, 50, 55–6,
    57–8
  Lord Lieutenant, deputation to
    55–6, 57–8
  Standing Committee of Catholic
    and Protestant
    Headmasters 55–6
Healy, Bishop of Clonfert (*later*
    Archbishop of Tuam) 12
Healy, T.M. 52, 108, 175, 177
Hemming, A.F. 172
Hennessy, John Pope 28
Hennessy, Peter 19, 20n6
Hicks-Beach, Sir Michael (Chief
    Secretary 1886–7) 28, 31
  Cardinal Cullen, correspondence
    with 47n12, 47–8,
    48n13–14
High School, Dublin 59, **60**, 187
Hillersdon Estate, Devon 210
Hobhouse, Charles (Post Master
    General) 109–10
Holy Ghost Fathers (Spiritans) 30
  Rockwell College, County
    Tipperary 46
  see also French College,
    Blackrock
Home Rule 4, 82, 108, 110, 120, 144
  dominion home rule 5, 114, 117,
    163, 170, 203
  perception of 117–18
Home Rule Bills 109, 114
homosexuality 138
Hopkinson, Mark, *Last Days of
    Dublin Castle, The* 164, 232
Horsman, Edward, MP 10
Hôtel de Crillon, Paris 171
House of Commons

Cope and 222
Duggan's visit to 202
Education (England and Wales)
    Act (1902) 25
Intermediate Education (Ireland)
    Bill (1878) 25, 36, 38
MacPherson and 41, 142
university education in Ireland
    18, 53
House of Lords
civil service headship debate
    137
Cope's actions referenced in
    222–3
Intermediate Education (Ireland)
    Bill (1878) 28, 35–6, 37,
    38
Howley, Edward 30–1
Hugh Lane Gallery, Dublin 217, *241*
hunger strikes 227
Hyde, Douglas 54

Inchiquin, Lucius William O'Brien,
    Baron 32n60, 33
Indian Civil Service 95, 122, 124,
    135, 200, 220
Bengal Civil Service 225
Insurance Corporation of Ireland 176
Intermediate Education Board for
    Ireland
assistant commissioners, role of
    36
Catholic members 52, *52*
commercial certificates and
    prizes 51
Commissioners (1879) 51–4, *52*
denominational representation
    36, 52, 53
expenditure (1879) *55*
finances 49–50, 54, 55, 56, 57
Lord Lieutenant and 25, 35, 36,
    55–6, 57
Protestant members 52, *52*
regulations, changes in 50, 54,
    56, 57, 59

report (1888) 72–3
reports (1879–1919) 48–50, 72–
    3
reports, publication of 44–5
results fees 49, 56, 72–3
results-lists, publication of 44,
    45, 49
see also headmasters;
    intermediate examinations
Intermediate Education (Ireland) Act
    (1878) 2, 10, 11, 211
Catholics, improved access for
    93
finance for the board 34–5
financial assistance for
    individuals and schools
    19
girls, inclusion of 8, 38, 47–8,
    57
guidelines for teaching 19
impact of 3, 7, 22, 58, 93
implementation of 44–5
payment by results 19, 30–1
Scottish act as a precursor to 33
secular nature of 58, 93
see also intermediate
    examinations
Intermediate Education (Ireland) Act
    (1882) 35, 50
Intermediate Education (Ireland) Act
    (1900) 54
Intermediate Education (Ireland) Bill
    (1878)
amendments 37–8, 50
conscience clause 32–3
cramming, issue of 39
debates on 30–40, 52
girls, inclusion of 37–8
House of Commons debate 25,
    36, 38
House of Lords debate 28, 35–6,
    37, 38
inspection of schools 39–40
religious instruction 32–3
schedule of prizes and

exhibitions 31–2
schedule of rules 31
subjects 32
Intermediate Education (Ireland) Bill
(1900) 29, 62–3
Intermediate Education Office 229
intermediate examinations 31, 32, 59,
177
boys, ratio of south to north
participation 74
boys' schools (1879/1880/1881)
60
Catholic schools' success in 59,
60
examination subjects 50, 54, 65
exhibitions and prizes 49–50,
61, 62, *64*, 67, 73
girls, ratio of north to south
participation 74
impact of 61–2
percentage of passes, girls and
boys 51n25
Protestant schools' success in
59, *60*
results (1879) *61*, *64*, 65, 75
student numbers
(1879/1880/1881) *49*
student numbers, decline in 50
Irish Church Act (1869) 34
Irish Convention (1917) 3–4, 117
Irish Dominion League 117
Irish establishment 82, 193
Irish history, boycott of 28
'Irish Question' 2, 4, 132, 185, 213
Irish Republican Army (IRA) 219,
221, 224, 231
Irish Statesman 117
Irish Times 47
Duggan's articles 186
Irish Universities Act (1908) 11, 179
Irish War Savings Committee 180

Jackson, Alvin 80, 81
Jacobs, W.W. 235
Jellicoe, Anne 9, 76

Jesuit College, Tullabeg *see* St
Stanislaus College
Jesuits 12, 46, 62, 81, 105, 112
see also Belvedere College;
Clongowes Wood
College; Sacred Heart
College, Limerick; St
Stanislaus College
Jones, Thomas 222–3, 237–8
Joyce, Colonel J.V. 84n17, 122n221,
174–5
judiciary, Protestants and 14
Junta *see* British cohort

Keawell, Patrick 99
Keenan, Sir Patrick (Commissioner of
National Education) 31
Kennedy, Conan 67
Keogh National Irish History prize
182
Kerr, Schomberg Henry (The Marquis
of Lothian) 22–3
Kildare Street Club 142
Killanin Report 40, 40n107
King's Inns 52
Kingussie School 101
Knights of Columbanus 176

Ladies Collegiate School, Belfast
(Victoria College) *61*, 65, 75–
6
Ladies' General Educational Institute
37
Ladies Intermediate School, Limerick
77
Ladies' School, George's Street,
Limerick 77
Land Act (1881) 14
Land Commission 88, 185, 186
Lansdowne Rugby Club 182
Laurel Hill Convent, Limerick 64
Lavery, Sir John
Cope, portrait of 217, *241*

Redmond and Carson, portraits
of 80–1
Leader 109, 112
Lecky, W.E.H. 117
Leipzig University 103
Leman, Revd Jules 30–1
Lewis, Charles, MP 35–6
Lewis, Rebecca 230
Leys School 225
Liberals 18–19, 26, 28, 53, 57, 102,
110, 224
Home Rule and 82, 108
Lloyd George, David 113, 116, 210
Archbishop Clune and 165–6
Churchill, letter to 140–1
Cope and 151, 165, 216, 218,
221, 224
de Valera and 169, 170
Dublin Castle and 165–6
Fisher report 146–7
Fisher's memorandum 146, 147
Irish Convention, establishment
of 3–4
policy of repression 4, 5
policy team (Garden Suburb)
132, 132n2
Sinn Féin and 5, 168
Local Government Board 48, 125,
176
Logue, Michael, Cardinal 16, 89,
108, 163, 166
MacMahon and 116, 168, 169
meeting with Lord Derby 168
perception of 166, 167
London Metropolitan Archives 213
Londonderry Academical Institution
(Foyle College) *61*, 64, 65, 66
Londonderry, Charles Stewart Henry
Vane-Tempest-Stewart, 7th
Marquess of 192
Long, Walter (Chief Secretary 1905)
112, 113, 115
Longhurst, C. 151
Lord Lieutenant of Ireland
abolition of office 173

Intermediate Education Board
for Ireland and 25, 35, 36,
55–6, 57
role of 15–16, 148
see also FitzAlan of Derwent,
Edmund Bernard
FitzAlan-Howard, 1st
Viscount; French, Sir John
Denton (1st Earl of Ypres)
Loreto Order 9
Loreto College, St Stephen's
Green 12, 74
Loreto Convent, North Great
George's Street 75
Loughnane, Denies I. 237
Loughnane, Norman Gerald 198, 201,
235, *240*
death 237
Dublin Castle, secondment to
236–7, 238
education 237
family background 237
press secretary to Greenwood
237
Lowther, J. (Attorney General) 37–8
Lucey, John 77
Lynn Committee 192

MacAuley, Charles J. 220
McBride, J.M., Archbishop 175
McBride, Lawrence W. 6, 16, 81–2,
142, 144, 178, 199
McCartney, Donal 12
McColgan, John 5, 143, 199
MacDonnell, Sir Antony Patrick
(Under Secretary 1902–8) 82,
83, 111, 118, 132–133
McDowell, R.B. 48
McElligott, T.J. 47, 60–1, 210–11
Secondary Education in Ireland
45, 46
McKee, Elizabeth (Lizzie) (*née*
MacMahon) 88, 89, 94
McKee, F.W. 89
McKee, H.J. 89

McKee, H.J., Snr 89, 94
McKee, James 89
McKee, Kathleen 94
McKee, Madeline 94
McKee, Margaret 94
Mackenzie, Andrew 91–2
Mackenzie, Chrissie (*later* Anderson)
    91–2, 103, 105–6
Mackenzie, Mary 91–2
Mackenzie, Nellie 106
McLorinan, James 46
MacMahon, Captain *196*
MacMahon, Charlie 88
MacMahon, Elizabeth (Lizzie) (*later*
    McKee) 88, 89, 94
MacMahon family (1887) *127*
MacMahon, Frank 88
MacMahon, Harry 88
MacMahon, James, Snr 86, 87–9
MacMahon, James Stanislaus 13,
    127, *129*, *195*, *196*
  Anderson and 84, 163
  Anglo-Irish Treaty and 119,
    162–3, 172
  Blackrock College, links with
    98–9
  Catholic Church, links with 84,
    89, 94, 113, 114, 176,
    177, 193
  Catholic hierarchy and 108, 111,
    114–15, 116, 118, 145,
    161, 163, 166–7, 193
  children 103–4
  civil service career 83, 90, 99,
    104, 106–14, *107*, 124,
    125
  Civil Service Committee,
    appointment to 172
  club memberships 145, 152, 176
  Collins and 219–20
  conciliation/settlement and 163–
    4, 168–9, 170–1
  confidential information, refusal
    to disclose 174–5, 186
  constitutional nationalism and

    113–14, 145, 146, 163–4,
    176
  Cope and 219
  death 98, 177
  directorships 176
  Dublin Castle, handover of 173
  Dublin Irish Blue Terrier Club,
    membership of 220
  education 13, 60, 81, 92, 93, 94–
    7, 98, 99
  examination prizes 96, 99
  family background 86–9
  Fisher and 121, 125–6
  Fisher Report's assessment of
    140, 143, 144–5, 147
  French's assessment of 118,
    147–8
  Government of Ireland Bill
    (1919), views on 5, 117
  GPO Chief Clerk 104, 124
  GPO Secretary 108, 109, 110–
    11, 112, 125, 145, 147
  home addresses 103–4
  marriage 103
  networks in Ireland 84, 115,
    145, 161–2, 168
  obituaries 99, 108
  papal audience 176–7
  perception of 175–6
  personality 86
  Post Office positions (1882–
    1918) 104, *107*, 108, 109,
    110–11, 112
  Redmond and 108, 109–10
  retirement 176
  St Vincent de Paul Society and
    161–2, 167n30, 176
  siblings 88, 94, 97–8
  Sinn Féin and 219
  social work 176
  Taylor's attitude towards 118,
    119, 120–1, 139, 149, 222
  Under Secretary (1918–20) 13,
    81, 82, 83, 85–6, 111–15,
    129, 198

Under Secretary (joint) (1920–
22) 121–2, 126, 160–1,
193, 198
Under Secretary, perception of
role as 85–6, 145–6, 162
Under Secretary's Lodge,
Phoenix Park 104, 116,
161, 174, 202
unionist perception of 114, 116,
164
Wylie and 161, 163, 184
see also British cohort ; Dublin
Castle administration
(1918–20); Dublin Castle
administration (1920–22);
Old Castle Gang
MacMahon, John 88, 89
MacMahon, John Rochford (Jack)
103, 104, 111–12, *129*
Jesuits and 105, 112
MacMahon, Joseph Aloysius 88, 89,
97–8, 190
MacMahon, Katie 88, 94
MacMahon, Maggie 88
MacMahon, Margaret Mary
(Marjorie) (*later* Manning)
103–4, 105
MacMahon, Mary (*later* Cromie) 88,
89
MacMahon, Mary McConnell (Molly)
(*later* Doolin) 103, 104, 105
see also Doolin, Mary
McConnell (Molly) (*née*
MacMahon)
MacMahon, Mary (*née* McConnell)
87–8, 166, *196*
MacMahon, Mary (*née* Rochford)
103–4
MacMahon, Teresa 88, 94
MacMahon, Vincent 88, 89
Macnair, John Charles Hirschfeld 123
MacNeill, Eoin 221
MacNeill, James 220
MacPherson, Anne (*née* Stewart) 101

MacPherson Bill (1919) 40–1, 42,
102
MacPherson, Ian (John James) (Chief
Secretary 1919–20) 16, 139,
142
appointment as Chief Secretary
116, 119–20
colleagues, views on 139–40
death 102
Dublin, departure from 41, 121,
137
education 101–2, 201
Education (Ireland) Bill (1919)
40–1, 42, 102, 192
Home Rule, support for 120
ill health 41, 121
MacMahon, ostracisation of 148
resignation 148
MacPherson, James 101
Macready, General Sir Cecil Frederick
Nevil 148, 164, 165, 166, 169
Cope, plans to arrest 219
Dublin Castle, assessment of
133, 141–2
Ireland, views on 119–20
MacMahon's perception of 173–
4
Madame de Prins' College, Limerick
77
Magee College, Londonderry 12, 66
Maguire, Martin 138, 174, 205, 227,
230, 232, 237
civil service reform 132–3, 142
Home Rule Bills 114
Lord Lieutenant, role of 15–16
Malvern College 106
Manchester Grammar School 231
Manchester Guardian 231
Manning, Dermot 105
Manning, Margaret Mary (Marjorie)
(*née* MacMahon) 103–4, 105
marriages (mixed), pre *Ne Temere*
decree 66, 70n109
Maume, Patrick 85, 86, 113, 114, 139

Maunder, Annie Scott Dill (*née* Russell) 65
Maunder, Walter 65
Maye, Brian 112
Maynooth, County Kildare 12
Medical Research Team 125
Merchant Taylor's School 225
Meredith, J.C. 63
Methodists 26, 55–6
Miller, David and Dinan, William 231
Milner, Alfred 132
Ministry of Education, Northern Ireland 189, 192
Ministry of Finance, Northern Ireland 189
Ministry for Health 232
Ministry of Information 230
Ministry of Pensions 214, 224, 237
Ministry of Reconstruction 232
Ministry of Shipping 125
Ministry of Transport 233, 234
model schools 77
Molloy, Revd Gerald 57
Montagu-Stuart-Wortley, Lady Rachel (*later* Sturgis) 208, **240**
Moody, T.W. 12
Mooney, J.J. 117
Moore, Lucy *61*, 75
Moran, D.P. 24, 109
Morant, Sir Robert 125
Moriarty, John Francis, KC 67
Morningside Board School, Edinburgh 100
Morris, Sir Michael 63
Morrow, Kathleen *61*, 75, 76
Morrow, Robert 76
Mount St Catherine's Convent National School, Armagh 94
Mountjoy Prison 221
Moylan, Hannah 76–8
Moylan, Jeremiah 77
Moylan, Mary 77
Moylett, Patrick 222
Murphy, Fintan 171

Murphy, Richard 4, 5
Muskerry, Lord 222, 223

Nairne, John James 123
Nathan, Sir Mathew 21, 110
National Archives of Ireland 105, 115
National Archives, Kew 120, 207, 229
National Education Office 42
National Health Insurance Commission 124, 125
National Health Insurance Scheme 125
National Library of Ireland (NLI) 179
national school system
    British 25, 30
    children, number enrolled (1850) 34
    Irish 18, 24, 25, 28, 30, 33–4, 71–2
    non-denominational 24, 33–4
    number of schools (1850) 33–4
    see also schools
National University of Ireland (NUI) 11, 12, 22, 66, 78, 179
Ne Temere decree 66, 70n109
Neligan, David 98
New Year Honours lists
    (1920) 215
    (1922) 210
    (1923) 177, 217, 227, 232, 237
Newtonmore Public School (Newtonmore Primary School) 101
Nicholls, Sophie 70
North London Collegiate School 69, 75
Northcote, Sir Stafford 19, 20–1, 202
Northcote-Trevelyan Commission 42
Northcote-Trevelyan Report 6, 13, 19–21, 96, 177
    Civil Service Commission (1855) 124n269
    patronage, elimination of 207

Northern Ireland
    civil service functions, transfer
        of 172
    civil service in 189
    Lynn Committee 192
    Ministry of Education 189, 192
    Ministry of Finance 189
    sectarian tension 170
Norway, A.H. 108, 109, 110, 171

Oath of Allegiance 183
O'Brien, Flann 68
O'Connor, Anne V. 8–9
O'Connor, James J. 219
O'Conor, Charles (The O'Conor Don)
    18, 19, *52*, 53
Odgers, Frances (*née* Hudson) 235
Odgers, Lindsey Noel Blake 198,
    201, 230, 235, *240*
    civil service career 235, 236
    death 236
    Dublin Castle, secondment to
        235, 236
    education 235–6
    family background 235
    First World War and 205, 236
    Home Office and 236
    Military Cross awarded to 236
Odgers, William Blake 235
O'Donnell, Patrick, Bishop of Raphoe
    108
O'Farrell, Edward 113
O'Hagan, Thomas O'Hagan, 1st
    Baron 29–30, 29n44, *52*, 53
O'Halpin, Eunan 4, 139–40, 142, 199
    Cope, assessment of 214, 216
    Fisher 136, 142, 144, 149, 200
O'Kelly, Sean T. 163–4, 175–6
Old Castle Gang 3, 5, 105, 149–50,
    160–2, 208
    Catholic background and 161,
        173, 176, 177, 178–9,
        180, 183–4
    educational backgrounds 161,
        178–9, 181–2, 184, 185,

        187–8, 199, 200
    Irish establishment 193
    key personnel 160
    ostracisation by unionist clique
        160
    Protestant background and 184–
        8
    Sturgis briefed about 208
    see also Brennan, Joseph
        Francis; British cohort;
        Doolin, Walter; Duggan,
        George Chester;
        MacMahon, James
        Stanislaus; Wylie,
        William Evelyn
O'Leary, C.E. 215, 218, 220
O'Malley, Sir Owen 136
O'Neill, Ciaran 9, 27, 45, 46, 191
    Catholics of consequence 8, 47
Oxbridge colleges 20, 21, 22, 23, 42,
    74, 206
    see also University of
        Cambridge; University of
        Oxford
*Oxford Dictionary of National
    Biography* 85, 207, 212
Oxford University Bill (1854) 22

Palles, Andrew 52
Palles, Christopher (Lord Chief Baron
    of the Irish Exchequer) 51–2,
    52, 53
Palles, Eleanor 52
partition 117
    Civil Service and 172
    Government of Ireland Act
        (1920) and 5, 114, 172
Pašeta, Senia 74
Pauline, The (school magazine) 225
Pearse, Padraig 182
Pease, H.P. 110
Peden, G.C. 84–5, 162, 204
Pembroke Cricket Club 182
Phelan Conan Ltd 68
Pihl, Brigadier Dame Mary

Mackenzie (*née* Anderson)
106
Pius XI, Pope 176–7
Plunkett, Horace 3–4, 114, 117, 171,
173, 174
Plutarch 200
De Liberis Educandis 44
Life of Alexander the Great, The
160
Parallel Lives 2, 18, 80, 132,
198
Portmarnock Golf Club 176
Post Master General 108, 109–10,
233
Post Office
Collins, post held by 107
salary scales *107*
see also General Post Office
(GPO)
Powis Commission (1870) 94–5
Presbyterian Churches 11
Presbyterian College Londonderry 12
Presbyterians 53, 55, 65, 86, 120, 184
Education (Scotland) Act (1872)
and 93
school attendance 45
Privy Council (Ireland) 144, 162,
174, 219
Promissory Oaths Act (1868) 183
propaganda 215, 224, 230n158, 231
Protestant Churches 41, 169
Protestant schools
boarding schools 27
endowment of 27n34, 58–9, 71
examinations, success in 59, *60*,
64, 74
girls' schools 8–9, 70, 74
school attendance 45
secondary schools 9, 45
Trinity, influence of 78
versus Catholic schools 45, 58,
59, 71, 74
see also English public schools;
George Watson's College;
grammar schools

Protestants
civil service and 14, 112
Dublin Castle and 82, 83, 109
education, access to 8, 184
governesses and 9
Intermediate Education Board
for Ireland and 52
judiciary and 14
MacPherson Bill (1919), views
on 41
middle class 66, 70, 71
mixed marriages 66, 70n109
Queen's Colleges and 10
sectarian tension 170
Prout, Ellen Linzee (*later* Wyse) 190
Provincial Bank 186, 187, 188
Provisional Government 162, 173,
174, 203, 242
public relations 230, 232, 234
public schools *see* English public
schools
see also superior Catholic
schools
Public Schools Act (1868) 27

Queen's College Galway 77, 78
Queen's College (Ireland) Act (1845)
11
Queen's Colleges 10, 11, 28, 78
Queen's Institute 9
Queen's University Belfast (QUB)
11, 12
Queen's University of Ireland 24

Ramsey, Sir Malcolm 151
redbrick universities 24
Redington, Thomas Nicholas (Under
Secretary 1846–52) 84, 118
Redmond, John 21, 29, 80, 81
constitutional movement 176
cramming, views on 39
MacMahon, promotion of 108,
109–10
Reeves, Cynthia Salome Caroline

(*later* Whiskard) 226
religious orders
　　education and 9, 71
　　fee-paying schools founded by
　　　46, 74
　　MacMahon family and 94
　　see also Benedictine Order;
　　　Christian Brothers;
　　　Faithful Companions of
　　　Jesus; Holy Ghost
　　　Fathers; Jesuits; Loreto
　　　Order; Ursuline Order;
　　　Vincentian Fathers
Rentoul, James, MP 39, 62–3
Republic, Sinn Féin and 168, 170
Restoration of Order in Ireland Act
　　(1920) 151
Richmond, Duke of 42
Robertson, George 102
Rochford, John 103
Rochford, Mary (*later* MacMahon)
　　103–4
Rockwell College, County Tipperary
　　46
Rotunda Hospital, Dublin 110
Rotunda Rink 110
Royal Belfast Academical Institution
　　(RBAI) 29n44, 30, 53, *60*
Royal College of Physicians, London
　　106
Royal College of Surgeons, London
　　106
Royal Commission (1864) 56
*Royal Commission on the Civil
　　Service (UK and Ireland)
　　1912–14* 111
Royal Dublin Society (RDS) 176,
　　177
Royal Engineers 233
Royal Fleet Auxiliary 204
Royal Infirmary, Edinburgh 99–100
Royal Irish Academy 192
Royal Irish Automobile Club 176
Royal Irish Constabulary (RIC) 4,
　　140, 142, 144, 150, 164

see also Smyth, Lieutenant
　　Colonel Gerald Bryce;
　　Tudor, Major General
　　Hugh
Royal Irish Yacht Club 176
Royal Marine Hotel, Kingstown 150,
　　151
Royal Military Academy, Woolwich
　　95
Royal Military College, Sandhurst 95
Royal School, Armagh *60*
Royal University of Ireland 7, 8, 191
　　Clerk of Convocation of 63
　　dissolution 11, 179
　　examination fees, payment of 66
　　examinations 12, 58, 66, 67, 98,
　　　178
　　female students 69, 74, 75
　　foundation of 11, 19, 23, 78
　　matriculation, female students
　　　(1885/1890/1895) 74, 77–
　　　8
　　preparation of students 98, 178
　　robes and caps, hiring of 68
　　University of London, modelled
　　　on 23, 191
　　women, degrees awarded to 23,
　　　69–70, 77
Ruane, Joseph and Todd, Jennifer 14
Rugby School 27, 235–6
Russell, Annie Scott Dill (*later*
　　Maunder) 65
Russell, Hessy (*née* Nesbit Dill) 65
Russell, Hester 65
Russell, James 65
Russell, Lord John 21
Russell, Samuel 65
Russell, William Andrew *61*, 64–6
Russell, Revd W.A. 65

Sacred Heart College, Limerick
　　(Crescent College) 46, *61*, 62,
　　63
Sacred Heart Order 9
　　Mount St Catherine's Convent

National School 94
novitiate, Roehampton 95
Sacred Heart Convent, Mount
    Anville 74
Sacred Heart Convent, Roscrea
    105
St Andrew's Church, Drumsheugh,
    Edinburgh 105
St Angela's College, Cork 74
St Columba's College, Dublin 27
St Joseph of Cluny Order 9
St Malachy's College, Belfast *64*
St Mary's College, Trinidad 30
St Mary's University College, Dublin
    77
St Patrick's College, Armagh (St
    Patrick's Grammar School) 93,
    94, 95, 96–7
St Paul's School, London 187n129,
    225–6
    Pauline, The (school magazine)
        225
St Peter's College, Westminster *see*
    Westminster School
St Philip Church, Kennington Road,
    London 213
St Stanislaus College, Tullabeg 46,
    60, *61*, *64*, 105, 112, 178
St Vincent de Paul Society 161–2,
    167n30, 176
St Vincent's College (Castleknock
    College) 12, 57, *60*, 95
Salmon, Revd George (Regius
    Professor of Divinity) *52*, 53
Samuel, Herbert (Post Master
    General) 108, 109–10
Saunderson, Edward 139
school inspectors 39, 64, 88, 98, 189–
    90, 191–2
schools
    attendance post-1878 45
    Belmore Commission and 192
    boarding schools, Irish 14, 46,
        71
    Church of Ireland schools 76,

184, 187
college entry provision 74
competition among 58, 71
continental schools 45, 47, 68
day schools 71
English public schools 7, 23, 27,
    56, 74, 137–8
fee-paying 46, 71, 73, 94–5
inspection of 39
Irish boarding school habitus 14
Irish primary curriculum, inquiry
    into 192
model schools 77
non-denominational 33–4
private schools in Ireland 29
professional classes, entry to 14
secondary schools 77
see also Catholic convents;
    Catholic schools;
    education; headmasters;
    national school system;
    Protestant schools;
    religious orders; teachers
Schools League 66
Scotland
    Catholic Church 26, 33
    Catholic schools 26–7
    denominational schools 27
    Education Department 42
    Education (Scotland) Act (1872)
        25, 26, 33, 81
    Education Scotland Act (1918)
        26
    Home Office 206
    Leaving Certificate examination
        26, 81, 102
    secondary education 26–7
    Secretary for Scotland 42
    universities *20*, 22–3
Scotland Yard 140
Searle, G.R. 26
Second World War 204, 210
    Anderson shelters 91, 204
    Ministry of Information 230
    propaganda posters 230n158

Shannon, Mr 215
Shortt, Edward (Chief Secretary 1918–19) 112, 113, 116, 117, 118, 119, 181
Simcox, Evelyn (*later* Brennan) 180
Sinn Féin 5, 151, 163, 167, 168, 171
    Cope and 216, 217, 218, 221–2, 223
    dominion home rule and 170, 203
    Dublin Castle hand over 174
    General Election (1918) and 4, 116
    Lloyd George and 168, 170, 216, 217
    MacMahon and 219
    Republic and 168, 170
Sisters of Mercy 94
Sloan, Sam 172
Smith, David R. Parke *64*
Smuts, General Jan Christian 169, 170
Smyth, Lieutenant Colonel Gerald Bryce (RIC) 150, 164–5
social class
    aristocracy 14
    British stratification 13–14
    Catholic middle class 3, 14, 44, 178
    class formation in Ireland 13
    clubs and 176
    education and 29–30, 70–1, 210–11
    lower middle class 210, 225
    middle class 3, 13, 14, 29, 30, 44, 57, 66, 70–1
    upper middle class 13–14, 29–30, 224, 225
    upward mobility 3, 8, 13, 57–8
    working class 13, 14, 210
social equality, education and 58
Soloheadbeg, County Tipperary 4
Staines, Michael 221
Stephen's Green Club 145, 152, 166, 175, 176

Street, Mr, telegram sent to 173, *195*
Sturgis, Gerald Boit 206, 207
Sturgis, Julian Russell 206, 210
Sturgis, Mark Beresford Russell 15, 86, 122, 149, 152, 164, *240*
    Anderson and 162, 164
    arrival in Dublin 198
    Asquith, private secretary to 207
    Assistant Under Secretary 209–10
    British cohort, social divisions among 200
    civil service career 200, 201, 206, 207–8, 209, 210
    Cope, perception of 218, 219, 222
    death 210
    diaries 164–5, 166–71, 185, 208–9, 227
    Dublin Castle handover 174
    Dublin Castle, secondment to 206
    Duggan, views on 170
    education 206–7
    family background 206
    Fisher and 206, 207, 208
    Grant-Sturgis, name changed to 210
    inheritance 210
    Irish people, contempt for 209
    KCB (Knight Commander British Empire) 210
    MacMahon and 162, 163, 164, 165, 166, 170–1
    marriage 208, *240*
    patronage 200, 201, 207, 211, 238
    personality 209, 234–5
    secretary (unofficial) to French 209
    Sinn Féin, views on 169–70
    social status 216
    Treasury and 210
    Whiskard, assessment of 227

Wylie's judicial appointment 185

Sturgis, Lady Rachel, (*née* Montagu-Stuart Wortley) 208, *240*

Sturgis, Roland Josslyn Russell 206

suffragettes 38, 69, 180

superior Catholic schools 7, 45, 46, 71, 199

   see also Catholic convents; Clongowes Wood College; Downside School; French College, Blackrock; Sacred Heart College; St Stanislaus College; St Vincent's College, Castleknock

superior (term), use of 7–8, *8*

Supreme Court 185

Sutton High School 106

Tallents, Sir Stephen 234

Taunton Commission (1864–67) 27

Taylor, Charlotte M. 23

Taylor, Sir John (Assistant Under Secretary) 115–16, 118, 119, *129*, 140, 141

   anti-Catholic bias 180–1

   departure from Dublin 121, 137, 139, 143

   Duggan's views on 188

   Fisher report's assessment of 146, 149

   Fisher's memorandum 221

   French leave ix, 121

   MacMahon, attitude towards 118, 119, 120, 139, 149, 188, 222

teachers 26, 40, 40n107, 57

Territorial Army 184

Thom's Directory 93, 95, 186–7

Tibbs, John Harding *64*

Tighe, James 72–3

Times 138–9

Townsend, Frank 228

Townshend, Charles 216

Treasury 136, 137, 199, 210, 229

Treasury (Ireland) 202–3, 227–8

Treaty *see* Anglo-Irish Treaty

Trevelyan, Sir Charles 19, 21, 202

   see also Northcote-Trevelyan Report

Trinidad

   intermediate education 30, 31

   St Mary's College 30

Trinity College, Dublin 10, 11, 52, 53, 62, 67, 188

   Catholic students and 78, 184

   Officer Training Corps 184–5

   religious bar, removal of 11, 22

   Wilkins Memorial Exhibition 77

Truce (1921) 4, 169, 170, 172, 223

Truscot, Bruce 24

Tudor, Major-General Hugh (RIC) 164, 165, 203

Under Secretary

   role of 16

   see also Anderson, Sir John; Burke, Thomas Henry; Dougherty, Sir James Brown; Harrel, David; MacDonnell, Sir Antony Patrick; MacMahon, James Stanislaus; Redington, Thomas Nicholas

unionism/unionists

   Dublin Castle and 145, 164

   MacMahon, perception of 114, 116, 164

   Southern Unionism 117

   Ulster Unionism 117, 143

universities

   English universities, privilege associated with 22, 23

   Irish civil service candidates *20*, 22

   Irish Universities Act (1908) 11, 179

   professional classes, entry to 14

redbrick universities 24
    Scottish 22–3
Universities Tests Act (1871) 22
University Bill (1873) 11, 28
University of Bristol 24
University of Cambridge *20*, 24, 66
    Christ's College 179
    civil service and *20*, 22, 23, 123,
        179, 182, 236
    Girton College 65
    Junior Cambridge local
        examination 233
    local examinations 233,
        233n173
    Pembroke College 106
    proportion of the population
        attending 23
    religious restrictions, removal of
        22
    St John's College 236
    sciences, neglect of 23
    Trinity College 54
University College Blackrock 67
University College Dublin (UCD) 8,
    12, 178, 179, 182
    foundation of 22, 78
    medical faculty 11
University of Dublin *see* Trinity
    College, Dublin
University of Edinburgh Journal 103
university education 9–11
    Catholic access in Ireland 42,
        178
    Catholic hierarchy and 9–10, 12,
        42–3
    civil service and 13, *20*, 22, 24
    clerical education 12
    denominational colleges 12
    first woman in Ireland to be
        conferred 76–7
    House of Commons debate 18,
        53
    Irish Catholics' access to 9–10,
        22, 200

Irish Universities Act (1908) 11,
    179
    non-denominational colleges 10,
        19
    O'Conor Don's motion 18, 19,
        53
    Protestants and 184, 188
    women and 23, 69–70, 75, 76–7
University Education (Ireland) Act
    (1879) 11, 19, 22
University Education (Ireland) Bill
    (1873) 10, 11, 28
University of Leeds 24
University of Liverpool 24
University of London 20n7, 23, 24,
    191, 237
University of Manchester 24
University of Oxford 24
    Balliol College 206
    Christ Church 229
    civil service and 13, *20*, 20n7,
        21, 23, 42, 123, 182
    'Greats', students taking 13, 21
    Hertford College 135
    proportion of population
        attending 23
    religious bar, removal of 22
    sciences, neglect of 23
    Wadham College 226
University of Sheffield 24, 40n103
Ursuline Order 9
    St Angela's College, Cork 74

Valentine and Sons, Dundee 91
Viceregal Commission on Education
    (1889) 52
Viceregal Commission on
    Intermediate Education (1919)
    40
Viceregal Committee of Inquiry into
    the pay and conditions of the
    police 180
Viceregal Committee of Inquiry
    (Killanin) *see* Killanin Report

Viceregal Lodge, Phoenix Park 166, 167, 209, 210, 219, 220
Viceroy *see* Lord Lieutenant
Victoria College, Belfast 74, 75, 76
Victoria, Queen 18, 75
Vincentian Fathers 93
    St Patrick's College, Armagh 93, 94, 95, 96–7
    St Vincent's College, Castleknock 12, 57, *60*, 95
Vinycomb, William Andrew *64*

W. Abbotts and Sons Ltd 224
Walkington, Letitia Alice 23
Walsh, William J., Archbishop of Dublin 52, 58–9, 62, 71, 72, 74
War of Independence (1919–21) 4, 116
    Truce 4, 169, 170, 172, 223
Warren Fisher, Sir Norman Fenwick *see* Fisher, Sir Norman Fenwick Warren
Warren Fisher Report *see* Fisher Report
Waterfield, Alexander Percival 149, 198, 201, 203, 224–5, 235
    academic achievements 229
    civil service career 227–8, 229–30
    Dublin Castle, secondment to 227–8, 229–30
    education 224, 228–9
    family background 228
    First Civil Service Commissioner 230
    Ministry of Information 230
    obituary 228–9
    Treasury (Ireland), Assistant Under Secretary 227–8
Waterfield, Matilda Rose (*née* Herschel) 228
Waterfield, William 225, 228
Watson, George 100
    see also George Watson's College
Watsonian, The, 'Side Lights on the Civil Service' 123–4
Waveney, Robert Alexander Shafto Adair, 1st Baron 37
Wedderburn, J.H. MacLagan 102
Weeks, Bridget 63
Wesley College, Dublin 59, *60*
West Cork Bottling 178
West, Trevor 117
Westminster Parliament 199, 202
Westminster School 27, 228, 229
Wharncliffe, Ellen Montagu-Stuart-Wortley-Mackenzie, (*née* Gallway), Countess of 208
Wharncliffe, Francis John Montagu-Stuart-Wortley-Mackenzie, 2nd Earl of 208
Wheeler-Bennett, John 84, 85, 91, 92, 99, 102, 122, 200
Whiskard, Cynthia Salome Caroline (*née* Reeves) 226
Whiskard, Ernest 225
Whiskard, Geoffrey Granville (Whiskers) 149, 168, 187, 198, 201, 216, 235, *240*
    assessment of 226–7, 234
    Cadet Corps 225–6
    civil service career 226–7
    Colonial Office 227
    Cope's views on 227
    death 227
    Dublin Castle, secondment to 226–7
    Duggan's assessment of 226–7
    education 224, 225–6
    family background 224, 225
    Greenwood, assistant secretary to 227
    High Commissioner to Australia 227, 233–4
    Home Office and 226, 227
    knighthood 227
    marriage 226
    personality 226

White, Henry G. 212
White, Mary 69
Whitehall
    Anderson and 83, 125, 201, 202,
        204
    civil servants seconded from 3,
        5, 15, 132, 149, 150, 162,
        198–201
    Cope and 222–3
    Dublin Castle, funding of 199
    Fisher's memorandum to 140,
        146, 147
    MacPherson and 16
    New Year Honours list (1923)
        177
    reorganisation, Fisher and 229
    Scottish Education Department
        42
Whitley Councils 142–3
Wilkins Memorial Exhibition 77
Winchester College 27, 56, 134–5,
    137
women
    astronomy and 65
    civil service, employment in 39,
        48, 111
    Federation of Women Civil
        Servants 111
    university degrees awarded to
        23, 69–70, 75
    see also girls; suffragettes
Woods, C.J. 118
Wrench, Frederick S. 165
Wylie, Ida 186
Wylie, Marion (*née* Drury) 184
Wylie, Robert Beatty 184
Wylie, William Evelyn
    British cohort, social divisions
        within 200
    called to the Irish bar 184
    Cope, perception of 218
    death 186
    death of wife 186
    dominion home rule 203
    Dublin Castle and 120–1, 139,

        152, 160, 163, 164
    Easter Rising leaders, trial of
        185
    education 161, 184, 185, 193
    family background 184, 193
    High Court judge 186
    Land Commissioner 185, 186
    Law Advisor to the Irish
        Government 120, 139
    MacMahon and 161, 163, 184
    policy implementation, views on
        185–6
    Stephen's Green Club and 152,
        166
    Supreme Court judicial
        appointment 185
    Territorial Army, lieutenant in
        184
    Trinity College Officer Training
        Corps 184–5
Wyndham Quinn, Captain 220
Wyse, Andrew Reginald Nicholas
        Gerald Bonaparte
    CB awarded to 192
    civil service career 189, 191–2,
        194
    education 190–1
    family background 190
    inspector of schools 191–2
    marriage 191
    Ministry of Education 192
    Royal Irish Academy, member of
        192
    teaching position 191
Wyse, Ellen Linzee (*née* Prout) 190
Wyse, Mariya (*née* Dmitryevna) 191
Wyse, Sir Thomas Bonaparte 18, 189
Wyse, William Charles Bonaparte
        190

kelan lowry o'reilly